MODERN ARCHITECTURE
1920-1945

Published in the United States of America in 1983 by
RIZZOLI INTERNATIONAL PUBLICATIONS, INC.
712 Fifth Avenue, New York, NY 10019

Copyright © 1983 A.D.A. EDITA Tokyo Co., Ltd.
3-12-14 Sendagaya, Shibuya-ku, Tokyo, Japan

ISBN 0-8478-0508-5
LC   83-61411

Printed and bound in Japan

MODERN ARCHITECTURE
1920-1945
KENNETH FRAMPTON/YUKIO FUTAGAWA

RIZZOLI
NEW YORK

CONTENTS PART 2 1920-1945

Cover: Daily Express Building by E. Owen Williams
Title pages: Villa Savoye by Le Corbusier
Photographs by Yukio Futagawa

MODERN ARCHITECTURE 1920-1945

6 The Modern Brick Vernacular in Northern Europe: Austria, Germany, and Holland 1914-1935

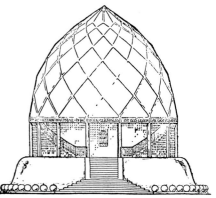

77   Taut, Glass Pavilion, Werkbund Exhibition, Cologne, 1914. Elevation.

1. The Glass Prologue

Glass architecture is unthinkable without Gothic. In the days when Gothic cathedrals and castles were rising, an architecture of glass was also tried. It was not completely realized, because iron, the indispensable material, was not yet available, and this alone enables the totally glass room to be constructed. In Gothic times glass was entirely unknown in most private houses. Today it is a principal factor in the architecture of every home. But it still lacks colour. Colour, however, will come.

The peculiar influence of coloured glass light was already known to the priests of ancient Babylon and Syria; they were the first to exploit the coloured glass hanging lamp in the temples, and the coloured glass ampulla was later introduced into churches throughout Byzantium and in Europe. From these were developed the stained glass windows of the Gothic period; it is not to be wondered at that these make an especially festive impression, but such an impression from coloured glass is inevitably inherent in glass architecture; its effect on the human psyche can accordingly only be good, for it corresponds to that created by the windows of Gothic cathedrals and by Babylonian glass ampullae. Glass architecture makes homes into cathedrals, with the same effects.

Paul Scheerbart
Glasarchitektur, 1914

These two passages drawn from Paul Scheerbart's *Glasarchitektur* of 1914 adumbrate the fundamental themes which were to inform Expressionist architecture after the war. In the first place, hints of a science-fiction culture, in the second an involvement with the Orient; on the one hand, the poetic possibilities of Western technology — the perfection of ferro-vitreous construction and the invention of electric light, on the other a feeling for mystical redemption with which the diaphonous haze of the Gothic cathedral could be readily associated. Already established as catalytic agents for the restructuring of German society, ecclesiastical and theatral form were first combined into a "cult" building in Bruno Taut's glass pavilion erected for the Deutsche Werkbund exhibition of 1914. As an agent for the redemption of an over-industrialized society, the cathedral was to appear after the Armistice, in one artistic manifestation after another; from Ernst Toller's play *Die Wandlung* (The Transformation) of 1919 to Fritz Lang's film *Metropolis* of 1926.

In 1914 the architect Taut and the poet Scheerbart reciprocally dedicated their seminal works to each other, the entablature of Taut's glass pavilion being inscribed with aphorisms drawn from Scheerbart's *Glasarchitektur* a year before his death in 1915. Such phrases as "coloured glass destroys hatred" called attention to the light filtering through Taut's faceted cupola to illuminate a seven-tiered chamber, lined with coloured glass. That this crystalline structure was modelled on the Gothic cathedral was confirmed by the Scheerbartian legend that Taut attached to the initial design: "The Gothic cathedral is a prelude to glass architecture." The glass pavilion was in effect a *Stadtkrone* or city crown; the form and institution that was postulated by Taut as being the necessary religious structure which, together with the faith it would inspire, was seen as essential to the rebuilding of society.

With the Armistice of 1918 Taut and his close associate Adolf Behne organized the *Arbeitsrat für Kunst* based on the concept of the worker's soviet or *Arbeiterrate*. This organization, comprising seven artists and eight architects, declared their anarchistic aims in Taut's *Architektur-programm* of December 1918, which advocated the creation of a new, total work of art, with the active participation of the workers themselves. The idea was that this anti-classical, anarcho-socialist architecture". . . should be enjoyed and experienced by the broad masses." In April 1919, Otto Bartning, Max Taut, Bernhard Hoetger, Adolf Meyer and Erich Mendelsohn staged an exhibition of visionary works under the title, "An Exhibition of Unknown Architects," to which Walter Gropius contributed an introduction. This text was effectively the first draft of the Bauhaus Declaration published in the same month. He wrote:

We must want, imagine and create the new architectural concept cooperatively. Painters, sculptors, break down the barriers around architecture and become co-builders and comrades-in-arms towards art's ultimate goal: the creative idea of the cathedral of the Future (Zukunftskathedrale) which will once more encompass everything in one form — architecture and sculpture and painting.

The suppression of the Spartacist Revolt in November 1919 put an end to the post-war, militant-anarchic phase of German revolutionary politics and prompted Taut to initiate a secret correspondence under the name of *Die Gläserne Kette* or the Glass Chain. At Taut's suggestion various artists and architects who had been affiliated in some way with the *Arbeitsrat für Kunst* — figures such as Gropius (Mass) or Hermann Finsterlin (Prometh) — started to correspond with each other under pseudonyms. This elite circle comprised not only Hermann Finsterlin, Walter Gropius and Bruno Taut but also the architects Adolf Behne, Max Taut, Hans Scharoun and Hans and Wassili Luckhardt. The artists August Hablik and Carl Krayl were also prominent members of the group. Apart from providing material for Taut's magazine *Frühlicht* (Early Light) — mostly in the form of fantasmagoric sketches and aphoristic texts — *Die Gläserne Kette* served primarily as a proving ground for the visionary ideas of the circle. Typical of this was Scharoun's letter of 1919 in which he wrote of the salient role to be played by the unconscious: "We must create just as the blood of our ancestors brought on waves of creativity and we shall be content if we are ourselves thereafter able to reveal a complete comprehension of the character and causality of our creations."

2. The Hanseatic Vernacular

In the received accounts of the history of the Modern Movement, modern architecture tends to be regarded as having suffered a simple evolutionary progression in which traditional load-bearing tectonics gave way, by degrees, to more advanced forms of building, comprised of lightweight industrial components arranged in such a way as to produce a sequence of interpenetrating volumes, structured about an open plan. While such a modernist architecture was universally realized during the inter-war period, a great deal of building was also achieved which served to extend cultural developments that had started before the interregnum of 1914. Among the European architectural cultures of the post-armistice period, mention must be made of

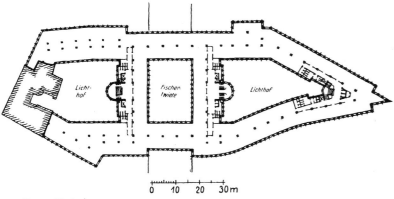

78 *Höger, Chilehaus, Hamburg, 1923. Ground floor plan.*

79 *Schumacher, a typical illustration from his book* Das Wesen des Neuzeitlichen Backsteinbaus *of 1920.*

the North German brick vernacular, not only for its subtle continuation of a late mediaeval "mega-structural" tradition (the vast dock-side warehouses of the Hanseatic League) but also for its unique reinterpretation of the seminal achievements of the American pioneers in the late 1880s. Although only one building, Fritz Höger's Chilehaus, Hamburg (1923-24), can be said to be directly related to the Chicago School — above all to the late Richardson and the early Sullivan — there is evidence that Höger was generally aware of the American "skyscraper-format." As Wolfgang Pehnt writes: "His office buildings of before the First World War are, like Schumacher's, marked by an austerity which admits few stylistic quotations. . . . They are in the tradition of the framed buildings articulated with giant pilasters erected in Hamburg by Erich Elingius, Henri Grell, Georg Radel, and others. Windows between the vertical members are gathered together in groups, not unlike the famous Chicago windows." Pehnt goes on to show how these regularly pilastered facades — interspersed with vertical lines of pierced fenestration — were reinterpreted in the twenties as vast, decorated megaliths, faced entirely in brick.

It would seem that once the Chicago formula had been assimilated (along with skeleton construction and the principle of locating service cores in the center of the plan) the Hamburg mediaeval tradition reasserted itself, largely through a conscious revival of the local brick vernacular, which was strongly advocated by Fritz Schumacher (Oberbaudirector of Hamburg after 1909) in his book *Das Wesen des Neuzeitlichen Backsteinbaus* (The Essence of the New Brick Building) of 1920. After dealing with the architectonic and

practical merits of brickwork — a material Höger regarded as the only possible medium with which to render the German soul — Schumacher went on to assert with greater sobriety that "anyone aspiring to a stern and stringent simplicity will find its full and lively realization in this material."

In the hands of the Schumacher school, the brick-encased, skeletal frame was rendered as a part mediaeval—part oriental style which in its obsessive reiteration of pilasters, shallow arches, and diagonally banded brick spandrels, seems to have responded, almost incidentally, to Scheerbart's call for a crystalline architecture, although where Scheerbart envisioned an exclusively *Glasarchitektur,* the North German architects built organic, crystallike megastructures entirely out of brick. Paul Bonatz's Stumm Building, Düsseldorf (1921-25), and at an institutional level, Wilhelm Kreis's Rheinhalle and Kunstmuseum, completed in the same city in 1926, are all works realized according to this crystalline sensibility.

But even this rather varied spectrum by no means takes into account the most talented architects, who were to derive their post-war manner from the German mediaeval brick vernacular. In various ways both Hans Poelzig and Peter Behrens, the one before and the other after the war, returned to the then unexplored capacity of this tradition; Poelzig in his industrial works, such as his Posen watertower of 1911, Behrens in his dyeworks built at Frankfurt-Hoechst for I.G. Farben in 1924.

As far as Behrens was concerned, the myth of the mediaeval cathedral was as much the underlying thematic of his post-war style as it had been the nostalgic inspiration informing the plan and profile of Bruno Taut's Glass

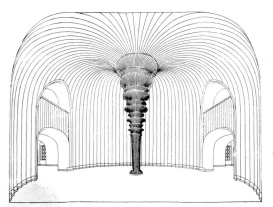

80 Poelzig, Grosse Schauspielhaus, Berlin, 1919. Foyer.

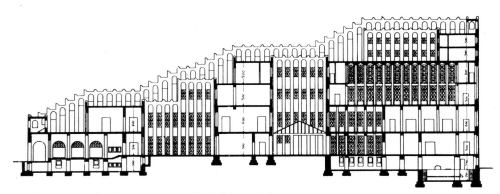

81 Poelzig, project for House of Friendship, Istanbul, 1916. Section.

Pavilion. This much is clearly confirmed by the Gothic parody he created for the Munich *Gewerbeschau* of 1922; his diamond-patterned, all brick Dombauhütte with its multiple pitched roof, making an evident allusion to the mediaeval masonic lodge or *bauhütte,* from which Gropius had already derived the term Bauhaus. An equally mediaeval image informs the entrance hall to the Hoechst dyeworks, with its crystalline, four-storey-high, stalactite volume in brick and glass; a form as indebted as Poelzig's Schauspielhaus to the stalactic vault of Islamic tradition. (Cf. the fourteenth-century Sala de los Abencerrages in the Alhambra.)

The format of Poelzig's post-war pilastered style was already established by 1916, with his House of Friendship competition entry, projected for a site overlooking the Bosphorous in Istanbul, where the repetition of a single elongated Romanesque arch organized into a reiterative format the aesthetic of this large courtyard complex, whose layered terraces were deliberately organized so as to suggest the legendary Hanging Gardens of Babylon.

The case that an orientalized brick style spontaneously emerged in Northern Europe between 1910 and 1919 is perhaps best advanced by two absolutely independent works which were both completed in 1919 and which each used well-established traditional motifs; the Hanseatic stepped gable in one case and the Romanesque arch in the other. The two buildings in question are P.V. Jensen-Klint's St. Hans Tveje Church in Odense, Denmark and Poelzig's Schauspielhaus built for Max Reinhardt in Berlin.

Like Max Berg's 67-metre reinforced concrete dome built as the Jahrhunderthalle in Breslau in 1913, Poelzig's Schauspielhaus was, to quote Wassili

Luckhardt, an effort "to furnish in architectural form an image of the cosmos that is more direct, more immediate, and more embracing than any furnished by earlier times." To this end Poelzig suspended a plaster stalactite dome, approximately thirty metres in diameter, within the existing shell of the old Zirkus Schumann which had previously served as a market hall. Poelzig's "tectonic cave," as it was sometimes known, was rendered pale yellow and illuminated in a manner to which only Luckhardt's contemporary account can really do justice:

The interior of the large dome is hung with an infinite variety of pendants which are given softly curving movement by the hollow of the cupola onto which they are fastened, so that especially when light is thrown against the tiny reflectors on each tip, the impression of a certain dissolution and infinity results.

This pendant syntax continued into the green foyer space, where it cascaded down from the ceiling, and even extended to the red exterior, where it was transformed into a low plaster relief of elongated arches, obsessively applied to every available surface. Reinhardt's arena stage, conceived by Poelzig as a "mosque" for the people, took over the sacred programme which Scheerbart and Taut had reserved for a glass architecture, and the irony is that in an architecture which was neither glass nor brick but plaster, Poelzig was able to combine into a single illusory volume not only the cave and the mountain, but also the image of the cathedral and the ritualistic stage. Not even Rudolf Steiner's First Goetheanum completed in Dornach a year later

82 De Klerk, Nautical Club, Amsterdam. 1922. Interior.

83 Nautical Club. Perspective.

could rival the spiritual rhetoric of this auditorium. Like Erich Mendelsohn's Einstein Tower built in Potsdam in 1921, the Schauspielhaus imparted religious connotations to an essentially secular programme.

Throughout the remainder of his career Poelzig continued to project one building after another as a kind of "stalactitic" mountain. Even when the overall building face was sheer, as in his Friedrichstrasse, Berlin competition entry of 1922, there was always an imperceptible setting back of the brick mullions as they rose vertically to the full height of the given mass. Although eminently realizable, this overall mullioned image remained as crystalline and as other-worldly as anything conceived by the visionary architects of *Die Gläserne Kette.* The overwhelming presence of Poelzig in Berlin at this time is surely testified to in other entries for the Friedrichstrasse building including those by Mies van der Rohe and Hugo Häring. Poelzig's influence may also be detected in the Chicago Tribune International Competition of the same year, where many entries were obviously indebted to the Breslau master, including, of course, the glass pyramidal skyscraper which was submitted by Bruno Taut.

3. The Amsterdam School

While the reinterpreted North German brick vernacular was largely achieved for corporate capital, in terms of factories like Poelzig's masterly chemical works built at Luban in 1912 or large office developments such as Fritz Höger's Chilehaus, Hamburg, of 1924, the Dutch brick vernacular came into being in the service of municipal housing and urban development. Once again the stylistic point of departure was American as much as it was European, for the brick architecture of the Amsterdam School arrived at its maturity under the leadership of Hendrik Petrus Berlage whose mature manner was due, in part at least, to the neo-Romanesque architecture of H.H. Richardson. But Berlage's contribution was not only the lucidity of his Rationalized Romanesque (cf. the Structural Rationalism of Viollet-le-Duc) but also his profound commitment to the dense European city, both as architectural form and social institution.

In his successive plans for Amsterdam South projected between 1900 and 1917, Berlage endeavored to maintain an emphasis on the spatial continuity of the street as an absolute prerequisite for the achievement of urbanity. Alone among the Socialist architects of his generation (categorically opposed in this respect to the Kropotkinian views of Bruno Taut), Berlage remained firmly against the compromise of the Anglo-Saxon garden city of Howard and Unwin, and it was this principle above all others that he succeeded in transmitting to the younger avant-garde architects of the Amsterdam School; to M. de Klerk, P.L. Kramer, J.F. Staal, M. Kropholler, C.J. Blaauw and, last but not least, H.T. Wijdeveld, founder of the Expressionist magazine *Wendingen* (Turnings) to which this group was affiliated.

To a degree Berlage participated in the emergence of the Dutch Expressionist "vernacular" in as much as his St. Hubertus lodge, built for the Kröller-Müller family at Hoenderloo (1914-20), was elaborately manipulated in order that its plan outline should symbolize a stag bearing a crucifix, a vision which according to myth had appeared to Hubert while hunting. Apart from the typical Berlagian brick aesthetic, little separates this work from the

84 Lauweriks, graphic compositions based on spiral, mandala themes, 1913-14.

grotesque, Javanese-influenced, and shiplike *Huize de Bark* and *Huize Benkenhoek* designed by Fritz Staal and Margaret Kropholler for the Park Meerwijk garden estate, built at Bergen-Binnen in 1918. But the most expressive possibilities, as far as the Amsterdam School was concerned, was to reside not in the plan form but in the manipulation of wall thicknesses in conjunction with the fenestration, and in this they were more indebted to Willem Kromhout and Johan Melchior van der Meij than they were to Berlage; the former for his American Hotel (1898-1901) and the latter for his Scheepvaarthuis (1911-16), both works being built in Amsterdam.

The fact that the Amsterdam revival of the Dutch brick vernacular occurred a decade before the equivalent North German movement is in part due to Dutch neutrality during the First World War and in part due to the *Wohnen Wet* or the Dutch housing law, which already in place by 1901, was fully operational by 1910. That some 10,000 houses were built in Amsterdam alone between 1910 and 1918 largely accounts for the precocious careers of Michel de Klerk and Pieter Lodewijk Kramer; the former's famous Eigen Haard estate already being finished by 1919, while the latter's De Dageraad housing complex was under construction from 1918 onwards.

Two broadly different forms of expression seem to be distinguishable within the public works of the Amsterdam School. On the one hand, there were bold undulating of brick surfaces designed so as to achieve wave formation and prowlike corners and situated so as to provide baroque emphasis as in De Dageraad or in Kropholler's Holendrechtstraat flats, both built in Amsterdam South in 1922. On the other hand there was the free sculpting of relatively independent brick episodes, in conjunction with syncopated and eccentrically shaped fenestration. This last was typical of the work of De Klerk, above all his Hembrugstraat and Zaanstraat sequences in the Eigen Haard estate.

As the years advanced, De Klerk abandoned his predeliction for whimsical symbolism, such as his false church spire in Eigen Haard, in favor of a horizontally rhythmic manner manifest, say, in his Amstellaan flats completed one year before his untimely death in 1923. This development brought the late Amsterdam School surprisingly close to Mendelsohn's horizontal, stream-lined street aesthetic of the late twenties, evident in the department stores that the German architect built in Breslau, Stuttgart, Chemmitz and Berlin. These works were conceived, as Reyner Banham has remarked, in terms of tidily profiled horizontal edges.

The craft discipline of the brick tradition and the propriety of Berlage's urbanism kept the public works of the Amsterdam School equally removed from both Mendelsohn's metallic dynamism and the figurative excesses of the Dutch *Landhuis* architects who were peripheral to the *Wendingen* circle — namely, P. Vorkink, J.P. Wormser, J.A. Snellbrand and A. Eijbink. The organic "folkiness" of this movement is typified in the thatched roof house built at Oostvoorne to the designs of the Dutch architects Vorkink and Wormser.

As peripheral to Amsterdam Expressionism, but even more distanced from these rambling country houses was the short-lived partnership (1895-1900) of K.P.C. de Bazel and J.L. Mathieu Lauweriks who, jointly influenced by

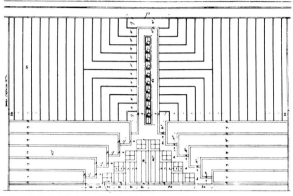

85 Oud, builder's hut for Oud-Mathenesse, Rotterdam. 1919.
Elevation design influenced by Lauweriks.

Theosophy and by the mathematical mysticism of their colleague J.H. de Groot, refused to subscribe to the sculptural license indulged in by such architects as De Klerk and insisted that all plastic invention must be governed by a geometrical/numerical rule system. For them, as for Rudolf Steiner, certain mathematical structures were seen as the literal embodiment of cosmic principles and in this respect they came close to the emotive mysticism that informed the crystalline structures envisioned by *Die Gläserne Kette.* The influence of these men can hardly be overestimated, from the impact of their proportioning methods on the facade of Berlage's De Beurs in 1898 to the later influence of Lauweriks as a teacher on more than one generation of architects; that is from the Neo-Quattrocento period of Behrens's work of 1905 to the early "theosophical" temporary, site hut built by J.J.P. Oud in 1919.

Equally grounded in mediaeval urban traditions, the primary differences between the Dutch and German wings of the Northern European vernacular are clear enough. Where the former was grounded in socialist municipal practice, the latter had little opportunity but to realize itself in free-standing corporate structures; where the one stressed the horizontal and the thrust of the traditional street, the other, with the exception of Mendelsohn and the later Taut, emphasized vertical attenuations; where the one celebrated the traditional craft elements of building, the other transformed these elements into unfamiliar crystalline features; where the one strove to achieve a general culture, the other attempted to render every commission in monumental terms; finally, where the Dutch found their exoticism ready to hand in their Indonesian colonies, the Germans cultivated an "oriental" myth and therefore tended to give an Islamic inflection to their vernacular forms.

4. The Viennese Superblocks
While Austria lacked a vital brick vernacular comparable to that which still obtained at the turn of the century in Holland, Scandinavia and Germany, the superblocks, or *Wohnhöfe,* built in Vienna by the Socialist City Council between 1919 and 1930 were, nonetheless, intended to be read as "vernacular" culture even if the specific form that this expression should take varied widely from block to block.

The chronic housing shortage at the end of the war, the demand to control the cost of living through rent stabilization and the need to reserve capital for investment in industry led to a situation in which the Social Democratic government was called upon to build 63,000 living units in approximately a decade; of which some 15,000 were accommodated in twenty-three superblocks, or *Höfe* of varying size, randomly located around the periphery of Vienna. The largest of these perimeter block developments, comprising multiple courtyards and a full range of ancillary facilities such as nursery schools, contained from 1,000 to 1,500 units, while the average superblock, rising from four to six stories, would house between 300 to 450 units around a single court.

Of load-bearing block and brick, partly framed and usually rendered on the exterior, the expression in each instance was extremely varied, ranging from a bastardized Neo-Baroque in the case of Winarskyhof (1924) to a collage

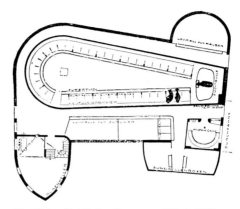

86 Häring, Gut Garkau Farm, near Lübeck, 1924.
Ground plan.

combining motifs drawn from Czech Rondo-Cubism and from Hoffmann. Such a combination is evident in the George Washington Hof, built to the designs of Krist and Oerley in 1927. In the main, however, the superblock architects adopted the format that Adolf Loos had first demonstrated in his Michaelerplatz store of 1910; occasionally enlivening the ground floor of their *Höfe* in a stripped *Rundbogenstil* rendered in a dark ochre or red. The style of Fuchsenfeldhof (1922) or Am Fuchsenfeld (1924), both being designed by Schmid and Aichinger, is typical in this respect and what is not Loosian – that is to say, the rhetorical fenestration and pilasters over the entryways – seems to have been drawn from the Prague school of Cubist architecture. It becomes increasingly clear that most of the Viennese superblocks were influenced by the experimental work of Josef Chochol and Josef Gočár, and never more so than in Karl Ehn's monumental Karl Marx Hof of 1927, accommodating some 1,400 units around five interconnected courts.

5. The Demise of the Brick Vernacular

The completion of Ragnar Östberg's National Romantic Stockholm Town Hall in 1923 – arguably the last "mediaeval" *Rathaus* in Europe – paradoxically announced the end of the Northern European brick vernacular as a fertile architectural source, although brick was to play a significant role in subsequent works by both Gunnar Asplund and Alvar Aalto. Nonetheless, neither Holland nor the Baltic was able to sustain a significant brick culture after the mid-twenties. Thus, the extraordinarily refined masonry forms documented by Schumacher in his seminal work of 1917 and elaborated by

such figures as Berlage, De Bazel and Poelzig in their architecture, fell into disuse after the mid-twenties, although there remained the occasional revivalist foray, such as Eliel Saarinen's all-brick Cranbrook Boys School built in Michigan, Illinois in 1925. To a degree it may be claimed that the German architect Hugo Häring continued to employ Northern brick vernacular in his Garkau farm completed near Lübeck in the same year, but Häring's output was too limited to have any issue, even in terms of his own development. The same may also be asserted in the case of Bernhard Hoetger whose highly sculptural Böttcherstrasse complex completed in Bremen in 1931 was certainly indebted to the stepped gable vernacular of that city, but here again the achievement is too isolated and the sense of vernacular is definitively dissipated by the time of Hoetger's Paula-Modersohn-Becker house of 1927, despite the continuing pro-Nordic and proto-Fascist sympathies of his prime patron, Ludwig Roselius. Even Aalto's large-scale excursion into brick with his Sunila Pulp Mill of 1935 hardly reflects any change in this architect's aesthetic preferences and one has to wait until his MIT Baker Dormitory built in Cambridge, Massachusetts in 1948 for any kind of conscious return to the expressive potential of brickwork – that is, to the spirit of Poelzig, Häring and Kramer.

Within the total spectrum of the inter-war years, only the Dutch made any serious effort to further the European brick tradition, first with the understated work of the Delft School led by M.J. Granpré Molière, and then with the efforts of those neo-Wrightian architects who, while variously influenced by the De Stijl movement, were distanced from its avant-gardism –

figures such as the early J.J.P. Oud, Jan Wils, the later J.F. Staal and, finally, W.M. Dudok, the municipal architect of Hilversum. In the case of Granpré Molière there is an unwavering adherence to a normative, petty-bourgeois stance already typified in his garden city, Tuindorp Vreewijk, built near Rotterdam in 1919. Brick in this instance simply assumes the role of an everyday material out of which a series of quite ordinary pitched-roof houses have been constructed (cf. Heinrich Tessenow's Am Schänkenberg Siedlung built at Hellerau in 1910). Nothing could be further from Schumacher's celebration of the rhetorical potential of masonry as published in his study of 1917. The case of Dudok is more complex for he tended to treat brickwork in a very abstract manner. Thus while enlivening the Delft syntax with Richardsonian rubbed brick arches as in, say, his Oranje School, Hilversum (1922), his later neo-Wrightian treatment of brick masses becomes increasingly planar as he passes from his Hilversum Town Hall started in 1924 to his masterly department store, De Bijenkorf, Rotterdam, of 1929. As with Wright, none of these works really derive their intrinsic expression from the fact that they are rendered in brick and however impressive Dudok's works are from a compositional standpoint, the brick of which they are made tends to remain totally inert, conveying, despite the articulation of its coursework, the feeling of a thin veneered mass which has been organized into planes.

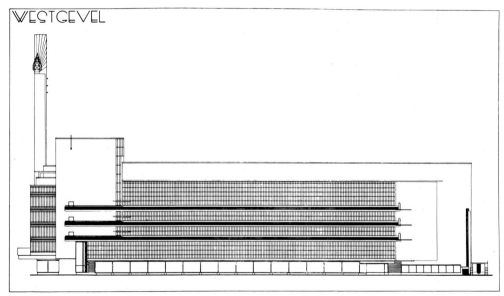

87   Dudok, De Bijenkorf Department Store, Rotterdam, 1929. Elevation.

PETER VILHELM JENSEN-KLINT
Grundtvigs Church
Copenhagen, Denmark

Although twenty-two years older than Asplund, the Danish painter/architect Jensen-Klint came to his creative maturity remarkably late, largely because he did not begin to practice architecture until 1905 when he was already over fifty. Jensen-Klint, whose unusual background included an engineering degree, devoted his belated architectural career to a single-minded reinterpretation of the Baltic brick tradition. Above all, he exploited the ziggurat-like form of the Hanseatic stepped gable, the characteristic profile of the Skåne churches to be found in Southern Sweden. From first to last this was the one expressive motif of his work, from the extraordinary grandeur of his Grundtvigs Church (supposedly first designed in 1913 and not complete until 1940) to the more modest silhouette of his St. Hans Tveje church, built in Odense in 1921. The same stepped motif even reappears in his secular work; in the YMCA that he built at Odense in 1923 and in the perimeter block housing that he erected around the Grundtvigs Church in 1926.

The undeniable power of these forms seems to derive from a deeply felt spirituality which may account for the strange affinity obtaining between the Grundtvigs Church and Steiner's Goetheanum built at Dornach near Basel between 1925 and 1928. While there is not the slightest formal resemblance between these two buildings, it is clear that a similar expressive energy is present in both and it is this, no doubt, that brings them to be classified as proto-Expressionist works. It is clear, however, that Jensen-Klint's formation lay outside the ideological development of Expressionism, for all that his work may be explicitly compared to the kind of forms that Hans Poelzig was creating around 1911.

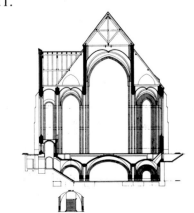

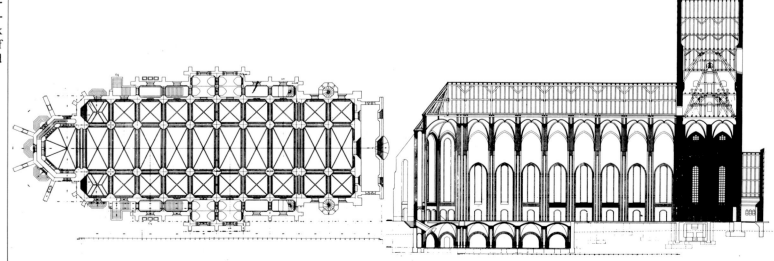

218 Above: front elevation
  Below, from left: cross section, plan and
  longitudinal section
219 Interior, view toward entry

MIES VAN DER ROHE
Projects:
Friedrichstrasse Office Building
and the Glass Skyscraper

Following his demobilization at the end of the First World War, Mies abandoned the Romantic Classical tendencies of his prewar career and began to apply himself to the creation of an architecture which would be predicated on new materials and techniques. During this immediate postwar period, when he was closely associated with the Berlin *G Gruppe,* Mies attempted to arrive at the phenomenological essence of a number of new tectonical forms, such as the reinforced concrete frame in his prototypical office building of 1922 and the hermetic curtain wall which he projected first in his entry for the Friedrichstrasse competition of 1919 and then in his hypothetical glass skyscrapers of 1920 and 1921. Where the concrete office building was reduced to a stack of cantilevered floor slabs, rendered in such a way as to stress the inert and dense nature of the material, Mies projected the glass skyscraper as a shadowless form; as an architecture in which all accentuation would derive from reflection rather than shadow. Thus he wrote of his glass skyscraper proposals in Expressionist magazine *Frühlicht* in 1922:

"At first glance the curved outline of the plan seems arbitrary. These curves, however, were determined by three factors: sufficient illumination of the interior, the massing of the building viewed from the street, and lastly the play of reflections. I proved in the glass model that calculations of light and shadow do not help in designing an all glass building.

The only fixed points of the plan are the stair and elevator shafts. All the other elements of the plan fit the needs of the building and are designed to be carried out in glass."

That the glass skyscraper was among the more prophetic insights of Mies's early career seems to be more evident than ever. In the early twenties Mies projected a technique and a mode of expression which could not be realised prior to the invention of the neoprene window gasket. The recently completed Lake Point Tower, Chicago built to the designs of George Schipporeit in 1968 is only one of a number of recent structures which suggest that the Miesian glass skyscraper has finally come into its own, now some fifty years after its initial invention.

220 Friedrichstrasse Office Building, Berlin. 1919
  Charcoal and pencil on brown paper mounted
  to board: 68 1/4″ × 48″
221 Glass Skyscraper. 1921

Photos: Collections, Mies van der Rohe Archive, The Museum of Modern Art, New York

A cursory comparison between De Dageraad and the last significant housing built by De Klerk at Henriette Ronnerplein, would unquestionably decide in favour of Kramer's monumental De Dageraad, rising to a full five stories at its corner so as to provide a suitable urban focus at the junction of Co-operativestraat and Pieter Lodewijk Takstraat. Unlike the self parody latent in De Klerk's final work, De Dageraad still carries conviction largely because its author was still committed to the possibility of recreating, after Berlage, the syntagmatic urban form of mediaeval Christendom. Kramer, who had worked on the Amsterdam Scheepvaarthuis with van der Meij, was clearly steeped in the Northern European brick tradition and the moulded brick "prow" roofline of De Dageraad (a marine metaphor for both the ship and its furrow) was clearly a rhetorical element which boldly condensed many of the themes first broached in the Scheepvaarthuis. In some ways De Dageraad equals and even excels the powerful monumentality of De Klerk's more elaborate community development built for Eigen Haard.

Below: corner of the block
Bottom right: site plan

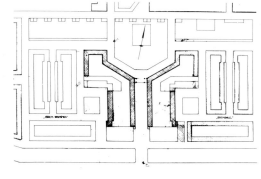

This astrophysical observatory built at Potsdam, at the expense of the German government for Einstein's personal use has its origin in an innumerable series of sketches (some of them no larger than a postage stamp) which the young Mendelsohn produced while he was engaged in military service during the First World War. These sketches reveal more certainly than any other testimony the sources from which the Einstein Tower was derived. Three related lines of development seem to have concerned the young architect during this period. The first of these was the mechanistic vision of the Futurist architect Sant' Elia as this had emerged in his Cittá Nuova drawings of 1914. The second was the Viennese *Wagnerschule,* above all the work of Emil Hoppe, who had also been a source of inspiration for Sant'Elia. Finally there was the specific example of Otto Wagner's prime pupil, Joseph Maria Olbrich whose Ernst Ludwig Haus and Hochzeitsturm at Darmstadt Mendelsohn greatly admired. Thus we find him writing to his wife in 1915: "... Yesterday I received an old issue of *Kunst und Dekoration* ... the Darmstadt Exhibition of 1901. Jugendstil manifestation. I must write why its course suddenly came to an end. It is only separated from my works by a single leap."

The leap in a more worldly sense as far as Mendelsohn was concerned seems to have come about in the spring of 1917, when he sent his astronomer friend E. Findlay-Freundlich a sketch for an observatory. After the Armistice, Freundlich was to be instrumental in launching Mendelsohn's career, since it was he who gained him the commission for the Einstein Tower.

In retrospect, however, two other buildings, both built for the Werkbund Exhibition of 1914, seem to have exercised a decisive influence on the actual shape of the tower. The first of these was clearly Bruno Taut's Glass Pavilion; the second was the extremely plastic volume of Henry van de Velde's Werkbund Theatre. Van de Velde is also the obvious source for Cubistic but organically distorted pieces of furniture with which Mendelsohn furnished the interior.

Curiously isolated from the ideological mainstream of the Expressionist movement (he seems to have had little contact with Bruno Taut and his circle) Mendelsohn became an Expressionist almost by accident.

The strong symbolic form of the Tower (reminiscent of Taut's concept of the *Stadtkrone*) seems to have been determined by Mendelsohn's naive enthusiasm for the romance of modernity and scientific progress. Antedating the powerful in-situ concrete mass of Rudolf Steiner's Second Goetheanum by more than four years, Mendelsohn had originally intended that the observatory should be built of concrete but in the end he was forced to settle for a reinforced concrete frame, filled with brick and rendered over so as to achieve the monolithic appearance which he had originally desired.

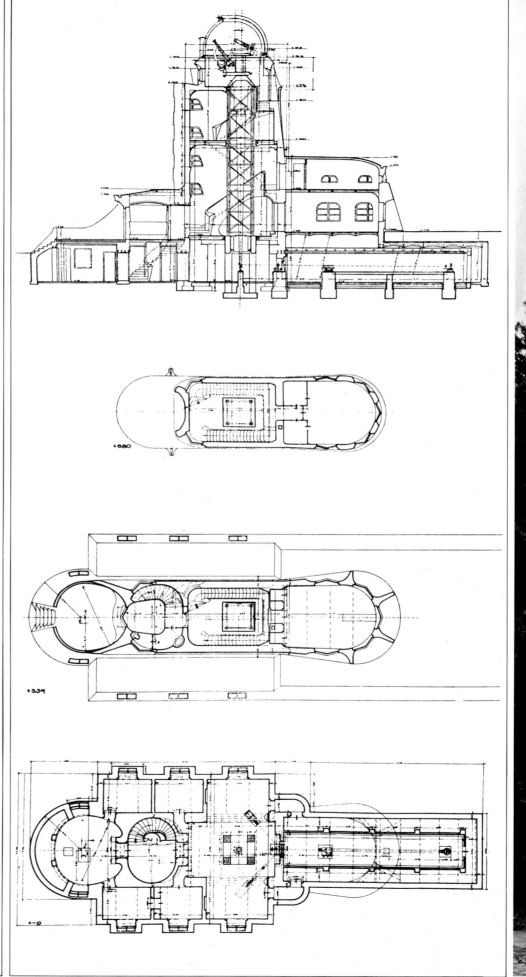

223 *Front elevation*
224 *Plans and section*
224-5 *Overall view*

Designed and built as a maquette in the intensely creative aftermath of the Bolshevik revolution, Tatlin's gargantuan, 1,500-foot-high tower, dedicated to the Third (Communist) International (the Comintern 1919–1943), was the only building which the famous Russian Cubo-Futurist artist was ever to project. As was often the case, in the immediate post-Revolutionary period, it was the artists and not the architects who were to create the canonical architectural images of the Socialist millenium. Clearly derived from the Eiffel Tower which Tatlin would have visited during his sojourn in Paris in 1912, it was at the same time a deliberate exaggeration, not to say violation of the engineering principles on which Eiffel's crowning achievement had been based.

In this sense it was a characteristic "transrational or "zaumy" work to coin the polemical language of the Russian Futurist poets Khlebnikov and Kruchonykh by whom Tatlin had been strongly influenced. For these Russian artists and intellectuals (the Russian structuralist critic Victor Shklovsky was to adopt a similar position in literature — his idea of estrangement or *ostraneje*). The transrational mode was seen as the sign of the millenium; an apocalyptic expression which was deemed to be the only form by which the fundamental break with bourgeois politics and culture could make itself manifest. Pyramidal forms such as classical pediments were regarded by the avant-garde as being quintessentially bourgeois and repressive while upward spiralling forms were seen as the universal dynamic trajectory of the liberated proletariat. One of the most succinct contemporary descriptions of the tower and of the ideological intent of its form may be found in Nikolai Punin's pamphlet of 1920, wherein he wrote:

"The main idea of the monument is based on an organic synthesis of the principles of architecture, sculpture and painting. It was to comprise a new type of monumental construction, combining a purely creative form with a utilitarian form. In agreement with this principle, the monument consists of three great rooms in glass, erected with the help of a complicated system of vertical pillars and spirals. These rooms are placed on top of each other, and have different, harmonically corresponding forms. They are to be able to move at different speeds by means of a special mechanism. The lower storey, which is cubic in form, rotates around its own axis at a rate of one revolution per year. This is intended for legislative assemblies. The next storey, which is pyramidal, rotates around its axis at a rate of one revolution per month. Here the executive bodies are to meet (the International's executive committee — the secretariat, and other administrative executive bodies). Finally the uppermost cylinder, which rotates one revolution per day, is reserved for centres of an informative character: an information office, a newspaper, the issuing of proclamations, pamphlets and manifestoes — in short, all means for informing the international proletariat; it will also have a telegraphic office and an apparatus that can project onto large screens. These can be fitted around the axes of the hemisphere. Radio masts will rise up over the monument. It should be emphasized that Taltin's proposal provides for walls with a vacuum in between (thermos), which will make it easy to keep the temperature in the various rooms constant."

is a noticeable shift in De Klerk's work between the urban idealism of the Eigen Haard estate built at Spaarndammer-burt, Amsterdam in 1918 and the far more sophisticated terrace blocks erected at Henriette Ronnerplein, in Amsterdam South between 1920 and 1921. Here De Klerk divided up the sides of a square into units which at first sight seem to indicate the presence of individual houses; exaggerated chimney shafts and flat pyramidal roofs serving to syncopate a continuous rhythm of peculiarly distorted facades throughout the terrace. These "houses" were nothing more than apartment blocks, each one serving six tenants although no one seems to have objected to the grotesque and obvious nature of this deception. In a profound sense the work adds little to what De Klerk had already achieved in the Eigen Haard development and within two years of completing Henriette Ronnerplein the moving genius of the *Wendingen* circle was dead.

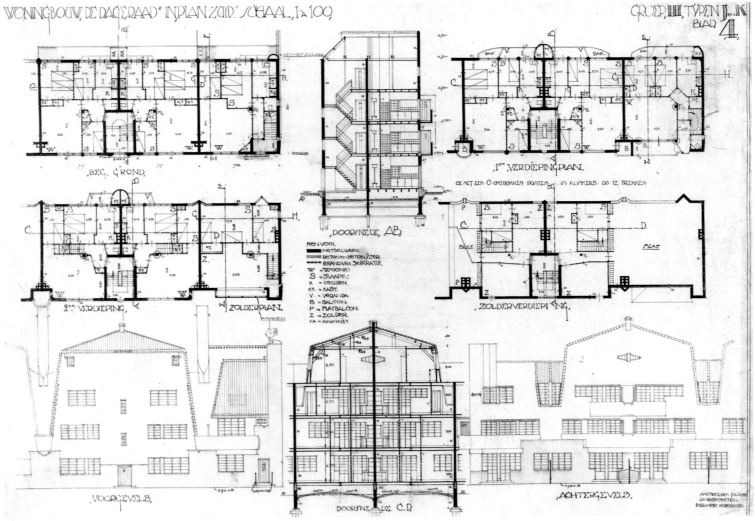

Above: view from forecourt
Below: working drawings

The First World War runs through the fabric of Western society like a knife and save for those neutral countries on the periphery of the struggle, European culture was totally transformed by the impact of the first industrialised conflict. There is no European architect of the period in whom this transformation is so pronounced as Peter Behrens. A complete ideological gulf separates the *Machtstaat* ethos of his prewar AEG Humboldthain complex built in Berlin-Wedding in 1912 from the cryptic, mediaevalized forms of his dyeworks erected for I.G. Farben at Frankfurt after the war. Where the one celebrated the evident triumph of a modern industrial state, (the victory of enlightened monopoly) in a manner which sought to render the glazed industrial shed, as Neoclassical "temple," the other was a return to the security of the North German brick tradition, to rubbed brick arches and narrow window openings, to massive walls, clock towers and bridges. With I.G. Farben Behrens also returns to the crystal myth which had informed the architecture of his youth in Darmstadt. The four-storey entrance hall to the main administration building is clearly rendered as the interior of a cosmic crystal and the facetted and corbelled brickwork which descends from its crystalline roof is surely sufficient evidence of a desire to return to the mystical religious space. While this entrance hall seems fortuitously close to Bruno Taut's concept of the cult building, there is little evidence of there being any ideological contact between the two. By this date, we may take it that Behrens had already withdrawn spontaneously from the mainstream of European modernism.

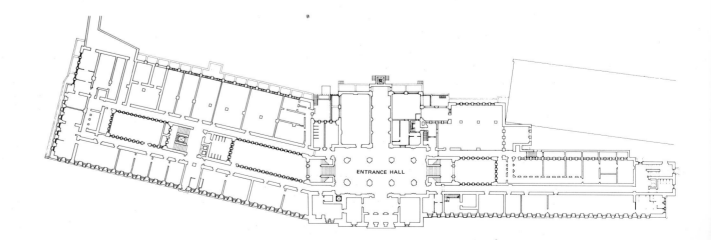

228 *Above: view from street*
     Below: ground floor plan
229 *Entrance hall*

230 Above: facade detail (charcoal drawing)
      Below: staircase
231 Left: entrance hall (charcoal drawing)
      Right: skylit over entrance hall

Strongly influenced by the classical and often anonymous Biedermeier works which were illustrated in Paul Mebes's book *Um 1800* of 1908, the so-called Scandinavian Doricist manner seems to have arisen out of a reaction against the highly rhetorical National Romantic expression of the Jugendstil; a style which was still evident in Asplund's Swedish church, projected for Paris in 1909. Soon after Asplund was to embrace a kind of classicized vernacular manner in his chapel for the Stockholm Southern Cemetery of 1918; a building which ingeneously combined a Tuscan peristyle in wood with a high-pitched, hard-edged, tightly shingled roof.

This crypto-classical *maniera,* conceived by its adherents as being the basis for a new nonreductive, nonhistorical mode of expression, was projected by Asplund on a monumental scale in his 1921 project for the Stockholm Public Library, where the domed and coffered section of the central, cylindrical reading hall was initially derived from E.-L. Boullée's Bibliothèque Nationale of the 1780's. While the plan and its circular placement in the middle of an enclosed courtyard had as a further antecedent Smirke's British Museum reading room of 1852, the reading room of the Stockholm Public Library (as a built in 1928) was ultimately indebted to the avant-garde architects of the Ancien Regime; above all, of course, its high cylindrical drum which was clearly taken from Ledoux's Barrière de la Villette of 1785.

On the other hand, the Egyptoid entry door was patently derived from a local tradition or rather from the Romantic Classicism of Gottlieb Bindesbøll's Thorwaldsen Museum, completed in Copenhagen in 1848. At the same time, the specific detailing of this entry is Asplund's own; its lightweight fenestration being profiled in a uniquely mannerist way so as to conceal the opening of the actual door.

Asplund's idiosyncratic, part classical, part metaphysical, part folklorique sensibility can also be felt in the Flaxman-like reliefs to the library foyer, in the secret stair access around the perimeter of the rotunda, and finally in the somewhat trivialised decor of the children's reading room. All this referential complexity is momentarily supressed in the library restaurant which, facing onto a landscaped park, was the last part of the complex to be completed. As early as 1927 this section was already being rendered in the so-called *Funkis* manner; that is to say, in the stripped functionalism which was to emerge in Asplund's work, in his designs for the Stockholm Exhibition of 1930.

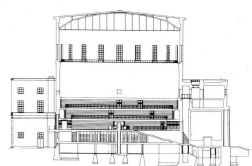

232 *Front facade*
233 *Above: section*
    Center: reading hall
    Below: plan

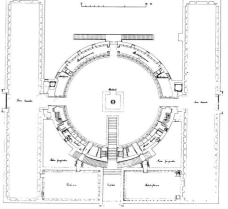

Although not finally opened until May 1935, a year after Berlage's death, this museum was effectively a product of the museum movement, dating back to the mid-nineteenth century and gaining special impetus in Europe after Alfred Lichtwark's reorganisation of the Hamburg Kunsthalle in the early 1890s. The idea of building a new museum for The Hague in order to amalgamate diverse municipal collections came from the City Archivist, H.E. van Gelder who, as early as 1896, initiated a frustrating and extremely protracted procedure which eventually, in 1920, led to the approval of a most elaborate design for the present site. This promising, not to say immodest, beginning was offset by an endless series of municipal reappraisals, including the solicitation of totally contrary outside advice, and the decision in 1924 to abandon the entire undertaking.

Thus the present building would have never seen the light of day had it not been for Van Gelder's threat of resignation which came in 1927. This dramatic stand had the effect of producing immediate action. In the following year Berlage submitted a much more restrained version of his original design; one whose scale was modestly modulated so as to articulate a programme of reduced scope. It is instructive to compare these two successive designs since the difference between them not only represents the final modernization of Berlage's style, but it also reveals the upper limit, so to speak, of his idealism. The first trapezoidally planned and multi-domed proposal (comprising full sized congress and concert halls, in addition to the museum itself) was clearly a miniature city of culture grouped about an inner expanse of water, like an exotic Zanadu — a kind of Romanized Venice unaccountably stranded on recently redrained land. The realized design on the other hand, assumed the then traditional format of a low-rise free-standing palace of culture set within a carefully landscaped park, with plenty of area left over for future expansion. However, certain fragments of Berlage's poetic intent were to remain, albeit in modified form; first in the wide stretch of ornamental water separating the museum from the main approach, second in the concatenation of the horizontal silhouette — a syncopation of pitched and glazed gallery roofs together with the flat topped public volumes; third, the provision of an adequate lecture hall whose profile is articiulated as such; fourth, in the persistence of the original minaret motif as exemplified in the twin chimney shafts to the central heating chamber and in the minarets flanking the main entrance; and last, but by no means least, the triple-height central hall, situated to the left of the low entry foyer, symbolically and spatially uniting the volumes of the entire museum. This last, which was a *tour de force* in trabeated concrete construction was evidently indebted in both its proportion and spatiality, to the interior of Wright's Larkin Building of 1904.

Interestingly enough, this was by no means the only American influence on the building, for the layout and the specific appointment of the structure and its parts had been worked out jointly by van Gelder and Berlage, under the influence of Benjamin Ives Gilman's classic study of modern museological methods, his *Museum Ideals of Purpose and Method* published in 1918. Gilman's concept of a popular didactic "megalo-museum" conceived as a cultural center for the entire community, is patently the precept behind the Gemeentemuseum in all the stages of its evolution, including such specific features as the unifying central hall, the deliberate introduction of spatial variety in order to overcome the tendency towards "museum fatigue" and above all, the location of the structure in a park, where nature and artifact are free to play one against the other.

Gilman seems to have been of the opinion that the ideal museum should be broken down into four separate but linked pavilions and something of this is reflected in the planning of the Gemeentemuseum about an inner green court, and in the provision of a free-standing café terrace-cum-tempieto in the park.

The organization of this approximately four-square plan is straight forward enough with the principal galleries being arranged around an inner courtyard on the ground and first floors and with the adjunct block set to one side, comprising the entrance hall, administration offices, and the large and small lecture halls. Constructed about a

reinforced concrete armature and finished in plaster and tile on the interior, and in brickwork on the facade, (with all the dimensions on the brick module) the Gemeentemuseum is the last major work of the Dutch master and his tectonic prowess and precision is in evidence everywhere. It is present, above all, in the fastidious detailing of the galleries themselves, Berlage painstakingly evolving, after endless consultations, the most optimum form of controlled and diffused top-lighting he could devise. Aside from this, Berlage applied the strictest rigour to detailing every technical provision, including the integration of radiant heating panels into the soffits of the maintenance catwalks.

As far as stylistic expression is concerned, it is obvious that this work is on the threshold of entering into the abstract, cubistic discourse of modernism. And yet the simplifying and liberating lessons of Wright's Froebel manner have been assimilated and transformed into a syntax which is as poetically dense as it is acerbic. The tectonic details are reduced throughout to the minimal profiles, as these are coincident with the necessities of construction and the laws of proportion. The result is that the glass monitors clip into position over the brick masses as though they are made of the same lithic substance, while the flat topped cubic forms cluster about the administration wing and interpenetrate in a manner which is profoundly

spatial and totally devoid of the sentimental Wrightianism which is often debilitating in the work of Dudok.

234-5 Views from garden court

236 *Left: gallery*
      Right: entrance hall
237 *Above: plan and section*
      Below: interior of the museum

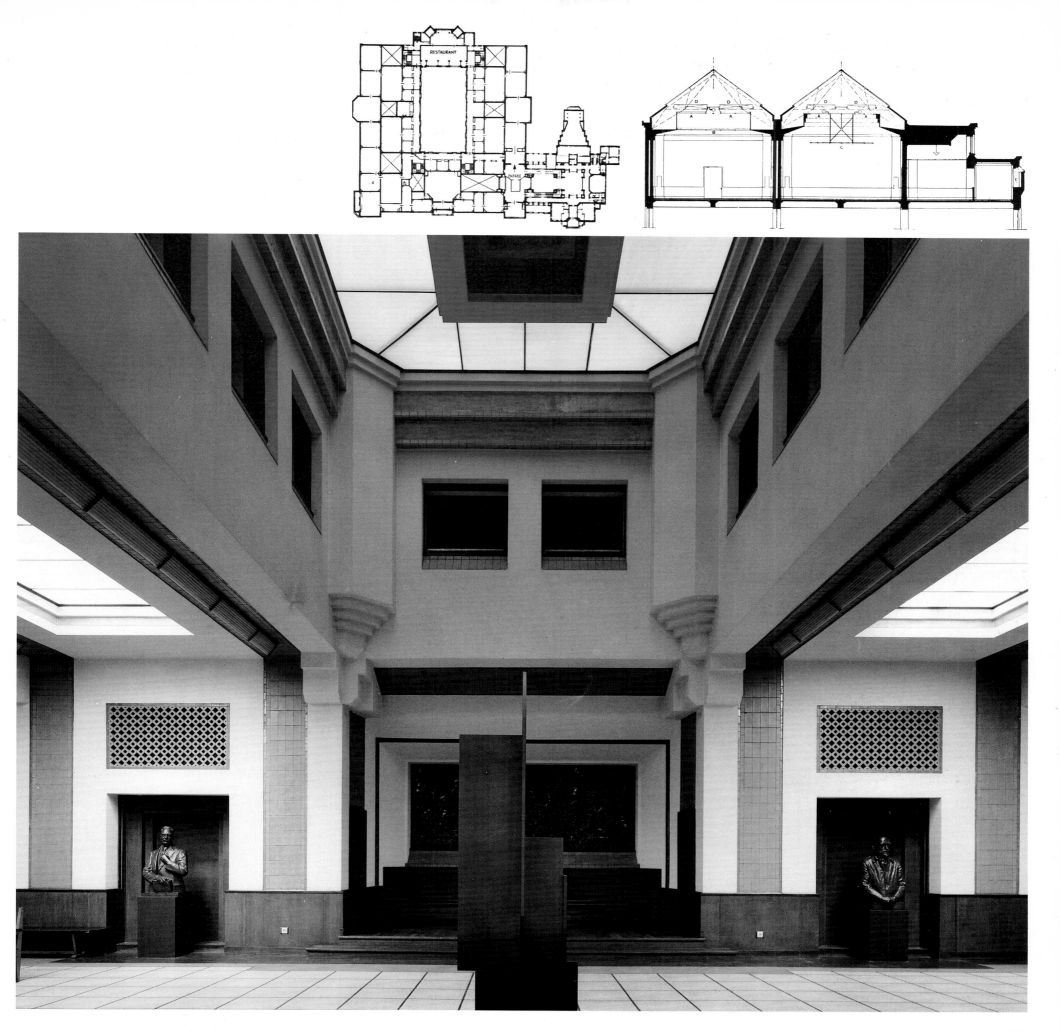

The Chicago Herald Tribune competition held for purposes of selecting an architect for the newspaper's editorial premises, ostensibly on the occasion of its seventy fifth birthday) had the unexpected effect of inaugurating a new era in American skyscraper design; one which continued as an unbroken line of development from the competition to the completion of Raymond Hood's Rockefeller Center in New York, in 1938.

It is one of the paradoxes of this occasion that while the first prize went to Hood for his Neo-Gothic design entered in collaboration with John Mead Howells, the most influential project remained the second prize; the design submitted by the Finnish architect Eliel Saarinen. The scope of Saarinen's influence may be judged from the fact that his part National Romantic; part Neo-Gothic design, setting back in three major tiers before terminating in a four-square flat crown, was to exert an immediate influence on Hood himself, as may be judged from Hood's black and gold American Radiator Building realised in New York in 1924, in the same year that the Tribune tower was completed. That Louis Sullivan should have recognized the outstanding quality of the Saarinen entry testifies to the perspicacy of his judgement just a year before his death, when he wrote of the competition in 1923: ". . . there remain, for some, two surprises: first, that a Finlander who, in his prior experience had had no occasion to design a soaring office building, should as one to the manner born, have grasped the intricate problem of the lofty steel-framed structure . . . second, that a 'foreigner' should penetrate to the depths of the sound, strong, kindly and aspiring idealism which lie at the core of the Ameri-

Eliel Saarinen. Perspective

Eliel Saarinen. Section

Howells & Hood

can people."

Sullivan's rhetoric aside, it is clear that Saarinen was able to extend and refine the Neo-Gothic high-rise formula already established by Cass Gilbert in his Woolworth Building of 1913. The difference between Gilbert and Saarinen (and this was an attribute totally lacking in the Hood and Howells's design) was that Saarinen was able to bring an effective degree of abstraction to the massing of his project, even if he was still to depend on traditional motifs. The base of his main tower was kept blocky and plain — simply pierced by five round headed elongated openings. At the same time the corners remained equally solid throughout, while the middle of his composition was articulated by seven Gothic pilasters which continued their course upwards through a series of set-backs to terminate in the crest of the tower. This was essentially the compositional formula that Hood was to abstract and extend throughout the rest of his career, from the Daily News and McGraw-Hill buildings of 1930 to the gradual completion of his Rockefeller Center complex during the first half of the thirties. The 263 national and international entries to this competition included many designs that were far more radical and modern than Saarinen's brilliant but nonetheless ultimately traditional solution. Amongst these, mention has to be made of four outstanding solutions, the Scheerbartian curtain-walled tower projected by Bruno Taut and terminating in a pyramid; two Neoplastic solutions — one submitted by Walter Gropius and Adolf Meyer in partnership and one by a Danish architect named Knut Lonberg-Holm — and finally a highly ironic entry by Adolf Loos, in which the main tower was projected as a giant Doric column standing on a rectangular base. With the singular exception of Loos, the decisive contribution of the European avant-garde to the skyscraper was that the traditional tripartite division adhered to by Sullivan was abandoned in favour of the "base-plus-shaft" format, this last terminating in a slight inflection rather than a capital-like cornice.

Bruno Taut

Gropius & Meyer

Adolf Loos

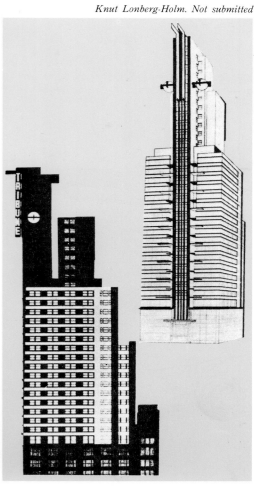
Knut Lonberg-Holm. Not submitted

Albert Kahn's career is inseparable from the rise of the automobile industry, Kahn receiving his first commission of consequence when he became sole architect to the Packard Motor Car Company in 1903, for whom he then designed a four-storey reinforced concrete factory. This plant was but the first in a series of industrial structures which included the Pierce Plant, built for the manufacture of the Pierce Arrow car in 1906, and Ford's reinforced concrete Highland Park Plant expressly built for the Model T. Ford in 1910. Three years later Henry Ford converted his factory to assembly line production and this necessitated the rebuilding of his entire system on a single-storey basis, which he finally achieved in 1917 with the Eagle Plant constructed by Kahn for the wartime production of submarines. To this 1,700-foot single-storey complex, divided into five bays, each 51 feet wide, Kahn added a free-standing glass plant in 1922 — Ford having decided in the interim to enter into wholesale production of glass.

This plant, designed for the continuous manufacture of plate glass, was organised about four great furnaces situated at the southern end of a 750-foot-long, single-storey, ferro-vitreous shed; the volume being top lit throughout by a series of large and small monitors. Each of the large monitors ventilated a *lehr*, that is to say a continuous band of annealing glass, while the small monitors gave light and ventilation to the processes of grinding and polishing.

Despite the utilitarian approach consistently adopted in all of these works, it is evident that Kahn was not beyond manipulating the exigencies of the programme for the purposes of ordering form. Thus the monumental transverse monitor at the south end of the plant not only serves to discharge the heat from the furnaces beneath, but also combines with the chimney shafts in such a way as to terminate the formal composition. In as much as its monitors face all directions, the glass plant represents a decisive break with traditional north light illumination and from this design on, Kahn is never to use the north light principle again. The prime reason for abandoning this single orientation was the restriction that it placed on future factory layout. The alternative strategy of opting for more even light distribution would also explain Kahn's preference for the two-way monitor. The other innovation which greatly contributed to the elegance of the plant was unquestionably the cladding which ran clear of the outer frame and was laid up in sweeps of corrugated sheet and steel sash. Apart from its clean appearance, this simple system facilitated construction and thus enabled the plant to come into early use.

240 *Overall view*
241 *Plan and section*
Photo: Albert Kahn Associates

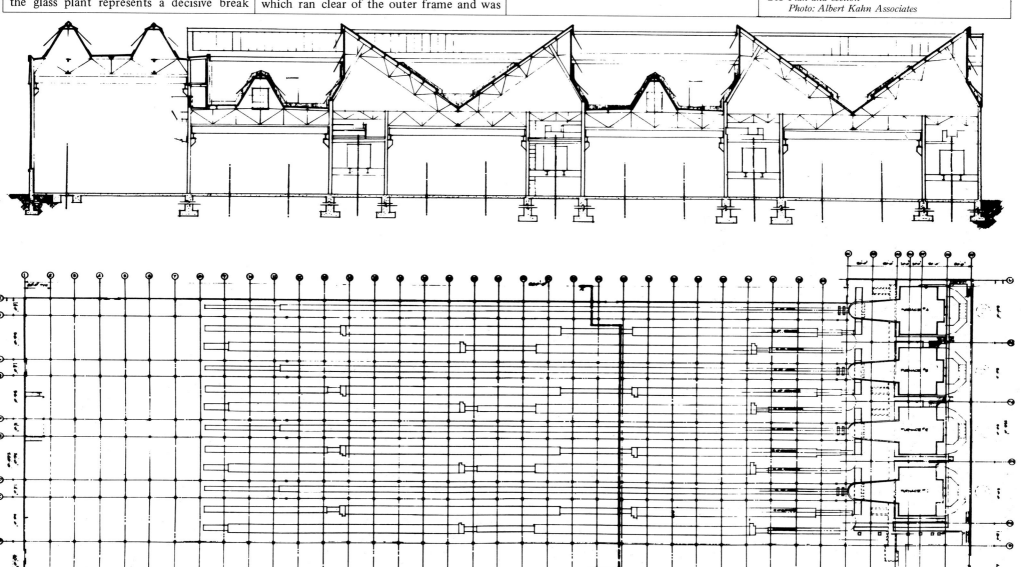

With this structurally lucid but typologically conservative building Perret was able to resolve the basic contradictions of the Greco-Gothic ideal. This post-Cartesian concern for combining the structurally explicit logic of the Gothic with the rational ideal of classical order had dominated French architectural theory from the mid-17th century onwards. J. G. Soufflot's Ste-Geneviève realised in Paris in 1755, and afterwards known as The Panthéon, may be taken as one of the earliest efforts at synthesising these opposing principles; the Gothic being largely hidden in the concealed arches and buttresses of its stone structure; the Classic being evident in the free-standing internal Corinthian peristyle which carried the domed and vaulted ceiling. In as much as the technique of iron reinforced stonework in Ste-Geneviève anticipated the invention of reinforced concerte, it is possible to argue that architects such as Soufflot had already shown the level of tectonic impurity which would have to be used in order to achieve this kind of synthesis.

From a typological point of view Notre-Dame du Raincy was a simple basilica or *hallenkirche* in which the aisles are in-variably the same height as the nave. Constructed entirely of reinforced concrete, twenty-eight of its extremely slender, cylindrical columns serve to support an elaborate reinforced concrete roof comprising five barrel vaults, running over each aisle — Cistercian style — and a continuous transverse shell running the full length of the nave. The total support system comprised thirty-two free-standing columns rising to a height of 37 feet and tapering upwards from a 17-inch diameter at the base to a 14-inch diameter at the crown. The Greco-Gothic synthesis is evident here even in the details,

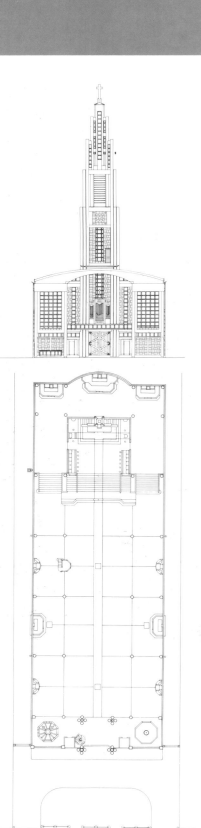

for the concrete columns are fluted by the formwork in such as way as to suggest both classical entasis and the Gothic composite pillar.

The body of the church itself comprises a precast concrete, perforated cage of glass which effectively floods its orthogonal volume with coloured light, varying from yellow at the entrance, to purple towards the shallow apse at the Western end. This membrane is built-up of 2-foot-square precast concrete *claustra,* panelled in coloured glass and organised about pictorial set pieces painted by Maurice Denis. This apparently colourless but highly textured exterior was achieved through the permutation of five standard concrete elements: a cross within a square, a circle within a square, a diamond within a square, a half square and a quarter square. By arranging these elements around the coloured glass set pieces, Perret was able to avoid the monotony that might have resulted from the external suppression of the structure. That Perret sought to achieve the same sublime effect as had been the intent in Soufflot's Ste-Geneviève is borne out by the following text which he published in the *American Architect* in 1924: "In this building we have entirely isolated these columns from the wall, permitting the walls to pass freely outside of them. By exposing all of the columns free-standing there are four rows seen instead of the usual two rows, and this greater number of columns in sight tends to greatly increase the apparent size of the church with a sense of spaciousness and vastness. The small diameter of the columns, their great height and lack of distracting detail, aid materially in producing this effect."

The same level of subtlety hardly obtained in the elevations, particularly at the Eastern end, which was given a psuedo-Gothic, spire-like silhouette through the clustering of reinforced concrete cylinders.

242 Left: ground floor plan and cross section
Center: overall view
242-3 View toward altar
243 Right: rear view

Wright eased into his second Eldorado career with Aline Barnsdall's Hollyhock House, built on Sunset Boulevard, Los Angeles in 1920, and he followed this tour de force in Pre-Columbian form with *La Miniatura* completed for Mrs. G. M. Millard in Pasadena in 1923. This is the first of Wright's concrete block houses of which some four more were built prior to 1929. The basic technique was to precast the necessary blocks bearing the imprint a limited range of different geometric cut-outs and to afterwards bind these elements into a monolith by interlacing the dry joints with steel rods and grouting the whole assembly into its final position. Wright invariably referred to this as his "textile block" system, having anticipated this development in the Midway Gardens of 1914 and in the ceramic inlaid stucco decoration applied to the spandrels of the Coonley House in 1908. In both instances it already appeared as though large sections of the facade were made of crystalized fabric.

As many have remarked, La Miniatura was not so much a house as it was a cultivated retreat; an aesthetic lair built at the bottom of a eucalyptus ravine. A middle-class neurotic impulse towards achieving total seclusion (shared in this instance by both Wright and his client) led to a main facade which was virtually blank, entry actually taking place on the middle floor of the three-storey section. From this *piano nobile* one either descended to the dining room and the poolside terrace, or alternately one rose to the bedroom floor and mezzanine overlooking the living volume. It is interesting to note how the windowless corner bastions, on the lowest level, were exploited as vaults for Mrs. Millard's valuable collection of books and pictures. For all the delicate poetic intimacy implied by the interior, one can never quite overcome the unreal aura of Hollywood in this work which seems to have been pervaded by a paranoid quality which may have had its origins in Wright's own insecurity. As Robert C. Twombly has written: "With little to offer in the way of a theory of family organization, several of the concrete residences were hardly homes at all. Significantly, the only California buildings he discussed (at great length!) in his autobiography were for two middle aged women — Miss Aline Barnsdall and the widowed Mrs. George Millard — who did not have families and who, like their architect (in his Miriam years) were socially vulnerable and personally unfulfilled."

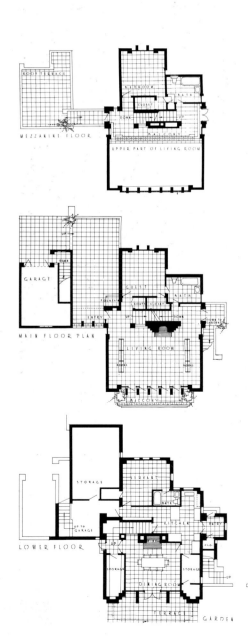

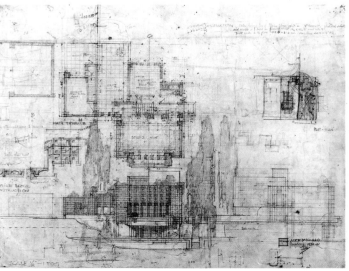

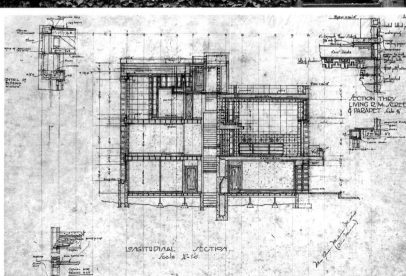

244 Left: plans
Above right: view from garden
Below right: drawings of plan, elevation, details and section
245 Balcony, view from living room
Photos: T. Kitajima

FRITZ HÖGER
Chilehaus, Shipping Headquarters
Hamburg, Germany

Chilehaus is but one of many so-called Expressionist brick-faced office buildings erected in Holland and North Germany between 1910 and 1926. Amongst these one would certainly have to cite J. M. van der Meij's Scheepvaarthuis, completed in Amsterdam in 1916, to which Chilehaus may be readily compared. Other examples would be Hans and Oskar Gerson's Ballin-haus, Hamburg of 1924, Paul Bonatz's Stumm Building, Düsseldorf of 1925, Harmann Distel's Montanhof, Hamburg of 1926, and last but not least, a further Höger building erected for the Hanover Anzeiger in 1928.

This strangely orientalized brick culture which was close, in many respects to Hans Poelzig's own *stalactite* style of 1917, clearly had its center in the Hanseatic city of Hamburg where Höger practiced throughout his life. We know that this curiously isolated architect had little contact with the intellectual Expressionist circles of Berlin, so that once again his works are only to be regarded as Expressionist for want for a more appropriate category. In any event, it becomes increasingly clear that the whole of this movement was masterminded by Fritz Schumacher who was *Oberbaurat* in Hamburg from 1915 to 1922. (See Schumacher's *Das Wesen des Neuzeitlichen Backsteinbaus* of 1920.)

Chilehaus is an exotic example of the mercantile office building or *Kontorhaus* which was first perfected as a type in the mid 1880s by Martin Haller. As a type this form lies curiously suspended between the mediaeval high-gabled Hanseatic warehouse and the modern office block. And yet for all these strong native affinities, Chilehaus, in its eccentric elaboration of Hanseatic detailing and through its ostentatious use of burnt seconds and vitrified bricks, now appears as some kind of cryptic but nonetheless homage to Louis Sullivan.

246 Overall view
247 Above: street facade
*   Below: plan*

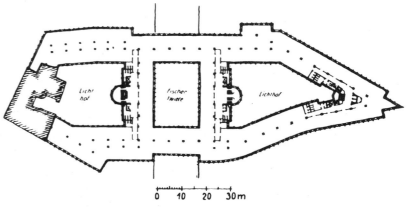

In this twin house (the third commission of his Parisian career) Le Corbusier was able to realise a version of his *rue à redent*, first sketched by him in 1920. His rather ambitious initial plan for four linked houses with separate garages and a lodge, had to be reduced, due to site restrictions, to two contiguous buildings set down at right angles to each other. In the final version of 1923 an entire wing was dropped from the original U-shaped scheme and Le Corbusier seems to have compensated for this loss of the "palatial" format by imposing a subtly displaced symmetry onto the lateral facade which was in any event divided into two residential quarters. This symmetrical displacement was then turned through ninety degrees by the device of a triple-height entry hall linking the La Roche house to the adjacent gallery. Thus the high bay window at the end of the long block was balanced by the raised bulging mass of the gallery whose floating form terminated the main approach, along the private gravel drive, set back from the frontage.

From a typological point of view the semi-detached house for La Roche-Jeanneret is a curious mixture; in part a Gothic Revival L-shaped house (cf. Morris's "Red House," Bexley Heath of 1859): in part a deconstructed Pompeian Villa complete with atrium. The three-storey entrance hall was used to synthesise these opposed typological origins into a single Purist vortex, where the major and minor stairs are treated as spatial slots together with their contiguous volumes. These Cubist *coulisse*-like spaces stand in strong contrast to the plastic energy of the curved ramp within the gallery itself.

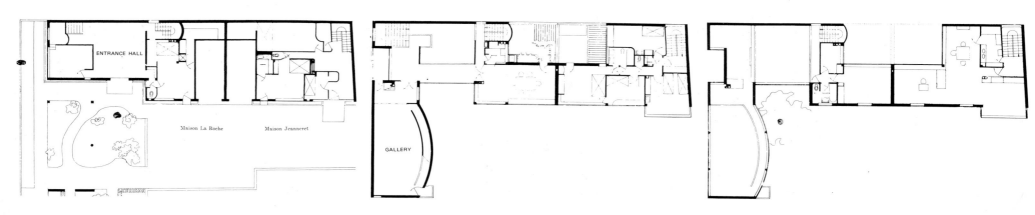

ENTRANCE HALL

Maison La Roche   Maison Jeanneret

GALLERY

248 Above: view toward gallery (La Roche)
   Below, from left: plans of ground floor,
   first floor and second floor
249 Gallery (La Roche)

It is symptomatic of the intimacy of the Dutch Neoplastic movement that a small two-storey house, tacked onto the end of a nineteenth-century terrace should come to serve as the canonical architectural work of the De Stijl movement. Neither before nor since have Theo van Doesburg's *16 Points of a Plastic Architecture,* first promulgated in 1924, been so explicitly and consistently embodied in a built work. Van Doesburg's polemical insistence that Neoplastic architecture should be both *dynamic* and *anti-monumental* and that it should also be anti-cubic and dedicated to the destruction of the box, seems to have been demonstrated in the Schröder House, designed in close collaboration with the owner Mme Schröder-Schräder.

A more complex work in the early history of twentieth-century architecture would be hard to find, since the Rietveld-Schröder house combines two fundamentally different traditions; on the one hand the influence of Frank Lloyd Wright in Europe (which was more decisive in Holland than elsewhere); on the other a mystical cosmology of abstract form, of which the most salient and important practioner was unquestionably the painter Piet Mondrian.

The first of these influences announces itself in the pinwheel organisation of the plan, in which all the components, irrespective of their scale and status, appear to be spiralling out from the central core which in this instance happens to be the access stair. Rietveld drew this notion from Robert Van't Hoff's reinforced concrete Wrightian house, built at Huister-Heide, near Utrecht in 1916. In the Van't Hoff house, as in most of Wright's domestic work, the central core included a chimney as well as stair.

The second of these influences derived in part from the autonomous evolution of post-Cubist painting at the hands of Piet Mondrian and Bart van der Leck and in part from the cosmology of a certain Dr. Schoenmaekers — a mystical mathematician, who in 1913, had determined the primary colours of De Stijl, on a cosmic basis. In his book of 1913 he wrote: "The three principal colours are essentially yellow, blue and red. They are the only colours existing ... yellow is the movement of the ray (vertical) ... blue is the contrasting colour to yellow (horizontal firmanent) ... red is the mating of yellow and blue." For Schoenmaekers the vertical ray was the sun falling on the earth, while the horizontal as the path of the earth around the sun.

Unlike the conceptually infinite canvases of Mondrian and Van Doesburg, whose linear elements theoretically extended beyond the picture plane, the Rietveld-Schröder house was predicated on the concrete notion of flexibility. In this respect it matched the dynamism of its three dimensional form (its centrifugal, sculptural energy) with a transformable layout which was literally dynamic in as much as it could be easily altered. Most suprisingly of all perhaps is the way in which the first floor plan could be opened up into one free space or alternatively broken down into four separate volumes. Various detailed elements reflected this overall transformation; the bathroom which was capable of collapsing its necessary volume into the confines of a small closet or the large composite, corner window of the main living volume which opened out in such a manner as to imply the literal destruction of the vestigal box. In this connection it is always something of a shock to realise that this house was built of traditional timber construction and that the apparently "floating" slabs were to depend upon cantilevered floor joists for their support. It is ironic that a cabinet-maker like Rietveld should design and build a timber structure in which jointing should play such a negligible role. Thus from a technical as well as a conceptual point of view the work remained uncompromisingly abstract.

250 Above: view from street
Below: ground floor plan (left) and upper floor plan (respectively enclosed by the sliding walls, and open)
251 Street facade

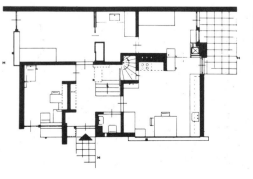
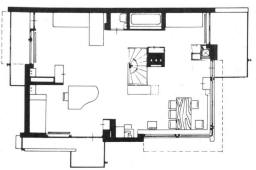
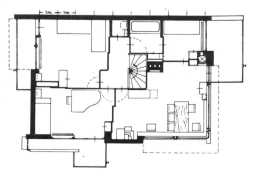

This complex of farm buildings is the only substantial realised work in Häring's seminal but relatively unproductive career. An ideologue first and an architect second, Häring's theoretical writings are extensive. Throughout the Weimar period he was involved in the struggle of the German Neues Bauen group against the reactionary policies of the then Berlin city architect Ludwig Hoffmann. In 1924 he participated in the foundation of the circle known as the *Zehnering* and a year later in conjunction. with Mies van der Rohe and other leading architects of the period, he organised *Der Ring*, of which he remained the secretary until it was dissolved by the Nazis in 1933. Having divided the architectural creative process into two separate but interelated phases, first the evolution of the *Organwerk*, that is to say the emergence of a supra-functional programmatic morphology (or what Louis Kahn later termed "what the building wants to be"), and second, the development of the *Bauwerk,* as the built or tectonic manifestation of this immaterial organic structure. Unlike such diverse figures as Jensen-Klint, Höger, Bonatz and Steiner, Häring (like Poelzig and Taut) may be regarded as an unrhetorical expressionist in as much as he consiously sought the direct expression of the *Organwerk* in built form. His position in this respect is extremely close to that of Hans Scharoun and the later Alvar Aalto. Both Häring and Scharoun, the one the thinker, the other the builder, took a somewhat Zen-like attitude towards the creation of built form. Unlike the *a priori* geometric paradygms of Le Corbusier, Häring sought to arrive at a suitable building shape without recourse to a preconceived notion or sectional profile. He wrote: "We want to search for things and let them unfold their own design. It goes against the grain to determine their shape from the outside, to subject them to a set of derived laws." To the extent that the physical image of building was to be determined by this "natural" process, Häring's method may be seen as an organic version of the eighteenth-century ideal of an *architecture parlante*. In this connection he wrote: "The identity of an object must determine the type of form appropriate to the individual building." For Häring, however, the ultimate reference was the vernacular rather than classical form.

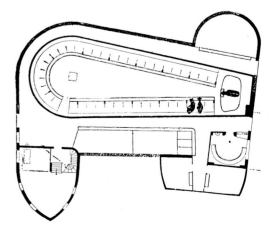

This remarkable block of flats completed for a socialist cooperative in the rue des Amiraux in 1924 is an elaboration of the *Maisons à Gradins* which Henri Sauvage had first realised in the rue Vavin, Paris in 1913. It may be claimed that Sauvage not only anticipated the Futurist city of Sant'Elia, but that he also realised an actual part of it. Even by today's standards the block in the rue des Amiraux is a remarkable achievement for it is a *unité d'habitation* realised over twenty five years before Le Corbusier came to build his *Unité* at Marseille in 1952. Its phased construction (built first as a section of set-back housing without the swimming pool at its core) and its ingeneous internal organization, merits more specific description. Flanked on three sides by streets and comprising some eleven flats per floor, the basic stacking principle is for the apartments to be accessed in pairs from four internal stair towers set close to corners. The larger three-room apartments with set-back terraces occupy the longer sides of the block, each one being situated on either side of a six-storey freight elevator, the form of which is given prominent expression.

The flats diminish marginally in size as they set back with each successive floor, and the resultant profile gradually occupies the space above the top-lit swimming pool situated in the core of the block. As in rue Vavin, the construction is of reinforced concrete throughout and while the apartment planning may be primitive by contemporary standards, it says something for Sauvage's ability and for the productive capacity of the time that the white and blue faience tiles facing the facade are still intact and in immaculate condition after nearly seventy years of use.

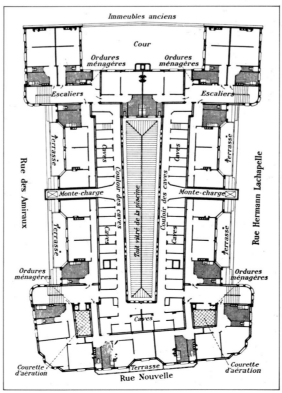

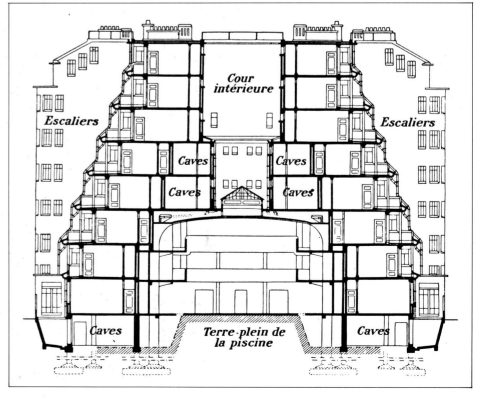

254 Above: perspective
    Below left: fifth floor plan
    Below right: section
255 View from street

This remarkable and in many ways unique structure, first outlined in 1924, is commonly regarded as the masterpiece of Dudok's brilliant but decidedly anti-avantguardist career. Dudok's achievement testifies to the strength of provincial culture since almost all of his work was realised in Hilversum; much of it being carried out while he was Director of Municipal Works between 1915 and 1927.

Prior to 1930, Dudok's approach remained an uneasy synthesis of a number of different lines of development. In the first instance, of course, there was Berlage, by whom his work was determined at the beginning, above all in the Secondary School that he built at Leiden in 1916. There was then the partial influence of the Expressionist *Wendingen* circle, evident in the Sevensteijn house built in The Hague in 1920. This was all soon overlaid by bold compositional devices drawn from J.J.P. Oud's De Stijl period such as we see in Dudok's Dr. H. Bavinck School built at Hilversum in 1921. Finally, Frank Lloyd Wright's influence became decisive, first in the Hilversum abbattoir completed in 1923, and then in the Hilversum Town Hall under construction from 1928 to 1931.

Set in relatively extensive grounds and rendered entirely in brick, the free-standing mass and landscaped surrounds of this structure immediately annouce the garden-city character of Hilversum. Despite the asymmetric, Neoplastically derived composition, the main representative elements were both traditional and monumental; the high clock tower over the entry and the three symmetrical windows signifying the council chamber. As far as the details are concerned, the influence of Wright is everywhere; above all in the understated entrance from the side, which consists of a long causeway leading to a cantilevered portico overlooking the lake. However, the syntax changes abruptly as soon as one enters the building. The Wrightian brick manner is at once dropped in the marble-faced entry hall whose formal order is closer to the Viennese *Wagnerschule* than to any indigeneous Dutch or American style. The eclectic nature of Dudok's formation (he was trained as an engineer rather than an architect) becomes evident at this juncture and reveals a conservative tendency in Dutch architecture which seems to come increasingly to the fore throughout the nineteen thirties.

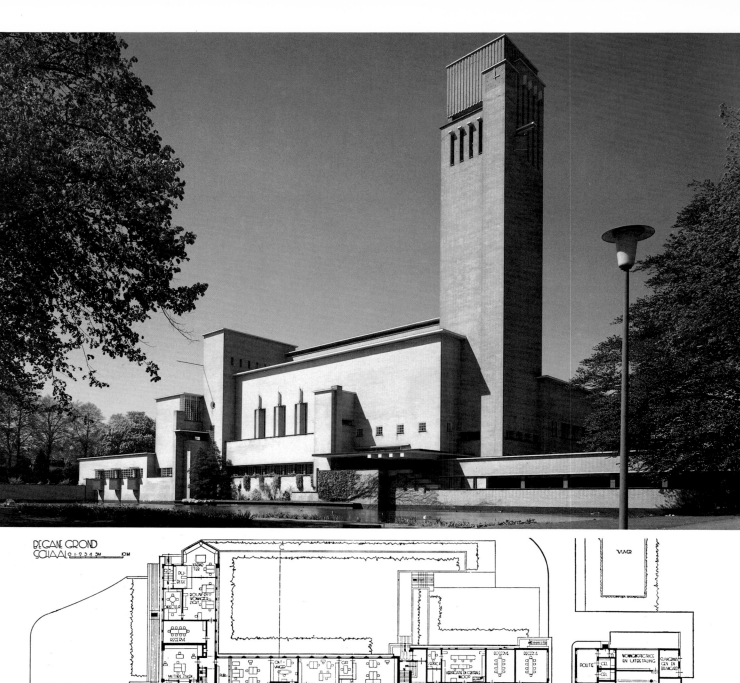

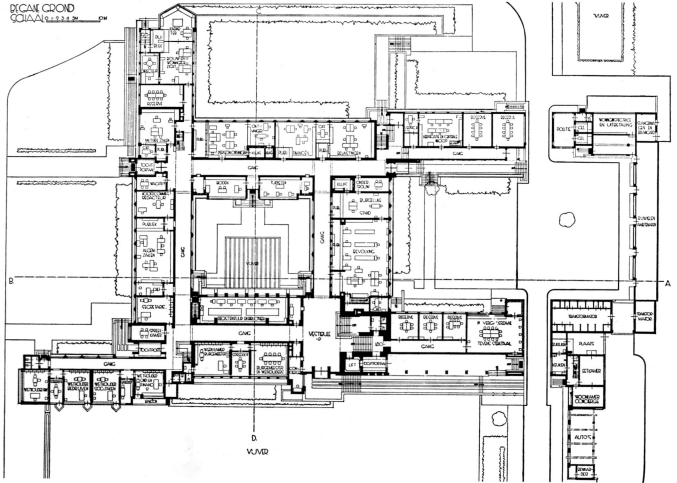

256 Above: overall view
   Below: first floor plan
257 Above: reception hall
   Below: council chamber

The small pavilion that Le Corbusier realised at the Exposition des Arts Décoratifs had both a traditional provenance and a polemical orientation. It was not just one more pavilion whose primary aim (at least as far as the national exhibits were concerned) was to demonstrate the sovereignty of France in the field of decorative art. Derived from the L-shaped courtyard of the traditional Carthusian cell which Le Corbusier had first encountered when he visited the Charter-house of Ema in Tuscany in 1907, the pavilion was a full size mock up of a typical unit for one of the hypothetical apartment blocks in his Ville Contemporaine of 1922. In three dimensional terms this prototype fused together two independent archetypes; the mediaeval monastic cell and the nineteenth-century double-height artist's atelier with mezzanine over; this last being a type which Le Corbusier had already incorporated into his Citrohan houses of the early twenties.

Reduced to its simplest level, the Pavillon de l'Esprit Nouveau was intended to be a two-storey house or villa suspended in the air. It was the building block of a hanging garden concept which was simultaneously incorporated at a more modest scale in Le Corbusier's Immeubles-Villas project of 1922. Here, however, the prototype was actually built as a double-edged propagandistic effort. On the one hand Le Corbusier wished to mount a strong polemic against the idea of decorative art; on the other he wanted to demonstrate the general viability of his

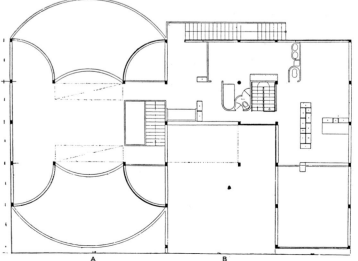

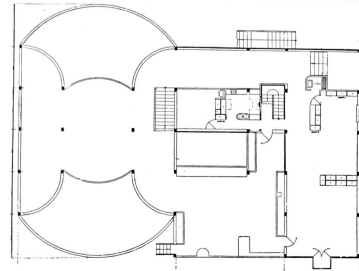

concepts on housing and urbanism. The former was largely indicated through the austere furnishings of the pavilion; the latter was eleborated in large scale drawings and didactic texts which were exhibited in the gallery adjacent to the prototype.

The policy taken towards equipment in the Immeubles-Villas was polemically anti-decorative. This is evident from the photographic record of the pavilion which indicates that every piece of furniture was carefully selected so as to conform to the Purist canon. Purism valued the spontaneously refined object type which according to Purist theory had come into being in response to a generic need or *besoin type*. This accounts for the Purist paintings, the Thonet chairs, the Anglo-Saxon upholstered armchairs, the Persian rugs, the model aircraft and the built-in cupboards. They are all seen as exemplifing Adolf Loos's anti-*Gesamtkunstwerk* cultural programme. Loos's prescription was reduced to a simple formula; namely that the architect should restrict his activities to the building and the built-in equipment and that thereafter the taste of the client for traditional craft production should prevail. This is exactly the policy of the Pavillon de l'Esprit Nouveau, except that "anonymous" taste now expresses itself in terms of standardised objects.

258 Above: overall view
.   Below: floor plans
259 Entry facade
    Demolished and reconstructed in Bologna, 1977.

7 The Classical Tradition and the European Avant-Garde: France, Germany, and Scandinavia 1912-1937

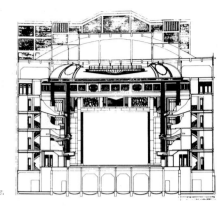

88   *Perret, Thêâter des Champs-Elysée, Paris, 1911-12. Section of the large auditorium, with reliefs by Bourdelle.*

1. Engineers Aesthetic and Architecture

The Engineer inspired by the law of economy and governed by mathematical calculations, puts us in accord with universal law; he achieves harmony. The Architect by the arrangement of forms, realizes an order which is a pure creation of the spirit.

You employ stone, wood and concrete, and with these materials you build houses and palaces, that is construction. Ingenuity is at work. But suddenly you touch my heart, you do me good. I am happy and I say: "This is beautiful." That is architecture. Art enters in. My house is practical. I thank you, as I might thank railway engineers or the telephone service. You have not touched my heart. But suppose that walls rise towards heaven in such a way that I am moved. I perceive your intentions. Your mood has been gentle, brutal, charming or noble. The stones you have erected tell me so. You fix me to the place and my eyes regard it. They behold something which expresses a thought. A thought which reveals itself without word or sound, but solely by means of shapes which stand in a certain relationship to one another. These shapes are such that they are clearly revealed in light. The relationships between them have not necessarily any reference to what is practical or descriptive. They are a mathematical creation of your mind. They are the language of Architecture. By the use of inert materials and starting from conditions more or less utilitarian, you have established certain relationships, which have aroused my emotions. This is Architecture.

Le Corbusier
Vers une Architecture, 1923

The First World War was catalytic in more ways than one; first, because it hastened the restructuring of bourgeois Europe; second, because it retarded developments which had been well underway by the time that the conflict started; and third, because it brought in its wake not only revolution but also the universal sense that the postponed millenium had at last arrived. The so-called "war to end all wars" was seen as leading to the prospect of a lasting and redeeming peace; a sentiment which found its most succinct expression in Le Corbusier's slogan — "A great epoch has begun" — which appeared first in 1920, in the inaugural issue of *L'Esprit Nouveau*.

As far as France was concerned, it was inevitable that the millenium would announce itself in classical form, first in the stripped classicism of Auguste Perret's Théâtre des Champs-Elysées, Paris, completed in 1912, and then in Tony Garnier's *Cité Industrielle* which, dating from 1904, was finally published in 1917. Both works constituted the primary point of departure for Le Corbusier's Classical Machinism, otherwise known as Purism; a style which permeated his early career from 1916 to 1928. Purism was the culmination of French Classical Rationalism in as much as it terminated a trajectory of thought running from J.N.L. Durand's *Précis des leçons données à l'Ecole Polytechnique* of 1801-05, to Julien Guadet's *Eléments et théorie de l'architecture* of 1902. Le Corbusier was to absorb this heritage through Perret and Garnier, both of whom had been star pupils of Julien Guadet during his tenure as professor of theory at the École des Beaux-Arts.

Two other lines of classical development are evident in the modern movement throughout the inter-war period. First, the German line of Romantic Classicism which, stemming from Durand, entered Prussian culture via Friedrich Gilly and Karl Friedrich Schinkel. This line was eventually

89 Garnier, Cité Industrielle, 1904.
Perspective of Neoclassic concrete courtyard house
showing Biedermeier environment.

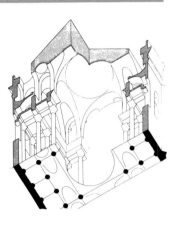

90 Choisy, Histoire de l'architecture, 1899.
Plate showing the structure of J. G. Soufflot's
Ste-Geneviève (the Panthéon), Paris, 1755-90.

reformulated by Ludwig Mies van der Rohe who declared his initial affinity for Romantic Classicism in his Bismarck Monument projected in 1912. The second was a strain which, resisting explicit definition, accepted certain aspects of the classical tradition and rejected others. This manifestation, which Demetri Porphyrios had called Doricism, intended at one and the same time both a feeling for rustic simplicity and a Dorian sense for primal order. In both Germany and Scandinavia its protagonist sought an *anti-machinist, anti-Jugendstil,* hybrid style which was neither classical nor vernacular, but a subtle compound of the two; a mixed expression which depended for its refinement on such protoclassical devices as axiality and regulating lines.

2. Auguste Perret and the Greco-Gothic Ideal

The most traditional of the Classical Rationalists was clearly Auguste Perret and in many respects the Corbusian dialectic of the Engineer's Aesthetic and Architecture was more strictly embodied in Perret's career than in his own. In some ways Perret's architecture may be seen as a final resolution of the Greco-Gothic ideal which had obsessed French architectural theory since the Abbé de Cordemoy's *Nouveau Traité de toute l'architecture* of 1706. In an effort to overcome Perrault's refutation of the divine rules of classicism, de Cordemoy attempted to ground the architecture of the proto-Enlightenment in a dual principle; that is to say, in the evident structural lucidity of the Gothic and in the trabeated orthogonal order of the Greek. The subsequent reworking of de Cordemoy's thesis by Abbé Laugier in his *Essai sur l'architecture* of 1753 was to be the inspiration behind J.G. Soufflot's Ste-Geneviève Church begun in Paris in 1755; the nave and aisles of which were covered by hemispherical domes, whose thrusts, bearing onto semi-circular arches, were apparently supported by a continuous peristyle of Corinthian columns. This premature realization of the Greco-Gothic ideal necessitated the use of hidden flying buttresses to resist the lateral thrust of the domes. An equally masked application of advanced technique is evident in Jean-Baptiste Rondelet's trabeated, stone *pronaos* built for Ste-Geneviève in 1770, wherein an elaborate system of iron cramps — comparable in their layout to the placement of modern reinforcement bars — were to prove essential to the stability of the portico.

Perret's particular resolution of the Greco-Gothic ideal was prefigured in many ways by the work of Henri Labrouste, whose Greco-Gothic essays were to depend for their architectonic probity on the structural capacity of cast and wrought iron. Labrouste's ferro-vitreous constructions were inserted like metal armatures into the load-bearing, masonry bodies of his Neoclassical buildings; his Bibliothèque Ste-Geneviève (1843-50) and his Bibliothèque Nationale (1862-68). But the full integration of the skeleton with the body, so to speak, that is to say, of the Engineer's Aesthetic with Architecture, had to wait on François Hennebique's perfection of the reinforced concrete construction in 1896 and on Auguste Perret's realization of the classical potential of the concrete skeleton in the evolution of his style.

Two seminal texts, both written by engineers, were to assist Perret in the development of an articulate *tectonic* for the rendering of reinforced

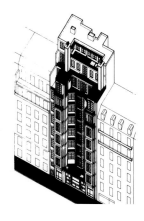

91 Perret, 25 bis rue Franklin, Paris, 1903-04.

concrete. While the first of these was largely technical, namely, Paul Christophe's canonical work, *Le Béton armé et ses applications* of 1902, the second, Auguste Choisy's *Histoire de l'architecture* of 1899 was conceptual and exercised an enormous influence on the way in which Perret was to arrive at a series of extraordinarily refined solutions.

Choisy, Professor of Architecture at the École des Ponts et Chaussées, was to argue that the various historical styles had arisen not as the sports of fashion, but as the logical consequence of developments in building technique. Among his preferred examples of such styles were the Gothic and the Greek, although it was his emphasis on the latter that made him the last great theorist of Classical Rationalism. Despite the incipient positivism of his method, Choisy still gave a certain primacy to intention and to the mediation of technique by cultural form. This is evident in his treatment of the Parthenon, of which he writes that: "Form was indeed the point of departure, and structure, far from having imposed upon it its exacting requirements, only came into harmony with it slowly; but the century of Pericles had the honors of effecting this concordance, even though it is only endured for a short time."

The proscriptive implications of Choisy's text were first followed by Perret in the block of apartments that he built at 25 bis, rue Franklin, Paris, in 1903, although on this occasion, while still under the anti-classical influence of the Art Nouveau, Perret rendered the frame in such a way as to resemble trabeated timber construction. He was to justify this idiosyncracy some fifty years later when he wrote: "In the beginning architecture is only wooden framework. In order to overcome fire one builds in hard material. And the prestige of the wooden frame is such that one reproduces all the traits, including the heads of the nails." While the rue Franklin block, clad throughout in ceramic tiles, was a tour de force in terms of exploiting the site and while its traditional *enfilade* plan embodied the potential of Le Corbusier's *plan libre* its subdividing partitions being entirely free from load throughout) the architecture itself gave little indication of the revitalized classicism which was to emerge with the parking garage that Perret Frères built in the rue de Ponthieu, Paris, in 1905. This four-storey structure, organized into a full-height nave for the gantry conveyor with car-stacking aisles to either side, was rendered as a fair-faced reinforced concrete frame, fully glazed between the spandrels and painted white throughout. And although the ornamental "rose" window which stressed the centrality of the nave can now be seen as already implying Perret's ecclesiastical manner, the important breakthrough was the classical profiling of the facade; that is, the flat overhanging cornice, the attic storey and the provision of intermediate sub-frames or *alettes* between the main structure and the infill glazing. And what was merely a beginning in the rue de Ponthieu became a fully fledged classical excursus in the Théâtre des Champs-Elysées built to Perret's designs on the avenue Montaigne in 1912.

Inaugurated with the premiere of Igor Stravinsky's *Rites of Spring,* no other structure realized on the eve of the 1914 War epitomized so poignantly that Symbolist swan song of cosmopolitan bourgeois culture which was literally destroyed by the conflict. By turns solemn, gracious and evocative —

92 Perret, Notre-Dame du Raincy, 1922-23.
Principal facade.

technically brilliant in its total mastery of monolithic concrete raft construction — the Théâtre des Champs-Elysées was Perret's first exercise in a stone veneered frame and this led him, by virtue of the material alone, to elaborate the reduced classicism that he had employed in the rue de Ponthieu. In this exercise he was paradoxically assisted by Henry van de Velde, whose crypto-classical facade, projected with his own proposals for the same structure, decisively influenced Perret's modelling of the final elevation. The neo-Palladian rhythmic structure of this austere front, the central bay of which was divided into three panels by Henri Bourdelle's Symbolist reliefs was faithfully echoed in the trabeated structure of the entry foyer, with its capital-less, free-standing columns supporting a subtly syncopated diaphragm of downstand beams. For all its mastery, the paradoxical significance of the Théâtre des Champs-Elysées resides in the fact that it was a prototype for the generic theater that Perret built in 1925 for the Exposition des Arts Décoratifs.

Four structures built by Perret in the early twenties brought him to develop that form of *Greco-Gothicism* which was to be the hallmark of his mature style; the church of Notre-Dame du Raincy, commissioned in 1922 to commemorate the First World War, the small house that he built for the painter Cassandre at Versailles in 1924 and the two temporary structures realized in Paris in the following year; the Palais de Bois on the Bois Boulogne and the Théâtre des Arts Décoratifs on the banks of the Seine.

Notre-Dame du Raincy evoked the Greco-Gothic ideal in a manner that surely referred to Soufflot's Ste-Geneviève, only now the basic plan form adopted — that is to say, the *hallenkirche* instead of the Greek Cross — was such as to stress, at the outset, a Gothic interpretation. Nevertheless, the component parts were far from Gothic in any strict sense and the hermetic, skinlike basilica, with its twenty-eight free-standing cylindrical columns, seems to have posited Le Corbusier's free plan *avant la lettre*. The thin outer skin of glazed concrete panels, just missing the peripheral columns, was clearly a liberating notion that facilitated Le Corbusier's invention of the Five Points of a New Architecture in 1926, and in this respect it is perhaps significant that Perret never returned to this arrangement, except for the Théâtre des Arts Décoratifs. In Notre-Dame du Raincy, save for clumsy clusters necessitated by the traditional frontality of the East facade, not a single column touched the glass-concrete *(claustra)* skin of the enclosure. Aside from this peristyle, the Greco-Gothic, even Roman quality of Ste-Geneviève was to find expression in the single shallow shell vault covering the entire nave and in the transverse vaults roofing the aisles. The same could be said of the columns which while cast directly from timber formwork and tapering towards the top so as to simulate classical entasis, were nonetheless formed as Peter Collins has remarked not of regular, "segmental grooves, as in antique columns, but an alternation of curved projections and angular fillets, more suggestive of Gothic composite piers." Perret made his attachment to the Greco-Gothic ideal explicit in 1924, when he declared his reasons for isolating the columns: "By exposing all of the columns free-standing, there are four rows seen instead of the usual two rows, and this greater number of columns in sight tends to greatly increase the apparent size of the church. . ." As Collins points out, this

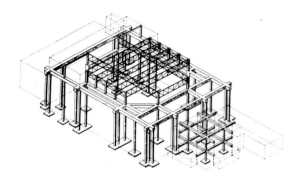

93 Perret, Théâtre des Arts Décoratifs, Paris, 1925.
Axonometric showing structure.

was exactly the precept behind Durand's criticism of Soufflot's Ste-Geneviève as demonstrated in Plate I of his *Précis des leçons* . . . of 1809.

Where the Palais de Bois, constructed out of standard timber scantlings, is a Japanese-like demonstration of much of the same principle, the impermanent Théâtre des Arts Décoratifs was one of the most lucid and lyrical statements of Perret's career. Eight free-standing columns support an octagonal ring beam which reflects at ceiling level the plan formulation of the seating below. This parterre is subdivided into three parts in order to conform to the outline of a tripartite stage. The ceiling is elevated so as to admit fenestration around its perimeter, and the resultant clerestory is inflected by pendentive elements at the corners, so as to produce a cruciform attic above the center of the auditorium. The conflict evident in Perret's work between the expressive primacy of the structure and the inherent representational quality of the facade, finds its momentary resolution in the Théâtre des Arts Décoratifs, where the free-standing, inner perimeter peristyle of the auditorium is duplicated on the exterior in advance of the otherwise blank enclosure. The reiterative blankness which had characterized the exterior of Notre-Dame du Raincy, is here animated by a fluted frieze and a peristyle of free-standing columns.

In subsequent work, Perret, in search of a new National Style, was to reserve the free-standing peristyle largely for the interior and to reconcile the rival claims of structure and facade through the time-honored strategy of *modenature,* whereby each relief element acquired its respective representational status through its degree of recession. It was decisive for the development of modern architecture that Le Corbusier rejected this compromise between the expressive claims of modernity and the *ordonnance* of tradition and that he subsequently exploited (through devices drawn from modernist painting) the absolute division between columnar structure and cantilevered skin. It is significant, in this respect, that stucco was to be the essential agent for Le Corbusier's de-construction of the modelled Perret facade into the layered membranes of Purism.

3. Tony Garnier and the Mediterranean Millenium
Sited on an escarpment in an undulating topography that corresponded to the Lyons region, Garnier's hypothetical industrial city for 35,000 people was not only a regional center, sensitively related to its physical and cultural context, but also a reinterpreted Hippodamian city that anticipated in its differentiated zoning the principles of the CIAM Athens Charter of 1933. It was in essence a Utopian Socialist city, without private property or established boundaries, without church or tribunal, without barracks or prison; an *open city* where all the unbuilt area was laid out as a continuous park. Within the residential zone Garnier projected a two- to three-storey housing typology to be constructed entirely out of reinforced concrete, according to certain criteria for light, ventilation and open space. A hierarchy of different schools dedicated to primary and secondary education were integrated into the residential fabric while the institutions for technical and professional education were located between the residential and industrial zones. The cultural and political center of the city was an assembly building of lozenge-shaped formation in plan

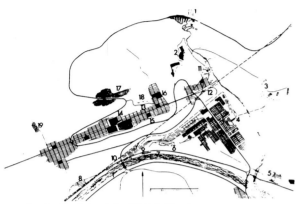

94 Garnier, Cité Industrielle, *1904-17. City plan.*

surrounded by a reinforced concrete arcade. This peristyle-promenade would have enclosed a cluster of union meeting rooms and auditoria dedicated to the accommodation of the various legislative organs of the city. Like the Athenian agora of which it was intended to be a modern counterpart, Garnier's assembly building was depicted as being populated by shadowy figures whose latter day Biedermeier clothing was designed to evoke an archaic, not to say classical, atmosphere. Unlike even the most modest houses projected by Perret, the residential stock of the *Cité Industrielle* was rendered in an extremely reduced form of crypto-classicism which was all but totally stripped of cornices and moldings. Apart from the occasional antique sculpture or relief, often rendered in the style of Bourdelle, the *Cité* was rendered in terms of the Engineer's Aesthetic (to employ Le Corbusier's phrase); a mode to which Garnier gave even greater freedom of expression in the therapeutic and utilitarian structures that he projected for the hospital and industrial quarters of the city; above all in the reinforced concrete sanitarium and in the three-hinged steel trusses over the ship yards that were located in the industrial sector.

The unique contribution of the *Cité Industrielle* stemmed from the fact that not only were its various zones open to independent expansion, but also that precise indications were given as to the organization and construction of a whole range of emerging building types. Nothing as comprehensive as this had been attempted since the publication of C.-N. Ledoux's ideal city of Chaux in 1804.

Garnier, like Le Corbusier after him, envisioned a millenialistic freezing of history in which a technically advanced civilization (already initiated in Lyons in terms of steel, reinforced concrete, automobiles, locomotives, ships, aviation and hydro-electricity) would attain some stable datum of perfection as the final fulfillment of the Western Enlightenment; that is, as the positive end of history and the return of civilization to its cradle in the Mediterranean.

4. Le Corbusier and Classical Machinism

The fourteen months that Le Corbusier (C.-E. Jeanneret) spent working for Perret in 1904 gave him a totally new outlook on architecture. Perret not only trained him to the technique of *béton armé* but also introduced him to Garnier whom he seems to have met in Lyons in 1908, while the latter was still preparing his plans for the *Cité Industrielle.* Garnier at once confirmed Le Corbusier's Utopian Socialist sympathies and encouraged his awakening interest in the normative potential of classical form.

Brought up in the Jura town of La Chaux-de-Fonds, close to the French frontier, Le Corbusier was caught between the technocratic and romantic traditions of the Teutonic north (which he experienced first hand while working for Behrens in 1911) and the poetic and rationally lyrical heritage of the Mediterranean which he first encountered while travelling in the Balkans and Asia Minor in 1913 — his famous *Voyage d'Orient.* This last took Le Corbusier to Greece where he was overwhelmed by the purity of the Parthenon which he first saw through the "eyes" of Ernst Renan's *Prière sur l'Acropole.* His immediate conversion from the Jugendstil values of his youth to the classicism of the antique world was seemingly influenced by Alexandre

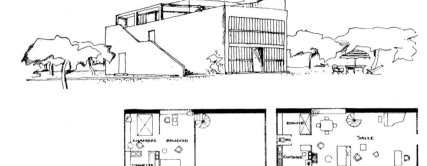

96 Le Corbusier, Maison Citrohan, 1920.
Perspective and plans.

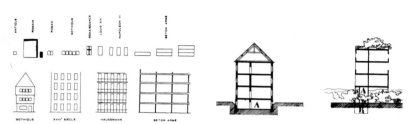

95 Le Corbusier, The Five Points of a New Architecture, 1926.

Cingria-Vaneyre's book *Entretiens de la Villa Rouet* in which the Swiss-Romand critic attacks Germanic culture for its romanticism and for its tendency towards Americanization and industrialism. For Cingria-Vaneyre, the cultural affinities of the Jura lay in the Mediterranean rather than in the Teutonic north.

Garnier and Perret prepared the ground for the two different aspects of Le Corbusier's Classical Machinism, the one anticipating the idea of the city as a plastic machine and the other articulating the basis of a reinterpreted classicism. The first was to manifest itself in Le Corbusier's Ville Contemporaine exhibited at the Salon d'Automne in 1922; the second was to become crystallized in Le Corbusier's *Les 5 points d'une architecture nouvelle* first published in 1926.

Although Garnier and the early Le Corbusier both projected Utopian Socialist cities, the difference in their visions turns on their loyalties to the two separate wings of the Utopian Socialist movement. Where Garnier stressed Fourierism — his city being projected without any repressive institutions whatsoever — Le Corbusier envisioned the Saint Simonian city of control. His Ville Contemporaine, formally structured like an oriental carpet, consisted of residential blocks, varying in height and arranged around a center of twenty-four, sixty-storey cruciform office towers; the whole being set in the midst of a vast park whose apparent purpose was to establish an absolute division between the proletarian suburb and the city of bourgeois capital. Separated from the city by a green belt, these satellite communities were depicted as loosely gridded structures which, like the residential quarters of

the *Cité Industrielle,* would have accommodated workers' housing in close proximity to the centers of industrial production. Le Corbusier was to realize such a community in 1926 when, under the patronage of the industrialist Henri Frugès, he managed to build the garden city of Pessac, close to Bordeaux. The residential sector of the *Cité Industrielle* is clearly the prototype for Pessac just as Garnier's individual housing types are to be the point of departure for Le Corbusier's own research into mass-produced housing.

The reinterpreted classicism variously evident in the immediate postwar work of both Garnier and Perret was to be transformed by Le Corbusier under the influence of the Parisian avant-garde; above all, under the impact of the painter Amédée Ozenfant, who made Le Corbusier aware not only of the de-construction of Humanist painting at the hands of Cubism, but also of the Futurist transformation of the world under the impact of industrialization. Contrary to the absolute and traditional Mediterraneanism of Garnier and Cingria-Vaneyre, Le Corbusier seems to have been suspended in the early twenties between a nostalgia for the classical world and an unqualified enthusiasm for the imminent triumph of the machine. In the map that he prepared of his *Voyage d'Orient* of 1913 he distinguished between three coexistent but inherently incompatible levels of cultural development — *classicism, industrialism* and *folk culture* — and from this point onwards his work became an endeavor to resynthesize the modern world without destroying the fundamental authenticity of these different cultural forms. In brief, he assumed the anti-*Gesamtkunstwerk* programme of Adolf Loos, but

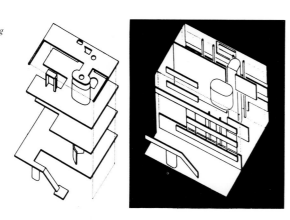

98 Le Corbusier, Villa Savoye, Poissy, 1929-31. Perspective of living room and roof deck.

this time on a much more global scale.

Alone among the pioneers of the modern movement, he conceived of his house types and buildings as though they were large scale pieces of industrial design. And yet the very title of one of his earliest prototypes, the Maison "Citrohan" of 1920, already suggests the curious ambivalence which was to run through his early work: on the one hand the assertion of the house as an industrial product, as a "machine for living"; on the other hand the Maison Citrohan was first projected as a *megaron* and as such it was obviously drawn from the vernacular of the Mediterranean. The Maison Citrohan was presented as a fusion between the industrial form of the late nineteenth-century atelier and the folk culture of the Levantine house. This conflation acounts, in part, for the strange inversions we encounter in the *Five Points of a New Architecture* and for the fact that an earlier version of this manifesto included a significant sixth point. In this version Le Corbusier advocated the elimination of the cornice; that is to say, the supression of the one sign that was capable of unequivocally indicating the presence of a classical building. In other words, the new syntax seems to have deliberately intended a certain ambiguity as to whether the work in question was *classical, industrial* or *folk.*

With the *Five Points of a New Architecture* as they are demonstrated in the Maison Cook of 1926, the representational facade is reduced to a pictorial membrane and that other essential element of classical architecture, namely the *peristyle,* is displaced in order to form the *piloti,* only to reappear in the partial column grid of the freely planned interior. By a similar token the *free facade* was now no longer the impasto skin of Notre-Dame du Raincy

but rather the stressed fabric. of a "grounded" machine whose principal mechanical element was the *fenêtre en longeur* — the horizontal repudiation, that is, of the classical *porte fenêtre* preferred by Perret. This strategy of Dadaist transposition attained its apotheosis in the *toit jardin,* where the original site reappeared as a floating foredeck hovering above a sea of trees; an elevation that denied the house not only its traditional roof but also its status of being rooted into ground. The ambivalence of this formula was reflected in Le Corbusier's Pavillon de l'Esprit Nouveau built for the Exposition des Arts Décoratifs of 1925, a building which was at one and the same time a free-standing suburban villa and a prefabricated monastic cell to be inserted into the skeleton frame of his Immeubles-Villas, first projected for his Ville Contemporaine of 1922.

This uncertainty as to whether the generic house was a production object or a cultural artifact attained its most contradictory expression in the Classical Machinism of the two canonical villas which Le Corbusier realized outside Paris in the late twenties — the Villa de Monzie (Stein) built at Garches in 1927 and the Villa Savoye completed at Poissy in 1929.

In both instances the machine appearance ("the impression is of naked polished steel," as he wrote of the Parthenon in *Vers une Architecture*) was achieved through the application of stucco which was the one "inauthentic" material which Perret abjured throughout his life. And yet while this material was antipathetic to the Greco-Gothic ideal, it was by no means unsympathetic to the neo-Palladianism which informed the plans of these villas; indeed, convincing parallels have since been drawn between these villas and their

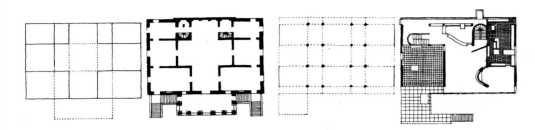

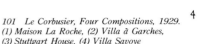

99 *Comparative analysis of the proportional rhythm employed in Palladio's Malcontenta of 1560 & Le Corbusier's Villa à Garches, 1927.*

100 *Le Corbusier, Villa de Monzie, Garches, 1927. Garden elevation with regulating lines.*

101 *Le Corbusier, Four Compositions, 1929. (1) Maison La Roche, (2) Villa à Garches, (3) Stuttgart House, (4) Villa Savoye*

respective sixteenth-century prototypes in the Veneto, with the Villa Malcontenta as the prototype for de Monzie and the Villa Capra as the corresponding model for Savoye. As Colin Rowe remarked of the first pair in his book, *The Mathematics of the Ideal Villa:*

In both cases six "transverse" lines of support rhythmically alternating single and double bays are established; but the rhythm of the parallel lines of support, as a result of Le Corbusier's use of the cantilever, differs slightly. At the villa at Garches, it is ½:1½:1½:½ and at Malcontenta 2:2:1½. In plan, Le Corbusier thus obtains a sort of compression for his central bay and interest seems transferred to his outer bays, which are augmented by the extra half unit of the cantilever; while Palladio secures a dominance for his central division, and a progression towards his portico, which focuses interest there. In both cases the projecting element, terrace or portico, occupies 1½ units in depth.

Rowe goes on to point out that the square plan, elliptical entry and central ramp of the Villa Savoye may be read as a displaced reference to the centralized, biaxial, domed form of the Villa Capra. There, however, all similarity ends, Palladio insisting on centrality and Le Corbusier asserting within the confines of the square the asymmetrical qualities of rotation and peripheral dispersal.

Both de Monzie and Savoye were significant for their implicit resolution of the cultural problem which had first been posited by Adolf Loos and which had been assumed by Le Corbusier after his *Voyage d'Orient;* namely how to combine the convenience of the Gothic Revival or Arts and Crafts house of *vernacular* provenance with the representative asperities of *classical* form. As

Le Corbusier's Four Compositions of 1929 would indicate, his villas of the twenties were able to achieve this with an intellectual elegance denied to Loos. By exploiting the dissociations of the free plan he was able to separate the irregular convenience of the asymmetrical interior from the regular deportment of the free facade. At the same time the precision of the rendered finish was complemented by the application of *industrial* components such as steel fenestration and hardware, marine balustrading and the occasional spiral or dog-leg free-standing stair in tubular steel.

The 1927 international competition for the League of Nations headquarters in Geneva had the effect of returning Le Corbusier to the Greco-Gothic principles from which his Classical Machinism had originally evolved. This is evident from the classical format that he and Pierre Jeanneret adopted for its overall organization, from the absolutely symmetrical arrangement of the assembly building and its approaches, to the facing of the entire complex in glass and coursed ashlar. That their Palais des Nations assembly building was literally a "classical-machine" is evident from the tense interaction of two entirely different architectonic systems: on the one hand a hierarchical enfilade of element drawn from the classical palace — the *peristyle,* the *scala regia,* the *pas perdu* and the *promenade architecturale;* on the other hand the equally hierarchical trussed-concrete and steel-frame structure carrying the roof of the assembly hall and the double-layered glazed curtain walls — the *pans verre* — flanking either side of the auditorium. A comparable tension was to exist in the four major monuments that the firm saw realized between 1932 and 1933 — the Maison Clarté apartments, Geneva, the Pavillon Suisse

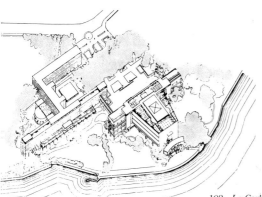

102 Le Corbusier & Jeanneret, League of Nations, 1927. Axonometric.

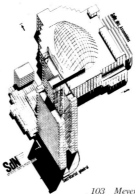

103 Meyer and Wittwer, League of Nations, 1927. Axonometric.

(Cité Universitaire), the Cité de Refuge and the Porte Molitor apartments; the last three being located in Paris. In each instance, glass, glass blocks, ashlar and ceramic tiles were treated as though they were equally thin membranes stretched across the surface of a plastic armature. This effect was comparable in many respects to the inversion of glass and masonry that appeared in the Walter Gropius and Adolf Meyer shoe-last factory built for Karl Benscheidt at Alfeld-an-der-Leine in 1911. The insertion of ferro-vitreous structures into the lithic corpus of stone-faced buildings or alternatively the application of vitreous membranes in the place of masonry revetment recalled in Le Corbusier's SdN proposal the work of Henri Labrouste. It is curious to note in passing that such a dialectical attitude was absent from the absolute functionalism of the Hannes Meyer and Hans Wittwer entry for the same competition, where a constructivist revetment in glass and asbestos cement stressed the non-hierarchical intention of the design. As Meyer wrote:

Our League of Nations building symbolizes nothing — its size is automatically determined by the dimensions and the conditions of the program. As an organic building it expresses unfeignedly that it is intended to be a building for work and co-operation. This building does not seek an artificial link with its park-like setting through the art of landscape gardening. As a deliberately contrived work of man it stands in legitimate contrast to nature. This building is neither beautiful nor ugly. It asks to be evaluated as a structural invention.

Nothing could be further from the SdN entry of Le Corbusier and Pierre Jeanneret, where every effort was made to represent the honorific status of

the work, where the building was landscaped into its site and where the architects took a Beaux-Arts "elementarist" approach to the design, as this had been formulated at the turn of the century by Julien Guadet, professor of theory at the École des Beaux-Arts at the time that Garnier and Perret were students there.

That Le Corbusier adopted this "elementarist" approach generally when dealing with large complexes is shown by his preliminary studies for his entry to the Palace of the Soviets competition of 1931. There under eight alternative layouts we read:

the various stages of the project, wherein one sees the organs, already independently established, the one from the other, take up, little by little, their reciprocal places to culminate in a synthetic solution.

We find a similar remark appended to an alternative sheme for his League of Nations entry, published in his book *Une Maison, Un Palais* of 1928. Under a symmetrical, and evidently more functional layout we encounter the caption: "alternative proposition employing the same elements of composition." The partially asymmetrical organization finally adopted suggests a conflict between the circulatory convenience of the symmetrical *parti* and the classical necessity of maintaining an axial approach to the representative, neo-Palladian facade of the assembly structure.

The League of Nations competition is the climax and the crisis point of Le Corbusier's early career. It represents the culmination of his Classical

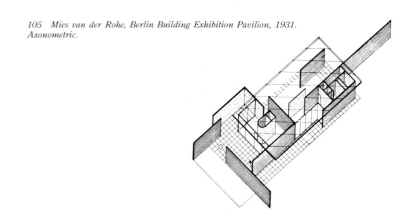

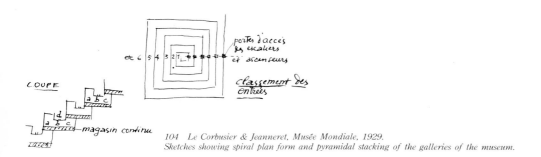

104 Le Corbusier & Jeanneret, Musée Mondiale, 1929.
Sketches showing spiral plan form and pyramidal stacking of the galleries of the museum.

Machinism, since it virtually coincides with the introduction of "realist," figurative elements into his Purist painting. From now on his public projects become increasingly classical and symmetrical. Thus his SdN proposal seems to have been a watershed, not only within his own carrer, but also in terms of his rapport with the international modern movement.

Le Corbusier's drive to inform structural utility with the traditional hierarchy of classicism, and vice versa, was soon to bring him into conflict with the socialist-functionalist designers of the late nineteen twenties, although the left-wing Czechoslovakian architectural critic Karel Tiege had publicly supported Le Corbusier on the occasion of his being disqualified in the League of Nations Competition. However, the classical monumentality of Le Corbusier's pyramidal Mundaneum museum proposed in 1929 for Paul Otlet's Cité Mondiale was sufficient to convert Tiege into the most vehement of his critics. Tiege wrote in *Stavba* in 1929:

According to Le Corbusier, architecture as art believes that its mission begins where construction ends... It aspires to eternity while the engineer responds to actuality. According to Poelzig, architecture as an art begins where it does not submit to any particular purpose; building *für den Lieben Gott*. In short, according to this argument, to become dignified as architecture, there must be added some "plus" to the rational solution... If we have occupied ourselves so carefully with the Mundaneum project, it is because we believe this work, whose author is a leading and foremost representative of modern architecture, should serve as a warning to its author and to modern architecture generally. The Mundaneum illustrates the fiasco of aesthetic theories and traditional prejudices, of all the dangers of the slogan "house-palace," and thus of utilitarian

architecture with an artistic "addition" or "dominant." From here it is possible to go all the way to full academicism and classicism, or ... to return to the solid reality of ... the motto, the "house as a machine for living in," and from there, once again to work towards a scientific, technical, industrial architecture.

5. Mies van der Rohe and the Schinkelschüle

Ludwig Mies van der Rohe's return to the *Schinkelschüler* tradition, in which he had been firmly grounded prior to the First World War (see his Kröller-Müller house project of 1912) came with his Barcelona Pavilion of 1929 which combined a number of diverse influences under the sign of a reinterpreted Romantic Classicism. First, there was the floating planar aesthetic that he had adapted from Wright's Prairie Style, as filtered through the Dutch De Stijl movement; second, there was his own version of the free plan, derived from Le Corbusier's *Les 5 points d'une architecture nouvelle* of 1926; third, there was the influence of the Russian Suprematist sensibility, most evident in the "fossilized" wall planes and in the glazed and chromed components of the fenestration; finally, there was the *Schinkelschüler* traditon itself (see Mies's Berlin Building exhibition pavilion of 1931). As far as the Barcelona Pavilion is concerned, this is evident in the vaguely Italianate composition and in the eight column grid of its loggia form, the whole being implanted on a Romantic Classical base of unfilled travertine.

The Tugendhat House, built in 1930 in Brno, Czechoslovakia, adapted the spatial conception of the Barcelona Pavilion to a domestic programme. It may be seen as combining the late Arts and Crafts plan of Wright's Robie

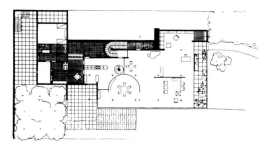

106 *Mies van der Rohe, Tugendhat House, Brno, 1928-30. Main floor plan.*

House with the typical loggia format of a Schinkelesque villa. Unlike Le Corbusier's Maison Cook (which also incorporated vestiges of the Arts and Crafts tradition), the free plan was reserved here for the living area which once again, as in Barcelona Pavilion, was structured about a grid of cruciform, chromium-plated columns. An enormous plate glass wall, capable of being mechanically retracted into the basement, opened the whole of the living area to the garden in good weather, and thereby directly evoked the idea of a Schinkelesque belvedere. Four other components can be identified as referring to Prussian Classicism. First, the chromium-sheathed cruciform columns themselves whose vertical highlights momentarily recalled classical fluting (cf. the .faceted fillets used in the fromwork of the standard Perret column); second, the shallow plate glass conservatory which served as a kind of living foil to the fossilized vegetation of the onyx panel which subdivides the main space and last but not least the classically profiled stairway to the garden.

Mies's reinterpretation of Prussian classicism was curtailed at this juncture as he moved closer to productive functionalism and to the ideal of *Baukunst* as this was embodied in the Neues Bauen movement. Mies seems to have committed himself at this point to the position which was emerging in German practice, namely that advanced technical production could be combined with the craft tradition to create a new bourgeois architecture — modern but solidly linked to the best of the burgher traditions. Mies had already demonstrated this thesis in his all-brick Hermann Lange house built at Krefeld in 1928 and he was to pursue this line further in his unbuilt courtyard houses of the thirties and in his Lemcke House, Berlin, of 1932 and in his

second project for the residence of Ulrich Lange in 1935.

This objective *Baukunst* approach — an attitude that was by no means alien to the *Schinkelschüler* tradition — assumed new levels of objectivity in the factory buildings that Mies van der Rohe realized for the Krefeld silk industry in 1932-35 and in his project for the Reichsbank competition of 1933. This last dramatically demonstrates the split running through his work in the thirties: on the one hand, the absolutely technical objectivity of the repeated office floors of the Reichsbank; on the other, a return to classical hierarchy in the elaboration of the entrance and the first floor banking hall — the anomalous emergence of the honorific entry sequence complete with *peristyle* and *scala regia*. Mies was to embrace these classical components with much greater assurance in the full flowering of his later Chicago period which occurred a full decade after the end of the Second World War.

6. Heinrich Tessenow: Craftsmanship and the Provincial City
Influenced by Hermann Muthesius's *Das Englische Haus* of 1904 and by Paul Mebes's study of the Biedermeier period, *Um 1800* of 1908, Heinrich Tessenow and his collaborator Paul Schultze-Naumburg began to reinterpret the German rural vernacular in terms of a purified vision of the English Arts and Crafts movement. In this they renounced the idiosyncratic artistic mannerism evident in the work of such architects as C.F.A. Voysey or Richard Norman Shaw (a "will to form" which had so clearly led to the hermeticism of the Jugendstil) in favor of accepting the resilience of rooted culture, whose traditional syntax was such as to make both the style and its

realization acceptable to all. They were to repudiate the *avant-gardism* inherent to an equal degree in both the crypto-classicism of the late Jugendstil (Behrens) and the modernized normative classicism that was emerging from the École des Beaux-Arts (Garnier). Instead, they accepted the normative authority of vernacular components — the house types, barns, roofs, gables, windows, shutters, steps, pergolas, fences, and casements which were seen as being comparable in their fixity to the received repetoire of Western Classicism. They posited a timeless *Baukunst* in which the existing reality of rooted production would prevail over the ideology of progress and would transcend that which they saw as the false dichotomy of classical and vernacular culture. Like certain Scandinavian architects who shared the same influences and impulses (the 1907 Skønvirke Organization, for instance), they sought a kind of *Ur-Kultur*, compounded out of vernacular building and the stereometric manipulation of pure form.

With his Dalcrose Institute and his Am Schänkenberg Siedlung, both built at Hellerau in 1910, Tessenow was able to demonstrate an ontology of building predicated to an equal degree on the architectonic constituents of the past and the craft capacities of the present. This ontological approach was oriented towards the everyday in the same sense that Jacques Dalcrose's technique in dance was based on the natural capacity of the body. It also regarded history in much the same way as Dalcrose, who as a disciple of the Swiss director Adolph Appia sought to recreate an archaic and universal theater based in the ritualistic movement of the body in architectural space.

Spengler's *Der Untergang des Abendlandes* (The Decline of the West),

already written by 1912, is paralleled in many respects by Tessenow's *Handwerk und Kleinstadt* (Craftmanship and the Provincial City) written in the summer of 1918. Located on either side of the first industrialized war, they both reflect on the climatic upheaval brought about by industrialism and monopoly capital. In different ways they each regard the emerging epoch as cataclysmic and decisive. As Julius Posener has written:

... Tessenow wrote that the extreme division of labor, brought about by industrialization, had already reduced man to an instrument long before the beginning of the war, which in its turn, had been the inevitable consequence precisely of this process directed against man. Mankind, therefore, "will have to go through hell" before getting back to the path of artisan work. ... Tessenow was influenced by Morris, whose writings he knew very well. Their conceptions are not, however, identical. Morris's protest was directed against industrial society, whereas Tessenow rejected both the big city and the village; in the city the individual works only with his head, in the country only with his body, almost without thinking. The provincial town is the place for craftmanship, and this is the activity best suited to man. It is in fact only through a craft that the individual completely fulfills himself .... Tessenow succeeded in expressing this outlook so convincingly precisely because he himself had been a craftsman and had grown up in a provincial town, ... (He) was the advocate of a petty bourgeois ideology, but middle class life was not an ideology as far as he was concerned; it was experience. Since this experience was therefore real life, the only life worth living, everyday objects were transfigured in his hands. His houses, his public establishments, his tables and chairs, irradiate an austere delicacy, a satisfaction with just life and this judicious work and salutary order. It was a type of life that already showed through so clearly in his drawings. Tessenow comments on this limited existence,

108 *Tessenow, Am Schänkenberg Siedlung, Hellerau, 1910.*

bestowing upon it a very much broader feeling of spaciousness.

Tessenow's practice was predicated on a small number of traditional types and components which were then assembled in such a way as to create simple, but nonetheless tense and vibrant forms, suffused with a restrained and uncanny sense of timelessness and warmth. In his theoretical text of 1916, *Hausbau und dergleichen* (House Building and Related Issues), he revealed his formal methods, of which the following comment on biaxial symmetry is typical:

Basically, the union of two figures gives rise to a new symmetrical image . . . the axis of which remains invisible; but the fact that in a double building of this kind the details are brought so strongly into relief bestows upon the whole an extraordinary force which, however, remains very contained without thereby being irrelevant.

It is no accident that Tessenow's buildings were finished in white stucco throughout, irrespective of their size and status. The grounding of his "vernacular" in the golden years of the German late eighteenth century celebrated by Paul Mebes — that is to say, in an architectural syntax where the glazing was almost flush with the surface of the stucco — enabled him to maintain tight control over the abstract placement or "dis-placement" of traditional components such as casement windows, doors, etc. The same choice also insured that the glazing bars would help to energize the facade and to create an invisible network of stereometric order, running over the surface of the work. These devices are already evident in the Am Shänkenberg row housing at Hellerau, and they recur again in the Sächsische Landesschule, built at Klötsche in 1925, in the Heinrich-Schütz Schule built at Kassel in 1927 and finally, in the Gagfah Siedlung realized at Berlin-Zehlendorf in 1928. Tessenow's craft abstractions led him in his public works to create certain surprising "displacements," such as the half-ironic simulation of a classical arcade in his Sächsische Landesschule of 1925 or more earnestly the realization of a technocratic precision, close to the *Baukunst* of Mies, in the indoor swimming pool, Stadtbad-Mitte, Berlin, of 1927.

The major inconsistency of Tessenow's career resides in the fact that for all his advocacy of the provincial city, he never once projected the potential order of its form. Instead he restricted himself to projecting one "garden city" colony after another, particularly after the rise of the Nazi Party in 1933, when his anti-avant-gardism and his classico-vernacular approach afforded a convenient style in which to render the *Blut und Boden* ideology of the Third Reich.

7. The Doricist Sensibility

The works of Mebes and Muthesius also had an influence in Scandinavia, where they encouraged a native movement to overcome the void left by the collapse of National Romanticism (Scandinavian Jugendstil) and to bring a new paradigm to serve in its place. The year 1907 saw the first of Vilhelm Wansher's Neoclassical articles and the independent organization of the vernacular-oriented *Skønvirke* movement by P.V. Jensen-Klint and Jens

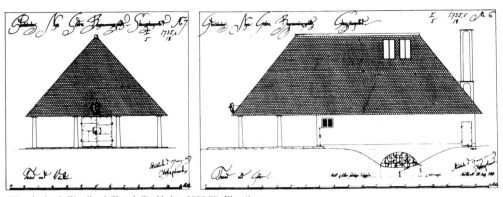

109 Asplund, Woodland Chapel, Stockholm, 1918-20. Elevations.

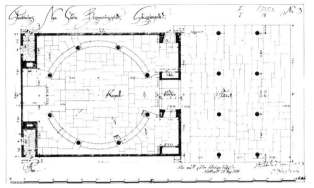

110 Woodland Chapel. Plan.

Moller-Jensen, while as early as 1906 Tens Norup stressed the syntactic aspects of architecture as opposed to the superficial semantic constituents of style. Only Tessenow, however, really demonstrated a method whereby a classico-vernacular mode of building might be brought into being, a method which had its most direct influence in Finland, above all in Martti Välikangas's all-timber Puu-Käpylä housing settlement completed outside Helsinki in 1920 and in Alvar Aalto's early housing and civil guard houses built in the region of Jyväskylä in the mid-twenties. In retrospect the 1920 Woodland Chapel built in the Southern Cemetery of Stockholm to the designs of Gunnar Asplund is to be seen as inaugurating the Doricist sensibility, a mode of building which was to endure for a full decade in Scandinavia following the end of the First World War. As Demetri Porphyrios has written of his invention of this term:

The ability and determination to continuously shift between classicism and vernacular without the slightest embarrassment that it might be mistaken as practicing an eclecticism, suggests that it is not stylistics that the architectural mind of the period is after. Architecture is situated not on the fleeting surface of visible representation, but on the fundamental act of the drawing up of the constructional and occupation map of shelter. Thus the vernacular or classicist looks of Asplund's or Lewerentz's chapels, do not refer to the associational mythology of the respective stylistic regions, but instead they point to the . . . "doricism" inherent in the austerity of both the shed and the temple.

In short, the Doricist architects were to return to the very origins of the Greco-Gothic ideal, as these were initially formulated in Laugier's primitive hut, depicted in the famous frontispiece to his *Essai sur l'architecture* of

1753. In this *répétition differente*, however, the mind was not allowed to reauthenticate abstract classic categories on the basis of a hypothesized fusion of nature and culture. Instead as in the case of Ledoux (only now with greater urgency), a culturally neutralized but nonetheless marginally referential architecture was seen as the vehicle in which to embody and celebrate that act which Porphyrios has called "the ontology of construction and shelter."

It is no accident that, like Richard Mique's Hameau designed for Marie Antoinette at Versailles in 1783, Asplund's Woodland Chapel had their origins in the cult of the Romantically picturesque *fabrique*, only in this instance the folly was a Hytten or hunting lodge built for the Liselund estate in at Moen, Denmark in 1795 to the designs of Andreas Kirkerup; a structure which the collaborators of the Danish architect Aage Rafn had already measured and published by 1918.

To evoke the Doricist sensibility is to paraphrase a complex movement which, as in the work of Tessenow, intended a return to an accessible culture of building; to an expression which, despite its modesty, aspired to a certain restrained monumentality and generally employed a sparse but nonetheless direct iconography (see Carl Milles's "Angel of Death" in Asplund's Woodland Chapel). The triumphant forms and elemental codes of Humanistic Classicism are recalled but not repostulated as such. Instead "vernacular" construction and a metaphysical sense of "dwelling" are permitted to attain a Doric authenticity whose surface, volume and profile may reflect the memory of a past culture, be this culture classical or high vernacular. One of the paradoxes of the Doric mode resides in the fact that such a conjunction is by definition

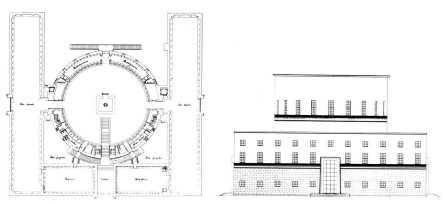

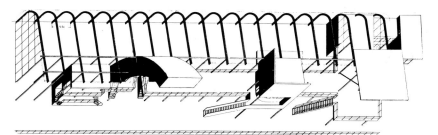

111　Asplund, Stockholm Public Library, 1920-28. Main elevation and plan.

112　Asplund, Stockholm Exhibition, 1930. A short lived Foray into constructivism.

atectonic; that is to say, indifferent to the apparent authenticity or otherwise of the revealed construction and hence opposed in some profound sense to a pure ontology of shelter and construction. The truth is, of course, that the Doricist sensibility was to vary more than in the expression of Tessenow, for where the German master hardly modified his *atectonic* syntax between house-form and public institution — specifically, let us say, between his Hellerau housing of 1910 and his Klötsche School of 1925 — Asplund was to shift the tone of his monumentality in a decisive way as he moved from the taut astringency of his Woodland Chapel of 1920 to the lithic solemnity of his penultimate scheme for the Stockholm Public Library, dating from 1920.

Asplund originally conceived his Woodland Chapel as a Neoclassic temple but on seeing the Liselund publication he immediately recast the design in the form of a shingle-covered pyramidal structure on an elevated base. Just under two-thirds of this form was enclosed by white-washed walls which accommodated within their volume a square chapel, domed over from a circular springing of six columns and illuminated from above in a surprising way. Nothing could have been more guaranteed to destroy the fragile illusion of a masonry tectonic than this skylight, evidently let into the timber trusswork of a traditional roof. The remainder of the pitch that extended beyond the chapel was supported by an open peristyle of eight Tuscan columns, turned out of timber and resting on the flat stylobate of a paved loggia. Much of the Doricist quality in this building derived from the *arationality* of its detailing — from say the enamelled wooden columns, whose capitals appeared to be slightly detached from the flush ceiling they mysteriously support or again

from the unlikely "weightlessness" and diminutive size of the dome suspended within the shelter of the vast roof. As Stuart Wrede has written: "Detailing the junction of the pitched roof and the flat ceiling so that they create a continuous flush joint on all sides, he (Asplund) presents the roof as a discrete solid out of which the dome appears to be carved."

A comparable self-consciousness pervaded the exquisite mediaevalized script applied to the presentation drawings. This calligraphy was of the same graphic genre as the wrought-iron gates with their death's head motif. In brief, there was an air of auto-suggestive hallucination about the entire piece as though the author imagined that he could induce both himself and others to believe that they had been momentarily transported to some other, preindustrial epoch, lying beyond the established cultural domains of history.

These domains could be specifically identified in the case of the Stockholm Public Library as realized in 1928, where the cylindrical drum, the half-cubic mass and the giant Egyptian door were readily decipherable in terms of the Enlightenment architecture of Boullée and Ledoux — the former for the library chamber itself lined with books, the latter for the employment of prismatic geometry, directly reminiscent of the prisms which appear in his Barrière de la Villette built in Paris in 1784. For Romantic Classical precedent, however, one need look no further than the main door, for here the source is surely the Egyptoid fenestration that articulates G. Bindesbøll's Thorwaldsen Museum completed in Copenhagen in 1848. And indeed, it is impossible to deny the influence of Romantic Classicism on the Doricist sensibility although this heritage was mediated by two entirely different

275

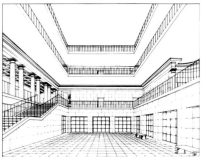

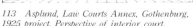
113 *Asplund, Law Courts Annex, Gothenburg, 1925 project. Perspective of interior court.*

114 *Law Courts Annex, Gothenburg, 1936. Penultimate facade.*

interpretations within the same cultural movement; on the one hand the whimsical *atectonic* theatricality of Ivar Tengbom's Stockholm Concert Hall (1921-26) or say J.S. Sirén's Finnish Parliament (1926-31), or for that matter Asplund's own Skandia Cinema bult in Stockholm in 1923; on the other, there is the more solemn and reductive monumentality evident first in Ivar Bentsen's Philharmonic Hall projected in 1919 and then returned to with Spartan vigor in Edvard Thomsen's Oregaard School of 1925 and in Asplund's Stockholm Public Library completed in the following year.

While Asplund never aspired to Thomsen's severity, he nonetheless pursued a reductive procedure which led him by degrees after 1928 to embrace the modernist aesthetic, particularly on the occasion of his design for the Stockholm Exhibition of 1930. The international style restaurant added to the library sometime after 1928 was already a move in this direction just prior to Asplund's total but short-lived conversion to the syntax of constructivism under the influence of the socialist critic Gregor Paulsson, who masterminded the Stockholm Exhibition. Of the ideological superstructure underlying this shift in taste Wrede has written:

Though the transformation of Swedish society had begun with the introduction of universal suffrage in 1911, the haute bourgeoisie had continued to exercise a cultural hegemony, especially in architecture, for the first three decades of the century. Asplund's library represented both its peak and its swan song. His Stockholm Exhibition of 1930 was to become the most striking symbol in Scandinavia of the advent of a new era. Two short years apart in terms of their completion date, the two projects became the prime architectural symbols of the "fundamental difference in mentality" of which Åhren spoke.

Wrede's reference is to Uno Åhren's criticism of the library which appeared in *Byggmästaren* in 1928 in which the Swedish functionalist insisted that the new classicism was dead. And yet what was of interest as far as the future of Doricism was concerned was its transformation into something other than mainline modernism, evident not only in the development of Asplund's work between the mid-twenties and the mid-thirties, but also evident much later in the post Second World War career of Alvar Aalto. In this respect we can see how a fundamentally Doricist type — namely an internal rectangular top-lit atrium with galleries above — was to persist through a series of transpositions, from Asplund's 1925 Neoclassic proposal for the Gothenburg Law Courts through to Aalto's Rautatalo office building completed in Helsinki in 1956. Thus while Doricism persisted in some form or other throughout the twenties and thirties, culminating in Asplund's Forest Crematorium completed in Stockholm's Southern Cemetery in 1940 and in the work of the Danish architect Arne Jacobsen — particularly in his town halls of virtually the same date — a more "brutal" concern for an ontology of shelter and construction would wait upon the later career of Aalto, although hints as to the possibility of this development had already been made by Aino Aalto, most notably in her timber-columned and thatched-roof Villa Flora, built at Alajari, Finland in 1926.

Aside from his work of Barnsdall while he was still employed by Wright, Schindler had already designed some ten buildings and countless projects by the time he had the good fortune to obtain Lovell as his client. Lovell, as David Gebhard has written, ". . . was a characteristic Southern California product. It is doubtful whether his career could have been repeated anywhere else.

Through his *Los Angeles Times* column, 'Care of the Body,' and through 'Dr. Lovell's Physical Culture Center,' he had an influence which extended far beyond the physical care of the body. He was, and wished to be considered, progressive, whether in physical culture, permissive education, or architecture."

Lovell basically wanted a house by the beach in which it would be possible to indulge in nude sun bathing, and this gave a certain priority to the open terrace on the bedroom floor; a provision which caused the house to be popularly known as the "upside down house." It was the necessity of cantilevering this terrace that influenced Schindler to base the structure of the house on a set of five reinforced concrete frames within which the rest of the dwelling was to be delicately cradled. It was typical of Schindler's passion for structural invention that he would hit upon this division of labor between rigid heavy-weight transverse frames and light-weight wooden skeletonal construction spanning in between. Once this principle was established the house seems to have evolved naturally as a kind of continual altercation between the long frontage oriented towards the street, and the short end facing the sea. This conflict imposed a rotational, plastic treatment on the intersection of the two primary facades, facing the street and the ocean, while the other two sides were rendered as solid, with the occasional fenestration to light the service sector of the house. One of the more unusual features introduced by Schindler, was the elevation of the main body of the house and the creation of a sand garden beneath, capable of serving not only as a playground for children, but also as a forecourt for people coming from the sea. This device was formally inflected by the concrete stairs giving access to the first floor; the one being a stepped ramp giving access to the living room balcony and the other being a short service stair leading to the kitchen. In this sculptural division, stabilized formally by the steady rhythm of the frames, one may speak of a situation in which form and content are united, for the ramp opens towards the public sector of the house while the short stair turns towards the kitchen, etc.

Schindler did everything he could to make this house into a total work of art, syncopating the subdivisions of the wooden fenestration in relation to the built-in furniture and commissioning a textile designer, Maria Kipp, to weave golden fabric for the curtains and the upholstery. Nothing could be further from the Neoplastic astringency of the Rietveld House and yet in certain respects the works are strangely comparable.

Left: ground floor plan   Right: overall view

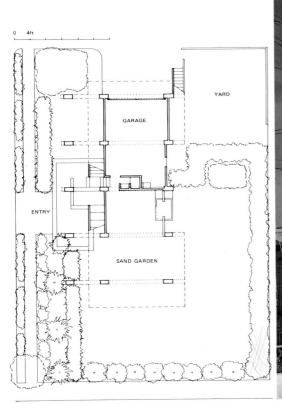

1925-27

KARL MOSER
St. Antonius
Basel, Switzerland

Karl Moser, like Auguste Perret by whom he was influenced, was destined to be the immediate patron of the Swiss Neue Sachlichkeit; indeed in one case, to become the actual father, since his son Werner Moser was to be a major participant in the movement. This church thus stands on the threshold of the functionalist era; an impeccable and authentic Perretesque essay which was to revolutionize church design in Switzerland. In this respect it is clear that both Fritz Metzger's St. Karl's church in Lucerne (1933-35) and Burkhardt and Egender's St. Johannes church is Basel (1936) owe a debt to Moser's vigorous reinterpretation of Perret.

Modeled on Perret's Notre-Dame du Raincy of five years before, St. Antonius follows the basilica paradygm in a way that is more direct, with one huge barrel vault spanning the better part of the nave and running for the full length of the volume. While Moser followed Perret directly in creating a structurally rationalist church, the exterior of St. Antonius was even more divorced than the curtain wall of Notre-Dame du Raincy from the trabeated and vaulted order of the interior. Thus the membrane of Moser's basilica presents itself as an in-situ concrete prism penetrated intermittently by totally glazed bays of stained glass which served to illuminate the nave. Indeed, unlike le Raincy, the traditional allusion here is to the simple brick basilica, roofed in timber, rather than to the architectonic sophistries of Perret's Greco-Gothic ideal. Thus the ribbed and coffered roof of St. Antonius resembles in its orthogonal precision the timberlike framework of Perret's apartment block of 1904. Other than the crypto-classical Zurich Kunsthaus started in the same year, Moser's reputation largely rests on this single masterpiece.

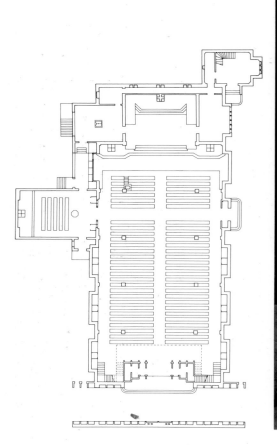

Left: ground floor plan
Center: street facade
Right: view toward entry

WALTER GROPIUS
ADOLF MEYER
The Bauhaus
Dessau, Germany

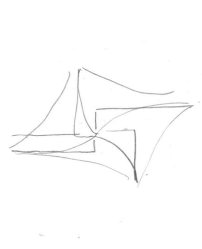

Main entry

Indebted to the universal asymmetrical aesthetic posited by the Dutch De Stijl movement, and being at the same time the only realised work of three projects designed by Walter Gropius and Adolf Meyer between 1922 and 1925, the Bauhaus building is the culmination of an intense period of architectural development. First broached in their Chicago Herald Tribune Competition of 1922, where a straightforward steel frame was transformed into an asymmetrical composition by the application of projected balconies and recessed terraces, this Neo-plastic aesthetic was developed in a much more integrated way in the Gropius and Meyer project for a philosophical academy at Erlangen (1924) and it is this horizontal, elongated, but nonetheless pinwheeling composition which becomes the essential point of departure for the Bauhaus.

While bridging an access road (cf. Duiker's Zonnestraal; 1927) the Bauhaus complex spiraled about its principal entry hall to project three pinwheeling elements, first, the five-storey student's dormitory block to the East, then the three-storey classroom block to the North, and finally the three-storey workshop block to the South. This complex mass was raised on a traditional half-recessed cellar floor; with the resultant podium being rendered black in order to give the illusion that the white, ochre and blue mass of the main structure floats above the ground. The Bauhaus's system of internal circulation was structured about two principal stairway entries to the North and South of the access road. These stairs served the classroom and workshop blocks respectively. Their opposing cores of equal volume appear to symbolise the Bauhaus's pedagogical strategy of balancing theory (to the North) with practice (to the South), the two being linked and controlled by the administration bridge spanning the road.

Of reinforced concrete and block infill throughout, the most intense rhetoric from a structural point of view obtained in the workshop wing which was built of haunched,

downstand beam and slab construction with a three-storey-high curtain wall spanning clear for the entire height of the building. Industrial standards prevailed throughout this wing including the radiators which were integrated with the glazing. Aside from this, the spiraling mass of the entire complex was subtly accentuated by the cantilevering balconies in the dormitory block, and by the projecting bands of glazing in the classroom wing. While breaking with the absolute canons of Neoplasticism, the Bauhaus none-theless reflected the De Stijl ethos in its furnishing, which was largely designed and built by the Bauhaus faculty and students, including Moholy-Nagy's neon lighting to the main public volumes, and Breuer's tubular steel furniture. On the other hand, the symbolic centerpiece of the interior, Oskar Schlemmer's famous painting of the Bauhaus staircase, was not so much Neo-plastic or Constructivist as it was close to that German materialist school of painting known as Magical Realism.

280 Exterior view, classroom block (left) and
     workshop block (right)
281 Left: second floor plan
     Right, from top: neon lighting on the ceiling,
     entry to main hall, detail of windows

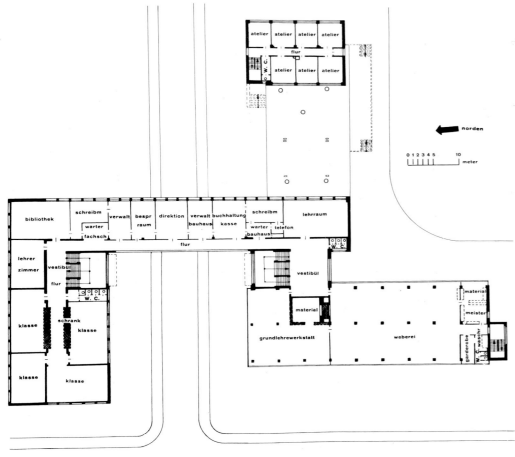

As inventive from a formal point of view as Melnikov, Ilya Golosov was encouraged by the Revolution of 1917 to abandon the constraints of the neoclassical manner in which he had been trained. In the immediate post-revolutionary era, classicism was associated with the superseded monarchy and as a result traditionalists such as Golosov felt called upon to create totally unprecedented forms. Golosov's first attempt at a new "millenialist" manner was his entry for the 1923 Palace of Labor competition which he projected as a curious mixture of colossal abstract prisms (auditoria shaped like thick cogwheels) and smaller elements drawn from crypto-classical and even Assyrian sources. Among these last it is surprising to note the presence of forms whose origins are as diverse as Behrens's high tension factory for the AEG Humboldthain complex of 1910 or battlements and staircases drawn from the Palace of Sargon at Khorsabad.

This eclectic exoticism is abruptly curtailed in the following year when Golosov adopts the received constructivist mode in a series of projects ranging from his House of Councils design, projected for Briansk in 1924 to his Telegraph Building and Zuyev Worker's Club, both completed in Moscow in 1926. From a stylistic point of view, Golosov's achievement, like that of others of his generation, remains strangely suspended between, on the one hand, somewhat superficial efforts to disrupt the monotonous regularity of the trabeated frame, and on the other, bold and freely inventive, three dimensional compositions carried out at a large scale. The Zuyev Club is typical of this last and as such it is Golosov's enduring claim to fame, since this unique corner treatment first posited in his Electrobank project of 1927 is in effect a modernized *bâtiment d'angle* derived from the Neo-Baroque fabric of the nineteenth-century city. Reinterpreted here in dynamic terms, it seems to have had considerable influence outside the Soviet Union, above all on the early work of the Italian architect Giuseppe Terragni. In some ways, this work represents Russian formalism at its most extreme, since apart from the corner stair shaft which is patently expressed as a glass cylinder, there is little relationship between the hierarchical morphology of the plan and the formal rhythm of the facade.

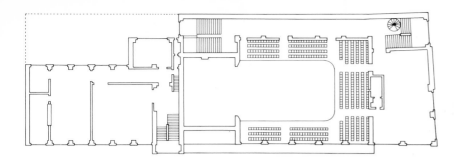

282 *Above: lower floor plan*
282-3 *Below: overall view*
283 *Above: upper floor plan*
    Below: interior of circular staircase
    Photos: M. Sekiya

It is hardly surprising that Loos's "architecture without qualities" (to paraphrase Robert Musil) should have directly appealed to the Hungarian Dadaist poet Tristan Tzara. How exactly Loos came to Tzara's attention is not known, but it is evident that Tzara was responsible for inviting Loos to Paris for the purposes of this commission. From an artistic point of view, the choice couldn't have been more felicitous, since Loos was the only architect of the twenties whose work was at all Dadaist in feeling. Judging from the photographs of the time, Tzara's collection of primitive sculpture went surprisingly well with Loos's disjunctive conception of space.

Among the Dadaist aspects of the house is the ruthlessly perverse planning which Loos's first exponent Heinrich Kulka had some difficulty accounting for in his classic study of the architect published in 1930. Without doubt this was one of the more extravagant versions of Loos's *Raumplan*; the fragmentary, split-level planning concept that he first advanced in the Rufer House, Vienna, of 1912. The irregular L-shaped Gothic Revival domestic plan, as documented in Hermann Muthesius's *Das Englische Haus* of 1904, clearly inspired Loos's notion of *Raumplan*, and yet due to his predilection for cubic form, he could not accept the picturesque massing that was its necessary consequence. From this contradiction came the tortuous manipulation of

the available volume in order to create a dynamic space within a static mass.

Loos's penchant for disjunctive planning was particularly stimulated in the Tzara House by the fall of the site, which 25 feet from the sidewalk, rose abruptly some 16 feet to establish a new datum. This upper level had poor load bearing capacity, with the result that it could only sustain a single-storey extension to the rear of the main five-storey volume. The floors of this pile were so eccentrically arranged as to merit an account of the way in which its services were disposed. The ground level was given over to a garage and a vestibule, with a heating chamber to the rear; on the first floor was a rented apartment which was by-passed by the main stair leading from the vestibule. At the second floor, another entry hall was introduced giving access to the principal living suite above. The main kitchen and cellar were also located at this level and linked to the outbuildings at the rear of the site. At the third floor the *Raumplan* finally came into its own with a split level separating the 33-foot-long lounge from a raised stage on the central axis of the plan. On this last, Tzara staged previews of his Dadaistic work.

The absolutely symmetrical organization of the facade was reinforced by the traditional subdivision of rusticated base below with rendered noble floors above. This base hardly lent itself to a traditionally honorific

interpretation since it was built of the same kind of rubble walling that was normally employed for the end walls of terraces. This deliberate dissonance was echoed on the monumental scale in the central opening which was curiously at variance with the scale of the clerestorey windows in the lower part, whose sills coincided in a disturbing way with the upper limits of the rubble work.

284 Section and plans
285 Main facade

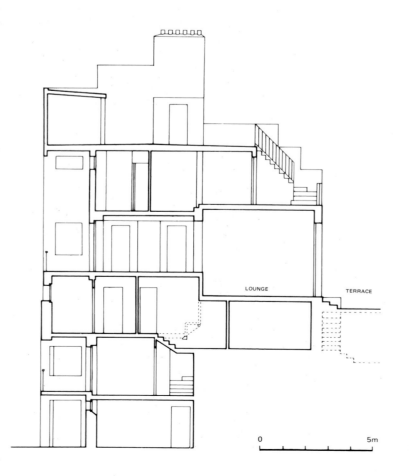

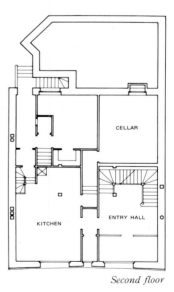

Second floor

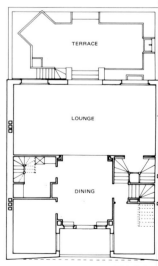

Third floor

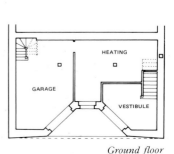

Ground floor

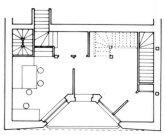

First floor

Hoek van Holland is unquestionably one of the most powerful formal statements of Oud's career, although he had been moving towards this level of achievement since 1917, the year of his set-back seaside terrace project designed while he was still associated with Theo van Doesburg and the Dutch avant-garde movement known as De Stijl. In the following year he became city architect to Rotterdam at the age of 28 and there followed, in rapid succession, a whole series of worker's housing schemes which were built

to his designs, beginning with the Berlagian brick, four-storey, perimeter blocks erected in the Rotterdam neighbourhoods of Spangen and Tusschendijken between 1919 and 1921. This was followed by the two-storey triangular worker's garden colony, built at Oud-Mathenesse, Rotterdam, in 1922. With its high pitched, Spanish-tiled roofs, its white-washed, rendered walls, its brick thresholds and string courses, its sharply profiled eaves and porches, its gridded fence-work and exquisitely proportioned fenestra-

tion, Oud-Mathenesse already displayed a level of formal mastery which has rarely been seen in public housing. Between Oud-Mathenesse and Hoek van Holland, designed but two years later in 1924, Oud's work passes through a decisive transition. On the one hand he is already gravitating towards the white, prismatic simplifications of the "new objectivity," on the other he remains under the influence of the theosophically based geometrical schemes of J. L. M. Lauweriks. This last is evident in the fore-

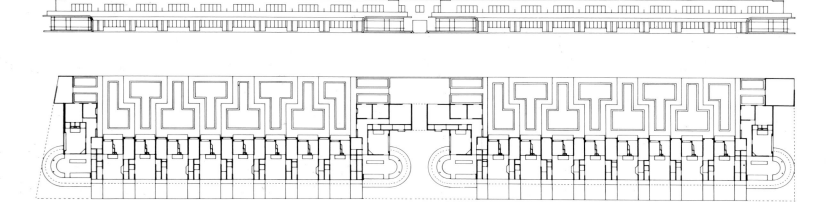

man's hut built at Oud-Mathenesse in 1923, in the Café De Unie, Rotterdam of 1925 and finally in the interlocking back gardens that run behind the stripped forms of the two-storey, white rendered, symmetrical terraces, under construction in Hoek van Holland, by 1926.

Apart from all these specific housing precedents, the Hoek van Holland housing is straightforward enough with its semi-circular, ground floor, corner shops, establishing terminal points in the centre and at either end. This split composition involves Oud in an uncharacteristic use of long horizontal first floor balconies, a device which enables him to unify the repetitive forms between the cylindrical terminals. This form entails, however, the somewhat awkward use of light metal grillage in order to separate the individual terraces precisely placed and proportioned metal windows, sharply profiled concrete overhangs and cornices and finally the syncopated geometrical ordering of the front and back gardens, complete plastic asperities of the scheme. And yet however modern his syntax became Oud never lost sight of the principle that the cultural charge of housing is to constitute the collective urban fabric of the city. This intention is implicit in his 1925 manifesto *Yes and No Confessions of an Architect*, wherein he wrote: "I expect a crystallization of form in a distinct style to result from the reduction to the typical of the subordinate parts of a building; but the standard house, prefabricated *en masse*, appears to me to be difficult to fit into the complex of a large city."

This sanatorium, bearing the appropriate name "Zonnestraal" or "sun's ray," and dedicated to the treatment of tuberculosis then prevalent among diamond cutters, epitomises in a subtle way, the transcendental wing of the Dutch functionalist movement which was polemically known as the Nieuwe Zakelijkheid, or the New Objectivity. Despite superficial resemblances, a subtle difference separates the deterministic functionalism of say a Marxist architect like Mart Stam, from the geometrical constructions projected by Duiker. For Stam the New Objectivity meant solely the determination of built form through the exigencies of production and technique; for Duiker it still meant, after the demands of function had been met, a cultural form brought into being through a higher order of economy. Thus we find Duiker writing in 1928: ". . . also in architecture 'functionalism', is the only means to obtain that great freedom; not a 'pseudo-functionalism' that is self-seeking and just playing with high-grade materials like iron, glass and concrete, that are the gifts of our age, but a 'functionalism' possessed of high moral consciousness, which finds the possibility in the immaterialisation of architecture (according to the cosmic law of economy) to give man in a future society the needed sunlight and the joys of nature in his immediate surroundings, from which he has been turning away since the dark ages."
Like all of Duiker's work after 1925, Zon-

nestraal was predicated on the idea of a dematerialised architecture. Its pavilionated hospital form set in the midst of a park near Hilversum, comprised one central building with four free-standing ward blocks set apart, in pairs, to either side of the central axis. Each of these ward clusters, planned on two floors, contained bed spaces for 50 people, divided between two terraced wings each with a slightly different orientation. This cluster planning was ordered according to a 1.5 metre grid with the standard bedroom measuring 3 metres by 3 metres. The ward blocks themselves were comprised of specific components which were arranged in the following spatial sequence; sun balcony, patient's room and access corridor. This last led to a service unit and after that to a bridge link connecting the pair of ward blocks to a single-storey common room.
The central administration building was split into two parts by an access road running through the site, dividing the medical suite to the north from the boiler room, bath house, kitchen and refectory to the south. The first floor, cruciform refectory and its terrace were evidently raised so as to afford views over the surrounding landscape.
The construction was the usual reinforced concrete frame, with rendered block work and industrial glazing as the basic elements of the infill. It is important to note, however, that Duiker and Bijvoet were to evolve a concrete architectonic which was entirely different from that developed by Le

Corbusier. Unlike the famous Dom-Ino skeleton to which the basic structure of their ward blocks may be readily compared, the Zonnestraal frame was to depend on the overt expression of each of its components; the square column, the haunched downstand beam and the cantilevered slab. Duiker was to exploit these components as different manifestations of the same structural and spatial order. Thus the haunched beams in the ward blocks established the lateral unity of the bedrooms stacked side by side, whereas the four cantilevered beams to the overhanging roof of the refectory helped to orient its volume towards preferential views. A comparable inflection also appears in the overhanging roofs to the single-storey lounges connecting the free-standing blocks. Like much of the work of Van der Vlugt and Mart Stam, this is clearly a canonical work of Dutch Constructivism and at Zonnestraal, just as in the Van Nelle factory, the building first appears to be projected as though it were a machine. However, among the differences between Stam and Duiker, one has to remark on the way in which Duiker's work, unlike that of Stam, uses structural components in such a way as to modulate the architectural space.

288 View of central building
289 Above left: site plan showing original project
Above right: detail of glass wall
Below: views of circular staircase

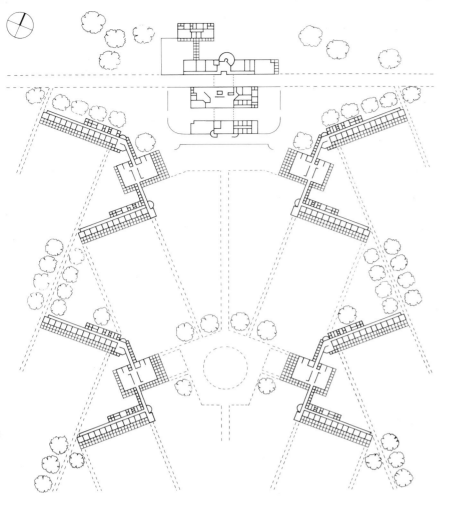

Initially conceived for the Woga development company as part of an urban cul-de-sac off the fashionable Kurfürstendamm in Berlin, the Universum Cinema was a small scale condensation of Mendelsohn's commercial style in the second half of the twenties.

In compositional terms, however, this urban fragment can hardly hold its own with Mendelsohn's magisterial department stores built in Berlin, Nuremberg, Stuttgart and Breslau between 1924 and 1928, or with his heroic Berlin proposals for Alexanderplatz and Potsdamerplatz, dating from 1931. The original "expressionist" sketches for the Universum promise a good deal more than was finally realized from the point of view of horizontal massing, and this was due, in part, to the fact that the urban whole for which it was originally projected had to be abandoned.

Thus the Universum is to be valued for its interior rather than its exterior; above all, for the brilliantly arranged auditorium which thereafter was adopted by the UFA company as the normative plan for their chain of cinemas. Hemmed in by shops on the perimeter frontage, Mendelsohn was able to impart a compensating sense of generosity to the foyer where a broad flight of steps gave access to both the parterre and the balcony — the auditorium being equipped with an access corridor and cloakroom spaces to either side. But the final triumph of this cinema was its indirect architectural illumination, where luminous bands of light imperiously directed the eye back to the centroid of the screen. Of this Mendelsohn wrote in July, 1928: "I have just come back ... from the first lighting test at the cinema. The ceiling lighting is splendid and I think we shall get the red mahogany, with soft shades of blue and yellow for the wall behind the circle, the austere and the delicate together. Everything there makes a unified and generous impression, despite the sparing use of materials and simple colouring."

Recently restored.
Photograph shows reconstructed building.
Elevations and plan are redrawn based on
Mendelsohn's original design.
Photo: W. Fujii

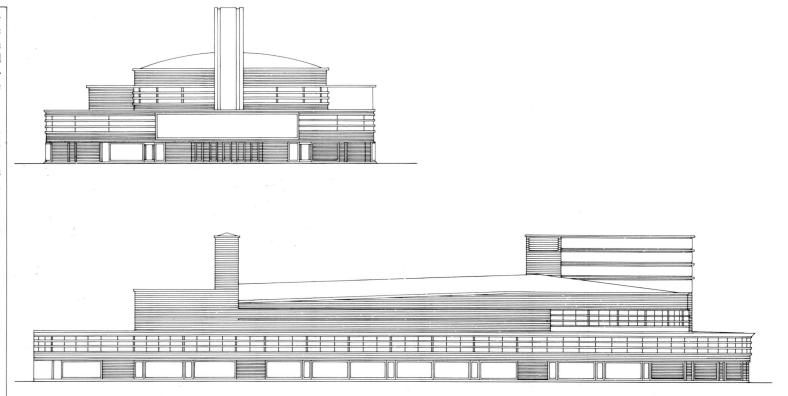

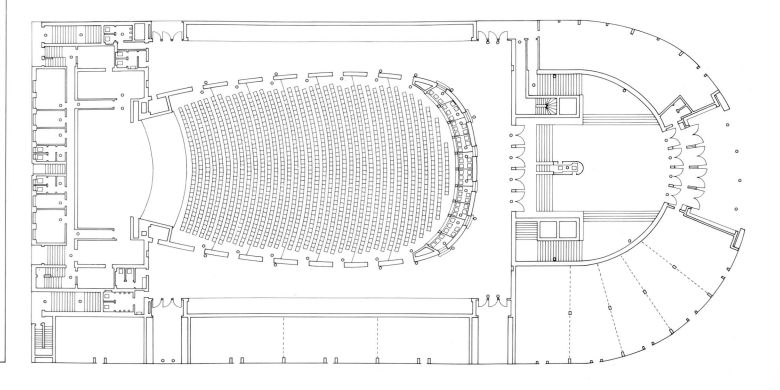

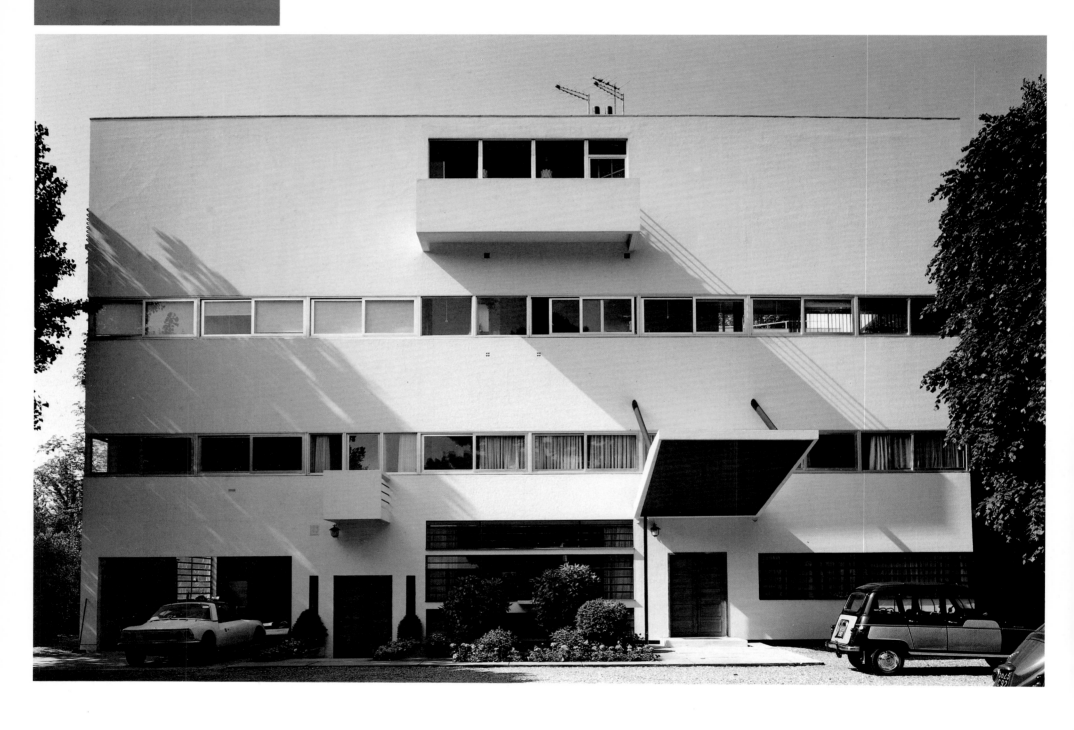

292 Entry facade
293 Garden facade
294 Above: main facades with tracé régulateurs
    overlaid and fourth floor plan
    Below, from left: plans of first floor, second floor
    and third floor
295 Above left: roof garden
    Below left: living room
    Right: stairs to upper level
    Photos: M. Sekiya

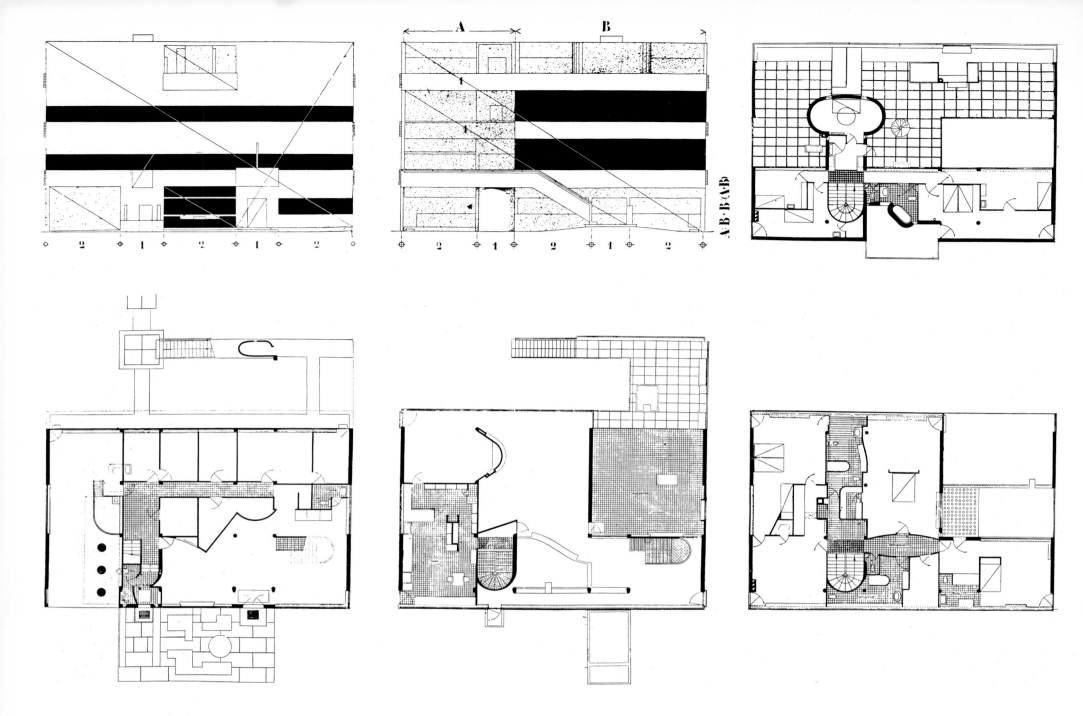

More usually known as the Villa Garches, this building started its life as the Villa de Monzie, according to the name of the original client, de Monzie who, as Minister of Culture, first invited Le Corbusier to design the Pavillon de l'Espirit Nouveau before proceeding to commission him with this villa. Just prior to the completion, de Monzie was compelled to sell the house for personal reasons, and the new owners — the Stein family — added their name to the various rubrics by which the house has since been known.

In retrospect, nothing served to tie Le Corbusier more firmly to the Humanist tradition of the Renaissance than this villa, realized in 1927, for its form was patently predicated on Palladian types and rhythms. This connection was first demonstrated by Colin Rowe in his remarkable essay *The Mathema-*

tics of the Ideal Villa (1947) in which he drew specific parallels between Palladio's Villa Malcontenta of 1560 and this villa built at Garches three hundred and fifty years later: "In both cases six 'traverse' lines of support, rhythmically altering single and double bays, are established; but the rhythm of the parallel lines of support, as a result of Le Corbusier's use of the cantilever, differs slightly. At the villa at Garches, it is ½:1½:1 ½:1½:½ and at the Malcontenta 1½:2:2:1½. In plan, Le Corbusier thus obtains a sort of compression for his central bay and interest seems transferred to his outer bays, which are augmented by the extra half unit of the cantilever; while Palladio secures a dominance for his central division, and a progression towards his portico, which focuses interest there. In both cases, the projecting element, terrace or portico, occupies 1½

units in depth."

The protracted evolution of the design for this villa at Garches and its particular synthesizing function within the overall body of Le Corbusier's early work, require some explication if we are to understand the cannonical significance of this villa.

The Villa de Monzie was first conceived as an L-shaped (Gothic Revival) plan and it was only by degrees that Le Corbusier was to bring himself to contain its still fragmented form within the confines of a Purist prism. Le Corbusier had first assumed the theme of the modern bourgeois villa in his Maison Cook of 1926 in which he formulated for the first time the "five points of a new architecture," namely: the *piloti* elevating the structure off the ground, the *free plan,* separating the load bearing columns from the partitioning of the volume, the canti-

levered *free facade* (this being the elevational corollary of the free plan), the *long horizontal sliding window* and finally the *roof garden* supposedly restoring to human use the ground area covered by the building. All these "points," save the *piloti,* are patently in evidence in the Villa de Monzie and are, in fact, the generating elements of its syntactical and spatial design.

One of the first things to be remarked on in the overall design of the de Monzie residence — particularly when viewed from the main approach — is its highly frontalized presentation where the entry facade appears like a diaphanous guillotine behind which the asymmetrical Purist volume can be partially perceived.

It would be hard to imagine a more didactic condensation of Purist aesthetics than this frontal membrane, for it combines both

literal and phenomenal transparency; the former being a self-evident attribute of glazing and the latter depending on the shallow space lying between the cantilevered facade and the line of free-standing columns, set some 80 centimetres behind its surface. Where post-Cubist, Purist painting was to exploit such an illusory shallow space as a way of compressing the perspectival, deep, space of the Renaissance (thereby challenging, so to speak, the reality of its illusion) Purist architecture was to exploit the illusory nature of this "compressed" three dimensional reality. In this way, once one penetrated beyond the shallow space of the frontal facade in the Villa de Monzie, one "unexpectedly" entered the highly configurated spatial depth of the villa itself. In the first case (painting) the shallow space can be thought of as revealing the illusory

nature of the represented depth, in the second case (architecture) the shallow space "conceals" the real depth of the volume.

Aside from *Les 5 points d'une architecture nouvelle,* the Villa de Monzie also displays the marine and aeronautical metaphors of Purism – devices with which Le Corbusier sought to incorporate the machine by association – thereby evading the apparent antinomy obtaining between architecture and industrial production. To this end the suspended *porche cochère* clearly alludes to aviation technology, the suspending rods being shaped like elliptically sectioned wing spars, while the canopy itself assumes the profile of an aerofoil. Similar intentions were apparent in the elliptically planned storage cabin on the roof terrace which referred, in a rather obvious way, to form of a ship's funnel.

The deconstructed Palladian structure of de Monzie is brilliantly achieved on the ground and first floors of the villa where the means of vertical access are directly related to the narrow bays of the Palladian tartan grid A-B_1-A-B_2-A. In this matrix the left hand service stair is rotated ninety degrees and displaced out of its bay – (B_2). The gyration induced by this displacement initiates the asymmetrical configuration of the first floor, where the living volume "zig-zags" between the kitchen situated on the left front and the inset terrace opening towards the garden at the right rear.

The Villa de Monzie is equally complex from a typological point of view, for within the context of Le Corbusier's development it is both the paradignmatic dwelling and the palatial monument. In the first place, it is an enlarged version of the standard dwelling

(*Pavillon de l'Esprit Nouveau*) which Le Corbusier had developed out of his Immeubles-Villas project of 1922 on the occasion of the Exposition des Arts Décoratifs of 1925. In the second place (as he demonstrated in his Société des Nations competition entry of 1927) it can also be regarded as a fragment part of a palace. This curious double intention, suspended between the banality of building and the honorific status of architecture, was a metaphorical embodiment of Le Corbusier's socio-cultural polemic, that is to say, it exemplified his belief that a house should be accorded all the formal dignity of a palace and a palace should be provided with all the domestic convenience of a house.

1927

MIES VAN DER ROHE
(Artistic Director)
RICHARD DÖCKER (Site Architect)
Weissenhofsiedlung
Werkbund Exhibition
Stuttgart, Germany

Initially conceived in 1925 as an Expressionist "hill-town," the Weissenhofsiedlung, Stuttgart, built as a permanent housing exhibition, effectively resuscitated the Deutsche Werkbund as a major cultural force; a revitalisation which had been gaining ground ever since the Württemberg *Form without Ornament* exhibition of 1924. Erected under Mies van der Rohe's direction with Richard Döcker acting as site architect, the realization of the Weissenhofsiedlung owed a great deal to the organizational capacity of Gustav Stoz, executive director of the Württemberg Werkbund. Projected as a modern sequel to the Darmstadt Artists'

Colony exhibition, *Ein Dokument Deutscher Kunst*, of 1901, the Weissenhofsiedlung not only attempt to demonstrate the Neue Sachlichkeit way of living, but also to prove the efficacy of modern constructional methods. While it was hardly successful in either of these aims, it nonetheless attracted over half a million visitors and the lessons learnt at Stuttgart enabled the Deutsche Werkbund to mount a more successful permanent housing exhibit at Breslau in 1929, under the title *Home and Workplace.*

For all its shortcomings, this exhibition provided a public focus for the ambitious housing programme of Weimar Republic

which had been underway for three years and which would continue to build extensively throughout Germany until the rise of the Third Reich in 1933. In addition, it also functioned as a show case for the European rationalist avant-garde, featuring private houses or terraces by the following foreign architects: Le Corbusier and Pierre Jeanneret (France); J.J.P. Oud and Mart Stam (Holland); Victor Bourgeois (Belgium) and Josef Frank (Austria). The German architects who participated in the Weissenhofsiedlung were mostly members of the powerful Berlin *Ring* group, including Mies van der Rohe himself, Richard Döcker, Walter Gropius,

Ludwig Hilberseimer, Hans Scharoun, Adolf Rading, the brothers Bruno and Max Taut, and two prewar Werkbund architects, Peter Behrens and Hans Poelzig. As certain critics have remarked, there were two notable omissions from this exhibition, Hugo Häring, who withdrew early after a quarrel with Mies and Erich Mendelsohn who was excluded for reasons which remain obscure. The most important contributions to the exhibition and by far the most prominent in terms of sheer size was the central apartment building designed by Mies van der Rohe and the small housing prototypes built to the designs of Le Corbusier and Pierre Jeanneret.

Mies's apartment building was clearly intended as an intelligent critique of the standard *zeilenbau,* rowhouse, then being built all over Germany. Mies simply introduced a number of modest refinements which clearly had advantages over the national standard. Above all, by maintaining a separation between the structural frames and the subdividing walls, he was able to provide apartments of varying shape and dimension. As he wrote at the time: "If we regard kitchens and bathrooms because of their plumbing as a fixed core, then all other space may be partitioned by means of movable walls." That Mies, unlike Le Cor-

busier, was not preoccupied at this juncture with expressing the frame is evident from the latter's communal prototype where a set of double free-standing columns awkwardly interrupt the living volume.

While some architects concentrated on developing advanced methods of modular construction, (see Gropius's steel frame, asbestos cement clad two-storey prototype) others such as Le Corbusier used the occasion to exhibit a new type of lower middle-class villa, as in the Stuttgart version of his Citrohan house. This three-storey unit raised on piloti, comprised a double-height living volume with auxilliary bedrooms and garden

terraces situated on the roof. In terms of both space standards and ideology, nothing could have been further from this version of the Citrohan house than Mart Stam's three-storey workers' row housing, where a garden-terrace workroom is provided below each living room. However, as with most of these exhibition prototypes, both Le Corbusier and Stam attempted to activate areas which in traditional houses had hitherto always been treated as 'dead' volumes; such spaces as the access stairs which in Oud's terrace were projected as auxilliary living volumes.

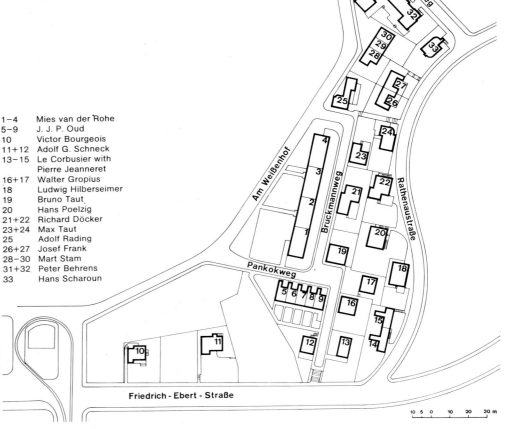

1–4	Mies van der Rohe
5–9	J. J. P. Oud
10	Victor Bourgeois
11+12	Adolf G. Schneck
13–15	Le Corbusier with Pierre Jeanneret
16+17	Walter Gropius
18	Ludwig Hilberseimer
19	Bruno Taut
20	Hans Poelzig
21+22	Richard Döcker
23+24	Max Taut
25	Adolf Rading
26+27	Josef Frank
28–30	Mart Stam
31+32	Peter Behrens
33	Hans Scharoun

296 Mies's apartment building
297 Left: Le Corbusier's apartment building
Right: site plan

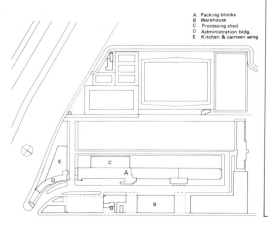

A Packing blocks
B Warehouse
C Processing shed
D Administration bldg.
E Kitchen & canteen wing

This factory, which still serves the same refining and packing processes for which it was originally designed, has remained virtually unchanged for over half a century; its appearance being as pristine today as when it was first erected. It endures as one of the masterpieces of the European Neue Sachlichkeit movement, otherwise known as the New Objectivity which was without doubt the most rigorous form of functionalism propagated in the twenties. The extraordinary elegance of this work seems to have derived from the unique collaboration of L.C. van der Vlugt and Mart Stam, the latter serving as job captain for the building. While Stam played a major role in the determination of the design, it is questionable as to whether it

would have attained such a high level of resolution had it come from his hand alone, since the doctrinaire nature of Stam's functionalism often imposed severe restrictions on the range of expression permitted. Stam's inhibitions in this respect are dramatically exemplified in the conflict which arose over the circular observation salon superimposed at one end of the packing complex. Stam was vehemently opposed to applying such a picturesque addendum to an otherwise functionalist slab and his subsequent departure from the firm seems to have been precipitated by his conflict with Van der Vlugt over the addition of his nacelle-like form.

In essence, the Van Nelle factory comprises two eight-storey, packing blocks, linked by

glazed, aerial conveyor tubes to a canalside warehouse, where the packed products — tea, tobacco and coffee — await their transhipment and delivery, either by water, road or rail. Three other curtain-walled prisms complete the complex. Of these, the first is a single-storey processing shed with a sawtooth roof attached to the rear of the leading block, the second is a curved administration building whose concave form helps to establish the principal entry into the compound, while the third and final envelope is a kitchen and staff canteen wing which projects beyond the rear of the administration building, at the point where it joins the leading slab. The canteen and administration wings are linked to the pack-

298 Bottom left: site plan
298-9 Overall view
299 Above: section of packing block
Below: third floor plan

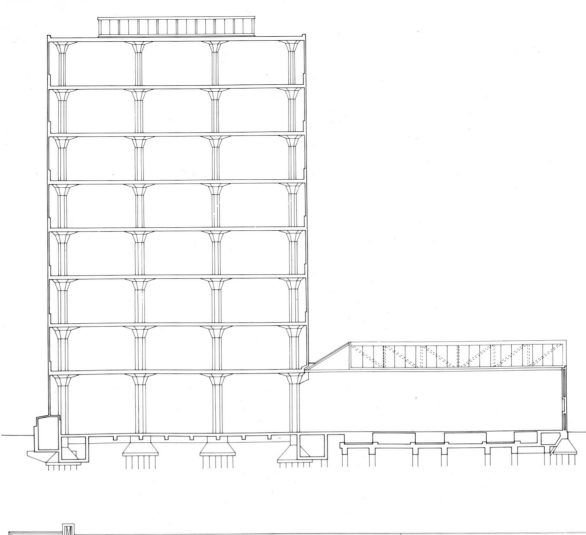

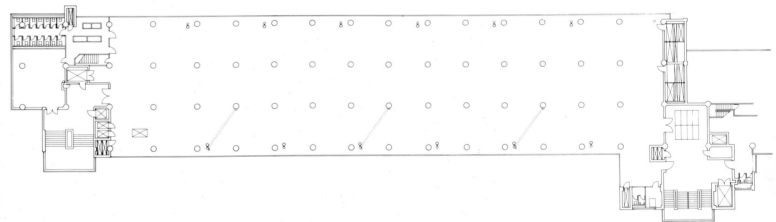

ing complex by glazed bridges whose tectonic order is close to that assumed by the aerial conveyors.

Like Owen Williams's Boots Factory in Nottingham, the Van Nelle plant is predicated on reinforced concrete slab and mushroom column construction, largely in order to provide optimum freedom for varying the production sequence, while still sustaining heavy floor loads. Thus, the curtain wall skin is cantilevered well clear of the support line so as to allow mechanical chain conveyors to pass between the columns and the outside wall. While the production space itself is finished throughout in fair faced concrete with fenestration bars and spandrel panels of galvanized steel, the Van Nelle factory attains its most elegant finish in the glass enamelled sheet steel and tubular chromium furnishings, applied to the free-standing semitransparent partitions, tables and chairs which equip the interior of the personnel wings. Despite this differentiation, the overall quality was remarkably high throughout as the following comment by Le Corbusier makes clear: "The road that runs into the factory is smooth, flat, bordered with brown tiled sidewalks. It is as clean and bright as a dance floor. The sheer facades of the building, bright glass and grey metal, rise up . . . against the sky. . . . The serenity of the place is total. Everything is open to the outside. And this is of enormous significance to all those who are working on the eight floors inside. . . . The Van Nelle tobacco factory in Rotterdam, a creation of the modern age, has removed all the former connotations of despair from the word 'proletarian.' "

This idealistic appraisal of the factory surely corresponded closely to the socio-cultural intentions of the owner, the industrialist Cees van der Leeuw, who was to remain a patron of modern architecture and industrial design throughout his life, including his ambitious patronage of the Van der Leeuw Research House, built to the designs of Richard Neutra at Silver Lake, Los Angeles, in 1934.

In many respects, the Van Nelle factory was the ultimate realisation of an international attempt to evolve a normative level of Constructivist design; the built equivalent of the canonical Hannes Meyer/Hans Wittwer project submitted for the Société des Nations competition of approximately the same date. Like the Meyer/Wittwer design, the Van Nelle factory was almost literally a *machine à produire,* its conveyor system circulating visibly throughout its transparent form; the conveyors containing a movement which projected itself as a dynamic sign above the access road into the plant. This image of a regional mechanism, was to inform the appearance of the Van Nelle at a distance, where, against the flat datum of the Dutch landscape, its giant silhouetted, neonlit roof top sky-sign served to locate its profile in the dark.

Dr. Phillip Lovell's Health House, built in Los Angeles in 1927 to the designs of the Austrian émigré architect Richard Neutra, may be regarded as the apotheosis of the International Style, its architectural expression deriving directly from a skeleton steel frame, clad in a lightweight synthetic skin. Set on a bluff overlooking a romantic, half-wild parkscape, its asymmetrical composition of dramatically suspended floors was reminiscent of Wright's West Coast block-house style of the 1920s, and this formal similarity already suggests the catholic sources from which the apparent homogeneity of the International Style derived.

The open-plan form of the house was an appropriate reflection of Lovell's expansive personality and served to represent his callisthenic lifestyle. As David Gebhard suggests in his study of Neutra's compatriot and early partner Rudolf Schindler (who had realized a house at Newport Beach for Lovell just one year before), Lovell could have been regarded as embodying the athletic and progressive attributes of the International Style in his own persona.

The ideology of Lovell and its direct expression in the Health House exercised a decisive influence over the rest of Neutra's career.

From now on his work was at its best where the building programme could be interpreted as making a direct contribution to the psycho-physiological wellbeing of its occupants. The central theme of both Neutra's work and his writings was the beneficial impact of a well-designed environment upon the general health of the human nervous system. And while his so-called 'bio-realism' rested largely on unproven arguments linking architectural form to overall health, it is difficult to discredit the extraordinary sensitivity and supra-functional attitude that coloured his whole approach.

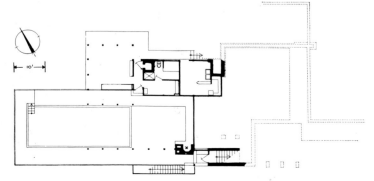

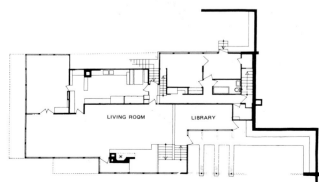

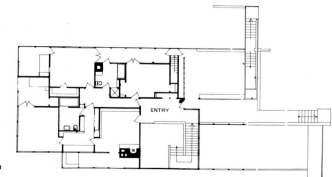

300 Above: overall view
  Below, from left: plans of ground floor,
  lower quarters and upper story level
301 Above: view from living room toward library
  Below: living room

302 View from large open court
303 Above: street facade
     Below: main elevation

Left: gate cut through the building
Above right: view of the facade
Below right: apartment entrance

Karl Marx Hof was but the largest and the most monumental of some twenty-three municipal housing blocks built around the periphery of Vienna in the so-called Red Ring between 1919 and 1934, beginning with the earliest sections of the Metzleinstaler Hof and culminating with Sandleiten Hof, a block which, with 1,587 units, was the largest development in the series. In general, the dominant configuration of these superblocks was the perimeter plan as this had emerged through a reinterpretation of the 17th-century *Hof*. This type was deliberately revived after O. Thienemann's second prize design in the Viennese People's Housing competition of 1896. However, the Austro-Hungarian Empire succeeded in building very little popular housing and by 1912, some 80,000 people were living in night shelters in Vienna; of which 20,000 were children.

Housing improvement, welfare planning and general Social Democratic reform came into being after the worker's riots of 1911 and the national strikes of 1917; in particular with the election of the Social-Democratic council of Vienna, which was to remain in power until 1934. This government purchased some 1,000 hectares of land between 1919 and 1925 and brought about an Apartment Requisition Decree and the Rent Control Acts of 1919 and 1922. This welfare programme was part of general strategy for economic recovery as a contemporary critic made abundantly clear: "Our competitiveness can only be maintained by relatively low wages, which are lower than those of other industrial nations. The quotas for food, clothing, education and the small portion for entertainment, cannot stand reduction. There is only one component that can be eliminated from the worker's wages without the necessity of stepping up his productivity. That is rent. In the prewar years rent abosorbed 25% of the worker's wages. When rent control ends, wages must rise. Our export industry, on which the fate of this country depends, cannot, in light of the described unfavourable production conditions, accommodate any such wage increases."

With 50,000 people living in Superblocks by 1934 — a figure which by then amounted to 1/10 of the city's population — it is clear that the Superblock had become a sociopolitical force of consequence; a radical potential which even escaped the control of its sponsors. This potential finally showed its colours in the Republican anti-Fascist rebellion of 1934, when the fortifiable nature of the perimeter block suddenly became manifest. However, this resistance only lasted for four days since it was soon clear that not even a Superblock could withstand the impact of modern artillery.

Political confrontation aside, the Superblock was correctly recognised by Josef Frank as being the anti-thesis of the garden city. To this end he wrote in 1934: "Despite all this we must never give up our ideal, the Siedlung house, an ideal to which we were once closer than we are today. One cannot stress often enough that the single family house is the basis of our city planning and our approach to modern architecture. . . . the moral force . . . radiating from a piece of land . . . cannot be replaced by anything. . .' Judging from the magisterial form of Karl Marx Hof, it is unlikely that Ehn would have had much sympathy for Frank's *Heimatstil* ideology. Ehn organised his eight-storey Superblock into two enclosed courts on either side of a single open forecourt; a vast complex which comprised some 1,382 apartments plus a full range of communal facilities; a laundry, a bath house, a kindergarten, clinics, shops, a health insurance facility, a pharmacy and a post-office.

8 The Millenialistic Impulse in European Art and Architecture: Russia and Holland 1913-1922

European architectural expressionism and the modern Neoclassical tradition, descending from the École des Beaux-Arts, were both equally removed from the radical abstract art produced by the European modernist avant-garde between 1918 and 1932. For reasons which are ultimately mystical if not religious this twentieth-century cult of the millenium was to be almost entirely of Russian and Dutch origin. In the years immediately before and after the First World War, this avant-gardist impulse gave rise to uncompromisingly abstract forms in both art and architecture; forms which could hardly have been more distant from the Realist and Historicist traditions of nineteenth-century bourgeois culture.

Part 1 The Russian Millenialist Avant-Garde: Constructivist Culture and Eschatological Vision 1913-33

After the liberation of the serfs in 1861, the Russian artistic and literary intelligentsia became increasingly obsessed with the idea of the millenium; that is to say, with that primitive notion of a cyclical break in the continuity of time, whose advent would be cataclysmically announced either by the coming of the redeemer or by the evident termination of the world, or by an awe-inspiring combination of both.

Alexander Malinovsky is a typical intellectual of this period. Styling himself Bogdanov, that is the "God-given," he founded The Organization for Proletarian Culture, later known as the Proletkult Movement as early as 1906, with the intention of encouraging an oppressed and backward populace to create a culture of its own. As far as Bogdanov was concerned, this expression had to be equally removed from both the obscurantism of the Russian Orthodox church and the superficial and imported culture of the Russian bourgeoisie. Inasmuch as Bogdanov was both a Bolshevik and an idealist, he personified the often ambivalent stance adopted by the progressive intelligentsia at this time. The idea that a largely illiterate citizenry would be able to create, *de novo*, a culture of its own was, to say the least, naive. It is evident that the project was largely an idealistic fiction, for aside from vernacular timber construction or traditional craftwork imbued with popular, religious, almost pagan iconography, there could be no culture of the people as such. Confronted with this impasse, the Russian intelligentsia assumed the "millenial task" of creating a new culture on its behalf.

This effort first became manifest with the well-meaning but nonetheless patronizing Realist art of the *Narodniki*, the so-called Wanderers, who seceded from the Academy of Fine Art in St. Petersburg in 1863. Fifty years later, this historic destiny fell to the Russian Futurist *avant-garde* who gathered in the summer of 1910 and for a few years thereafter, on the Black Sea estate of the Burliuk family. This group, composed almost equally of poets and painters and known as The Hylea, harboured in their midst one Velimir Khlebnikov, the pioneer avant-gardist poet of Russian Futurism who was to inspire the next decade of Russian avant-gardist art. As Vladimir Markov has remarked in his study *Russian Futurism* (1969), it was Khlebnikov who initiated the so-called "transrational," a "trans-sense" or *zaum* poetry of 1910, and this proto-Dadaist word play led at once to the almost equally

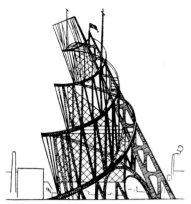

115 *Tatlin, Monument to the Third International, 1920.*

"transrational" poetry of Alexei Kruchonykh and Vladimir Mayakovsky, and, above all, to Kruchonykh's seminal science fiction opera, *Victory Over the Sun* of 1912. This last was to be the prime inspiration behind the canonical Productivist work, Vladimir Tatlin's Monument to the Third International, first exhibited in 1920 on the occasion of the All Russian Revolutionary Congress.

It is one of the paradoxes of twentieth-century culture that Suprematism was able to exercise such a compelling influence over the development of Russian avant-garde architecture, since it is difficult to imagine a more ethereal art form in all its initial manifestations. This paradox is revealed, in Malevich's essay *Die Gegendstandslose Welt (The Non-Objective World)*, published in Berlin in 1928, where, in a series of polemical illustrations, the author compares the environmental reality which has stimulated three different categories of modern art; namely, the agrarian, vernacular environment which is seen by Malevich as triggering Realist art; the noisy, urban industrialized environment which is regarded as stimulating Futurist production; and finally, the silent, cosmic, aeronautical environment which is seen as the experiential source of Suprematism. One may conclude after Malevich's visual comparisons that the objects which represent these three environments most intensely were respectively a timber windmill, an iron locomotive and a bi-plane; the latter, built out of light struts and stressed fabric, being the most ephemeral of the three. Perhaps the most surprising thing about this taxonomy was that Malevich chose to relegate the dirigible to the province of Futurism, thereby making it explicit that it was aircraft alone which possessed

the capacity to intimate the ethos of Suprematism. For Malevich, it was as though aeronautics was the sole agency through which the cosmic scale of his vision could be achieved. He appears to have seen the plane as the Suprematist icon par excellence, as the sole industrial tool, whose essential attributes could transcend Futurism. He saw aviation as a millenialistic experience through which the tyranny of Renaissance perspective over art could be finally vanquished. Unlike Realism, Futurism (or even Le Corbusier's Purism), it was not the airplane *in se* that Suprematism cherished, but rather the distant aspect of such a craft flying in formation, at high altitude or, alternatively, the prospect of the earth itself when seen from great height. The fact that the bi-plane invariably assumed a cruciform silhouette when seen from a distance was presumably relevant to the spiritual aspirations of Suprematism, given the traditional iconography of the Russian Orthodox church.

However, the ultimate intention of Suprematism resided in the irrational non-objectivity of universal space rather than in any obvious iconocity, and what Malevich intended by this evocation seems to have been close to the *beinahe nichts* or "almost nothing" of Mies van der Rohe, a concept which Malevich expressed, in most unequivocal terms, in his famous *White on White* painting of 1918. Part science-fiction polemicist, part phenomenologist, Malevich projected a millenialistic panorama consisting of sub- and supra-atomic particles. He created a kind of "trans-rational" *Gesamtkunstwerk*, and with this he tried to recast the universe, whether natural or not, in the Edenic light of Suprematist appearance.

116 Lissitzky, Lenin Tribune, 1920.

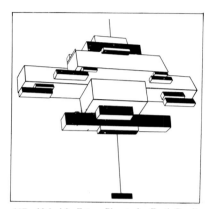

117 Malevich, Future Planets for Earth Dwellers, 1913-24.

It was largely left to Malevich's disciples and collaborators to adapt this vision to the design of everyday objects and it is clear that the products of the UNOVIS design school, which Malevich founded in Vitebsk in 1919, were unavoidable vulgarizations of the fundamental Suprematist idea. Thus Lazar (El) Lissitzky's agit-prop graphic poster of 1920, entitled *Beat the Whites With the Red Wedge*, is already a simplification and popularization of Suprematist forms and spatial concepts and the same can be said for the Lomosov cups designed by Malevich himself in 1923 or for the painted Suprematist chinaware designed by Nikolai Suetin between 1920 and 1925.

However, the Vitebsk UNOVIS school — the acronymic title standing for the *affirmation of the new art* — continued as a vital force throughout the twenties and affected the work of a number of talented artists, including V. E. Ermolaeva, E. Lissitzky, I. Chashnik, N. Suetin, and, for a brief while, even the Constructivist G. Klutsis. As far as architecture was concerned, Suprematism took off in two rather different directions. The first was an exploration which was largely internal to the UNOVIS school, represented in the main by the *arkhitektoniks* models created by Malevich, Suetin and Chashnik, between 1924 and 1928. The second was the adaptation of Suprematist precepts to the freer-ranging architectural work of El Lissitzky.

Lissitzky's Lenin Tribune project of 1920 immediately distinguished his output from that of his fellow Suprematists inasmuch as it was a synthetic product. It was, in fact, a collage, combining into a precarious unity both empirically engineered structures and floating Suprematist forms, with Lenin photo-montaged into position under the slogan "Strike" at the head of the Tribune. Not in itself realizable, this proposal demonstrated how Lissitzky's contemporaneous *PROUN* paintings (this acronym being compounded out of PRO [for] and UNOVIS) could be construed as models for a new kind of "weightless" architecture. This synthetic expression evoked the Suprematist ethos, without resorting to the replication of Suprematist space and form. The priority and meaning which Lissitzky attached to the suspension of structures in defiance of gravity and the consequence that this would have for traditional architecture and urbanism is evident from his book *Russland, Die Rekonstruktion der Architektur in der Sowjetunion* of 1930, wherein he wrote in a section entitled *Old Cities — New Buildings:*

The urgent need for offices for the centralized economy . . . had to be satisfied first. A number of such buildings have been constructed in Moscow. . . . All these were conceived as modern office structures . . . Nevertheless, all this still belongs to the past. Just as in the past, houses follow a continuous street line, as if the individual lots of private owners still existed. There is no suggestion whatsoever of the new situation in land ownership. The new houses put up so far give us no indication of the new concept of the open street, or of the city as the expression of a relationship of new associations as a result of which mass and space may be organized in a different way — even in the old parts of the city.

Elsewhere, in a chapter entitled "The Future and Utopia," he wrote:

The idea of the conquest of the substructure, the earthbound, can be extended even further and calls for the conquest of gravity as such. It demands floating structures, a physical-dynamic architecture.

118   *Lissitzky and Stam, Wolkenbugel project, 1924.*

119   *Lissitzky, Prounenraum, Berlin, 1923.*

Lissitzky made his most dramatic attempt at an anti-gravitational building form in his Wolkenbugel or "cloud hook" proposal of 1924, wherein he projected an "anti-skyscraper" — the term Wolkenbugel being an obvious play on Wolkenkratzer.   However, as the disposition of these projected structures makes clear, this form was not only an "anti-skyscraper," but also an "anti-gate" gateway.   Located at radial intersections about a circular boulevard, the *Wolkenbugel* were in effect dematerialized *propylea*, elevated above the main thoroughfares leading to the Kremlin. Each of these asymmetrical, pinwheeling masses consisted of horizontally layered office floors ranging from two to three storeys in height and elevated in the air on three "four-square" pylon clusters. Aside from accommodating the essential elevators, stairs and services, these clusters supported giant verendeel trusses, each being a floor height in depth and cantilevering well beyond the pylons themselves. The whole constituted a so-called Suprematist-Elementarist composition which was designed to be read or rather "deconstructed" from many different aspects. Lissitzky was well aware of the radical nature of this proposal when he wrote of it in 1929:

In comparison with the American skyscraper the innovation here resides in the fact that the utilized space which is horizontal is clearly separated from the "service and support" space which is vertical.

Nevertheless, such "anti-gravitational" devices were not regarded as being absolute prerequisites for the appearance of a Suprematist architecture. More

fundamental to the concept, as far as Lissitzky was concerned, was the idea of a kinetic syntax, as this was to be exemplified for him in two canonical works of the early twenties: in his own Proun room built for the Greater Berlin Art Exhibition of 1923, and in the Pravda newspaper building projected in the following year to the designs of the architects Alexander and Viktor Vesnin.

As in the Lenin Tribune of 1920, Lissitzky's *Prounenraum* attempted to combine objective machine-made forms with non-objective, Suprematist elements, thereby combining utilitarian components with kinetic abstract forms. In the first issue of magazine *G*, Lissitzky wrote:

The space was designed by using elementary forms and materials: line, surface and rod, cube sphere, black, white, grey, and wood: in addition, surfaces were applied flat to the walls (color), and other surfaces were placed at right angles to the walls (wood) . . . Thus the organization of the wall cannot be conceived as anything like a representative picture-painting. Whether one "paints" on a wall or whether one hangs pictures on it, both actions are equally wrong. New space neither needs nor demands pictures . . . I am aiming at a spatial equilibrium, both mobile and elementary, that will not be upset by the introduction of a telephone on a piece of standardized office furniture. *Space exists for man — man does not exist for space. . . . We reject space as a painted coffin for our living bodies.*

Lissitzky attempted to dematerialize the existing, cubic materiality of the *Prounenraum* through the continuous application of a Suprematist relief construction. While this intent was more intellectual than the "machinism" of

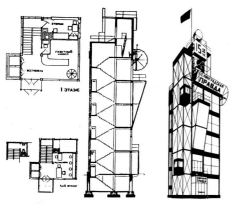

120 *Vesnin brothers, Pravda Building, Moscow, 1924.*

the Vesnin brothers' Pravda project of 1924, they were both activated by extra-tectonic components — by the movement of the body in space in the case of exhibition room and by the mechanized movement within the building itself in the case of the Pravda tower. Of this last, Lissitzky was to write in *Russland*:

All accessories — which on a typical city street are usually tacked onto the building — such as signs, advertising, clocks, loudspeakers and even elevators inside, have been incorporated as integral elements of the design and combined into a unified whole. This is the aesthetic of Constructivism.

Where Lissitzky and Malevich tended to be preoccupied with the latent "immateriality" of form and light, Tatlin concerned himself with the obdurance of material and its fabrication and his first *contre-reliefs*, exhibited after abandoning painting in 1915, were literally contructed from the debris of the street. It was this *trans-rational* (Khlebnikovian) obsession with resonant materiality which no doubt led him to compose and sign *The Program of the Productivist Group* of 1920, a manifesto which asserted that:

The task of the constructivist group is the communistic expression of the material, constructive work . . . Among material elements are — (1) Matter in general. Recognition of its origin, its industrial and productional changes. Its nature and meaning. (2) Intellectual matter: light, plane, space, color, volume. The constructivists treat intellectual and solid materials in the same way.

It is significant that this text concluded with a series of anti-art, anti-religious slogans, such as "Down with Art! Long live Technic! Religion is a lie! Art is a lie!", etc., and that it eschewed such traditional terms as architecture, painting and sculpture. Evidently construction was seen as an activity which transcended all previous forms of plastic culture. Tatlin regarded himself as an "artist-engineer" and there is no doubt that in certain sense he was. Throughout the twenties his activities as a designer had a very wide scope and included the design of workers' clothing, demountable furniture, ceramics, and even a stove designed to give off a maximum amount of heat for minimal input. And yet there remained an irreducible *arationality* about his work, a kind of primitive, proto-Dadaistic irony, which one critic was to describe as "technological Khlebnikovism." Tatlin was as much a part of the Russian eschatological and mystical traditions as Malevich, and his 400-metre-high Monument to the Third International was as millenialistic a sign as Malevich's quasi-astronautic image, *Future Planets for Earth Dwellers* of 1924. Tatlin's interlocking of two ascending spirals, his distortion of the space and technique of the Eiffel Tower into the mythical profile of the ancient Babylonian tower, his superimposition of suspended Platonic, glass-sided prisms — a cube, a pyramid, a cylinder and a hemisphere — each one rotating at a different speed, all point to an overriding apocalyptic intent.

The one architect who immediately combined in practice both the ethos of Productivism and something comparable to the millenialistic formal attitude of Suprematism was Konstantin Melnikov, whose Makhorka Tobacco pavilion, built for the All-Russia Agricultural and Craft Exhibition of 1923,

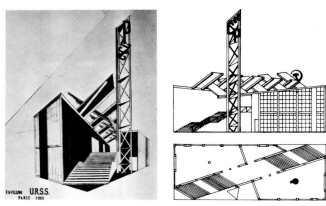

121 Melnikov, USSR Pavilion, Exposition des Arts Décoratifs, Paris, 1925.

initiated the primitive Constructivist phase of Soviet architecture. Melnikov combined, in a fresh and entirely "structuralist" manner, elements drawn from the Russian agrarian vernacular, such as exposed-frame construction, monopitched roofs, spiral stairs, gridded fenestration, horizontal, vertical and diagonal boarding juxtaposed together for the purposes of decorative effect, plus large block lettering stencilled straight onto undressed timber. This extraordinarily vigorous and inexpensive aesthetic seems to have directly paralleled the primitive Constructivist phase of Soviet typography, where rudimentary typefaces, of different font and size, were combined together for rhetorical effect. It is close in spirit to Alexander Rodchenko's early covers for the magazine *LEF* or Lissitzky's first "constructivist" book – his 1923 design for Mayakovsky's poem, *For Reading Aloud*. An almost identical ethos can be sensed in Productivist stage sets, such as Vsevolod Meyerhold's 1922 "bio-mechanical" presentation of *Tarelkin's Death*, with timber-framed acting machinery built to designs of Rodchenko's wife, Varvara Stepanova. As Christina Lodder has recently argued, the Constructivist stage and, above all, the polemical October theatre of Meyerhold afforded a ready laboratory in which the unprecedented Constructivist aesthetic could be rapidly postulated and developed and indeed Liubov Popova's 1922 sets for Crommelyck's play *The Magnificent Cuckold* and Alexander Vesnin's acting machine for Chesterton's *The Man Who Was Thursday* did just exactly that.

While subtle differences are discernible, the most extraordinary thing about all of these works is the commonality of both style and technique; the same battened and braced timber framing, the shared preference for inclined planes, dynamic stairs and diagonal, contrasting geometry, the introduction (in the sets, at least) of simple moving devices such as wheels and windmills, and finally the ubiquitous Constructivist finish of undressed timber, black and red components and stencilled lettering.

The apotheosis of all this work, at least as far as architecture was concerned, was Melnikov's USSR Pavilion, built in Paris, for the Exposition des Arts Décoratifs of 1925. Aside from its primitive structural rhetoric, the *parti* of this building was closer than anything by the Constructivist artists (Rodchenko, Vesnin, Gan, etc.) to the rhythmic and dynamic formal principles which had been in the throes of emerging in the *Vkhutemas*, or Moscow's Higher Artistic and Technical Workshops, from 1920 onwards. Somewhat along the lines of the literary Structuralism evolved by Shiklovsky and Eichenbaum, the architect N. A. Ladovsky attempted, in his *Vkhutemas* ateliers, to found the syntactical rules of a totally unprecedented architecture, based upon perceptual constancy (anti-perspectival) and upon the dynamic plastic rhythms that are engendered by receding geometrical progressions.

To this end the conventional rectangular plot of Melnikov's USSR Pavilion was "dynamicized" by a *scala regia* which cut the available site along its diagonal and hence divided the structure into two halves. This staircase, which rose and fell under an open timber "arcade," suspended at roof level, gave access to the first floor which was furnished as a typical worker's club. The intersecting roof form of the arcade over the stair had already appeared in J. Volodko's market hall projected in the Vkhutemas in 1923, and this form was destined to become as prevalent a geometric device in the Soviet

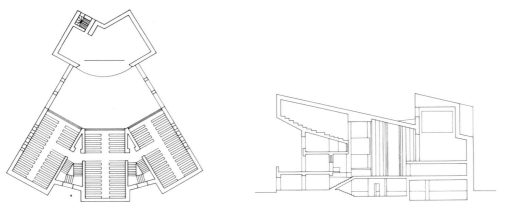

122 *Melnikov, Rusakov Club, Moscow, 1928. First floor plan and section.*

avant-garde as the logarithmic spiral embodied in Tatlin's tower. Melnikov's 1925 pavilion initiated that phase of his career which was to be devoted to the building of new "social condensers"; that is to say, to the remarkable workers' clubs that he designed in the late twenties, of which is Rusakov Club, built for the transport workers' union of Moscow in 1927, is possibly the most dramatic and successful. In this structure Melnikov attempted for reinforced concrete what he had already achieved for timber, namely, a Constructivist syntax appropriate to the material. The tripartite spread-eagled plan of Rusakov Club, with its three cantilevered lecture halls, unequivocally announces the end of the primitive Constructivist phase of Soviet architecture and establishes the truly Modernist period of Russian architecture, which lasted from Moisei Ginzburg's foundation of OSA (Association of Contemporary Architects) in 1925 to the Party Ukase of April, 1932, which curtailed, once and for all, the perennial factiousness of Soviet avant-garde architects.

Despite his proven capacity as a practitioner, Melnikov's energies were exclusively devoted to the invention of unprecedented forms of architectural expression and he never addressed the wider issue as to what could be the most appropriate form of architectural practice in a revolutionary society. As with the rest of the ASNOVA group (the Association of New Architects), to which Melnikov was affiliated, it was simply assumed that these broader issues of production and distribution were not strictly architectural concerns. ASNOVA, founded in 1923 by the Ladovsky's Vkhutemas circle (including in its membership such figures as N. Dokuchaev, V. Krinsky, T. Varentsov, and,

at some remove, Lissitzky) never really questioned the socio-economic, functional or cultural destiny of their forms.

For all the awkward machine Romanticism, evident in his eclectic project for the Palace of Labor in 1923, Moisei Ginzburg clearly came from a cosmopolitan background. Son of an architect in Minsk, he was professionally educated as an architect at the Academy of Arts in Milan and graduated from this institution in 1914. During the First World War he studied engineering at the Rizhsky Polytechnic in Moscow, and after the war he moved definitively to Moscow, where he joined the faculty of the Vkhutemas, becoming professor of architectural history and theory there in 1923 — the year that his first theoretical text, *Rhythm in Architecture,* was published.

Ginzburg's second collection of essays issued under the title *Style and Epoch* in 1924 can be seen as an interpretation of Le Corbusier's *Vers une Architecture* in terms of the apocalyptic Soviet situation. Ginzburg would have become familiar with Le Corbusier's thesis through the serialized publication in *L'Esprit Nouveau* in the early twenties. He was to reinterpret its classical machinist thesis in terms of the Constructivist architectural position which was evolving at that time around the charismatic figure of Alexander Vesnin. As S. O. Khan-Mahomedov has written:

In its early stages, the architectural Constructivist movement was under the influence of Constructivism, a larger movement in Soviet art of the 1920's, concerned with the creation of mass-produced art for the people. . . . A working group of Constructivists was formed in Inkhuk in March 1921; among its members were A. Gan, A. Rodchenko, V. Stepanova and

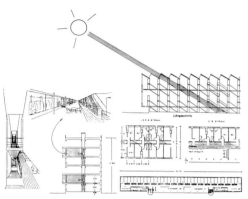

123 *Ginzburg and the Building Committee of the Economic Council of USSR, Type E dom-kommuna.*

V. and G. Stenburg. The views of these Constructivist artists were closer to those of Vesnin than those of the architects who joined the committee of Inkhuk architects, headed by N. Ladovsky. But an architectural group gradually formed around Vesnin, composed mainly of Vkhutemas students – M. Barschch, A. Burov, I. Sobolev, L. Komarova, N. Krassilnikov – to whom were allied a number of prominent members of LEF (Leftist Art Front) led by V. Mayakovsky, O. Brik and A. Lavinsky.

In slightly different ways, both Vesnin (in his *Credo*, delivered before the Inkhuk group in April 1922) and Ginzburg (in *Style and Epoch*) saw the necessity of grounding a new Socialist art and architecture on the achievements of engineering and on the dynamism and formal order which was to be found in the machine, but they differed somewhat in the role that they assigned to the imperatives of economy. Thus, Ginzburg gave a marginally more determinant role to economy when he wrote:

Exceptional economic stringency required the maximum possible economy of material in that "delimiting" and therefore a maximizing of the constructive work done by building elements. But it also happened that the principles on which every branch of contemporary life were organized or aspired to be organized, were precisely those embodied par excellence in the machine; the principles of honesty, structural simplicity, objectivity, precise organization, and thus economy of all means. The essence of this machine, which is beginning to play such an exceptional psychological role in our lives, consists in the naked constructiveness of its component organisms.

By and large the OSA group (Association of Contemporary Architects), founded by Vesnin, Ginzburg, Y. Kornfeld, V. Vladimirov and A. Burov in 1925, dedicated itself to a Functionalist/Constructivism as opposed to the Rationalist or Formalist/Constructivism advanced by ASNOVA. Of this split within the Russian architectural avant-garde and of its subsequent development throughout the twenties, Khan-Mahomedov has written as follows:

The aesthetic and formal explorations of these years determined to a considerable degree the development of Soviet architecture. But the formal problems were by no means adequately resolved; both the relationship between form and functional and structural requirements and that between form and all verifiable principles of perception, remained in doubt. These were the subjects of particular Rationalist and Constructivist study – and contention. But though the two parties diverged in their interpretations they were, ultimately, complementary in their approach.

Khan-Mahomedov goes on to show how the OSA Constructivists later became disturbed by the incipient tendency towards "style" and how their anxiety became the subject of the extensive polemical debate that appeared in the pages of the OSA magazine, *Contemporary Architecture*, between 1926 and 1930. As Khan-Mahomedov has written:

Ginzburg as editor laid most stress on "Functionalism" as a means of avoiding stylistic excess. ... By (this) was understood the integration of rational principles of planning with advanced building techniques. Functionalists – and the Constructivists in particular – stood for standardization, the industrialization of the building industry, the introduction of assembly line principles and prefabrication. Overenthusiastic in their faith in technology,

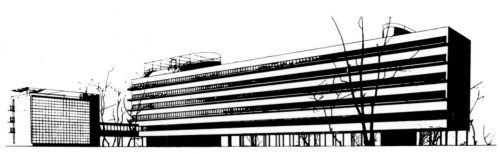

124   Ginzburg, Narkomfin Apartments, Moscow, 1928-29.

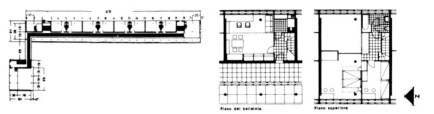

125   Narkomfin Apartments, block plan & plans of typical units: gallery and bedroom level.

they exaggerated perhaps the possibilities of rationalized methods of construction.

In 1927 *Contemporary Architecture* devoted a great deal of space to discussing the problem of the new communal dwelling or *dom-kommuna* and this debate finally led to an OSA competition devoted to this subject. The intent was to arrive at a new set of residential prototypes, where the aggregation of the units and the integration of common facilities would reflect the transformed nature of society. To this end many of the OSA submissions comprised interlocking duplex units, whose one-and-a-half or two-storey accommodations would pass either under or over the internal access corridor situated in the center of the block, at every three floors. This sectional device appears to have been an attempt at symbolizing the integration of the society in the spatial order of the building itself, and as such it was to reappear in the 1932 cross-section employed by Le Corbusier for the typical apartment slab of his *Ville Radieuse*. The polemical force of this invention projected it beyond the closure of the Soviet avant-garde and thus it reemerged in numerous housing blocks built after the end of the Second World War — most notably in Le Corbusier's *Unité d'Habitation*, under construction in Marseille, from 1947 to 1952.

The OSA competition encouraged the formation of a research group led by Ginzburg. This group, known as the Building Committee of the Economic Council of USSR, developed a series of prototypical communal dwellings, including the famous Stroikem units and blocks, one of which was to be adopted by Ginzburg for his experimental Narkomfin apartments built in Moscow in 1929. Despite the provision in all these studies of a wide range of communal facilities, including a collective dining hall, gymnasium, nursery schools, etc., Ginzburg remained aware that collective living could not be imposed on the residents without regard for their prerevolutionary habits and for their local culture. Thus he wrote:

We can no longer compel the occupants of a particular building to live collectively, as we have attempted to do in the past, generally with negative results. We must provide for the possibility of a gradual, natural transition to the communal utilization of a number of different areas. That is why we have tried to keep each unit isolated from the next, that is why we found it necessary to design the kitchen alcove as a standard element of minimum size that could be removed bodily from the apartment to permit the introduction of canteen catering at any given moment. We considered it absolutely necessary to incorporate certain features that would stimulate the transition to a socially superior mode of life, *stimulate but not dictate*.

Perhaps no text from the late years of the Soviet avant-garde is able to convey more succinctly than this the tensions and conflicts of the period; on the one hand, we have the continuing faith in the Constructivist capacity to devise flexible solutions to meet rapidly changing social conditions and, on the other, one senses the growing awareness that doctrinaire functionalism and collectivization will have to be subtly mediated if they are to prove acceptable at all.

The polarities within OSA in the late twenties oscillated between a hypothetically functionalist approach to   urbanism which dedicated itself

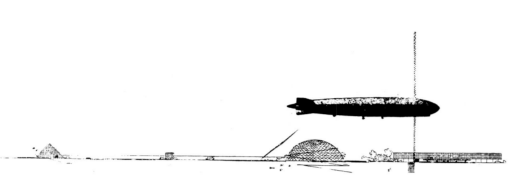

126 *Leonidov, project for a Palace of Culture, from the cover of* SA, *1930.*

127 *Leonidov, Lenin Institute, 1927.*

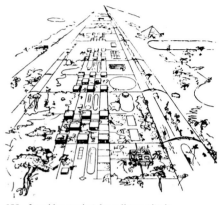

128 *Leonidov, project for a linear city in Magnitogovsk, 1930.*

(after the 1868 Communist Manifesto) to the "gradual abolition of the distinction between town and country, by a more equable distribution of the population over the country," and a relaxation of Ginzburg's dogmatic functionalism that had initially insisted that buildings must be designed as though they were large machines.

The first of these poles found its most doctrinaire expression in the work of N. A. Milyutin who advanced his linear city theory in the book *Socialist Towns* of 1930, wherein a virtually continuous pattern of land settlement was posited — made up of six parallel zones, arranged in the following order: (1) railway zone; (2) industrial zone, comprising education and research as well as production; (3) green zone with autoroute; (4) residential zone, plus communal institutions; (5) park zone with sport facilities and (6) agricultural zone.

The second pole, amounting to a crack in the OSA functionalist line, came with the emergence of Ivan Leonidov and his subsequent acceptance within the Ginzburg fold. Once again, as in the foundation of OSA, Alexander Vesnin was to play a salient role, inasmuch as Leonidov is to arrive at his unique style, under Vesnin's tuition in the Vkhutemas. Nothing could have been further removed from OSA's orthodox functionalism than Leonidov's graduating Vkhutemas thesis of 1927. This composition, which was ostensibly a research institute for a site on the Lenin Hills outside Moscow, was comprised, in the main, of two strongly contrasting and totally glazed forms: a vertical, rectangular shaft housing the book stack, and a spherical auditorium with a seating capacity of 4,000. This dualistic complex, complemented by a horizontal library block and five research units, was projected as being connected to Moscow by an elevated monorail. The principal forms plus an adjacent radio tower were supported on pylons and held in place by guy wires, the whole approximating Lissitzky's ideal of a "gravity-free" architecture. Leonidov's determination to render the "new social condenser" as though it were a Suprematist megastructure — a vision patently influenced by Malevich — was to reach its climax in 1930, in his Palace of Culture proposal, whose glazed auditoriums, planetariums, laboratories and Wintergardens were laid out on a gridded rectilinear matrix that made few concessions to traditional landscaping. Its metaphysical aura was relieved by luxuriant vegetation and by Platonic prisms, whose translucent or transparent forms were not functionally determined. The airship and mooring mast depicted in the elevation were clearly meant to celebrate the same lightweight technology as would be employed for the buildings themselves. In retrospect the space-frame technology envisaged for most of these structures seems to have anticipated in a remarkable way the mid-twentieth-century work of designers such as Konrad Wachsmann and R. Buckminster Fuller. This was truly an expression of "almost nothing" within which the process of societal reeducation would be enacted, in terms of athletics, tattoos, demonstrations, sports, flying, science and research. It was symptomatic of the changed ideological climate that the utopianism of this vision should at once expose Leonidov to public criticism from the pro-Neue Sachlichkeit Soviet faction known as VOPRA or the All-Russia Association of Proletarian Architects founded in 1929. Of this internicene struggle V. Khazanova has written:

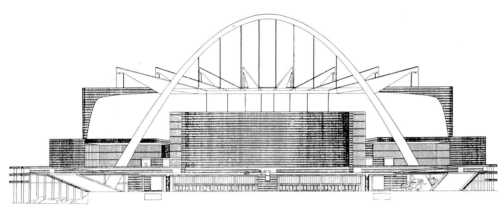

129 Le Corbusier, project for Palace of the Soviets, 1931. Elevation of large hall.

VOPRA refuted eclectic policies which hampered architecture and considered OSA to have gone too far left, over-rating the use of technology and rejecting art ... To VOPRA architecture had to be proletarian in its form and content – a synthesis of social, economic, emotional, ideological and structural elements. It was the application of dialectical materialism to planning and experimental work.

The eclipse of the Soviet avant-garde came with the Palace of the Soviets competition which was conducted as an excessively protracted contest and debate between June 1931 and May 1933. The idea of building a new congress complex, with the intent of representing the young Socialist state, both to itself and the world at large, had been around since the previous Palace of Labor competition conducted under Sergei Kirov's auspices in 1923, wherein the Vesnin brothers first elaborated their Constructivist syntax. The second contest for a "socialist palace" was at first closed, with as few as twelve architects being invited to participate, of which nine were foreign and three were seasoned Russian professionals of academic background and persuasion; Ivan Zholtovsky, Boris Iofan and G. B. Krasin. The outside architects invited to compete were Le Corbusier and Erich Mendelsohn, who had already built in the Soviet Union, and Walter Gropius, who had taken third place in the Kharkov Theatre competition of 1930. The remainder were Auguste Perret, Hans Poelzig, Armando Brasini and two relatively unknown American architects, Max Urban and Thomas W. Lamb. After these designs had been received, the competition was then extended into an open contest lasting until July 1931.

While the official results of the competition were declared in February 1932, with Zholtovsky and Iofan gaining the special first prize and other conciliatory prizes going to Hector Hamilton (USA) and various design teams drawn from the obviously ascendant VOPRA faction, a general dissatisfaction was expressed on behalf of the Stalinist commissioning body which was then chaired by V. Molotov and comprised, among other dignitaries of note, L. Kaganovich and K. Voroshilov. That this adjudicating body was absolutely nationalist and anti-Western in its general disposition is borne out by E. H. Carr who has written of the Stalinist circle after the death of Lenin in the following terms:

The absence of any significant Western influence in the formation of Stalin's mind and character distinguished him sharply from the other early Bolshevik leaders. Alone among them he had never lived in Western Europe, and neither read nor spoke any Western language. This peculiarity colored his personal relations as well as his political opinions. He never seems to have felt entirely at ease with colleagues steeped in a European tradition and outlook; ... Those who stood closest to Stalin in later years — Molotov, Kirov, Kaganovich, Voroshilov, Kuibyshev — were as innocent as himself of any Western background.

The narrow solidarity of this group would go some way towards explaining the rather uncertain, edictive, ambiguous and often contradictory judgements issued by the Stalinist Palace Construction Council from August 1932 onwards, ranging from their questioning Iofan's "skyscraper pylon" motif for being too capitalistic, to their condemnation of Le Corbusier's quite bril-

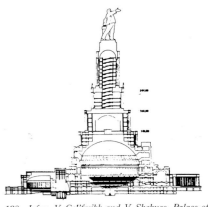

130 Iofan, V. Gel'freikh and V. Shchuco, Palace of the Soviets: revised winning scheme, 1934. Section.

liant entry because it embodied " . . . the aesthetic of a complicated machine, that is to 'turn over' huge masses of humanity."

In other words, despite the specially premiated award given to Hamilton's rather Art Deco composition (cf. the Rockefeller Centre of virtually the same date), the council were as much disturbed by Iofan's *moderne* syntax as they were absolutely antipathetic to the left wing formalist machinism, which, while it was manifest in Le Corbusier's entry, was equally evident in the Ladovsky or the ASNOVA entries, to cite only a few of the Constructivist schemes submitted.

The result of this impasse was to hold a third and closed competition in the spring and summer of 1932, this time inviting "predictable" entrants such as Iofan, Zholtovsky and two of the previously placed VOPRA teams to submit. While Ginzburg and Ladovsky were permitted to participate in this third round, the real effect was to compel Iofan to simplify his design into the form of a vast wedding cake which incorporated both of the conference halls within its somewhat bulbous mass. Part way through this process of design by committee, left-wing formalism was officially suppressed in the Soviet Union by the Central Committee Resolution of April 23rd, 1932, which effectively eliminated all the rival architectural factions of the Soviet Union and combined them into one Union of Soviet Architects, who from henceforth would adhere to the party line in culture. This line emerged, so to speak, with Iofan's revised design, submitted in May 1933, as yet a further stage in this protracted undertaking. This project, rising to some 220 metres in height, was finally regarded as being sufficiently classical and monumental, although even

this "prescribed" solution was to suffer further modification, at the hands of Stalin himself, who insisted that Iofan's surmounting statue of the "liberated proletarian" should be greatly enlarged and in any event transformed into a colossal statue of Lenin. Thus the avant-garde came to an abrupt end, in a proto-Social Realist scheme, which, while it was never built, nonetheless influenced the course of Soviet architecture throughout the next two decades.

Part 2 Dutch Elementarist Architecture: The De Stijl Movement 1917-31

The Dutch De Stijl movement, otherwise known as Neoplasticism was primarily based on the work of four men: the painters Bart van der Leck, Piet Mondrian and Theo van Doesburg, and the cabinetmaker Gerrit Rietveld. Most of the other artists who were founder members in 1917 — including the poet Anthony Kok, the painters Georges Vantongerloo, and Vilmos Huszar, and the architects J. J. P. Oud, Robert van 't Hoff and Jan Wils — played less salient roles, or, in any event, began to withdraw from the movement for various reasons after their initial enthusiasm waned.

The initial architectural paradigms of the movement came from Hendrik Petrus Berlage and from Frank Lloyd Wright, whose work had been published by Wasmuth in 1910 and 1911. Robert van 't Hoff had, in any event, seen Wright's work, during a visit he had made to the United States prior to the First World War, and in 1916 he built a remarkably convincing Wrightian villa on the outskirts of Utrecht. Yet aside from this pioneering reinforced concrete house, with its pseudo-Wrightian furniture designed by Rietveld and

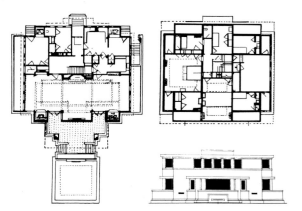

131 *Van't Hoff, Huister Heide, Utrecht, 1916. Plans and elevation.*

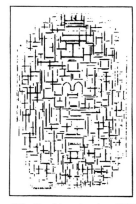

132 *Mondrian, drawing, 1917.*

a number of marginal Wrightian works by Wils and Oud (above all, perhaps, Wils's Daal en Berg estate, built in The Hague in 1925), there was little Neoplastic architecture prior to the canonical Schröder-Schräder house built in Utrecht in 1924.

Dutch Elementarist painting came into being as a result of a metaphysical cultural impulse (Christosophic) which had its origins in the Neoplatonic philosophy of the mathematician M. H. J. Schoenmaekers, whose major works, *The New Image of the World* (1915) and *The Principles of Plastic Mathematics* (1916) were to exercise a decisive influence on Mondrian and Bart van der Leck, during the long period that the two spent in daily contact with Schoenmaekers, throughout the interregnum of the First World War. From Schoenmaekers came the term "Neo-Plasticism" as well as the orthogonal and primary colour palette of the movement. While rendering his mystical cosmology in terms of colour and form, Schoenmaekers enunciated the principles of Neoplasticism in the following terms:

The three principal colors are essentially yellow, blue and red. They are the only colors existing . . . yellow is the movement of the ray (vertical) . . . blue is the contrasting color to yellow (horizontal firmament) . . . red is the mating of yellow and blue. . . . The two fundamental, complete contraries which shape our earth and all that is of the earth are: the horizontal line of power, that is the course of the earth around the sun, and the vertical, profoundly spatial movement of rays that originate in the centre of the sun.

Yet while Schoenmaekers isolated the primary elements of Neoplasticism,

the role played by Theo van Doesburg in the initial formulation was absolutely essential. Van Doesburg wrote regularly for the magazine *Eenheid* (Unity) between 1912 and 1914 and it is during this period that he first projected the idea of an international, orthogonal, abstract art. Berlage's *Studies on Architecture, Style and Community* of 1910 and Umberto Boccioni's *Technical Manifesto of Futurist Sculpture* of 1912 were major influences on Van Doesburg's thought at this time; from the former came, amongst other things, the title of the movement itself — *De Stijl* (The Style) — while from the latter came the stress on the straight line.

The other important influence at this time, and a total antithesis to the superficial socio-cultural programme of Italian Futurism, was Wassily Kandinsky's *On the Spiritual in Art*, published in 1912, Van Doesburg being greatly impressed by Kandinsky's description of the way in which Russian peasants live their lives surrounded by art. Thus while Van Doesburg was to be strongly influenced by and even involved with the two most "destructive" movements in modern art, which emerged in full force around the time of the First World War — namely Italian Futurism and Swiss-German Dadaism — the core of his work and thought remained tied to the positions established by Mondrian and Kandinsky and to the somewhat idealistic insight that he disposed himself of in 1916 when he wrote in the *De Avondpost* that: "In fact, what happens is nothing but the shift from an Eastern into a Western notion of art. Today this is possible now that materialism has annulled itself."

The year before, prior to his actual meeting with Mondrian, he had written of the latter's work in the following terms:

133 Oud, project for Strandboulevard housing, 1917. Perspective.

The feeling I obtained from (his) painting was of a purely spiritual, almost religious character, which, however, possessed no zeal ... To reduce the artist's means to such a minimum and to produce an impression of pure art using only black paint on a white canvas and horizontal and vertical lines is most extraordinary.... The other works of Mondrian could be described as colored architecture.

1917 was a seminal year for Van Doesburg, for not only did he summate his own theoretical activity in a text entitled *The New Movement in Painting* published at that time, but he also effectively founded the De Stijl movement by producing the first issue of the *De Stijl* magazine which carried Mondrian's theoretical statement on painting – his *Neoplasticism in Painting*, reworked for the third and last time in 1937, as *Plastic Art and Pure Plastic Art*, in which he was to conclude:

Art is only a substitute while the beauty of life is still deficient. It will disappear in proportion, as life gains in equilibrium.

The transcendence of painting by architecture and vice versa was also categorically declared in this first issue inasmuch as Van der Leck, Van Doesburg and Anthony Kok wrote on this theme and J. J. P. Oud produced his essay entitled "The Monumental Town," which appeared as an extended caption to his project for a *Strandboulevard* published at the same time.

The year 1918 saw Van Doesburg enter directly into architecture, first by designing stained glass, walls and titled floors for various projects by Jan Wils

and Oud – above all for Oud's "De Vonk," Noordwijkerhout development of that year, and then by submitting a project for the Leeuwarden monument, where he was apparently influenced by Wrightian concepts as these had been reinterpreted by Van 't Hoff. It is clear, as Baljeu has suggested, that Van 't Hoff's *Plastic Stairpost*, reproduced in *De Stijl 7*, is closely related to the spiralling composition of Van Doesburg's Leeuwarden project. 1918 is also the year of the first *De Stijl* manifesto, unsigned, incidentally, by Oud. This begins with an attack upon the pathological individualism of Romantic art. The first four clauses of the manifesto read as follows:

1. There is an old and a new consciousness of the age. The old one is directed towards the individual. The new one is directed towards the universal. The conflict of the individual and the universal is reflected in the World War as well as in art today.
2. The war is destroying the old world with all that it contains: the pre-eminence of the individual in every field.
3. The new art has revealed the substance of the new consciousness of the age: an equal balance between the universal and the individual.
4. The new consciousness is ready to be realized in everything, including the everyday things of life.

Van Doesburg's hyperactivity, constantly oscillating between his central Neoplastic position and his Dadaist (I. K. Bonset) and Futurist (Aldo Camini) personalities, distressed the more Calvinist members of the De Stijl circle and a rapid series of defections occurred, the architects ostensibly abandoning the camp because of the impracticality of Van Doesburg's vision, an artist like

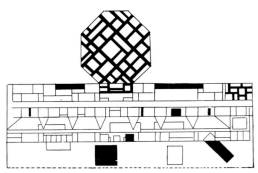

134 *Van Doesburg and Van Eesteren, project for a university hall, 1924.*

Van der Leck leaving because the constant polemicism did not agree with his aristocratic personality. Van Doesburg's over-heated polemicism struck out in all directions, including an attack on Berlage, which appeared in *Bouwkundig Weekblad* in 1920, wherein Van Doesburg accused him of being a rationalistic naturalist. Dadaism was valued by Van Doesburg as a cleansing force and his conviction was such that for a while he was able to persuade some of his more sober colleagues to add the affix "dada" to their surnames, hence Mondriandada, Kokdada, etc.

In many respects Van Doesburg embodied the movement in himself, for by 1921 the composition of the group had radically altered. Van der Leck, Vantongerloo, Van 't Hoff, Oud, Wils and Kok had all by then disassociated themselves from De Stijl, while Mondrian had reestablished himself as an independent artist in Paris. This Dutch defection convinced Van Doesburg that it was necessary to proselytize for De Stijl abroad. Thus of the new members of that year only one was Dutch, the architect Van Eesteren; the others were Russian and German — the architect, painter and graphic designer El Lissitzky and the film-maker Hans Richter. It was at Richter's invitation that Van Doesburg first visited Germany in 1920, and from this visit followed an invitation from Gropius to come to the Bauhaus in the following year. Van Doesburg's brief stay in Weimar in 1921 engendered a crisis within the Bauhaus, the repercussions of which have since become legendary, for the impact of his ideas on the students and faculty was both immediate and marked.

In the five-year period between 1917 and 1922, Dutch Elementarism transformed itself from being a crystalization of a pre-war Dutch avant-gardist impulse, to becoming an international movement, inextricably entwined with the equally international Suprematist-Elementarism, sponsored by El Lissitzky — an artistic movement which, as we have seen, had its own mystical origins in Russia and the East. The differences between the two were to lie in subtle nuances, for as Baljeu has written: "Whereas Lissitzky limited himself to advocating that Constructivist architecture should embody aesthetic values, Van Doesburg attacked 'constructive and solely functional architecture.' "

The catalytic ground on which these two impulses met to work out their short-lived synthesis was first and naturally enough Germany, but, more specifically and strangely, it was Walter Gropius's Weimar Bauhaus which, because of its Expressionist ideology, functioned as an unwitting foil to the other two highly intellectual and revolutionary movements. In *De Stijl 9* of July 1919, Van Doesburg was to distance himself from the Bauhaus by reprinting and then criticizing, for its Expressionist tendencies, the founding Bauhaus proclamation of April 1919, in which Gropius had exhorted fine artists to reject salon art and "to go into buildings, endow them with fairy tales . . . and *build in fantasy* without regard for technical difficulty." Surprisingly enough for one who was so committed to international art, Van Doesburg did not go to Germany until December 1920, when he met for the first time Hans Richter, Viking Eggeling, Bruno Taut and, above all, Walter Gropius and Adolf Meyer, who at that moment apparently invited Van Doesburg to come to the Bauhaus as a Constructivist artist. What transpired thereafter is somewhat lost in the fog of history, for while Van Doesburg

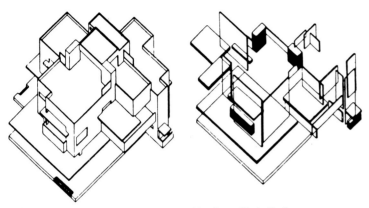

135 *Van Doesburg, Van Eesteren and Rietveld, private villa in the form of a counter-construction, 1922.*

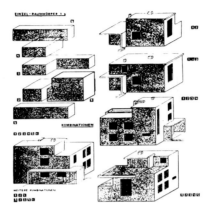

136 *Gropius, Baukasten permutable and extendable house system, evolved with Bauhaus students, 1922.*

eventually established himself in Weimar in April 1921, he did so not as a member of the Bauhaus faculty, but rather as a critical outside influence. Thus he wrote to Anthony Kok:

At Weimar I have turned everything radically upside down. This is supposed to be the most famous Academy with the most modern teachers! Every evening I have talked to the students and spread the vermin of the new spirit. Within a short time De Stijl will reappear in a more radical way. I have tremendous energy and know now that our views will achieve victory over anyone and anything.

That Van Doesburg was indeed to transform the Bauhaus is borne out by the works of the period, by the projects of such students as Farkas Molnár and Marcel Breuer, by the work of the furniture department in general, and even by the 1923 interior produced by Gropius himself for his own office. Perhaps the sharpest testimony to Van Doesburg's extraordinary influence at this moment is the Gropius and Meyer entry for the Chicago Tribune Competition of 1922, wherein a trabeated skeleton frame was to be "dynamicized" by the imposition of pin-wheeling Neoplastic elements.

The year 1922 was the *annus mirabilis* of international Constructivism, with the first issue of the three-language Constructivist magazine *Veshch/ Gegenstand/Objet* then under the joint editorship of El Lissitzky and Ilja Ehrenburg, and the International Congress of Progressive Artists being held in Düsseldorf in May of that year, resulting in the *Proclamation by the International Seciton of the Constructivist Artists,* signed by Van Doesburg, Lissitzky, and Richter, declaring " . . . art to represent a general and real expression of creative energy, organizing man's progress, that is to say, it is a means of the process of labor in general." These contacts led in the same year to the publication of Lissitzky's work in *De Stijl* and to the publication of Van Doesburg's article on "Monumental Art" in the first issue of *Veshch.* This was soon after followed by the publication in *De Stijl* of the manifesto "K. I.: International Union of Creative Constructivists" signed by Van Doesburg, Richter, Lissitzky, Maes and Burchartz.

Around this time, Van Doesburg was also to demonstrate the difference between his own "four-dimensional" space-form approach and Neoplastic work carried out inside the Bauhaus, as in the serial *Baukasten* which Gropius evolved with his students in 1922. These cubistic but *additive* compositions lacked the pin-wheeling spatial depth characteristic of the so-called Weimar models for small houses, carried out by the students Sturzkopf and Vogel, under Van Doesburg's supervision.

Under the impact of the Proun aesthetic of Lissitzky, Cornelis van Eesteren and Van Doesburg began to project (as axonometric drawings) a series of hypothetical architectural constructs, each comprising an asymmetrical cluster of articulated planar elements suspended in space about a volumetric centre. Van Doesburg invited Lissitzky to become a member of De Stijl and in 1922 Lissitzky's abstract-typographic children's fable of 1920, "The Story of Two Squares," appeared in the pages of the magazine. It is significant that the magazine itself changed its format at this juncture, Van Doesburg replacing the frontal composition and woodcut logotype designed by Huszar with an asymmetrical, Elementarist layout and a "Constructivist" logo.

In 1923 Van Doesburg and Van Eesteren managed to crystallize the architectural style of Neoplasticism in an exhibition of their work, at Léonce Rosenberg's Paris gallery, *L'Effort moderne*. This show was an immediate success and in consequence was restaged elsewhere in Paris and later in Nancy. Apart from the axonometric studies previously mentioned, it included their project for a house for Rosenberg and two other seminal works, their study for the interior of a university hall and their project for an artist's house.

Meanwhile in Holland Huszar and Rietveld collaborated on the design for a small room to be built as part of the Greater Berlin Art Exhibition of 1923, Huszar designing the environment and Rietveld the furniture, including the important Berlin chair. Simultaneously, Rietveld began to work on the design and detailing of the Schröder-Schräder House in Utrecht. This house, built at the end of a late 19th-century terrace, was in many respects a realization of Van Doesburg's *Tot een beeldende architectuur* (16 Points of a Plastic Architecture) published at the time of its completion. It fulfilled his prescription, being elementary, economic and functional; unmonumental and dynamic; anti-cubic in its form and anti-decorative in its colour. Its main living level on the top floor, with its open "transformable plan," exemplified, despite its traditional brick and timber construction, his postulation of a dynamic architecture liberated from the encumbrance of load-bearing walls and the restrictions imposed by pierced openings. Van Doesburg's eleventh point reads like an idealized description of the house:

The new architecture is anti-cubic, that is to say, it does not try to freeze the different functional space cells in one closed cube. Rather, it throws the functional space cells (as well as the overhanging planes, balcony volumes, etc.) centrifugally from the core of the cube. And through this means, height, width, depth, and time (i.e. an imaginary four-dimensional entity) approaches a totally new plastic expression in open spaces. In this way architecture acquires a more or less floating aspect that, so to speak, works against the gravitational forces of nature.

The last phase of De Stijl activity was announced by Mondrian's split with Van Doesburg in 1925, over the latter's introduction of the diagonal into his paintings, in a series of "counter-compositions" that he had executed in 1924. While Van Doesburg regarded these "oblique" works as paintings of his "counter-constructions" in architecture, Mondrian merely viewed them as an arbitrary modification of Neoplastic principles.

From his association with Lissitzky, Van Doesburg had come to regard social structure and technology as among the prime determinants of form, irrespective of any concerns he might still entertain for the De Stijl ideal of universal harmony. By the mid-1920s he realized that universality could, by itself, only produce an artificially delimited culture, which by virtue of its antipathy of everyday objects could only be against the initial De Stijl concern — subscribed to even by Mondrian — for the unification of art and life. Van Doesburg seems to have opted for a Lissitzkian solution to this dilemma, whereby both the environmental scale and status of the object should determine the degree to which it may be manipulated in accordance

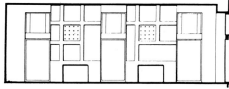

138 *Café L'Aubette. Wall relief in cinema.*

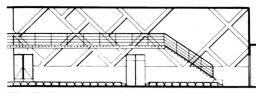

137 *Van Doesburg, Café L'Aubette, Strasburg, 1928-29. Wall relief in ballroom.*

with an abstract conception. Thus, while furniture and equipment as produced by the society at large ought to be accepted as the ready-made objects of the culture, the built environment itself could and indeed should be made to conform to a higher order.

Van Doesburg and Van Eesteren gave an idealized version of this position in their essay *Vers une construction collective* (Towards a Collective Construction), published in 1924, in which they tended towards a more objective and technical solution to the problem of architectural synthesis:

We must realize that life and art are no longer separate domains. That is why the "idea" of "art" as an illusion separate from real life must disappear. The word "art" no longer means anything to us. In its place we demand the construction of our environment in accordance with creative laws based upon a fixed principle. These laws, following those of economics, mathematics, technique, sanitation, etc., are leading to a new plastic unity.

Later one reads, under the seventh point of the manifesto, the essence of the spirit that was to inform Van Doesburg's last major work, the Café L'Aubette of 1928:

We have established the true place of colour in architecture and we declare that painting, without architectural construction (that is, easel painting), has no further reason for existence.

By the time that Van Doesburg received the commission through Hans Arp for the interior of the café-brasserie, L'Aubette, in Strasbourg in 1926, the De Stijl architects had come to embrace a reduced functionalism, a kind of nieuwe zaklikheid or "new objectivity." This much was evident in such works as Rietveld's "productivist" tubular metal and bent plywood chair of 1927, or in Oud's Hoek van Holland housing, under construction from 1924 to 1927.

The Café L'Aubette in Strasbourg, fully complete by 1928, was a large undertaking by De Stijl standards, involving a sequence of some seven rooms plus a galleria on the ground all set within an eighteenth-century shell, originally designed by Francois Blondel. This whole complex was designed and realized by Van Doesburg, in collaboration with Hans and Sophie Tauber-Arp. While Van Doesburg controlled the general theme each artist was free to design his own room. With the single exception of Arp's mural, all the rooms were modulated by shallow abstract wall reliefs, colour, lighting and equipment being integrated into each composition. Van Doesburg's own scheme was, in effect, a reworking of his 1923 project for a university hall, in which a diagonal Elementarist composition had been deliberately imposed on all the surfaces of a partially orthogonal space. Van Doesburg's interior in L'Aubette was similarly dominated and distorted by the lines of a huge diagonal relief or counter-composition, passing obliquely over all the internal surfaces. This fragmentation through relief — an extension of Lissitzky's Proun room approach of 1923 — was complemented by the fact that the furnishing was free of any Elementarist pieces. In their place Van Doesburg designed "standard" bentwood chairs and elsewhere employed extremely

323

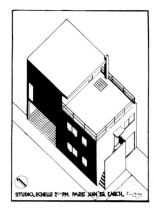

139 Van Doesburg, House in Meudon, 1929. Axonometric.

objective detailing. The tubular railing throughout was simply welded, while the main lighting consisted of bare light bulbs bracketed off two metal tubes suspended from the ceiling. Of this design he wrote:

The track of man in space (from left to right, from front to back, from above to below) has become of fundamental importance for painting in architecture.... In this painting the idea is not to lead man along a painted surface of a wall, in order to let him observe the pictorial development of the space from one wall to the other; the problem is to evoke the simultaneous effect of painting and architecture.

The Café L'Aubette was the last Dutch Elementarist architectural work of consequence and as such it was a victory of the principle of "counter-composition" over "counter-construction" or, translating Van Doesburg's terminology, of Neoplastic painting over Neoplastic architecture. This much Van Doesburg seems to have realized in his diary entries of 1928, where for the first time he expressed doubts about the possibilities of continuing with Elementarism and even suggests that the "new objective" functionalism may well be the way of the future. This shift in attitude seems to coincide with his recognition that the ultimate form of environmental art may be the "participatory" film to which he referred in his essay "Film as Pure Form," which appeared in the journal *Die Form* in May 1929. Of this environmentally "expanded cinema" he wrote, somewhat after Lissitzky's concept of the *Prounenraum*, that: "The spectator space will become part of the film space. The separation of 'projection surface' is abolished. The spectator will no longer observe the film, like a theatrical presentation, but will participate in it optically and acoustically."

That he was, in his heart, already convinced of the impossibility of continuing to aestheticize the elements of use and production in terms of a transcending Neoplasticism is borne out in the preliminary and final designs for his own studio-house, built at Meudon in 1930. The shift between the first design of 1927 and the final project of 1929 is an absolute *volte face*, for the former is essentially a pinwheeling "counter-construction," while the latter is almost a Purist composition, close in its stripped, white rendered, frontalized and rectangular form, partially raised on piloti, to Le Corbusier's Citrohan prototype of the early 1920s. From now on, Van Doesburg seems to accept that there must be a split between the world of painting and the world of architecture. The one text in which he was finally to admit this schism dates from 1930. In that year, in a hitherto unpublished essay entitled "The New Architecture and Its Consequences," he was to opine, somewhat ambivalently, that:

All object-form emanates from function, the best form being the one which corresponds with its function in as economical manner as possible. Though the "orthogonal style" may provide the most useful forms and express our age most clearly, curved form is more suitable to objects of illumination, lamps or wheels. If functional form is confounded aesthetically with creative form, decoration replaces the architectural constructive principle. *Function* and *decoration* are diametrically opposed.

The energy released by the Russian Revolution had the effect of totally transforming the work of many Russian architects whose output prior to 1917 had been largely conditioned by crypto-Classical or National Romantic conventions. This is evidenced in the case of Melnikov by his pseudo-Classical AMO (now Likhachev) authomobile factory erected in Moscow in 1917. Apart from transforming the general scope of professional work by shifting the emphasis to the design of worker's housing, the Revolution initially demanded a new "millenial" syntax for architecture; one which was neither classical nor vernacular, and to this demand Melnikov responded with an extraordinary fertility, designing one dynamic, quasi-Futurist work after another, particularly in 1923 when he passed from his famous housing Serpukhovskaia Ulitsa to the very strong iconic quality of the Makhorka Tobacco Pavilion erected for the First All-Russia Agricultural Exhibition staged in Moscow in that year. Makhorka, the Suk-harevka Market of 1924 and the Soviet Pavilion built for the Exposition des Arts Décoratifs in Paris in 1925 represent the apotheosis of Melnikov's primitive-constructivist manner.

The commissioning of the Rusakov Club in 1927, by the Union of Municipal Workers initiated the second phase of Melnikov's career and was but the first of six workers clubs which Melnikov designed between 1927 and 1929. Rusakov was exceptionally well worked out from both a formal and

functional standpoint since it seems that its acoustics were more than adequate and the devices installed for modifying the volume of the hall so as to accommodate audiences of various sizes, were to prove to be a useful provision. (Cf. Adler and Sullivan's Auditorium Building, Chicago 1899.)

The 1,200-seat hall broke down into the following seating areas; a 360-seat lower parterre, a 270-seat tier and three higher rectangular halls each with a capacity of 190 seats. Each of the upper halls could be closed off from the main volume by sound-proof, sliding panels. This tripartite plan form, comprising three rectangular volumes set within a larger triangle, was in fact, fed by two sets of triangular access stairs, rising upwards from an elevated triangular shaped foyer. These stairs became important architectural features, each one dividing the upper halls whose cantilevered masses established the basic *gestalt* of the building. The foyer to the club was elevated one storey above the street and fed by external access stairs. Once inside, the spectators either climbed upwards to the halls or descended to the parterre or to the two small 120-seat self-contained mezzanine lecture rooms. The realization of Rusakov, with its assertion that a workers club needs little more than a flexible auditorium, was sufficient to provoke a long drawnout controversy as to the appropriate form and content for the so-called "new social-condenser."

325 Overall view
326 Above left: section
Above right: hall, view from stage
Below, from left: plans of first floor, second floor, mezzanine level and third floor
Photos: M. Sekiya

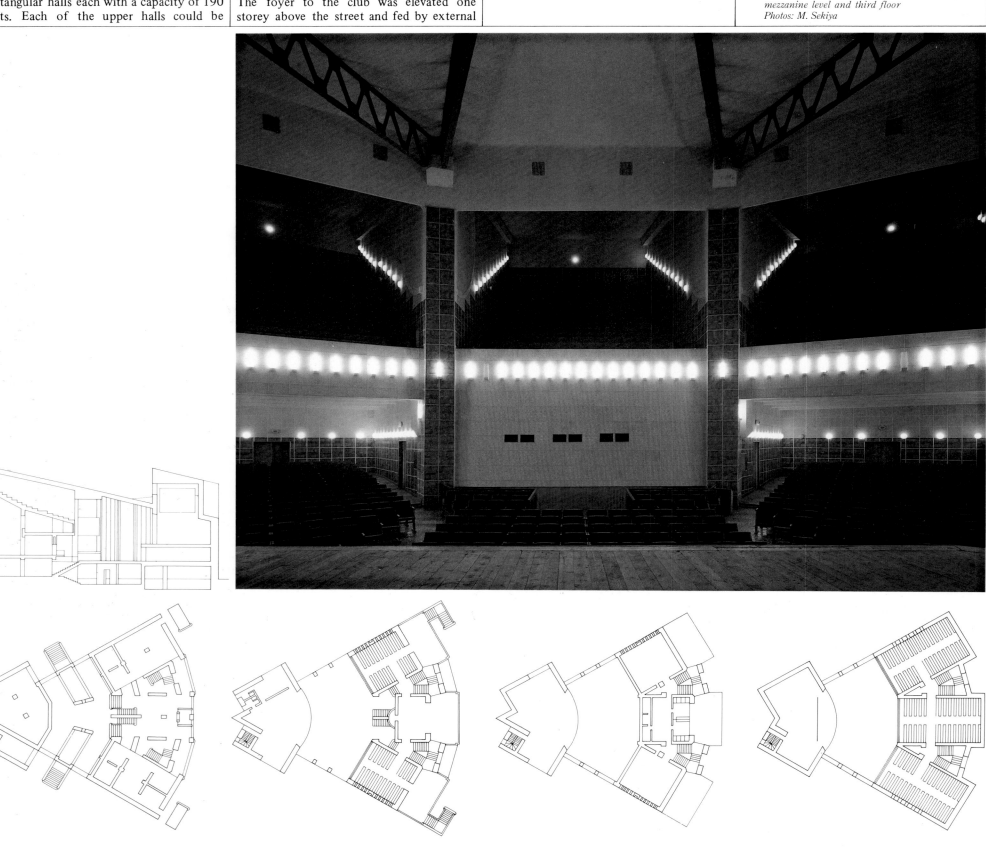

1928

J.W.E. BUYS & J.B. LÜRSEN
Cooperative Store, "Die Volharding"
The Hague, Holland

This cooperative store set into the conservative urban fabric of The Hague was rendered as an apotheosis of modern glass construction and as such was at its most spectacular at night when its surface was entirely illuminated from within. Very generally influenced by Vesnin's Pravda building of 1923, Die Volharding was a skeleton framed, vaguely constructivist composition comprised of different planar elements and built out of translucent and transparent glass surfaces; that is to say, gridded glass lenses were applied to the lower spandrels and to the corner staircase and service towers, while alternately translucent and transparent horizontal curtain walling was applied to the upper floors. From the point of view of massing however, this construction lies well within the Dutch tradition in as much as its pinwheel, pivoting corner, owes a good deal to the Wrightian-cum-Neoplastic exercises of Dudok. This relatively small department store attempts, like Duiker's Cineac Cinema of 1934, to transform street architecture into a spectacle; the built form becoming overwhelmed by other semiotic elements such as illuminated sky signs or back-lit glass billboards, both of which are featured here. That this fell short of the pure standards of Dutch Constructivism is evidenced by J.B. van Loghem who haughtily wrote of the building in his book *Bouwen* (1932) that "the architecture still being decorative, does not enter the scope of this book."

THEO VAN DOESBURG
HANS ARP
& SOPHIE TAUBER-ARP
Café L'Aubette
Strasbourg, France

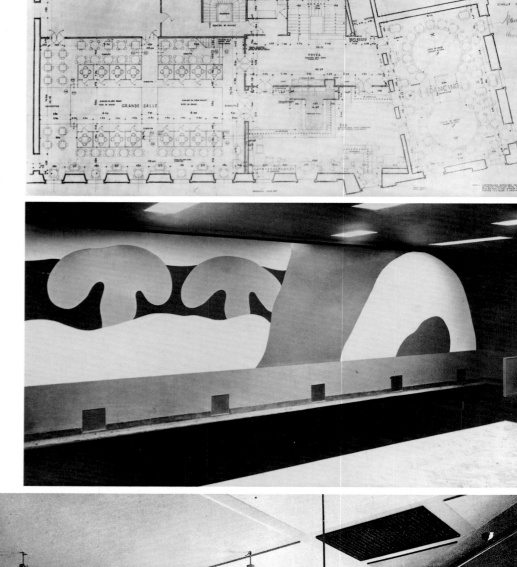

The Café L'Aubette in Strasbourg, designed in 1928, comprised a sequence of two large public rooms and a set of ancillary spaces, all encased within an 18th-century shell. These rooms were designed and realized by Van Doesburg in association with Hans Arp and Sophie Tauber-Arp. While Van Doesburg controlled the tenor of the overall work, each artist was free to design his own room. Thus, with the single exception of Arp's mural in the *cave dancing,* all the rooms were modulated by shallow abstract wall reliefs; the colour, lighting and equipment being integrated into each composition. Van Doesburg's own scheme was a reworking of his 1923 project for a university hall, in which a diagonal Elementarist composition was projected onto the surfaces of a partially orthogonal space. Van Doesburg's main interior in L'Aubette was similarly dominated and distorted by the lines of a diagonal relief or counter-composition passing obliquely over the internal surfaces. This fragmentation through relief (an extension of Lissitzky's Proun-room concept of 1923) was complemented by the fact that the furnishing was free of any Elementarist pieces. In their place Van Doesburg designed 'standard' bentwood chairs (after Thonet) and elsewhere employed extremely objective detailing. The tubular railing throughout was simply welded, while the main lighting consisted of bare lightbulbs bracketed off two metal tubes suspended from the ceiling.

Top: plan
Center: Cave dancing *with a mural by Arp*
Bottom: cinema and dancing hall
Photos: Musées de la Ville de Strasbourg (center),
Dienst Verspreide Rijkskollekties te den Haag (bottom)

This school is the consequence of a development which originates in an asymmetrical wooden house, built in Aalsmeer in 1924. Two years later this asymmetrical predeliction is transformed into the spread-eagled plan which Duiker first adopts in Zonnestraal and which he is then to repeat, in a more curtailed and symmetrical form in his high-rise prototype *Studie over hoogbouw* of 1929 and in his entry for the 1927 Société des Nations competition.

Superficially, this school is a characteristic product of the Dutch Nieuwe Zakelijkheid, with its directly expressed reinforced concrete spandrels and its horizontally proportioned glazing. On closer scrutiny, however, Duiker has been able to render this butterfly plan as a total image; this is to say, as a unified whole in which the stairtower, the classrooms, the structure and the glazed volume all seem to fuse into a single *gestalt*. At this juncture in his career, Duiker seems to be close to an architectural approach which in retrospect is similar to that embraced by Louis Kahn some twenty years later.

Each typical floor is symmetrically arranged with two square classrooms on either side of a square terrace of the same shape and size. All three squares are, in fact, squares derived from the rotation of an inner square whose side is a third shorter than the larger square. Since the columns coincide with the intersections between the smaller and larger squares, the basic geometry and the structural system are totally integrated.

Four stories high, this school only provides for seven classrooms with each classroom accommodating about thirty-six children. The ground floor is asymmetrically arranged with a standard classroom to one side and a gymnasium to the other. The simplicity of this arrangement is complemented by the sculptural complexity of the structure which consists of a network of haunched concrete beams. Since the columns occur in the center of the sidewalls, each of the haunched beams cantilever out towards the exterior corner and this cantilevering profile is compounded by the floor slabs which extend beyond the beam line. The skin tight glazing and the re-entrant corners combine with the structure to yield a strong sculptural profile, while the diagonal axis and the projecting stairtower produce a surprising sequence of changing crystalline planes and volumes.

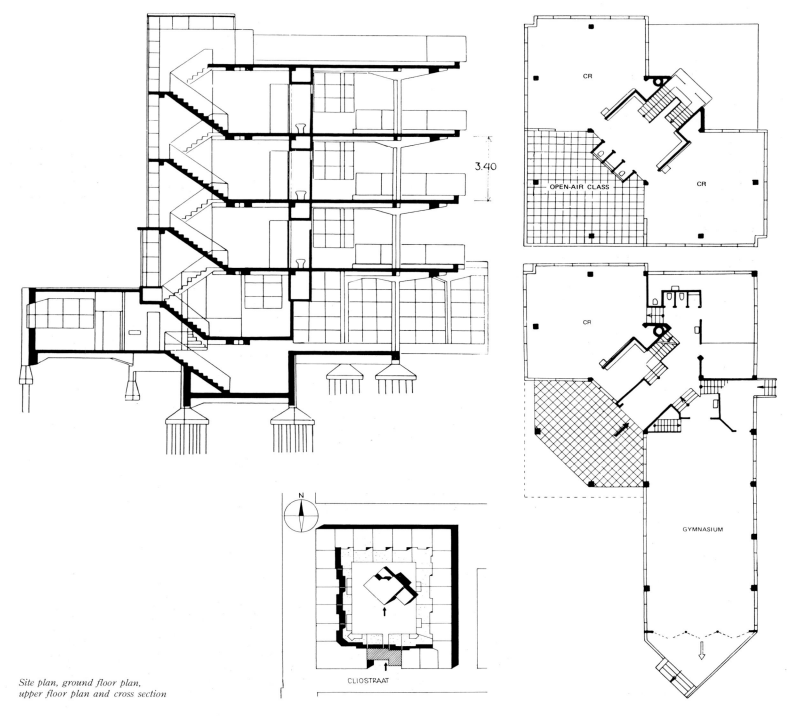

Site plan, ground floor plan,
upper floor plan and cross section

331 *Above: view from street*
    Below: lower floor plan (left) and upper floor plan (right)
    Pen and ink on illustration board. 76.5cm × 102cm
332 *Living room*
    Photos: Collections, Mies van der Rohe Archive,
    The Museum of Modern Art, New York

The Tugendhat House, built in 1930 on a steeply sloping site in the suburbs of Brno, adapted the spatial conception of the Barcelona Pavilion to a domestic programme. One may also see it as an attempt to combine the layered planning of Wright's Robie House — where the service wing slides past the main living block — with the organisation of the typical Schinkelesque Italianate Villa. In any event the free plan was reserved here solely for the horizontal living volume (50 ft. by 80 ft.) which, modulated by chromium columns, opened on its long side to a view of the city. The automatically retractable long glass wall had the effect of converting this living volume into a belvedere. Meanwhile, the conservatory acted as a mediator in a symbolic scheme, where the prospect of the panorama from the main living room presented nature in all her picturesque vitality, while the sub-dividing wall between the living and the study areas displayed the dead nature of the fossilized flora in which it was faced; that is, the polished onyx sheathing covering the partition. It was as though the conservatory sandwiched between two sheets of plate glass at the end of the room, was nature rendered as a middle term between these extremes; that is as an exotic specimen suspended between the living and the dead. In a comparable manner, the plywood dining alcove, faced in ebony veneer suggested the sustenance of family life to which it was dedicated, while the rectilinear onyx plane in the living room signified through its classical associations, the worldliness to be found in the sitting area and the study. This kind of rhetoric effected through surface treatment, seems only to have been obtained on the lower ground floor, for the bedrooms at the entrance level were simply treated as hermetic, functional volumes.

As in the Barcelona Pavilion, the steel columns are sheathed here in chromium casings so as to yield a cruciform section in plan, although where, in the Barcelona Pavilion, this cruciform amounts to a pure orthogonal cross, in the Tugendhat House the ends of the cross are semi-circular so as to effect a point support rather than an intersection. As one might expect, the columns are only faced in the honorific areas, and beyond these they are simply left as unclad steel.

Needless to say, the Tugendhat House also occasioned the design of a classic piece of furniture; namely the Tugendhat chair which was originally finished in blue and acid green fabric. Once again, Lily Reich would have played a salient (if "back-room" role) in advising Mies on the furnishing of the house, and it is almost certain that this colour scheme is largely due to her.

More of an insertion into an existing urban fabric than a completely new structure in its own right, the Maison de Verre occupies a unique place in the history of twentieth-century architecture; one which it is really impossible to describe adequately in the space of an extended caption. Suffice it to state that its character as a work of architecture is as rich and as unclassifiable as Marcel Duchamp's *Large Glass* in the field of fine art. Indeed, the case can be made that both works are located at an unexpected intersection in the history of contemporary art, where the apparent rigor of Constructivism meets the deceptively arational logic of Dadaism. This cultural miscengenation is such that a utilitarian emphasis suddenly seems to be transformed into a poetic uselessness. In this specific instance we are confronted with a kind of Parisian avant-gardist parallel to that *zaumy* trans-rational sensibility which first manifested itself in modern architecture with Vladimir Tatlin's monument to the Third International, although, aside from a common machinism, neither the Maison de Verre nor the *Large Glass* bear any resemblance to Tatlin's tower.

Conceived as a three-storey steel-framed and glazed box inserted into a two-storey eighteenth-century masonry void, it is the excessive functionalism of the Maison de Verre which causes one to question the poetic motives which may have triggered its realization. And yet, however unusual its opaque and totally glazed facade may appear to be, the basic organization of the house is fairly traditional with the ground floor allocated to entry and medical practice, and the first floor being given over to the salon — that is, to reception and dining. Above there is a second floor which overlooks the double-height salon and is again, conventionally allocated to bedrooms and services.

On entering the house, the most startling feature, apart from the diffused quality of the light, is the total transformability of the volume, evident at once in the principal stair where a pivoting, curved glass screen permits or restricts access to the first floor. Suspension is such an obsessive motif in the Maison de Verre that there is hardly a conventional hinge to be found throughout the house; every door being opened or closed through the action of pivoting or sliding components. The other surprising feature which imposes its character on the interior is the fact that the entire fabric of the house has been rendered as a *collage* and it is this perhaps, that ultimately evokes a comparison to Duchamp's *Large Glass*, particularly in the context of the obsessive mechanization. The technique of collage is most evident in the constantly and subtly changing floor levels and materials, so that the house seems to be *encoded* in terms of three intersecting coordinates; the code of mechanized or suspended movement, the code of differentiated finishes and finally the code of artificial energy as this manifests itself in the mechanical services.

As far as the encoding of floor finishes is concerned one may cite by way of example, the differentiated passage from the reception, to the dining, to the doctor's study via the studded rubber of the first, the wood block floor of the second and the black tile of the third. As far as machinism is concerned, a sexual opposition is implied in the contrast between the two forms of "marine" staircases employed to link first, the doctor's consulting room (male) to his study above, and second, Madame Dalsace's bedroom (female) to her boudoir below. However coincidental the parallel may be, the fundamental theme of Duchamp's *Large Glass* is too close to this antimony to be ignored. Finally, there is an opposition which is expressed almost exclusively in terms of mechanical services; namely, the electrical power which passes from floor to floor through *vertical* pipe standards and the hot air which is diffused throughout all three levels, via *horizontal* floor ducts.

The Maison de Verre is unique in the body of Chareau's work and neither before nor after does he attain a work of comparable richness. This is largely due to the exceptional circumstances under which the house was executed; the very generous budget, the intimacy obtaining between architect and patron, and finally the progressive attitude adopted to the modern world by Doctor and Madame Dalsace. Credit has also to be accorded to Bernard Bijvoet who served as an assistant to Chareau from 1925 onwards and who, coming from the idealistic wing of the Dutch Nieuwe Zakhilijkeid, no doubt contributed a great deal to the density of the form and the refinement of the details.

In the end, however, the poetics of the Maison de Verre reside in the complexity of Chareau's personality — a figure who was at once an aesthete and an inventor, a dandy and a dedicated member of the Parisian avant-garde. In conscious terms, Chareau certainly intended that the Maison de Verre should serve as a prototype for a new form of industrialized building; unconsciously, however, this intention was mediated by his feeling for decor and, above all, by certain psychological compulsions. Thus, aside from a passion for Japanese culture, evident in the red oxide finish to the interior steel and the liberal use of black lacquer, and apart from his taste as a *decorateur* for the tapestries of Jean Lurcat, the house radiates an aristocratic sense of subversive sexuality and it is this, no doubt, that evokes the spirit of *La Marieé mise a nu par ses Célibataires, même* (1915—23). Last but not least, no account of the Maison de Verre can be concluded without mentioning the contribution of the artisan Dalbet who having worked with Chareau throughout the twenties, attained his own *magnum opus* in this house of glass.

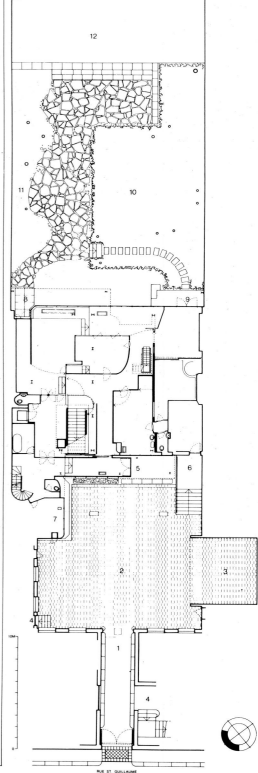

Site plan with ground floor

Legend
 1 Tunnel entrance
 2 Forecourt
 3 2-car garage
 4 Existing 18th century building
 5 Entrance to house
 6 Entrance to house above
 7 Service wing
 8 Garden access
 9 Consulting room terrace
10 Ground ivy
11 Grass and shrubs
12 Gravel play court

334 *Front elevation*
335 *Looking down at salon from second floor gallery*

1928-40
RAYMOND HOOD
in collaboration with Fouihoux,
Reinhard, Hofmeister, Corbett,
Harrison and MacMurray
Rockefeller Center
New York, N.Y., U.S.A.

Motivated by the New York Metropolitan Opera Company's desire to build itself new premises in a prominent location and later realised as a daring piece of speculation in the midst of the depression, Rockefeller Center still stands today as one of the most remarkable pieces of urban design in the twentieth century. The story of its realisation, without an opera house, but with a primary institution of the then newly flourishing communications industry, is surely one of the heroic myths of the Jazz Age. Thus, instead of being focused about an opera house as in B.W. Morris's 1928 design, it was soon to be reinterpreted as a Radio City; that is to say as a "city within a city" remotely comparable to the lat eighteenth-century Palais Royal development built in Paris to the designs of Victor Louis.

The Rockefeller Center management were only too aware of the economic threat that such a huge development would represent in the midst of the financial crisis and they therefore went out of their way to present it as an unequivocal contribution to the public weal. To this end they encouraged the Radio Corporation of America to commission the vaudeville and radio personality, Roxy (S.L. Rothafel) to work in collaboration with the architects in creating the 6,200-seat Radio City Music Hall for the presentation of a hybrid form of entertainment comprising vaudeville and film. The generally popular flavour of Radio City — the city of illusion and distraction in the midst of crisis (note

Roxy's slogan that a visit to Radio City was as good as a month in the country) was reinforced in 1936 when the failure of the shops in the sunken plaza led to the substitution of an open-air skating rink with restaurants situated to either side.

It is to the lasting credit of Hood, as the prime designer of the Center that he was able to control not only the overall composition and the detail, but also a good deal of the programme; it was he, for instance, who first suggested the idea of roof gardens. Under his supervision, the Center, including the seventy-storey RCA slab and the mammoth Radio City Music Hall, came to be completed in just eighteen months; in time for the gala opening of 1932.

Roxy's formula of the Rockettes plus a movie was as conciliatory in its nature as the artistic programme of the entire Center, where one work after another, be it a sculpture or a mural took as its subject such themes as light, sound, radio, television, aviation and progress in general, culminating in two major setpieces on the central axis of the composition. These were Paul Manship's gilded Prometheus, surrounded by the Zodiac, overlooking the sunken plaza and Diego Rivera's ill-fated mural to the entrance hall of the RCA Building, entitled "Man at the Crossroads." This mural, with its unequivocal revolutionary iconography, including even an image of Lenin, had the effect of placing his patrons in an impossible position in which they had no choice but to

insist on its removal. This contradictory New Deal gesture of monopoly capital commissioning an emblematic Communist work seems now, almost half a century later, to be as remote and fictitious as Hugh Ferriss's vision of Manhattan transformed into an endless sequence of Rockefeller Centers.

336 Left: plan in effect between Spring 1932 and January 1934
Right: promenade between La Maison Française and British Empire Building
337 Aerial view

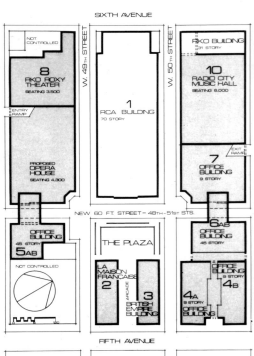

1929
MIES VAN DER ROHE
LILY REICH
German Pavilion
International Exposition
Barcelona, Spain

The apparently simple form of this pavilion, with which Mies arrived at his initial maturity, was, in fact, derived from many different sources, amongst which mention surely has to be made of Wright (as filtered through Dutch Neoplasticism) and of Schinkel, who is evident in the hierarchial use of materials and in the form of the eight-columned "belvedere-temple" type concealed within the body of this asymmetrical scheme. Despite these Romantic Classical associations the Barcelona pavilion was also undeniably influenced by Suprematism (cf. Malevich's *Future Planets for Earth Dwellers* of 1924 and the neo-Suprematist work of Ivan Leonidov).

Contemporarary photographs reveal the ambivalent and ineffable quality of its spatial and material form. From these records we may see that certain displacements in its volume were brought about by illusory surface readings such as that effected by the use of green tinted glass screens which then emerge as the mirror equivalents of the main bounding planes. These planes, faced in polished green Tinian marble reflect, in their turn, the highlights of the chromium vertical bars holding the glass in place. A comparable effect in terms of texture and colour was created by the contrast between the internal core plane of polished onyx (the equivalent of Wright's centrally placed chimney) and the long travertine wall that flanked the main terrace with its large reflecting pool. Here, bounded by travertine and agitated by the wind, the broken surface of the water distorted the mirror image of the building. In contrast to this, the internal space of the pavilion, modulated by columns and mullions, terminated in an enclosed court, containing a reflecting pool lined with black glass. In this implacable, perfect mirror, there stood the frozen form of Georg Kolbe's *Dancer*. And yet, despite these asymmetrically displaced spatial sequences, the building was simply structured about eight free-standing cruciform columns that supported its flat roof.

The Barcelona Pavilion was the occasion for Mies's first foray into the design of modernized Romantic-Classical furniture, namely the Barcelona chair, which was one of five neo-Schinkelesque pieces that the architect designed prior to 1930 – the other four being the Barcelona stool and table, the Tugendhat armchair and a classically profiled buttoned-down leather couch. The Barcelona chair, framed in welded and chromium-plated bar steel and upholstered in calfskin, was to be as essential to the aesthetic of the pavilion as Rietveld's Berlin chair had been to the room he designed for the Greater Berlin Art Exhibition of 1923.

338 Overall view
339 Left: plan. Pen and ink and pencil/heavy beige. 57.6cm × 98.1cm
    Above right: water court
    Below right: interior
    Photos: Collections, Mies van der Rohe Archive,
    The Museum of Modern Art, New York

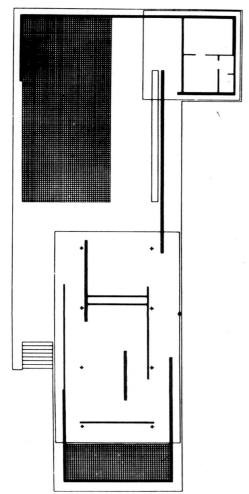

HANS SCHAROUN
Hostel Building
Werkbund Exhibition
Breslau, Germany (now Poland)

In spite of Scharoun's "fantastic" beginnings as a member of Bruno Taut's *Die Gläserne Kette,* the hostel which he designed for the Werkbund, "Home and Workplace" Exhibition staged in Breslau in 1929, was anything but anarchistic. Instead, it was rationally organized into two spread-eagled wings both facing south and linked by a raised lounge hall which served as the main entrance to the complex. The brilliance of this composition unquestionably resides in the surging organic movement of its basic form, comparable in many ways to a similar project by Hugo Häring – his Prinz-Albrecht Garten development in 1924. In this instance, the two living wings are predicated on two different bay dimensions, with the smaller bay housing bachelors and the wider one accommodating childless couples. Both wings (comprising some 48 units in all) are structured about a similar two or three-storey section with the access corridor being placed on the northern side; midway between the two living levels. In both cases one alternately enters a split-level apartment which conducts one either down or up to a living-bathroom-bedroom sequence, the bath being on the same level as the bedroom and the bedrooms locking over or under the corridor. In the bachelor type, each split-level stairway affords direct access to a shared roof deck, while the family apartments are equipped with individual balconies. In effect, this building was a prototypical "social-condenser" and as such it seems to have been possibly more advanced as a prototype than Moisei Ginzburg's Narkomfin block built in Moscow in 1929. This much seems to be clear from the organic way in which a communal restaurant is neatly housed under the shorter of the two wings and the way in which a stairway/lounge hall connects this public volume to the extensive roof terraces above.

340 *Above: view from garden*
   Below: ground floor plan
341 *Above: overall view*
   Below: view from roof terrace
   Photos: Scharoun-Archiv, Sammlung Baukunst, Akademie der Künste, Berlin

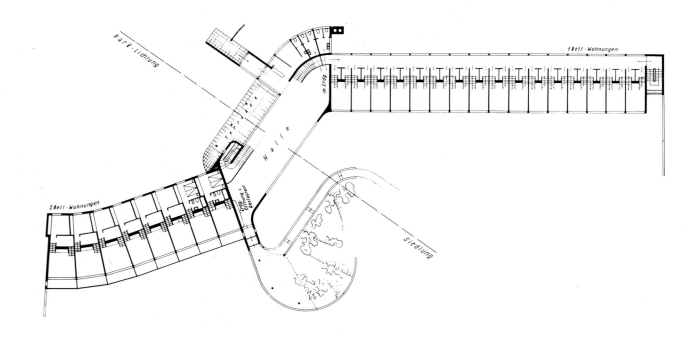

This 295-foot-span bridge over the Salgina valley near Schiers was in many respects a culmination in Maillart's long career as a pioneer of reinforced concrete bridge construction. The Salginatobel bridge was to have its origins in a 128-foot-span concrete bridge which Maillart erected at Zuoz in the Engadine in 1901. This was the first in a series of triply articulated bridges to be built by Maillart over the next thirty years. The term triple articulation refers to the design of hollow concrete bridges where the road bed becomes integrated with the load bearing section. Thus the spanning section at Zuoz already comprised three concrete "webs" separated by two hollow cores — these voids serving, of course, to reduce the overall dead weight of the structure. Some two years after its completion, the Zuoz bridge developed a series of expansion and contraction cracks in its concrete side walls, close to the abutments, and these defects brought Maillart to eliminate such features in his design for the three-hinged, 170-foot-span, Tavanasa bridge, built in 1905. With this work, Maillart reduced his prototypical bridge form to a deck and an articulated arch; the two elements being stiffened and linked by the sectional depth of monolithic concrete girders.

Maillart gained the commission for the Salginatobel bridge in a competition of some nineteen entries and it affords an idea of the growing popularity of concrete construction that only seven of these entries were projected in steel. The primary advantage of concrete was the fact that it required no maintenance and it was this plus Maillart's experience that helped him carry the day. As David Billington has written: "Only the designs of Maillart and Luscher were appropriate to the sharp vertical drop and relatively weak supporting capacity of the Salginatobel rock walls. A deeper arch would have required very much longer piers or cross walls between arch and deck and a larger amount of concrete, while an arch made heavier at its supports would have necessitated more rock excavation."

The key to the reduction of the arch rise in both Tavanasa and Salginatobel was the situation of the concrete hinges, one at the apex and one at each of the abutments. This unlikely invention by Mernager and Freyssinet at the turn of the century depended on reducing the sectional area of concrete at the hinge, thereby displacing the stress into the reinforcement. At Salginatobel the hinge at the abutment is only 80 centimetres deep and padded with cork inserts so as to cushion the movement induced by settlement, deflection and expansion.

While not the most sculptural of his works, Salginatobel, perched high in the Alpine landscape, was certainly one of the most heroic of Maillart's conceptions as Sigfried Giedion's appreciation makes clear; "There is something out of the ordinary in the way Maillart succeeds both in expressing and in sublimating the breadth of a chasm cleft between two walls of rock.... His shapely bridges spring out of shapeless crags with serene inevitability of Greek temples. The lithe, elastic resilience with which they leap their chasms, the attenuation of their dimensions merges into the coordinated rhythms of arch, platform, and the unended slabs between them."

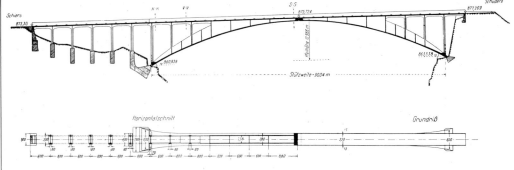

342 *Above: overall view*
Below: section and ground plan
343 *Distant view*

The Villa Savoye (Composition No: 4) is intimately bound up with the evolution of Le Corbusier's *Four Compositions* first published in 1929, and while none of these paradygms are necessarily linked to any specific programme, they are all evidently part of a progression towards a new type of bourgeois villa. Thus, where the first of the four, the Maison La Roche (1923) is modelled after a typical L-shaped Gothic Revival plan and the second is conceived as an abstract cubic form — Le Corbusier went on to posit his Stuttgart House of 1927 (Composition No: 3) as a mediation between these extremes; that is to say, as a "mean" between functional convenience on the one hand and stereometric purity on the other — or as a mediator between the irregularities of vernacular form and the asperities of classical order. One salient device was to prove essential to integrating these two otherwise incompatible propositions, and that was the *free plan* in which cantilevered reinforced concrete construction was exploited for its capacity to differentiate between free-standing columns and non-load bearing partitions. In the Villa Savoye, however, Le Corbusier took an entirely different approach in which the L-shaped irregular plan was simply laid into a square "tray" which was then elevated above the ground to serve as a patio-cum-roofdeck. The Villa Savoye was thus the ultimate projection of a "machine-for-living-in," since this mechanism was literally suspended within a Vergilian landscape. While its precise mode of access celebrated the automobile as the ultimate modern vehicle, its raised living floor synthesized most of the themes which had preoccupied Le Corbusier over the previous decade; the house as a "ship" floating above the landscape as though it were the sea; the house as a modern amplification of the Carthusian monastic cell, and finally, the house as a generic *promenade architecturale* where the occupant moves almost imperceptibly from one warped plane to the next. In the Villa Savoye this plane is a central ramp which ascends in a continuous sweep from the ground floor and service level to the *piano nobili* — living level and finally to the roof and solarium at the apex of the composition. In many respects the Villa Savoye fulfilled the poetic aims which had first been set out by Le Corbusier and Pierre Jeanneret in the famous letter that they wrote to Madame Meyer in 1925: "These ideas ... these architectural themes which carry with them a certain poetry have been made subject to the most rigorous structural rule ... columns of reinforced concrete carry the floors economically. In the concrete cage thus formed, the plan plays with such naturalness that one is tempted to take it for an animal ... for years we have been used to seeing plans of such complication that they give the impression of people with their viscera uncontained. We have held to keeping it within classified, set in order, only a single limpid volume appearing."

This after all, was and still is, the final sign of the classical tradition, namely that all the secondary, service components are firmly embedded within the core of the building, leaving the "body" of structure free to express its own intrinsic architectural value; that is, to cite Le Corbusier in *Vers une Architecture*, to arrange for, "... the masterly, correct and magnificent play of masses brought together in light."

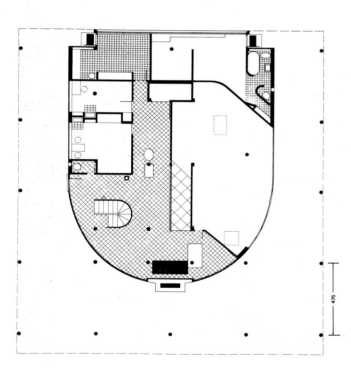
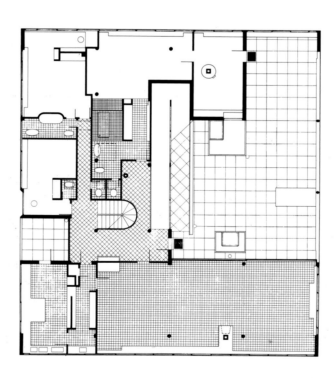
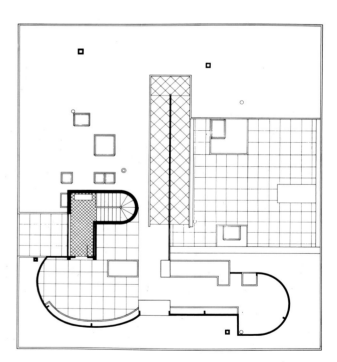

344 *From left: first floor plan,*
   second floor plan and roof plan
345 *East elevation*

346 *Above: view of terrace from living room*
Below: ramp to roof level
347 *Above left: ramp*
Above right: staircase
Below left: staircase
Below right: bathroom

GEORGE HOWE
WILLIAM LESCAZE
Philadelphia Saving Fund Society Bldg.
Philadelphia, Pennsilvania, U.S.A.

Howe and Lescaze's 32-storey, Philadelphia Savings and Fund Society building completed in Philadelphia in August, 1932, is a primary transitional work bridging the monumental ideals of the American Beaux-Arts and the functional efficiency of European modernism. William Jordy placed this work in its full historical context when he wrote: "In the development of the bare-bones aesthetic of modern skyscraper design, the PSFS is the most important tall building erected between the Chicago School of the eighteen-eighties and the metal and glass revival beginning around 1950."

The design of the PSFS was one of those rare instances when a collaboration directly reflects the specific differences of the personalities involved; Howe already being established as a traditionalist by the time he received the commission, and Lescaze being a Swiss émigré (a pupil of Karl Moser) who had joined Howe for the express purpose of developing the design. Credit also has to be accorded to two other seminal figures; the client James Willcox whose intelligent criticism led to the mullioned facade of the 27-storey slab, and the German émigré, Walter Baerman, who was evidently responsible for a great deal of the elegant metal furniture with which the interior is still equipped.

While various German buildings may be cited as influencing the design, from the Gropius and Meyer entry for the Chicago Tribune competition of 1922 to Mendelsohn's department stores of the late twenties and works as arcane as E. Otto Osswald's Tagblatt tower projected for Stuttgart in 1927 (published in America in 1929), the initial *parti* for this design clearly stems from Howe's proto-modernist, Art-Deco sketch of 1929 which in its turn obviously owes something to Raymond Hood.

The detailed planning of the final version was clearly a tour de force and it would be difficult today, to find a comparable commercial structure which is so brilliantly organized. Howe and Lescaze were able to exploit the two adjacent sides of a downtown corner site as a means of obtaining separate entires to the office tower and the first floor banking hall off Market Street. Where the former, on 12th street, gave access to a vertical service spine situated to the rear of the tower like the short cross bar of a T, the latter, on Market Street, led directly to the elevator/escalator hall feeding the banking floor above. The layout of this floor was felicitously related to the rows of columns carrying the slab over, thereby permitting a serpentine layout to the banking counter. This ingenious design necessitated the provision of a sixty-nine foot span, sixteen and a half foot deep steel truss above the banking hall, the interstices of which were filled with the air-conditioning equipment. Faced in granite and limestone, as well as in grey and semi-glazed black brick, the PSFS was the second skyscraper in America to be fully air-conditioned, the first being the twenty-one storey Milan building completed in San Antonio in 1928. All the necessary techniques for a fully air-conditioned high-rise structure, were first refined in the PSFS including the provision of full height mechanical spaces at the third and twentieth floors and the introduction of returns and cooling towers on the roof. These perenially unsightly objects were ingeniously screened in this instance by a rooftop billboard bearing the scarlet, neon lit inscription PSFS, etched out against the sky.

348 *Distant view*
349 *Above, from left: plans of first floor, second floor,*
   typical floor and rooftop
   Below: corner detail

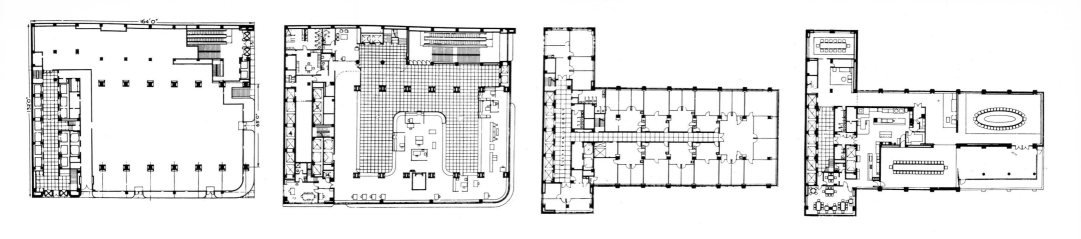

Won in open competition in January 1929, Paimio Sanatorium was based on the helio-therapeutic principles which had governed the treatment of tuberculosis from the turn of the century. It was a Swiss doctor named Sarasin who first posited, around 1900 the stepped and terraced sanatorium as a therapeutic instrument; a postulation which led to the proliferation of such sanatoria throughout the first decades of the century, particularly in Switzerland and Germany. The German architect, Richard Döcker, was a pioneer in this field and his Waibligen hospital of 1925 was the first to posit the typical "head versus tail" sanatorium plan, with the head housing the public and medical suite and the tail accommodating the patient's wing. Aalto was to modify this

format by splaying the head and the tail about a U-shaped entry court; a *parti* which was to reoccur in his work thereafter.

Subject equally to the influence of Dutch and Russian Constructivism, the Paimio Sanatorium designed late in 1928, consolidated Aalto's reputation as a public architect. On a visit to Holland in the May of this year, Aalto met Johannes Duiker who took him to his recently completed Zonnestraal Sanatorium in Hilversum. Built entirely of reinforced concrete construction, Zonnestraal was broken down into four free-standing spread-eagled pavilions grouped about a central administrative and treatment building and it is this angular layout, inflected towards the sun which exercised a direct influence on the form of Paimio.

More of a self-sufficient community than a hospital, Paimio comprises a number of interconnected blocks, each one dedicated to a different function. These consist of a seven-storey patients wing, a sun deck, a nurses dormitory combined with a four-storey communal wing, a three-storey services block, a boiler house and finally, at some remove, low-rise terraced housing for the doctors and employees.

From a typological point of view, one of the most original aspects of Paimio, is the location of the sun terraces at one end of the complex instead of stacking them in step-back formation, in front of the patient's bedrooms (cf. the sanatorium type projected by Tony Garnier in his *Cité Industrielle* project of 1917). This innovation not only

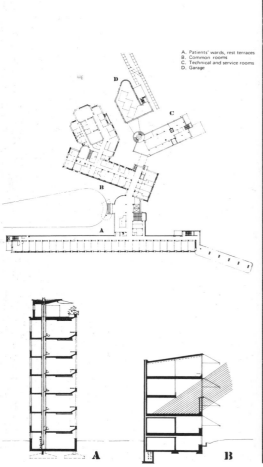

A. Patients' wards, rest terraces
B. Common rooms
C. Technical and service rooms
D. Garage

permitted the building of a vertical block but it also afforded Aalto an occasion for displaying the plastic character of reinforced concrete, since the sun-decks consisted of a series of concrete trays cantilevered off a columnar spine and tied back into a vertical wind-break wall located to the rear of the stack. From an organizational standpoint the planning of Paimio is straight forward with the access tower being centrally located with regard to the ward block, while the main entry is appropriately placed between patient's wing and the public facilities.

It is typical of Aalto, however, that he should approach the internal organisation of this institution as though it were a large house. This is evident from the grouping of the public elements around the main approach so that the *porte cochere*, not only leads to the ground floor reception and treatment rooms, but also serves the double-height refectory above. As the principal living room of the "house," this dining space is lit from both sides and has an open terrace at the west end together with a separate drawing room situated at the eastern end. The integration of service units and related accommodation is ingeniously handled with the kitchen servery entering between the dining hall and the drawing room. The double-sided refectory is inflected towards the south by a mezzanine library which extends for half its width on the northern side. This mezzanine also accommodates a cinema projection room.

Aalto approached the servicing with a great deal of ingenuity from the provision of separate vehicular access, to the provision of a draught-free and tempered ventilation for the patient's rooms. This careful attention to the micro-environment was to be characteristic of his work hereafter. At Paimio it was to include such features as profiling the wash hand basins so that the discharge made little noise. Paimio was also the occasion for the design of a classic piece of furniture — namely the Paimio armchair, fabricated entirely out of bent plywood. Aalto's description of the evolution of this piece merits reiteration here: "The purpose of these essays was to develop light, washable and hygenic chairs which, due to the springing characteristics of the material, could at the same time, provide comfortable seats. In the first series of furniture tubular steel was used, however only in such a manner that it never came in contact with the human body. Later came the bent wood structures. One of the first attempts to make wood elastic consisted of bending the wood in such a way that, under load, each radius of a curvilinear form had the tendency to become shorter, so that the various glued-up lamina became pressed together. The conventional techniniques for bending wood, such as steaming, etc., were not employed; only the natural moisture of the wood was used."

350 Left: sections and ground floor plan
Right: view from main approach
351 Left: dining hall
Right: reception room

The Chrysler Building is one of the most dazzling twentieth-century pieces of high-rise construction in America. If the PSFS was affiliated to Constructivism, the Chrysler Building took the 1925 Exposition des Arts Décoratifs in Paris as its point of departure. Where the PSFS simulated the forms of industrial production, the Chrysler celebrated the myth of modern luxury, as this had been already embodied in the streamlining of the automobile.

The Chrysler Building was a definitive statement in the Art Deco "look," enriched with mythic components drawn from American industry. Typical of this were the flying hub caps of its corner acroteria which were blown up to monumental proportions. The shaft of the fifty-seven-storey steel framed tower was covered entirely in a "fabric" of light and dark grey brick, becoming increasingly metallic as it rose towards the spire. Partly expressionist, partly Art Deco mixed up with Egyptoid forms, the iconography of the building was repeated in the public interiors in the form of a fresco to the ceiling of the lobby. The craftsmanship in this space was superlative, particularly the inlaid decorative veneer to the insides of the elevator cars which far surpassed, in their exquisite metalwork and polished wood, the techniques of industrial production to which the building was dedicated.

The Chrysler Building was eventually the subject of rather childish rivalry in as much as Van Alen secretly constructed a steel spire inside the uppermost shell of the structure; an element that just before completion was pushed through the inner core, thereby making the Chrysler, at 1,046 feet, the highest structure in New York until the toping out of the Empire State Building a year later.

Aerial view

1930-32
E. OWEN WILLIAMS
*in collaboration with Herbert O. Ellis,
W.L. Clarke and Robert Atkinson
Daily Express Building
Fleet Street, London, England*

As in most of the works in which Owen Williams played a decisive role (see his aborted collaboration with Curtis Green on the design of the Dorchester Hotel, Park Lane, London), the Daily Express pioneered the now ubiquitous curtain wall, which in this instance was made entirely out of glass (transparent and black vitrolite) and held in place by *Birmabright* chromium steel gaskets. This immaculate self-cleansing skin was assembled in such a way as to simulate a symmetrical, not to say, classical, facade — the Palladian narrow bays and the spandrels being faced in vitrolite, while the openable steel lights were filled with polished and occasionally ultra-violet glass.

This office building-cum-warehouse was in fact an addition to a pre-existing structure behind Fleet Street. It comprised a six-storey, 93-foot-high building supported by a reinforced concrete frame, consisting of 58-foot-wide central spans, with 13-foot and 19-foot side spans, the wider of these being cantilevered out over the truck entry on the western side of the building. The heavy duty floor slabs spanned 24 feet between the frames, while the load at the line of the facade was carried on 9-foot-wide piers, with each pier being faced in three, 3-foot-wide vitrolite panels. Once again, as in the Empire Pool, the building is planned on a standard module — three feet in this instance — and this fact would be sufficient to indicate that Williams, rather than the architects of record, was primarily responsible for the building. Publicly acknowledged as a work by Ellis and Clarke was the elegant helicoidal spiral on the central axis of the entry hall, which nonetheless lacked, as far as Serge Chermayeff was concerned, "the magnificent airiness of such staircases as Mr. Erich Mendelsohn puts into his buildings..." Nonetheless, despite the ponderousness of the *poché* surrounding it, (compounded out of vertical air ducts and elevator shafts) this reinforced concrete stair-core faced in Biancola terrazo, was in fact extremely dynamic and served to unite the space of the upper office floors with the grand entrance level. This last volume, measuring some 48 feet by 58 feet and rising for 21 feet, was largely the work of Robert Atkinson who embellished the interior in a brilliant Art Deco manner, which for Chermayeff was once again, more suited to a provincial "picture palace" than to the headquarters of a national newspaper.

Be this as it may, this decorative shell still survives as one of great English Art Deco interiors of the period with its "wavy" banded rubber floor in blue, black and green, and its walls variously faced in black marble, figured ebony and travertine, and highlighted here and there in chromium-steel. A similar range of luxurious contrasts occur in the purpose-made desks, telephone kiosks and newspaper racks, including a remarkable "modern" writing table, simply constructed to the design of Betty Joel out of stainless steel cylinderical supports and a plate glass top. Atkinson was to reserve some of his more exotic effects for the elevator lobby which was faced in chromium steel with emerald green "rustications," and for the recessed plasterwork "star burst" ceiling rendered in silver and pale green. As if all this were not enough, the whole was finally focused about a large plaster relief on the east wall, featuring the muse of the Empire protecting the British Imperium, with various representative figures picked out in gold and silver.

The ingenuity with which Williams incorporated the printing plant itself merits some comment, since it was all discretely housed in a 40-foot-deep basement below the office block, with two reel conveyors feeding the paper down from the trunk dock to the printing floor, forty feet below Despite this discretion, Williams nonetheless placed the building under the sign of the machine by attaching what was virtually his signature to the facade — namely, the tell-tale continuous window cleaning carrier rail at the fourth floor.

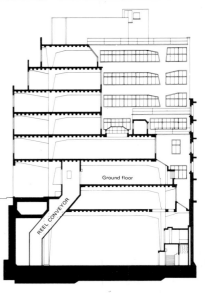

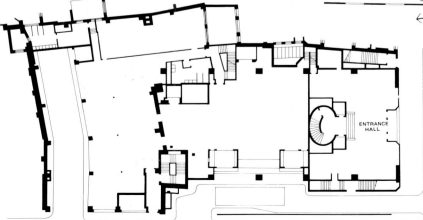

353 *Above: street facade*
    Below: section
354 *Entrance hall*
355 *Above: ceiling of entrance hall*
    Below: ground floor plan

This design for a stadium with a capacity of 35,000 was executed in two phases and won by Nervi in an open competition. This is Nervi's first work of national consequence and it is clear that his reputation was assured thereafter. Like Maillart and Freyssinet, Nervi sought a fusion between statical structure and architectural form. "I maintain," he wrote, "that a good structural organism worked out passionately in detail and in general appearance is essential to good architecture, structural architecture leads to that synthesis of static-aesthetic activity, technical knowledge and mastery of execution which produced the masterpieces of the past." The running tracks of the Berta Stadium naturally provide the basic form around which the shell of the stands are structured, establishing not only the overall continuity, but also the secondary inflections. A straight 657-foot track to one side thus provides the rationale for the asymmetrical plan-form while the flattened U-shape of the continuous perimeter is bounded by an uncovered grandstand of reinforced concrete tiers. On the straight side of the stadium, the covered *tribune d'honneur* is flanked by two short sections of an open tribune as well as two smaller curved corner pieces, cantilevered out in the form of concrete radii. Similarly, the roof of the covered stadium is cantilevered in a sweeping radial curve some 15'6" in diameter, and tied back into the skeleton below. The articulation of these sections exhibit the perculiar fusion of structural and formal factors which is so characteristic of Nervi's work. The exposed sections follow the dictates of the force diagrams, thickening out where the stresses are concentrated and tapering where they diminish. But these diagrams are nonetheless tectonically mediated by Nervi's detailing which reveals a profoundly intuitive sense of statically appropriate form which is somewhat independent of the calculable result. This understanding was most patently evident in the bracing to the helical access stair that projects out from the back of the stadium. Since this was a statically indeterminate structure, precise calculation was impossible and simplified formulas were used to test Nervi's conviction as to the profiling and reinforcement of the form. Thus Nervi's artistic and symbolic sense always complemented his technical skills. As in the provision of the so-called Marathon Tower which celebrated the sense of excitement and prowess appropriate to a structure whose sole purpose was to glorify athletic achievement.

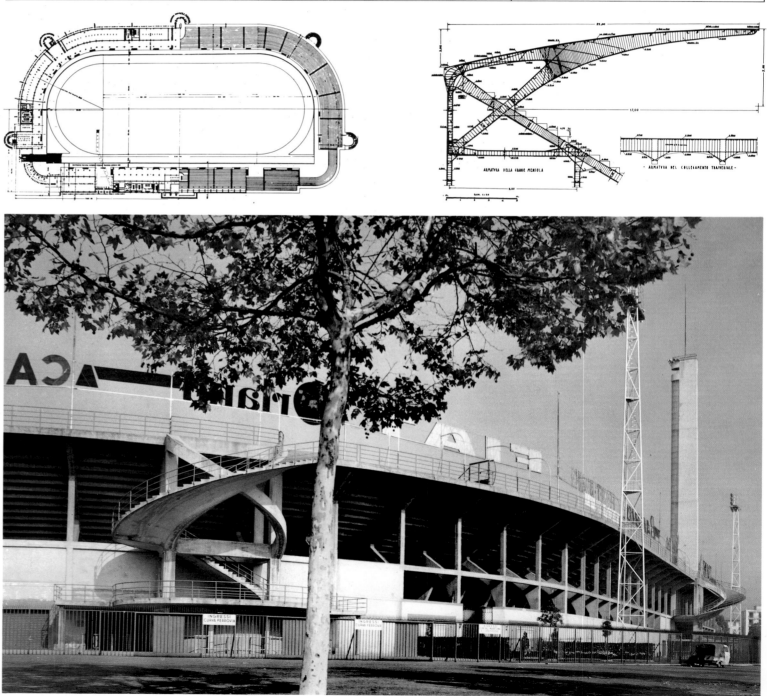

356 Above: plan and section of curved grandstand
   Below: exterior with helical access stairs
357 Above: side view of covered grandstand
   (under construction)
   Below: covered grandstand
   Photos: Studio Nervi (p.357)

Like many other remarkable engineers who pioneered reinforced concrete in the first half of the twentieth century, Owen Williams rapidly became an architect of world stature in the 1930s, not only because of the extraordinary sculptural power of his work, but also because he had a capacity for approaching modern programmes in such a way as to invent the forms of unprecedented institutions. This is the case in this industrial complex built at Beeston, near Nottingham, where pharmaceutical goods were processed, packed and distributed on a scale which, as far as England was concerned, was totally without precedent. Thus this four-storey processing plant was organized for "flatted" production, about a central toplit packing hall, the southern flank being allocated to raw materials and packing goods, and the northern one to finished products. Truck docking facilities and rail spurs were aligned with these long southern and northern facades for the express purpose of delivery and distribution. While the west face of the building received the personnel and contained the workers facilities, a repetitive sequence of circulation bays alternating with four work bays stretched off to the east, with a north/south section that directly translated the movement of materials into the production process. A continuous loading dock on the south side received materials from both rail and van. The raw materials then moved north, first to a raw materials storage, then to the manufactory and across the four-storey toplit packing hall which formed the main spine of the building to rest, finally, in the stores before dispatch and transhipment from the north side of the plant. Most of the horizontal movement of materials and goods was by conveyor belt, with the vertical movement of various commodities prior to packing effected by a system of lightweight metal chutes shaped like helter-skelters, which contributed to the general architecture of the central hall.

With the exception of this hall which was roofed by glass lenses set in concrete and

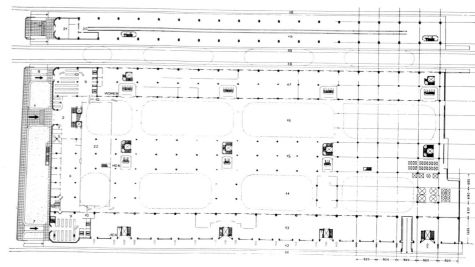

supported by exposed steel trusses each spanning 69 feet, reinforced concrete mushroom column construction was employed throughout on the basis of a bay system whose dimensions varied from 23 feet by 29 feet to 32 feet by 36 feet; the springing of the vaults occurring fairly low and giving a sense of massive power to the structure. The very remarkable plasticity of the overall form was to stem largely from these diagonally chamfered columns and from the diagonally faceted internal and external corners, together with the oversailing concrete cornices from which a metal track was hung as a continuous rail for cleaning cradles. This device provided for the general maintenance

of the glass and metal fenestration which save for the exposed concrete slabs, enveloped the entire exterior surface. Like the horizontal heating pipes which doubled as guard rails, this continuous metal "cornice" completed the image of the factory as an integrated object.

Of the sharp contrast between heavyweight concrete superstructure and lightweight ferro-vitreous cladding, Alfred Roth was to write in the following terms:

"The various forms of the elevation have arisen naturally from different functional requirements: the West elevation with the main entrances is a great glazed surface, 390 feet long; the north and south elevations are

partially cut back from the first floor upwards and are characterized by the cantilever effect over the loading docks. The characteristic internal spatial effect is produced by numerous light wells which pierce the various floors. These wells are constructed with rounded angles of large radius for structural reasons.

From an aesthetic point of view one of the most important considerations is the way in which the reinforced concrete has been freely allowed to remain visible in its structural forms. The visibility of the structure is accentuated by the glazed walls ... It is the forms of the reinforced concrete, which give to this building its richness of architectural

expression."

These formal characteristics were at their most dramatic on the northern and eastern facades, where the cantilevering slabs sprouted dentil-like projections which were intended to facilitate future extension to the north and the east. As with the rest of Williams's pioneering work, the architect/engineer attempted to invent a new building type, not only with regard to its structural form, but also through the provision of upgraded programmatic elements such as the canteens incorporated into the first floor service bays, and the provision of medical facilities on the roof.

358 Above: exterior view
    Below: plan
359 Toplit packing hall
    Photos: M. Sekiya

9 The Regional City and Corporate Urbanism: Architecture and American Destiny 1913-1945

Part 1 Frank Lloyd Wright and Cult of Usonia

In order to understand Wright's evolution and his later adherence to the agrarian position, it is necessary to bear in mind this double allegiance, this suspension between the mythical world of the pioneer, dear to the transcendentalists, and the daily reality of work in Chicago. Wright lived in direct contact with the main figures of the city's intellectual life. The lectures he gave at Hull House were a real contribution to the development of ideas concerning the necessity of working to "civilize" urban life. But his position in regard to this intellectual environment was always uncertain; he could neither adhere to it fully nor detach himself from it completely, and he oscillated between the atmosphere of Oak Park, where he lived with his family, and the city, which he reached each day by rail . . .

Wright found himself between two worlds, that of Hull House and all it implied, and that of the clan that included his clients, who were often his neighbors and to whom he tried to attune himself. Both were attached to the city, one criticizing it in order to improve it, the other drawing from it its own well-being — those who wanted to transform the city and those who were actually transforming it. Between the life of the city with all its cultural implications and that of suburbia as an expression of human contacts, Wright sought a higher synthesis, but between the intellectual society and the clan of family life there neither was nor could be any relationship.

Giorgio Ciucci
'The City in Agrarian Ideology and Frank Lloyd Wright'
The American City: From the Civil War to the New Deal, 1979

The perennial American unease with the metropolis and the simultaneous nostalgia for the greatness of past urban civilizations finds a certain personification in the career of Frank Lloyd Wright who, while rejecting the city, hankered constantly after its public glory and its moments of architectural grandeur. This dichotomy is already evident during his Oak Park period when, while enjoying the first fruits of his practice in an upwardly mobile society, he nonetheless commuted each day (at least as long as he was in Louis Sullivan's employ) to the harsh reality of Chicago's heroic downtown. Although he displayed little interest at this time in developing a theory of urbanism Wright remained, nonetheless, aware of the problem posed by the American city, which around the turn of the century was either atrociously overcrowded or otherwise hardly existed. This dilemma is reflected in the larger civic buildings of his pre-First World War career, in the Larkin Building, Buffalo of 1904 and in Midway Gardens, Chicago of 1914, which are in effect paradygmatic "cities in miniature" for their public facades face inwards, leaving their outside walls largely blank.

It is difficult to interpret the significance of this introspection. Was it that Wright wished to deny the existence of the urban fabric in which the building was situated or was in that the American city, as a public place could not be depended upon? Whatever the answer, from this point onwards most of Wright's public works turn inwards and they suggest by virtue of their internal modenature, ornamentation, and inscription the myth of a utopian communality; a kind of inner public realm set against the barbarism of the world.

Such introspection was absent from the domesticity of the Prairie house suspended amid the unspoilt verdure of the passified frontier; a landscape, which, impregnated with centuries of unrestricted natural growth, still

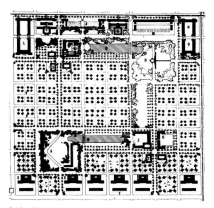

140 *Wright, Chicago City Club land sub-division competition, 1913.*

retained an Edenic aura. Hence, the idyllic intensity of Wright's early vision which is perceivable even today in the idealized renderings of his Oak Park and River Forest houses. Although Wright remained aware of the appalling conditions of the industrial urban poor, through his association with the Chicago School of Urban Sociology, yet it was his rebellious spirit rather than his consciousness that finally released him from the claustrophobic dream of the liberal-minded suburb. The catalyst that finally forced him to abandon Oak Park and even to leave the country was the wife of one of Wright's middle class clients; a certain Mrs. Cheyney, who in 1909, eloped with Wright to Europe.

Distressed by the local scandal which attended his infidelity, Wright and Mama Borthwick Cheyney returned from their sojourn in Europe, not to Chicago, but to Wright's family roots in Spring Green, Wisconsin, where in 1911 he built his first self-sufficient agrarian settlement, given the Celtic title, *Taliesin* or *Shining Brow*, thereby putting into practice, albeit, in isolation, the anti-urban, economic and cultural theories set forth by Henry George in his book *Progress and Poverty* of 1879. Taliesin was only the first of three ostensibly self-sufficient communities founded by Wright, in which his architectural acolytes were expected not only to assist the master, but also to cultivate the land and to busy themselves in the continual construction of the homestead.

Having established this rustic retreat, Wright turned his attention to resolving this perennial conflict between a Jeffersonian conception of nature and the burgeoning industrial city, not in this instance by designing a suburb like Oak Park, but by projecting a segment of a hypothetical regional city, in his unofficial entry to the 1913 Chicago City Club competition for a new pattern of residential settlement.

Wright's Chicago City Club project anticipated, almost to the letter, his more comprehensive Broadacre City thesis which he first started to elaborate in the late nineteen twenties. It transcended the suburban ideal to the degree that it integrated public institutions with single family homes; the whole being articulated and subdivided by the intervention of monumental axes, lined with trees. The basic residential unit (taken from his 1901 proposal entitled "A Home in a Prairie Town") consisted of four Prairie houses, pinwheeling about a central core, within the confines of a square lot. This suburban superblock — implying intra-family association — was to be repeated *ad infinitum*, save for the civic institutions evenly distributed throughout. While the urbane nature of this settlement pattern was to be assured by its public buildings, its regionality was guaranteed by its poly-centrism and its capacity for limitless extension. Wright's Elysian ideal was the infinite penetration of this tartan fabric into the virgin territory of the prairie.

Despite this model, Wright's nostalgia for civic grandeur was to be given uninhibited expression in his Imperial Hotel, Tokyo, under construction from 1916 to 1922. Here, in what was ostensibly his last "city in miniature," until the building of the Johnson's Wax headquarters at Racine, Wisconsin in 1936, Wright indulged in the exoticism of an instant culture; instant in the sense that it was invented *de novo* in every respect, from the carved cornices and finials executed in lava stone, to the great trusses and tentlike ceiling elements

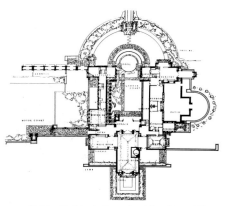

141 *Wright, Hollyhock House for Aline Barnsdall,*
Olive Hill, Los Angeles, 1917-20. Plan.

covering the ballroom interior, outrageously decorated in vaguely Pre-Columbian abstract designs which had as little to do with Japanese culture as they did with the Western tradition.

This predilection for some kind of inevitable trans-historical and transcontinental modernity, as prevalent in Wright as in the American progenitors of the Beaux-Arts Jazz Moderne, was to reach its apotheosis in Wright's work for Aline Barnsdall and above all, in Barnsdall's palatial Hollyhock House built to Wright's designs on Olive Hill, Los Angeles in 1920. The magisterial composition of Hollyhock, only recently restored to its former glory, suggests, even today, the stronghold of a Mayan or Assyrian princess, with its long blank, battered walls and half-hidden windows, with its garden court and fountain pool and its monumental living room fireplace magically surrounded by a shallow moat; with its extensive, elevated roof terraces, looking out, between sphinxlike finials at the prospect of the expanding city to the South and the Santa Monica mountains to the North. Barnsdall was just as enthused as Wright with the idea of creating an alternative American society and with this in mind she dedicated Hollyhock to the memory of her father, with the words: "our forefathers mined the wealth of this country, it is for us to mine its beauty." It was to this end that she was to espouse various progressive and socialist causes throughout her life, while as early as 1915 she had already begun to assume her role as an artistic patron by commissioning a large theater from Wright for the Hollyhock estate in which she intended the director Ordynsky and the designer Norman Bel Geddes, to create, at her behest, the theatrical festival of the new culture. She seems to have imagined

that Hollyhock might bring to a twentieth-century Pacific civilization, what Bayreuth had bestowed upon nineteenth-century European culture.

Disaffected with the hermetic lushness of the Midwestern domestic suburb, Hollyhock evoked for Wright the promise of a new Eldorado, the mirage of a sparse desert culture within which a timeless civilization of unprecedented modern grandeur could emerge, a culture of shimmering citadels rising from the arid desert floor or from the lush foothills that could be found in abundance along the edge of the Pacific Basin.

In 1921, he projected just such a citadel for the Sierra Madre Mountains; the Doheny Ranch development, comprising a whole settlement of concrete block houses scattered about a panorama of foothills and ravines. And while this ambitious Xanadu was never realized, Wright began to build out its component "textile block" houses, piece by piece, first in 1923, in the Storer and Millard houses, in Hollywood and Pasadena, respectively — the latter of the two also being known as *La Miniatura* — and then in the following year in the Freeman and Ennis houses erected on bluffs, overlooking the configurated canyons of Los Angeles. Finally, in 1927, he projected a large settlement for Chandler, Arizona known as San Marcos-in-the-Desert; a terraced hotel running along a ridge and emulating the Doheny Ranch proposal at a more modest scale. It was this project that occasioned the building of Wright's first desert encampment, in anticipation of Taliesin West to be erected at Phoenix a decade later. Wright seems to have decided to learn how to build in the desert by literally living and working in it. Hence, he set up his canvas and wood Ocatillo Desert Camp at Salt Range, near Chandler in 1927 and

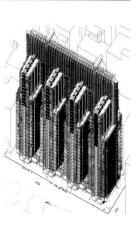

142 *Wright, National Life Insurance Building, Chicago, 1924. Axonometric.*

continued to work there intermittently for three years until the camp was broken up in 1930. It was no doubt this desert experience that he had in mind when he wrote in February 1928:

As he takes the trail across the great Western deserts – he may see his buildings – rising in simplicity and majesty from their floors of gleaming sand – where organic life is still struggling for a bare existence: see them still, as the Egyptians saw and were taught by those they knew.

For in the stony bone-work of the Earth, the principles that shaped stone as it lies, or as it rises and waits to be sculptured by winds and tide – these sleep forms and styles for all the ages of man.

Nonetheless, when Wright was offered the opportunity to realize his Eldorado vision in the city, he certainly accepted it, as his 1923 high-rise project for the National Life Insurance Company offices would indicate. And yet, while Wright was as familiar as a fashionable architect like Raymond Hood with the double standards of the American middle class, oscillating daily between the cosy suburban home and the monumental downtown, he did not, like Hood, gratify this scenographic desire with Neo-Queen Anne for the country and Gothic or Beaux-Arts Jazz Moderne for the city. Instead Wright took his development of the concrete block mosaic as a point of departure from which to cultivate *productive method* as a source of style and it was this that gave a remarkable unity to his work in the twenties, be it the textile block houses or his copper and glass faced skyscraper projected for Chicago. The fact is that Wright hit upon the felicitous idea of imprinting decorative motifs on what were otherwise quite standard concrete blocks. Of this integration of "textile patterning" into load bearing concrete blockwork Wright wrote:

As an artificial stone, concrete has no great, certainly no independent, aesthetic value whatever. As a plastic material – eventually becoming stone-like in character – there lives in it a great aesthetic property, as yet inadequately expressed.

To design a concrete pattern for a casting that would feature this flow of the material might be possible and so all its plastic nature to come through the process into artistic expression, thus distinguishing concrete from stone. I have seldom seen it done unless by accident.

There is another plastic possibility in treatment. The material *en masse* may be printed, "goffered," while fresh and wet, as the printer's die embosses his paper – and such effects had as may be seen in stone where fossil remains of foliage or other organic forms, either cameo or intaglio, are found in it. And this treatment would be nearer to its nature, aesthetically, than is any casting whatsoever.

This element of pattern, however it may mechanically be made to occur, is therefore the salvation of concrete in the mechanical processes of this mechanical age, whenever it rises as a material above the mere mass into which it may naturally be thrown on the ground and where it serves as such better than any other material.

Given that this invention stemmed from Sullivan's decorative use of terra cotta, Wright was immediately aware of the potential for applying such a mosaic irrespective of whether the walls were load bearing or not. Thus, he applied the textile principle with equal efficacy to the lightweight, non-load-bearing skin membrane of his National Life Insurance project, thereby

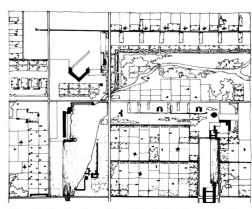

generating an ephemerality of which he wrote:

The exterior walls, as such, disappear — instead are suspended standardized sheet copper
screens. The walls themselves cease to exist as either weight or thickness. Windows become
in this fabrication a matter of unit in the screen fabric, opening singly or in groups at the
will of the occupant. The vertical mullions (copper shells filled with non-conduction
material) are large and strong enough only to carry from floor to floor and project much or
little as shadow on the glass may or may not be wanted.

There is, as many have remarked, a marked similarity between Wright's
National Life Insurance project and the Rockefeller Center, designed by the
firms of Reinhard and Hofmeister and Raymond Hood, and associates. To
some extent this may be explained by fact that both works were inspired by
the Chicago Tribune Competition of 1922 and above all, of course, by Eero
Saarinen's second prize winning entry for this competition. And yet aside
from a similar play of a modulated verticality in both designs they each went
far beyond the accepted paradygm of the free-standing skyscraper and posited
instead of the ziggurat as a new kind of "city in miniature"; a format which
Hood was to elaborate in his *Manhattan 1950* proposal of 1929 (see also
Hugh Ferriss's vision of Manhattan as a ziggurat city in his book *The
Metropolis of Tomorrow* of the same year). At this point, however, apart
from their mutual enthusiasm for an heroically modern citadel, Wright and
Hood could not have been further apart, for at a tectonic level, Hood's
Rockefeller complex was predicated on a conventionally stone-faced, steel
frame, while Wright's tessellated fabric was to be hung off a treelike concrete
structure consisting of vertical pylons and cantilevered floor slabs.

In Wright's work, the reinforced concrete cantilever was to become
increasingly associated with the idea of an organic architecture and from the
mid-twenties on Wright tends to use this unorthodox form of construction for
most of his larger works; notably for his high-rise, St. Mark's Tower of 1929
(eventually built out as the Price Tower in Bartlesville, Oklahoma in 1955)
and above all, for the Johnson Wax Administration Building. The Johnson's
Wax headquarters of 1936 may be seen as a fusion between the structural
brilliance of the National Life Insurance project and the introspective
communal realm evoked by the Larkin Building.

For all his occasional forays into the invention of new urban forms, Wright
never relinquished his preoccupation with evolving a more suitable pattern of
land settlement and in 1932, with his book *The Disappearing City*, he was
able to formulate his theoretical notion of the Usonian alternative; the term
Usonia being apparently derived, *not* from Samuel Butler as Wright claimed,
but from an alternative acronym for the United States, proposed around
1910. For Wright, Henry Ford's Model T car, first mass produced in 1903,
was to be *deus ex machina* of Broadacre City. In a later version of his urban
thesis, published in 1965, under the title *When Democracy Builds*, Wright
wrote:

The door of the cage is opening as one consequence of the motorcar invasion and of
collateral invention. The actual physical horizon of the individual immeasurably widens.

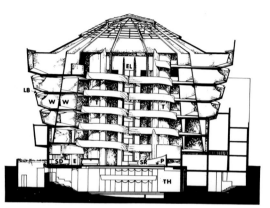

145   Wright, Guggenheim Museum, New York, 1943-59.
Section. TH = theater

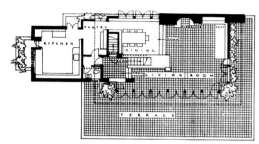

146   Wright, Malcolm Willey House, Minneapolis, 1932.
Wright's prototypical Usonian House.

And it is significant that not only have space values entirely changed to time values, with the new standard of measurement, but that the new sense of spacing is truly based upon Mobility.

For Wright, the new system of measurement was one single family homestead per acre, with the acre in question being reserved as a birthright for future generations. As Robert Fishman has pointed out, at this rate the entire population of the United States, in 1930, could have been comfortably accommodated in the state of Texas.

The prime example of regional planning already under way in the United States, namely the Tennessee Valley Authority, together with the disaster of the stock market crash of 1929, convinced Wright on the occasion of his Kahn lectures at Princeton University in 1930, that it was time to start anew. This he then set about doing by arguing in favor of the total decentralization of existing urban development in America. Against all rent of any kind, which he saw primarily as rent for land, for money (interest) and for ideas (patents), Wright based his economic thesis on the "single-tax" of Henry George, on the monetary reform, advocated by the Swiss economist Silvio Gesell, and on the anarchic-socialist model of decentralized development, first advanced by Peter Kropotkin in his *Factories, Fields and Workshops* of 1898.

As far as Wright was concerned, Broadacre City could continue, as an orthogonal subdivision, for as much as 100 square miles without having any specific center. Distributed throughout this territory would be such institutions as schools, sports arenas, airports, small industrial centers, racetracks,

tourist camps, museums, churches, universities, zoos, seats of government, roadside markets and above all, automobile objects, that is to say, centers of popular instruction combined with leisure activity; exactly the type of building which he first projected as a ziggurat planetarium in 1925, and which he reworked as a helicoidal art gallery in the Guggenheim Museum, New York, completed in 1959 — the year of his death. From time to time there would be the occasional high-rise (St. Mark's Tower) built as Wright put it, to accommodate, "those untrained urbanites desiring to enjoy the beauty of the country and yet unable to participate in creating it or operating it." For Wright there were three primary agencies who would assure the emergence of his ideal American civilization; universal light, power and communication (Edison); universal mobility (Ford); and finally, standard machine-shop production (Taylor). As he put it, "America needs no help to build Broadacre City, it will build itself haphazardly."

The broad scope of this rather generalized prophecy has been redeemed by history to the degree that the last thirty-five years of American urbanization has largely realized Broadacre City, except (and these are critical exceptions) for the vague anti-Capitalism of Wright's economics and the specific poetics of his architecture. It was exactly this possibility for misinterpretation which motivated Wright's late career, for with his first Usonian, Malcolm Willey house (1932) erected in Minneapolis in 1934, he began to build out the components of Broadacre City, piece by piece.

Everything that comes from his hand from this date forth is really conceived as part of his general policy for agrarian dis-urbanization, from his

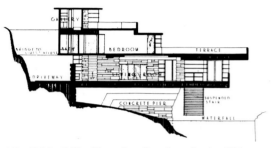

147 Wright, Falling Water, Bear Run, Pennsylvania, 1936.
Section.

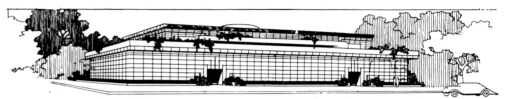

148 Wright, Capital Journal Building, Salem, Oregon, 1931. Prototype for the S. C. Johnson Building built at Racine.

famous masterpiece Falling Water, built in 1936 for Edgar J. Kaufmann in Bear Run, Pennsylvania, to the long sequence of relatively inexpensive Usonian houses realized during the late thirties, forties, and fifties (some seventy houses in all) of which the Goetsch-Winkler house built at Okemos, Michigan, in 1939, is perhaps one of the most typical.

The importance of Wright's Usonian domesticity is only now coming to be appreciated, for it surely represents the last concerted effort to render the small individual house as the irreducible element of a civilized environment. In the one-off Usonian houses and in the projected and partially realized Usonian communities such as Okemos and Pleasantville, New York, Wright tried to demonstrate the horizontal integration of the house into the landscape; the realization of the invisible city, by building *with* the ground rather than *on* it. However, paradoxical it may appear for a patriarch, Wright's Usonian houses can also be seen as liberative at another level, in that he rendered the kitchen — workspace as a differentiated, but spatially integral part of the main volume.

The Usonian house was not only designed to modulate light, ventilation and aspect according to orientation and situation, but also to be economically produced and open to the necessities of growth and change. Self-finishing materials, mostly brick and timber, were utilized as much as possible, so as to eliminate plastering once and for all. By the same token, the typical Usonian house was structured about a simple module in order to facilitate machine-shop production and optimize repetition. To this end also, only three basic types of windows were employed; clerestories for back light and cross-ventila-tion, full-height French doors for access to the garden and the occasional pic-ture window. Unforeseen future changes were allowed for, mainly by restrict-ing the house to a single storey wherever possible and by otherwise employing elongated, L or T shaped plans to which additions might be easily made. One of the most characteristic Usonian devices employed by Wright was to lay tubular heating elements along with the reinforcement in the ground level slab and to cast the floor with Cherokee Red, coloured cement. The resultant floor, which could be polished and waxed so as to heighten and unify the colour, also functioned as a climatological fly-wheel, in as much as it stored heat in the winter and provided a refreshingly cold surface in the summer.

Aside from the modest Usonian houses which Wright continued to build throughout the period and the occasional Usonian mansion, which he had the fortune to receive as a commission in the midst of the Depression — above all the famous Falling Water — Wright's most quintessential Broadacre piece was the new administration building which he designed for S.C. Johnson & Son in 1936 and which was completed in Racine, Wisconsin in 1939. Once again as in the Larkin Building (1904), Wright was to interpret the workplace as a place of sacrament and as a form of "social-condenser" for the community as a whole. This accounts for the large fireplace in the entrance hall of the Larkin Building and the placement of an organ on the top floor of its central space.

This determination to use the office building as the center of a community finds reflection in Wright's repeated efforts to persuade Herbert Johnson to move the company headquarters out of Racine and to relocate the firm in open countryside where it could be surrounded by low density worker's

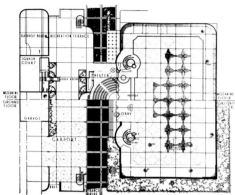

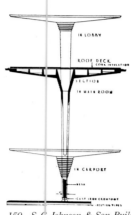

149 Wright, S. C. Johnson & Son Building, Racine,
Wisconsin, 1936-39. Plan.

150 S. C. Johnson & Son Building.
Section through lily-pad pier.

housing. Wright hoped that this proposition would enable him to demonstrate Broadacre City but Johnson remained unmoved and Wright had to design and build the headquarters building in Racine. Nonetheless, he was able to persuade his client to build a theatre-cum-dining room facility in the center of the complex so that in effect Johnson's Wax would be focused about a central theatrical place.

From the mid-twenties on, the term "organic architecture" which Wright had just coined as early as 1908, came to imply above all else, the expressive use of reinforced concrete cantilevered construction. This is first evident in Wright's National Life Insurance building projected for Chicago in 1924, wherein the inner concrete cantilevered skeleton assumes that branchelike "growth" structure which Wright, like Sullivan before him, recognised as the very essence of the organic. That he regarded such a form as an extension of Louis Sullivan's vitalist, "seed germ" metaphor (cf. Sullivan's *A System of Architectural Ornament According with a Philosophy of Man's Powers, 1924)* seems to be confirmed by Wright's characterization of the pool to the foyer of his Guggenheim Museum of 1943, as being symbolic of "the oval seed pod containing globular units."

The conceptual origin of Wright's masterpiece of the thirties — namely his S.C. Johnson Administration Building erected at Racine, Wisconsin in 1939 — lies somewhere between his National Life Insurance project of 1924 and his *Capital Journal* Building, projected for Salem, Oregon in 1931. This polarity is indicative of an oscillation in Wright's work in the last half of the twenties; on the one hand he is clearly trying to bring his work into line with the simple organisational and formal efficacy of European modernism, on the other, he evidently wishes to achieve this without sacrificing the syntactic and poetic potential which had been so evident in the Prairie Style. Within this schema the *Capital Journal* project, like the *House on the Mesa* of the same year, gravitates towards the values of Cubistic functionalism, whereas the continuously fused glass and copper, tesselated skins of the National Life Insurance project points towards the further evolution of a modern, exotic and specifically American culture; comparable in its faceted radiance to the great cultures of the Pre-Columbian world or to the antique civilizations of the Mesopotamian basin. The Johnson Administration Building seems to have synthesised these paradygms into a new whole, thereby combining the top-lit hypostyle hall of the one, with the continuous crystalline skin of the other. The proof of Wright's organic architecture turns, at this juncture, on the intensity of this romantic synthesis wherein highly sophisticated reinforced concrete construction is combined with equally advanced glass technology, evident in the intersticial vitreous membrane, set into the roof and the sides of the building, like a gossamer inlay, emanating light. Here the quintessence of the "organic" finds itself embodied in the sixty, thirty-foot-high mushroom columns, supporting the "lily-pad" roof of the central office hall and tapering down to nine-inch-diameter bases set onto pin-jointed bronze hinges. These slender supports which induce zero bending at the floor level, flatten out at the roof into broad circular discs of mesh-reinforced concrete, between which is woven a double-layered roof light of intersecting pyrex glass tubes. Each disc is connected to the next by a short beam, the whole system acting as a kind of multi-support, two-way system. The roof structure is supported by these discs while the hollow cores of the columns serve to drain the storm water from its surface.

This was the science-fiction essence of Usonia; a poetry of miraculous technique arising out of new materials and methods and out of a daring inversion in the hierarchy of traditional elements. Thus where one would have expected solid (the roof) one encountered transparency and where one would have expected transparency (the walls) one found an impenetrable perimeter. Of this inversion Wright wrote:

Glass tubing laid up like bricks in a wall composes all the lighting surfaces. Light enters the building where the cornice used to be. In the interior the box-like structure vanishes completely. The walls carrying the glass ribbing are of hard red-brick and red Kasota sandstone. The entire fabric is reinforced concrete, cold-drawn mesh being used for the reinforcement.

While Johnson Wax, like the Larkin Building, reinterpreted the sacramental place of work, Falling Water, built at Bear Run, Pennsylvania, in 1936, embodied Wright's ideal of the place of living fused into nature. Once again, reinforced concrete afforded the point of departure; only this time the cantilevering gesture was extravagant to the point of folly, in contrast to the implacable calm of the mushroom structure of Johnson Wax. Falling Water projected itself out from the natural rock in which it was anchored, as a free floating platform poised over a small waterfall. Designed in a single day, this dramatic structural gesture was Wright's ultimate romantic statement. No longer restricted by the extended earth line of his Prairie Style, the terraces of this house appeared as an agglomeration of planes miraculously suspended in space, above the trees of a densely wooded valley.

Wright declared that Usonia would eventually be everywhere and nowhere and that "it will be a city so greatly different from the ancient city or from any city of today that we will probably fail to recognize its coming as the city at all. Elsewhere he stated: "America will need no help to build Broadacre City. It will build itself, haphazard."

By far the most polemical building ever projected for Broadacre City was the Walter Davidson Model Farm of 1932. This unit of agrarian reform, designed to facilitate the economic management of both home and land, was critical to the overall urban theory, where every man would have his "small-holding" acre miraculously reserved for him at his birth. Aside from the fictitious political nature of this provision, Wright like Henry Ford, refused to recognize that individualistically structured agrarian reform would neither guarantee the sustenance of uprooted populations nor ensure that they would receive the benefits of a planned economy. As the next fifty years would unequivocally prove, the production of food would have to be just as industrialised as the manufacture of goods. While Wright was prescient enough to acknowledge the coming of the Megalopolis as a Pandora's Box — as a new nature in which the artifactual world would be distributed — he refused to recognize that an organic architecture would hardly be the consequence of such a random dispersal.

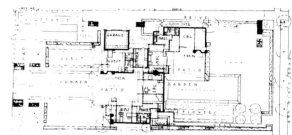

151 Schindler, Kings Road House, Hollywood, Los Angeles, 1922. Ground floor plan.

Part 2 Rush City Reformed: Schindler, Neutra and the International Style

Los Angeles' unmatched residential dispersal was only one manifestation of the community's anti-urban ethos. Its unprecedented business decentralizaiton was another, though it was barely evident as late as 1920. By then, suburbanization had brought about a thorough, extensive and permanent land use segregation in the metropolis. For the thousands of Mexicans, Japanese, and Negroes who lived amidst commerce and industry in the small ghettos of central Los Angeles and San Pedro there were a million white Americans who resided in the suburbs sprawling north to Hollywood, east to Pasadena, south to Long Beach, and west to Santa Monica. Moreover, greater Los Angeles extended so far into the countryside that only electric trains and motor cars connected its homes, stores and factories — a pattern not only preferred by the populace and imposed by developers, but also sanctioned by the city and country authorities.

Robert M. Fogelson

The Fragmented Metropolis: Los Angeles 1850—1930

By the time the Austrian émigré architect, Rudolf Schindler arrived in Los Angeles in 1919, to work as supervising architect on the Hollyhock House, he was, after his two year apprenticeship with Wright, so familiar with the master's syntax as to be able to simulate the house style. Thus all the ancillary works built in the grounds of the Hollyhock House are almost certainly made by Schindler in Wright's name, including the director's house completed on the side of Olive Hill in 1920. Schindler was as much committed to the development of a Californian architecture as Irving Gill had been a decade earlier, and as Wright was to become in his California concrete block houses of the twenties. What Schindler had in common with both Gill and Wright was the determination to create an unprecedented architectural expression from the available materials and techniques; from the specifics of the climate and from the, as yet, still evolving Californian lifestyle. Of this last, Schindler wrote in 1928: "The sense for the perception of architecture is not the eyes — but living. Out life is its image."

In building his own Hollywood house in 1922, Schindler was to distance himself from the concrete block tectonics of Wright, by identifying with the work of Gill; above all, by employing Gill's "lift-slab" system pioneered in the building of the Women's Club at La Jolla in 1913. From certain aspects, the Kings Road house seemed to be as introspective as the adobe house which Schindler had projected for Taos in 1915. Here, however, the enclosing walls were of four foot-wide, battered concrete slabs, cast on the ground and lifted into position, with glass or cement inserted into the narrow vertical slots left betwen them. The *parti* comprised two single-storey, L-shaped court houses rotating about the pivot of an independent guest suite, in such a way as to provide each living unit with its own patio. The arrangement clearly implied an experiment in living, since all three units shared the same kitchen in the center of the complex and each member of the respective families had his or her own domain specifically identified as such. Like Gill before them, Schindler and his wife Sophie Pauline Gibling were patently radical aesthetes — Schindler being an artist in the anarchic-bohemian tradition and Gibling a music teacher from Evanston whose progressive posture was explicitly socialist. It was through Gibling's friendship with Leah Lovell that Schindler

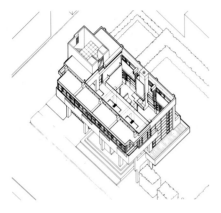

152 Schindler, Lovell Beach House, Newport Beach, California, 1925-26. Axonometric with roof removed.

received the most important commission of his early career; namely the Lovell house built at Newport Beach between 1925 and 1926.

As David Gebhard has suggested, Dr. Phillip Lovell was able through his public advocacy of exercise, stress-free lifestyles and drugless medicine, to embody the ideals of a progressive modernity in his own persona. Gebhard writes:

Dr. Lovell was a characteristic Southern California product. It is doubtful whether his career could have been repeated anywhere else. Through his *Los Angeles Times* column, 'Care of the Body,' and through 'Dr. Lovell's Physical Culture Center,' he had an influence which extended far beyond the physical care of the body. He was, and he wished to be considered, progressive, whether in physical culture, permissive education, or architecture.

What Lovell, Schindler and Schindler's then newly arrived colleague Richard Neutra wished to achieve in Southern California has been perhaps never more explicitly stated then in the articles which Schindler wrote, for Dr. Lovell's Care of the Body column in the *Los Angeles Times*. Thus, we find him writing in April, 1926:

Our high mechanical development easily controls our living conditions. Our knowledge about our own bodies releases us from slavery, and Nature becomes a friend. The house and the dress of the future will give us control of our environment, without interfering with our mental and physical nakedness.

Our rooms will descend close to the ground and the garden will become an integral part of the house. The distinction between the indoors and the out-of-doors will disappear. The walls will be few, thin, and removable. All rooms will become part of an organic unit, instead of being small separate boxes with peepholes. How petty the attempt to erect each one of different materials and to decorate them separately in different "styles!" Each house needs to be composed as a symphony, with variations on a few themes.

Our present scheme of social life in which we drudge behind the scenes most of the time in order to present an "impressive" face for a few moments of company is outworn. In driving out the king, we have lost the careless instigator of fashionable social manners. Our own everday actions must achieve the dignity of the past ceremonials. Each one shall create his own fashions — but only for himself.

Our house will lose its front-and-back-door aspect. It will cease being a group of dens, some larger ones for social effect, and a few smaller ones (bedrooms) in which to herd the family. Each individual will want a private room to gain a background for his life. He will sleep in the open. A work-and-play room, together with the garden, will satisfy the group needs. The bathroom will develop into a gymnasium and will become a social center.

A simplified cooking will become part of a group play, instead of being the deadly routine for a lonely slave.

The architect will try to divine the possible development of his client, and will design a building which may grow with him. The house will be a form-book with a song, instead of an irrelevant page from a dictionary of dead form dialects.

Despite the Wrightian ring of this last sentence, it is clear that Schindler was much more capable than Wright of launching a total critique of late bourgeois culture and its architecture and of offering an explicit and more open counter-thesis to its pretentious, repressive cultural references. Unlike his former master, Schindler was able to liberate both himself and his architecture

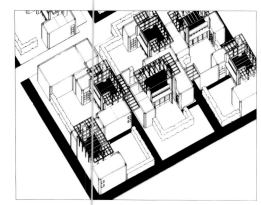

153 Schindler, El Pueblo Ribera Court, La Jolla, California, 1923. Axonometric.

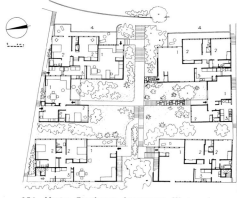

154 Neutra, Strathmore Apartments, Westwood, California, 1938. Ground floor plan.

from the oppressive aestheticism latent in Wright's work.

The Lovell Beach House is a pivotal building in Schindler's career as an architect. It clearly marks that point of departure in which he liberates himself from both the *Wagnerschule* by which he was educated and from Wright, with whom he had served an intense apprenticeship, although building is still indebted to Wagner and Wright in its use of structure as the primary expressive element, especially in the five reinforced concrete, transverse frames which support and impart their rhythm to the entire house. From the street, one initially encounters these frames as though they were a vestigial colonade, but this appearance of formality dissipates as the exposed circulation breaks asymmetrically left and right; a service stair towards the kitchen in the first instance and a ramp towards the sea in the second. Some debt to Wright also remains in the detailing of the fenestration, but thereafter, the break is decisive and the concept of both space and light is entirely different. The main double-height living volume is suspended above the beach, like a giant lantern-cum-light modulator, while the sleeping porches on the top floor clearly assume an open, alfresco approach to even the more traditionally private functions of the house. In addition this summer house is unexpectedly enriched by one of Schindler's earliest "play-courts," in which he was to prove himself a master gardener. There is, here, at Newport Beach and in other projects made by Schindler at this time — such as his brilliant Manola Court, Silver Lake apartments (1926-40) or his 1927 "translucent house" projected for Aline Barnsdall at Palos Verdes — an overtly Japanese sense of space and texture; an anti-monumental preoccupation with tessellated, diaphanous screens capable of modulating both light and movement.

As far as the evolution of a new Southern Californian lifestyle and settlement pattern was concerned, a continuous line of development may be detected from Gill's Lewis Courts, built for working class occupation, at Sierra Madre in 1910, through Schindler's unbuilt Bungalow Court designed for J. Korsen in 1921, to his remarkable 12-unit Pueblo Ribera community built at La Jolla in 1923. In fact, the line of development extends even further in that Richard Neutra's Strathmore Apartments erected in the Westwood district of Los Angeles in 1938, may be considered as an extension of the site planning notions first realized in Schindler's Pueblo Ribera complex.

At the same time, the planning principles of the Pueblo Ribera are related to the *parti* adopted in Schindler's Kings Road House of two years before and, although the more radical notions of the communal kitchen and the autonomous apartment are not carried over, the same basic principle of organization prevails; namely, the "pinwheeling" inflection of each house towards its own patio. Furthermore, the innovations in the use of structural concrete, pioneered by both Gill and Wright, are here complemented by Schindler's own *collage* approach to the production of building. Thus, the basic load-bearing reinforced concrete walls of the Pueblo were cast, course by course, from timber formwork secured against vertical guide rails. The result was a mass whose surface was striated throughout by horizontal lines; first by the grooves left by the formwork and then by the horizontal transoms of the sliding steel sash windows. Perhaps the most unorthodox aspect of this whole complex was the provision of sun-screened, sleeping porches on the roof, which in effect provided each family with three alternative living spaces; the living room itself, the garden court and the roof terrace.

After the Lovell Newport Beach House and Manola Court, the initiative as far as the California "modernism" was concerned, passed from Schindler to Schindler's compatriot and partner Neutra. David Gebhard has provided us with an account of this transition which can hardly be improved upon:

Almost immediately after Neutra came to Los Angeles in 1925, he and Schindler began to collaborate on a number of projects. Their association continued, in one degree or another, until 1930. The relation between the two (and later with the urban planner Carol Aronovici) varied from project to project. From 1926 on, their joint efforts carried the signature of the Architectural Group for Industry and Commerce. Considering the general scarcity of realized commissions, for both men during the late 1920s, the give and take between the two must have produced some effect on each other in their independent work. It would not be unreasonable to assert that Neutra's presence was one of the forces which helped Schindler rid himself of crotchety Wrightian details which he carried over into his early independent work of the 1920s. The cleaned-up quality of Schindler's buildings of the 30s, his reliance on hard, machine-like, non-tactile material, his rejection of the 'warm' material, especially of wood, during much of his De Stijl phase of the 30s might never have occured without Neutra.

Neutra's independent career begins with the Health House which he designed for Phillip Lovell and which was built on a bluff overlooking Griffith Park, Los Angeles, between 1927 and 1929. This lightweight, steel-framed, structure, clad in "gunned" cement and steel fenestration, was built on top of a reinforced concrete undercroft and retaining wall which also embodied a swimming pool, a playcourt and an open-air gymnasium extending beneath and beyond the main body of the house. Once again, as in Lovell's beachside residence, open-air sleeping porches and patios lead off various bedrooms and secondary living rooms as the main body of the building descends the slope. Access to the house is from a service road running along the top of the bluff, with the result that one enters on the principal private floor (study, sleeping, etc.) and descends to the main living level below. A certain ingenuity was to be exercised in arranging this lower level so that at night the client could enjoy both the benefit of an open fireplace and a panoramic vista towards the sea. Neutra's immodest, staccato description of the furnishing of this living-library suite gives a fairly fresh and distinct idea of the progressive character and stylistic preoccupations of the period:

Library for a thousand volumes, shelves adjustable. Cosy corner with exit to lawn patio. Light trough (chromium steel) for half direct and half indirect lighting; length 52 feet, 30 daylight bulbs, 30 watts each. Built-in telephone with adjustable shelf, accessible from living room and hall. Colors and materials: natural colored window drapes, mouse grey carpeting, deep blue upholstery goods, black lacquer woodwork, chairs and tables. A forerunner of modernly finished interiors in America.

The dissolution of the Schindler/Neutra partnership was to be followed by a series of remarkably progressive proposals, most of them unrealized which were to characterize the energetic and probing nature of Neutra's early career.

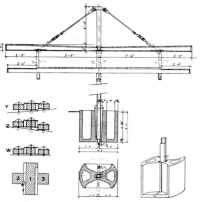

155 Neutra, One-Plus-Two prefabricated extendable family house, 1926.
Details of structural support and assembly pattern.

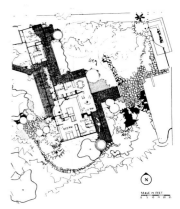

156 Neutra, Nesbitt House, Brentwood,
California, 1942. Ground floor plan.

In this respect it is possible to cláim that Neutra was even more pragmatically engaged than the European pioneers, in attempting to evolve a lightweight, industrially produced, but flexible architecture appropriate to the machine age. In a series of experimental and partially prefabricated homes, projected between 1923 and 1926, Neutra anticipated not only the General Panel Corporation work carried out by Walter Gropius and Konrad Wachsmann in the forties, but also, and more seminally, the single-storey "stressed-skin" prototypical houses developed by Jean Prouvé in the fifties. As in Prouvé's later work, Neutra's One-Plus-Two prefabricated settlement housing of 1926, included such innovations as cast-iron, point-support, adjustable foundations and cantilevered, cable-tensioned, lightweight roofs. It is interesting to note that at a more pragmatic level similar concerns were manifest in a small Long Island house built to the designs of Lawrence Kocher and Albert Frey in 1934.

The difference between the temperaments and careers of Schindler and Neutra are most decisively marked at this juncture. Above all, Schindler was the Bohemian artist, architect and general contractor, who, however pragmatic and ingenious, never manifested any interest whatsoever in rendering his work generally available or in orienting his production towards truly industrial methods. Neutra, on the other hand, was antithetical to this withdrawal of Schindler's, for in his own work of the twenties and thirties he was invariably motivated by socio-economic concerns and by a biological, not to say prophylactic attitude, towards human culture and the survival of the species. As he was to write much later in his book *Survival through Design*:

It has become imperative that in designing our physical environment we sould consciously raise the fundamental question of survival in the broadest sense of the term. Any design that impairs or imposes excessive strain on the natural human equipment should be eliminated or modified in accordance with the requirements of our nervous, and more gradually, our total physiological functioning.

It was exactly this kind of sensitivity that informed his Ring Plan School project of 1926 and all his subsequent school work, including his Activity Classroom project of 1928, his Corona School, in Bell, Los Angeles, of 1935 (designed with Gregory Ain), his Emerson Junior High School, in Westwood of 1938 and finally the Puerto Rican rural and urban school programmes to which he contributed a number of prototypical designs in the mid-forties.

At one level Neutra was to become the fashionable architect of the enlightened bourgeoisie and nouveau riche as they escaped to their exclusive hedonistic retreats, in the Hollywood hills or on distant offshore islands. In this instance, the expression varied from the rather simplistic machinism of, say, the vast Brown House that was built to his designs on Fishers Island in 1936 (complete with drop-in prefabricated bathroom elements designed by Buckminster Fuller), to the tactile and highly place-conscious sensibility evident in such works as the extraordinarily poetic Nisbitt House built in Brentwood, in 1942; or the more grandiose house, verging at times on vulgarity, that he produced at the end of the forties; the Kaufmann House in the Arizona desert of 1946 and the Warren Tremaine House built at Santa Barbara, California in 1947. These millionaire residences are distinguished by

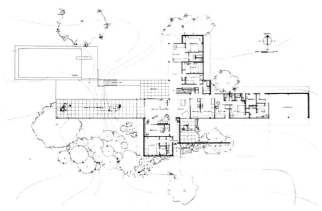

157 Neutra, Tremaine House, California, 1947. Floor plan.

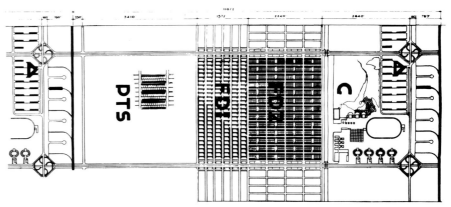

158 Neutra "Rush City Reformed," Los Angeles, 1923-35.
A = light industry, C = educational, FD2 & FD1 = family dwellings, PTY = prefabricated single family dwellings.

being a specific kind of "almost nothing" in which the landscape itself, desert in the first instance and rock scree in the second, penetrates into the very heart of the dwelling, where it is checked by sun screening, sliding doors, plywood veneered panels and built-in seating. One may think of this expression as a unique genre of its own in which interior design and landscape architecture fuse together so as to eliminate architecture as it is commonly understood. In this sense, Neutra elevated Wright's fusion of nature and culture to a hitherto unimaginable level of integration, so much so that, even now, these "dream houses" seem to hover on the threshold of an alternative Western culture; an anti-Cartesian, tactile expression, close to the Islamic cult of the paradise garden, but based, at the same time, on a more benevolent concept of nature.

At another level, Neutra's belief in the inevitability of the welfare state was no doubt strengthened by the New Deal and there thus emerges in his work a strain of socio-democratic concern which permeates his output in the thirties and forties. This much is evident in the various fragmentary proposals made for Rush City Reformed between 1923 and 1935 wherein, as opposed to the rather generalized Broadacre City, Neutra posits a more differentiated policy in which specific regional centers are emphasized rather than the general grid, with each center having its own nature and rules of development, contingent upon topography and specific use. Thus one configuration appears in the municipal vacation beach, another in the decentralized business districts and yet another in the harbor areas, etc. Neutra did, of course, propose that a tartan system of zoning should be applied to Los Angeles, thereby imposing a

syncopated system of land-use on the existing subdivision; alternating between (1) light industrial zone with rail access, (2) highway, green belt with educational and recreational facilities, (3) residential zone divided into two different densities and then again the industrial zone and so on. What distinguished Neutra's concept of residential land settlement, from, say, Ludwig Hilberseimer's proposals of the mid-forties, imposing courtyard housing over entire regions, is a thesis which he most probably worked out with the planner Carol Aronovici, whereby different kinds of accommodation are provided for different family groups; ten-storey apartment slabs for bachelors, two-storey patio houses for large families and single-storey patio houses for childless couples. Either way round, as in Wright's Broadacre concept, the model is *motopian* for every family unit was to have been provided with a two car garage, thereby placing the main burden of distribution on the automobile. In Rush City Reformed the contradictions of Megalopolitan development are hardly reckoned with. The cut-away perspective through Neutra's Futurist rail/air transfer terminal, projected for Rush City in 1925, fails to recognize the consequences of optimizing automobile usage. Above all, it doesn't foresee the total elimination of suburban rail transit in the Los Angeles and its replacement by federally subsidized freeways running along the same rights of way.

Nevertheless, the New Deal did bring Neutra his welfare state and the government sponsored housing schemes which were intended to fulfill the mandate of its social programmes. In 1939, he started to work for exactly those alienated Mexican and Black minorities alluded to by Fogelson in his

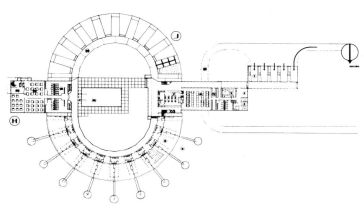

159 Neutra, Ring Plan School in Rush City, 1926.
Plan of unit, the sector C of general plan shown fig. 158.

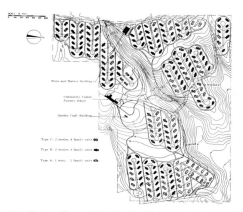

160 Neutra, Channel Heights, San Pedro, Los Angeles, 1942.

book *The Fragmented Metropolis*; first in an unrealized project for Jacksonville, Florida, then in a project for Maravilla in East Los Angeles, and finally the realization of a housing estate in the same district appropriately entitled Hacienda-Village. In the same year Neutra planned a so-called "finger park" community under the rubric Avion Village in Texas. In the following year came the masterwork of his low-cost housing career, the 600-unit community of Channel Heights, built at San Pedro, California, complete with nursery school, community center, supermarket and garden craft building.

All of Neutra's garden housing schemes were based on the Radburn principle of segregating the pedestrian from the car, first evolved by the planners Clarence Stein and Henry Wright for Radburn, New Jersey, in 1929. In fact, such is the similarity between Neutra's "finger park" system and the Greenbelt New Towns, of which the most successful was Greenbelt itself, completed in Maryland in 1938, that one has to acknowledge the success of the New Deal in evolving a nationally coherent policy for residential communities; an approach which sensitively reinterpreted the mechanistic garden city principles which had been first advanced by Raymond Unwin in his book *Town Planning in Practice* of 1909.

Superbly planned in relation to varied topography, Channel Heights breaks down into a series of regularly disposed "chevron" formations whose grouping often appears picturesque due to the undulation of the land. For all the cheapness and simplicity of the design, a pleasant contrast obtains between the white plastered bearing walls and the exposed red wood structure, siding, and roofing of the typical semi-detached one- and two-storey houses. Despite

this undeniable elegance and the favorable orientation towards both sun and sea, the dense urbanistic patterns of Pueblo Ribera and the Strathmore Apartments have been clearly lost. The highly urban, bungalow-patio typology of Southern California; a pattern so evidently capable of effectively integrating the automobile with housing and one which was central to the highly cultivated tradition of Gill, Schindler, Zwibel, and even Neutra's designs for Rush City, is here quite inexplicably sacrificed to an ideology which is patently suburban. The subsequent FHA mortgage regulations, the post-war GI Bill and the federally subsidized inter-state and state freeway systems were sufficient to turn this suburban model into a normative reality throughout the post-1945 period.

Perhaps the most influential Rush City image produced by Neutra in the late twenties was his design for a prototypical office building published in his book *Wie Baut Amerika?* of 1927. As William Jordy has suggested, this tray slab construction with its projecting exterior columns seems to have anticipated the final form of the Philadelphia Savings Fund Society building erected in Philadelphia to the designs of Howe and Lescaze between 1931 and 1932. Actually, the thirty-four-storey PSFS tower synthesized in its own evolution the intra-professional debate as to the appropriate form for a modern skyscraper; that is to say, it mediated (as it developed) between the translucent hermeticism of Wright's National Life Insurance project of 1923 and the various horizontal and vertical fenestration schemes, introduced by Hood into both his McGraw-Hill and Daily News buildings, as these where built in New York by 1930.

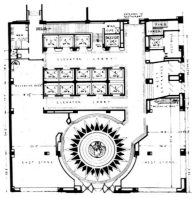

161 *Hood, McGraw-Hill Building, New York, N.Y., 1929. Ground plan.*

The PSFS design was developed in three stages, the first being initiated by George Howe as a more integrated version of the stripped Beaux-Arts Moderne style employed by Hood in his design for McGraw-Hill. In 1929, Howe attempted to resolve the horizontal-vertical schism by off-setting the unavoidable repetitiveness of the spandrels with unifying vertical accents. Despite this manipulation, the essentially horizontal banding of the floors prevailed, with the result that when the young Swiss architect, William Lescaze became Howe's partner, a second proposal was submitted in 1930, which emphasized the repetitive horizontality of the floors. This obsessively striated solution was checked by the intelligence of the client who recognized that the design lacked any unifying principle and so a third and final scheme was posited in 1931 in which the projection of the columns (as in Neutra's Rush City office structure) counterbalanced the reiteration of the spandrels and unified the whole into a vertical tower.

In works such as these, an emergent America confronted the cultural consequences of its industrial triumph, rejecting, to an equal degree, the nineteenth-century, transcendental aestheticism of Wright and the regressive, stone faced, fantasy of the Beaux-Arts Jazz Moderne. Thus, prior to the Hitchcock and Johnson exhibition, *The International Style*, staged at the Museum of Modern Art in 1932, certain American architects had already arrived at a non-monumental, industrial expressiveness, superior in many respects to the Neue Sachlichkeit style which was then being practised on the European continent.

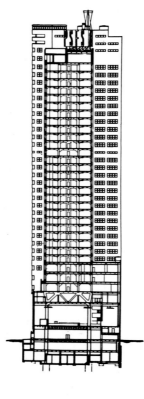

162 *Howe & Lescaze, PSFS Building, Philadelphia, Pennsylvania, 1929-32. Section.*

376

Built as the Swiss students dormitory in the Cité Universitaire, and housing some 45 students, the Pavillon Suisse was in some ways the building out of a fragment part of Le Corbusier's Radiant City. With a curtain wall on one side — his famous *pan verre* — and a corridor wall with small pierced windows, on the other, it resembled a segment of a typical *redent* block for *La Ville Radieuse*. Apart from this common treatment, the Pavillon Suisse was very much a building in its own right, as is seen from the subtle organisation of the complex which comprised of a five-storey residential slab plus an access tower and a single-storey communal building located to the rear.

The seminal importance of this structure in the history of the modern movement resides primarily in the plastic dynamism of its three dimensional order; in the fact that it can be read as a guillotine-like, elevated, frontal slab with a sculptural conch-like form behind. It is obvious from the preliminary sketches for the Pavillon Suisse that most of the work went into an elaboration of the communal element since it was originally designed as a five-storey box.

As finally built, a prominent harmonic curve serves to unite not only the thrust of the main stair as it rises out of the splayed volume of the entrance hall, but also the rubble stone wall of the refectory and the flanking wall of the stair tower above. Le Corbusier exploited the negative of this splayed form as a device with which to expand the apparent limits of the foyer, which at grade, gives access to the refectory, the kitchen and the director's office. At different times in his career Le Corbusier decorated this public volume; at first with a photographic mural celebrating the structure of natural form and later, after the Second World War, with a painted mural derived from his *Poeme de l'angle droit*. Somewhat hermetic acoustical metaphors are present in the sweeping angular plan form of the foyer, not the least among which is the fact that its configuration seems to have been derived from the auditorium building of his entry for the League of Nations Competition.

Refectory

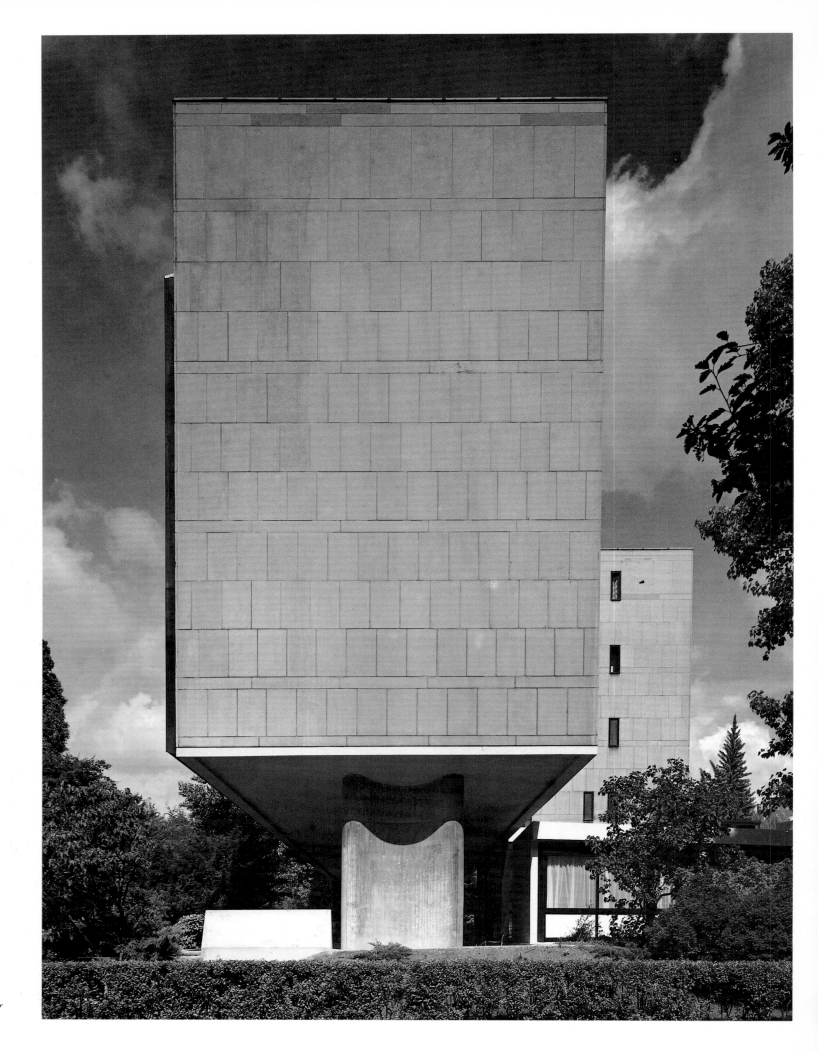

378 *East elevation*
379 *Above: plans of ground floor and typical floor*
   Below: overall view

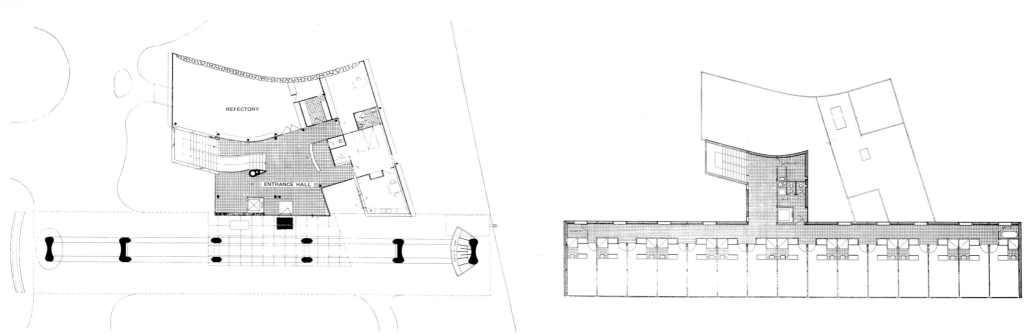

Commissioned under the patronage of the Princess de Polignac as part of the Salvation Army's building programme of the late nineteen twenties, this is one of three major buildings realised by Le Corbusier during the first half of the following decade; the other two being the Maison Clarté, Geneva, 1932, and his own Porte Molitor apartments, Paris, completed in 1933. These steel and glass structures were to exemplify his concept of a machine-age architecture. Like his Swiss students dormitory for the Cité Universitaire, this building may be seen as a residential fragment drawn from the utopian city proposal which he published under the title *La Ville Radieuse* in 1934. Faced in a curtain wall on one side and rendered as an opaque facade on the other, this slab is in effect a segment of Le Corbusier's prototypical *bloc à redent.* Inserted into a narrow and awkward site, this "radiant city" *parti* divides into a portico building with dormitory accommodation to the rear. The portico sequence took the form of a series of objects arrayed before a glass slab.

The derelicts for whom this building was commissioned have to be processed on entering the institution, and this finds reflection in the graduated volumes of the portico. Thus the transient enters via the canopy, turns right across the bridge and arrives in the large cylindrical vestibule faced in glass lenses. This space in turn leads to a large rectangular hall flanked by reception offices. The cross axis of this distribution sequence *(promenade architecturale)* connects directly to the elevator lobby of the dormitory slab at the same time affording direct access to the refectories above. The dormitories themselves divide into male and female sections with the higher floors dividing into *chamberettes* allocated equally to women and children on the left and men on the right.

In its original form the whole slab had some 900 bed spaces, but since 125 of them were equipped with cot spaces, the full complement of the structure was some 1,500 people. To service such a large infant population, a nursery school was provided on the roof.

This population, sometimes stacked as many

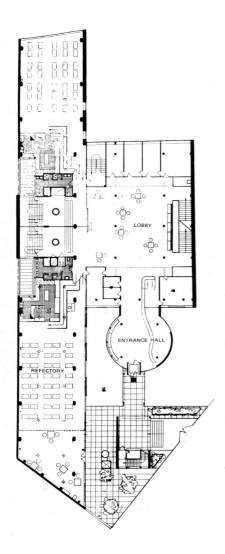

380 *Left: ground floor plan*
   Right: entrance porch
381 *Left: first floor plan*
   Above right: reception, view toward entrance hall
   Below right: refectory

as six beds deep, placed a burden on Le Corbusier's air-conditioning system — his so-called *respiration exacte* which, installed during a time of economic duress, was less than satisfactory in its operation. Above all, there was no provision for cooling the building in summer, with the result that the "greenhouse effect" created intolerable conditions for the occupants. This failure was typical of Le Corbusier's prewar career; where his passionate but naive determination to exploit advanced technology was often met by the incapacity of the building industry to provide such solutions at a reasonable cost.

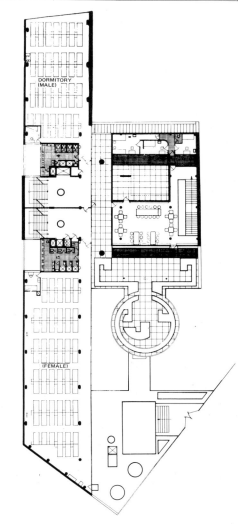

HANS SCHAROUN
Schminke House
Löbau, Saxony, Germany

For all the manifest differences in their general appearance, an ideological bond links Scharoun's Schminke House of 1932 to the farm which Häring had realized at Garkau some eight years before; Scharoun being committed to Häring's "organic approach" throughout his long career. There is, however, a peculiar lightness of touch and even a suggestion of whimsy in the steel-framed Schminke House which is characteristic of Scharoun and, while the main body of the structure has an essentially orthogonal organization, this is suddenly twisted towards the main view; the "head" of the house being organically emphasized as in Aalto's Villa Mairea. This head or belvedere form was appropriately occupied by an elevated formal dining room on the ground floor and a master bedroom above. Both the dining area and the bedroom were provided with generous terraces and these elements are projected as cantilevered flying forms which extend towards the vista.

The Schminke House has much in common with equally idiosyncratic elements employed in Scharoun's Mattern House, built in Bornim, near Potsdam, in 1934, and it may be argued that the enclosures of these houses function in both cases as sensitive light modulators; the wire mesh tubular steel, serpentine balustrading of the Schminke House agitating the reflected light in much the same way as the ambient light is filtered by the square-gridded fenestration in the living room at Bornim. This characteristic Neues Bauen fenestration is in fact liberally used in both houses as are certain "poetic" elements which are highly responsive to light and which give a luminous feel to the internal volumes; a conservatory-cum-wintergarden in the case of the Schminke House and a strange curved couch built into the concave gable wall of the Mattern House living room.

382 Overall view
383 Above: conservatory
Below: plans of ground floor and first floor
Photos: Scharoun-Archiv, Sammlung Baukunst,
Akademie der Künste, Berlin

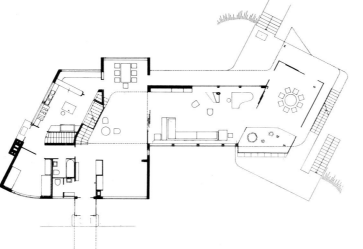

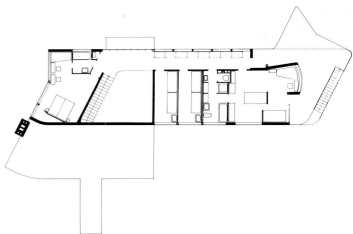

Initially projected in a number of early sketches as a palazzo and rendered at first with elements drawn from the Lombardy vernacular, including traditional tiled roofs, the Casa del Fascio eventually evolved into the canonical work of the Italian Rationalist movement; a modernist position which began with the declaration of the Gruppo 7, published in the *Rassegna Italiana* in December 1926. This group of young graduates from the Milan Polytechnic, which included such figures as Luigi Figini, Adalberto Libera, Gino Pollini and Giuseppe Terragni, sought to achieve a fusion between the classical heritage of the Mediterranean and the architetonic logic of the machine age. Thus the detailed articulation of the half-cube mass of the the Casa del Fascio was as much influenced by the stripped classical manner of Giovanni Muzio's Ca'Brutta, Milan apartment building of 1923 as it was by the Platonic machinism advanced by Le Corbusier, in the same year, in the pages of *Vers une Architecture.*

As far as classification is concerned the influence of Humanism is inescapable in the proportioning and alignment of the building; its facades being modulated throughout by root two rectangles and its central axis being aligned with the apse of Como Cathedral. On the other hand, machinism is equally evident in the battery of fifteen doors which serve to link the covered *cortile* with the open public square extending towards the Duomo. These electrically operated, steel-framed, plate glass openings, were to be activated simultaneously, so as to permit the immediate exit of fascist militia into the political arena of the piazza. Similar mechanical devices abound throughout the building, in the adjustable fenestration to the secondary access stair and in the numerous sliding windows and full-height glazed doors used throughout. However, the most striking and original feature of the Casa del Fascio is indutiably the way in which its surface is striated so as to afford layered readings of the principal internal volume in terms of the facade. Thus where the main elevation to the piazza is initially broken down into a solid flanking wall — and a five bay, four-storey-high trabeated frame, the second level reading, at the plane of the recessed entry door, denotes the volume of the three-bay-wide

courtyard on the interior. On turning around the building, one discovers that this three-bay volume is subtly indicated on every facade with the exception of the southeast elevation which gives priority to the main stair. While symmetrically situated with regard to the northwest-southeast axis, this three by three bay, two-storey-high inner volume is symmetrically set back from the piazza (then called the Piazza del Impero) in such a way as to afford a set of sluicelike thresholds; first the advanced stylobate of steps, then the recessed porch before the doors, then an anti-foyer before the first row of internal columns, then the foyer proper, (one structural bay wide) running between the main stair and the memorial to the 1922 Facist March on Rome and finally the hall itself. Preliminary studies reveal that like other works by Terragni, such as his Sant' Elia School of 1936, the Casa del Fascio was originally planned around an open court. In the course of its development this volume became the double-height hall, top-lit through a "lenscrete" roof (glass lenses set into concrete) and surrounded on four sides by galleries, offices and meeting rooms.

The latent classicism of this otherwise modern monumental work — the Rationalist concern for the expression of *mediterraneita* — is evoked by its revetment in Bolticino marble and by the free-standing trabeated construction, the beams and pillars, deployed around the perimeter of the hall. As in Mies van der Rohe's Barcelona Pavilion of 1929, its representative stature is acclaimed in a traditional manner, that is to say by its elevation on a podium or stylobate. On the other hand, there remains an abstract rigour and complexity to the architecture which denies its interpretation in terms which are exclusively classical. As its 1936 publication in the magazine *Quadrante* would indicate, the building was intended to be perceived as though it were as Escher-like matrix, with multiple orientations, apart from the one ultimately insisted upon by the laws of gravity and the necessities imposed by human occupation. The normal axial references of "up-down" and "left-right" are challenged throughout by a number of literal and phenomenal mirror effects, such as the foyer pillars which are reflected in the polished marble revetment to the foyer ceiling and floor or the stepped soffit of the main staircase which, aside from the decisive clue of the glass balustrade, may be read equally as an inverted space.

The political and ideological cause to which the Casa del Fascio was dedicated was represented on the interior, in a cut-out plaque embellishing the hall, bearing the inscription *Justicia, Ordine* and *Patria* and in Mario Radice's abstract photo-mural relief to the *Sala del Direttorio*, featuring a large blow-up of Mussolini.

384 Left: section
Right: front elevation
385 Left: first floor plan (below)
and third floor plan (above)
Right: entrance hall

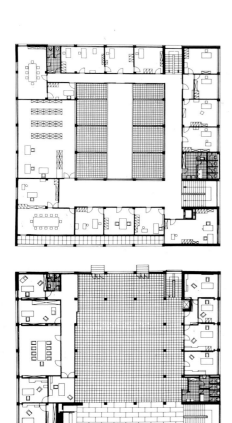

As in other European traditional societies recovering from the aftermath of the First World War, modern architecture was first introduced into England through the activity of émigrés beginning with Peter Behrens who was commissioned to build the house "New Ways" at Northampton in 1926 by the toy train manufacturer W. J. Bassett-Lowke and with the young New Zealand architect Amyas Connell who designed the tripartite reinforced concrete villa High and Over at Amersham, Buckinghamshire, for the distinguished archaeologist, Bernard Ashmole, whom Connell had met in the British Academy in Rome.

High and Over completed in 1929, was but the first work of a remarkably prolific and brilliant modern practice carried out under the partnership of Connell, Ward and Lucas — Basil Ward being a fellow New Zealander, and Colin Lucas being British. From the very outset the firm tended to propagate two somewhat different versions of the so-called "international style," the one spread eagled and dynamic as in Connell's Grayswood house of 1933, the other rendered in more subtly Cubistic manner as in Lucas's reinforced concrete house realized at Wrotham, Kent, in the very same year.

This small house incisively situated in the extreme corner of a pre-existing orchard with desirable views over a garden to the south and the east, was constructed entirely out of in-situ concrete and ingeniously organised so that with a bed-sitting space on the first floor, there would be one living area on each floor.

Aside from having advantageous views over the site, this dwelling, set into the corner of the lot, also afforded an appropriate plastic context for the chosen formal order of the work, with the diagonal thrust of the external reinforced concrete stair cutting back into the form of the implied cube. The counter thrust of the oversailing flat roof, extending as far as the first floor balcony, together with the horizontal fenestration to the living room bay window, checks the implied penetration of the stair and imparts to the entire form of the cube, a pin-wheeling counter-point volumetrically reminiscent of the Rietveld-Schröder House realized a decade earlier.

Above: overall view
Below: plans of ground floor and first floor
Photo provided by Colin Lucas

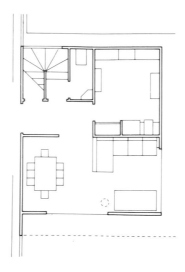
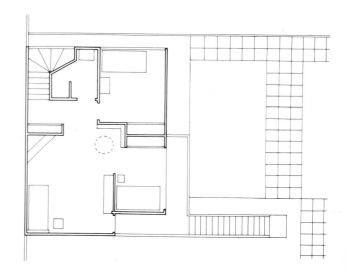

0   5   10   20ft

By far the most influential émigré architect to enter England in the late twenties
was the Russian Berthold Lubetkin whose
impact on the development of modern architecture in England has never been adequately appreciated. Lubetkin, who came from a
modest but brilliant career in Paris, brought
to Tecton (the firm that he founded in
1932) a capacity for logical organization
which has rarely graced English architecture.
His 1935 block of flats in Highgate, London,
Highpoint 1, remains a masterpiece even by
the standards of today; its internal layout
and disposition on an awkward site being a
model of both formal and functional order.
Despite the success of their susequent work
for the London and Whipsnade Zoos, Lubetkin and his Tecton team — Chitty, Drake,
Dugdale, Harding and Lasdun — never
attained this level again. Their Highpoint 2
block, built in 1938 already shows a decided
mannerist reaction. One is left to speculate
on the extent to which Lubetkin, as an
architect of anarcho-socialist persuasion, had
become sensitive to Soviet Social Realism,
for certainly his essays on Soviet architecture written in the 1950s reveal a sympathy
in this direction. The shift in expression
between Highpoint 1 and Highpoint 2 was
noted at the time, and the ensuing discussion
established the ground rules for the ideological struggles of the 1950s.

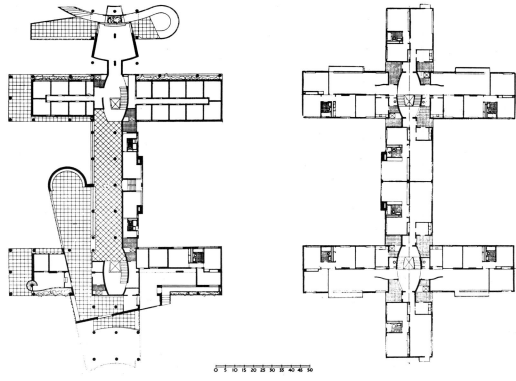

Above: overall view
Below: ground floor plan and upper floor plan
Photo: M. Sekiya

1934

LUBETKIN, DRAKE & TECTON
Penguin Pool, Regent's Park Zoo
London, England

Insufficiently appreciated at the time of its completion and even dismissed by some as a folly, this penguin pool has since become a popular classic. One of a series of buildings designed for the Regent's Park Zoo, by the newly created firm of Lubetkin, Drake and Tecton, this work was above all a brilliant demonstration of advanced reinforced concrete construction, comprising two interlocking, four-foot-wide spiral ramps, each having an unsupported length of 46 feet and tapering from the center to yield a six-inch slab at the core and three inches at the outside. These ramps are in fact helicoidal beams on which the penguins are at liberty to disport themselves.

In many respects this elliptically planned arena may be classified as a display machine, in which the inmates are able to exhibit the full range of their natural talents, from elegantly plunging into the transparent sided diving tank, to awkwardly waddling down the ramps. An account published soon after its completion in July 1934, reveals the ostensible rationale for the section and for the varied surface treatments employed in the design: "A genuine attempt has been made to preserve the birds from the boredom which generally overtakes all zoo inhabitants. They have necessary protection from the sun since the surrounding trees have been preserved and a cover is provided over part of the circumference of the pool. They have a variety of surfaces for their feet, ranging from plastic rubber on the flat paths to slate on the steps, and the concrete of the ramps is permanently wetted by a revolving fountain. The bottom of the pool is painted bright blue which is clearly visible in the water."

More influenced by the Purist vision of Léger, Ozenfant and Le Corbusier than by the formal dynamics of Russian Constructivism which had played a salient role in Berthold Lubetkin's formation, this zoological compound was but a dry run for a more elaborate and theatrical form of penguin arena designed by the same architects, in 1937, for the Dudley Zoo. In this last instance, however, a one-sided panorama plan form was adopted; the interlocking spiral ramps of the original now being dispersed to either end of an elevated esplanade.

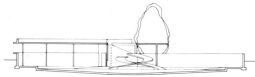

Left: section
Right: Penguin Pool in use

Having served as the chief engineer to the British Empire Exhibition staged at Wembley in 1924, Owen Williams was understandably chosen as the designer for this Olympic size swimming pool completed at Wembley in the incredibly short time of nine months. To judge from the official brief, this structure was intended to fulfill vaguely imperialist ambitions. Thus we read in the prospectus of the time: "One of the main objects, therefore, of the new enterprise was . . . to create for Great Britain the opportunity . . . of establishing itself second to none in the swimming world . . . the promoters will do everything in their power to make Wembley, in very truth, the preeminent sports center of the British Empire."

Aside from housing Olympic scaled swimming facilities, the Empire Pool was also designed to serve as a multi-purpose hall which would be suitable for a wide variety of events including circuses, boxing, equestrian displays, industrial exhibitions and popular, not to say national demonstrations. Above all, it was ultimately conceived as an indoor arena which would be dedicated to the arts of popular distraction and entertainment. As to this last, the prospectus was quite explicit: "On the wide terraces at either side, there will be a dance floor and fully licensed buffets. A dance band will play every afternoon and evening, while cabaret entertainment will be staged from time to time. From the seats above these terraces spectators will be able to watch the swimming, dancing and entertainments. . ."

To meet these multiple requirements Owen Williams designed a large concrete shed some 420 feet long and 250 feet wide, the inside span of the the three-hinged arches supporting the roof being 236 feet 6 inches exactly. This dimension was derived from the modular unit employed throughout. This unit was predicated on the seat width allocated to each spectator, namely 33 inches, so that the spacing of the concrete arches was based on an eight module interval or 22 feet. These 9-inch-wide, hinged frames were profiled in the lower section in such a way as to support the raked concrete seating which flanked the arena on either side and which, together with the stadia at the gable ends, had a total capacity of 100,000 people.

The knife-edge pivoting device employed for the lower hinges together with the counterbalancing provided by the projecting concrete fins, were designed to reduce the horizontal reaction at mid-span, although this would have been more efficiently achieved had the initial semicircular fin been retained. We have, from this alone, evidence that Owen Williams, despite his reputation as an anti-aesthetical engineer, was not averse to modifying the form of his works for reasons which were ultimately formal.

Exterior view
Photo: M. Sekiya

Torroja is probably the only concrete engineer of the inter-war period who is comparable to men like Nervi, Freyssinet and Maillart. Torroja's first building of consequence was his 156-foot-diameter domed market hall, built for the town of Algeciras in 1933. This was his earliest shell construction employing a thickness of 3½ inches; a feat which was to be overshadowed by his stands for the Madrid Hippodrome completed in 1935. At Madrid, a hyperboloid, 2-inch concrete shell in the form of a cantilevered vault, is the principal structural element for the main canopy over the stand itself. These vaults extend 42 feet on the track side and 28 feet behind, in order to cover the seating of the stadium. The total span of the two cantilevers is thus 70 feet for a rise of not more than 10 feet. The larger cantilever is prevented from overturning by a steel tie rod which balances the system by anchoring the smaller cantilever to the ribbed structure which covers the betting hall situated beneath the stand. The construction is in reinforced concrete throughout and includes an underground foyer and gallery entrance covered by concrete barrel shells running in the opposite direction to the vaulting over the stands.

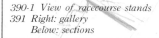

390-1 View of racecourse stands
391 Right: gallery
Below: sections

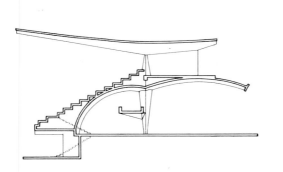

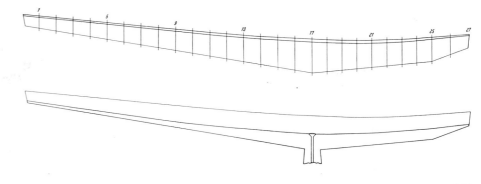

The four-storey, steel-framed, reinforced concrete Doldertal apartments, sponsored by Sigfried Giedion as a demonstration, amount, in many respects, to the apotheosis of the Swiss Neue Sachlichkeit. In Switzerland, the so-called functionalist approach was to assert itself suddenly, as the only reasonable style and was soon to become widely accepted as a normal mode of practice. This was in part due to a subtle inflection of the style, so that in the collaborations of Alfred and Emil Roth —

above all, in their work on the Siedlung Neubühl, designed with other architects a few years earlier — the harsher details of the style are effectively mediated, particularly as this affects the transition from inside to outside space.

It is clear that Marcel Breuer, then working in London with F.R.S. Yorke, contributed sculptural flair to this design, while both Alfred Roth and Breuer brought a certain warmth to Teutonic functionalism, partly as a result of their experience in Northern

Europe; Roth having worked in Sweden while Breuer was in England. There is in this respect something pecularliarly Swedish (even Asplund-like) about the wintergarden entry to these apartments just as there is something pragmatic and English about the vertical timber siding of the penthouse. But the plastic manipulation of the whole composition, the identical twin blocks stepping down the slope, in sequence, with their separate entrances and garages tucked into the undercroft and the splayed forms of

their generous terraces extending towards the South (both gestures contrasting with the orthogonality of their envelopes) these are all surely touches which may be attributed to Breuer's plastic imagination. Clearly Giedion's Doldertal development posited a new paradygm for middle class suburbia for while this site was hardly overbuilt, these six apartments certainly suggested a denser pattern of settlement than the nineteenth-century suburb into which they were inserted.

The interior planning demonstrates a level of well-serviced domesticity which for a while became a Swiss standard; a standard which has been rarely equalled in recent years. In the first place, it is the spatial criteria and the dimensions employed which impart to these modest four-bedroom apartments (1,500 square feet each) a feeling of extraordinary ease. It would be inappropriate here to dwell at length on all the refinements of the internal organization, but the practicality of certain features merits some comment, if only because it exhibits a functionalism which, far from being reductive, evidently contributes to the poetic and hedonistic aura which permeates the scheme. Amongst these simple, but effective devices employed in these apartments one needs to cite: the long diagonal views across the L-shaped living volume to the terrace, the ease of serving food to both the inside and outside dining spaces, the generous entry, bathroom and storage areas, etc., the generous criteria employed in determining the furnishability of bedrooms and last, but not least, the easily modifiable fenestration and sun screening.

Of the normative nature of all this, Alfred Roth was well aware when he wrote in 1940: "Aesthetically the oblique angle of the partitions gives a pleasing contrast with the right angles of the structure.... The walls of the flats are various colors all light in tone — beige, grey, blue. The plaster surfaces and the columns in the studios are painted white. The birch three-ply finish to the walls is wax polished. Joinery, in general — doors, cupboards, insides of window frames — are white-grey. Having in mind changes of tenants, no special accents of bright color were used."

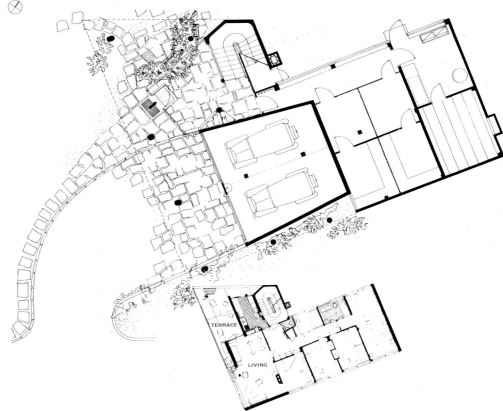

392 *Exterior view*
393 *Above: entrance*
Below: ground floor plan (with upper floor plan)

Built on an island in the Gulf of Finland, for the Ahlstrom combine, the Sunila cellulose and pulp plant took its architectural and organizational format from Väinö Vähäkallio's Kaukopaa mill, designed for Enso-Gutzeit in 1935. Of this, David Pearson has observed: "In its crisp, separated brick-clad masses, standing tall against the shoreline and linked by covered conveyors and hoppers whose exposed surfaces were finished in light-toned metal and concrete in contrast to the dark brick, it closely resembles Aalto's plant built two years later at Sunila, as well as others that came before it."

In Sunila then, Aalto employed an established syntax, but his experience in doing so made him acutely aware of the plastic potential latent in large uninterrupted brick masses. Aalto's retrospective description of this complex, testifies to the social and poetic nature of this new found sensibility: "The contours of this rock island have been left in their natural form so that the production process starting on the highest level can step down in its various individual stages to the level of the harbour. The center of the plant is built up into a terrace from which all phases of production can be observed. Here

are located the administrative offices, laboratories, etc. The terrace also forms, at the same time, a garden thereby creating a quiet atmosphere for the administrative center. Throughout the entire periphery of the various factory buildings, which are connected to each other by means of 'open-air corridors,' the pine forest has been left untouched. Every worker in the various departments therefore has the possibility to go out of his building directly into nature. Instead of an uniform monotony, an attempt has been made here to endow in a natural way, each department with its own

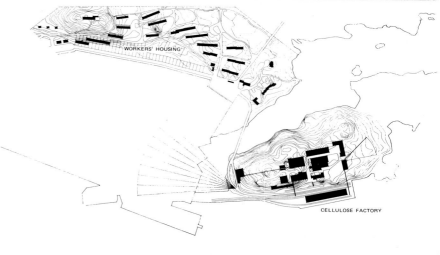

character. The result is a pyramidal building mass, rich in contrasts."

Structured in reinforced concrete throughout, a change of revetment was initially employed at Sunila in order to distinguish the production buildings faced in red brick, from the transportation, power station and warehouse structures finished in white fair-faced concrete. Compositionally, Sunila is grouped asymmetrically about its tall central chimney, below which one finds, to one side, the principal representative facade, topped by bowstring parabolic arches and stabilized by large squarish area of top-hung, gridded industrial fenestration — an emblematic front, asymmetrically accentuated by the placement of a clock. This is typical of the strategy of contrasts and balances employed throughout in order to characterize the various prisms of which the complex is irregularly composed; here exposed concrete pilasters or slots of vertical fenestration, there, widely spaced square openings or elesewhere, horizontal strip fenestration.

Sunila, in the end, constituted a world in microcosm, for as soon as the factory was complete, Aalto started to work on a nearby housing complex which was not finally occupied as a settlement until 1938. The workers' housing at Sunila was the first time that Aalto employed a topographically inflected form in which, while the southern slopes are given over to housing, the valleys are reserved for gardens and pathways and the northern terraces are left forested.

The prototypical dwellings developed for Sunila constitute Aalto's most serious contribution to modern housing after the severity of his Tapani apartments built in Turku in 1929. At Sunila the contours are allowed to displace the parallel order of the row-house form, while the apartment building for the supervisory staff radiates outwards in a fan-like configuration. A similar kind of fragmentation is introduced in section, where certain blocks step back as they rise to form apartments with deep balconies, occupying the full frontage of each unit.

394 Above: factory
    Below: site plan
395 Above: row houses for workers
    Below: plan of row houses for supervisory staff

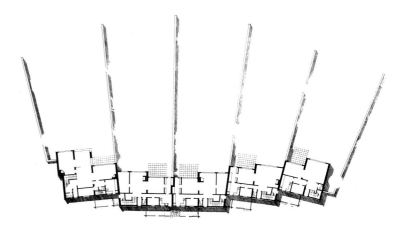

The Stockholm Southern Cemetery, more commonly known as the Woodland Cemetery, marks the alpha and the omega of Asplund's twenty-five-year long career. This coincidence manifests itself in a number of ways at once. In the first place, the Woodland Cemetery established Asplund's practice since it was the result of a competition held in 1915, in which Asplund (in collaboration with Sigurd Lewerentz) secured the first prize. In the second place, the crematorium which was eventually built in this cemetery between 1935 and 1940, happened to be the last major work of Asplund's career; a work which came to its

completion in the year of his death. There is a further irony involved in the fact that Asplund was one of the first persons to be cremated here.

The Woodland Cemetery is one of those rare instances in twentieth century wherein an extremely subtle and resonant relationship is established between a structure and its surrounding landscape. As far as this is concerned, the crematorium site consists of four primary "scenic" elements, the extraordinary undulating terrain itself, the long monumental causeway leading to the main loggia, raised high on the horizon, the adjacent cross which inflects the lower part

of the ridge and finally the meditation grove planted on a moundlike hill some distance from the complex.

Like Asplund's Stockholm Public Library of 1926, the conception of the crematorium is basically Neoclassical and as such it represents a move away from the functionalism which is still a persistent theme in, say, Asplund's State Bacteriological Laboratories of 1933 or his Gothenburg Law Courts Annex of 1934; although, even here, as at Emskede, as Stuart Wrede points out, modernist form still remains as a latent reference: "Asplund's use of essentially abstract walls as the organizing compositional ele-

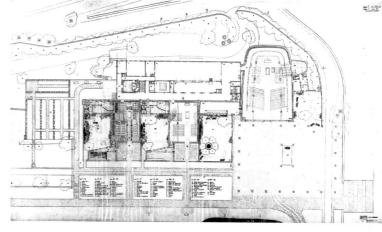

ment derives from traditional sources, yet there is a clear modernist-cubist influence in its implementation. The high, planar front walls of the small chapels serve to tie together the low mass of the waiting rooms in front of them. They also echo the freestanding walls, which serve as backdrops for graves, further down the hill. Contrasted to the planar composition of the front of the small chapels, is the great centralizing and static form of the open loggia, its roof inverted towards the impluvium at its center. The main facades are faced with an intricate pattern of unpolished white marble, while the building volumes attached to the back of these stone facades are clad in warm yellow stucco, giving the building an unusual lightness and intimacy."

In order to solve one of the characteristic problems of the type, namely, how to accommodate a virtually continuous flow of funerals, in close proximity to one another, Asplund provided two parallel chapels, each with its own forecourt and circulation, so there was no risk of two separate groups of mourners encountering each other. The crowning element of this linear complex, set at the head of the hill, consists of two parts; first, the cavelike, main chapel, seating 300 people and known as the Chapel of the Holy Cross, and second, the Neoclassical loggia with its open-air impluvium. This monumental complex was naturally intended to accommodate large funeral processions and the more public type of cortege.

Asplund was no doubt aware that a Christian crematorium is a contradiction in terms; a split which modern society has to be conscious of since it categorically denies the doctrine of resurrection. It is possible that this is the anomaly behind the curiously pagan atmosphere which permeates the complex. Thus as Wrede points out, the shape of the main chapel is basically that of a primitive burial cave and would have been more so had Asplund been allowed to curve the floor continuously into the wall surface as it was initially projected. In a similar way, the mound beneath the meditation grove unmistakably alludes to an archaic tumulus, and indeed, one may argue that despite the presence of Christian iconography the whole crematorium is finally dominated by the Neoclassical loggia which imparts an unmistakably Greek and hence pagan tone to the entire fabric. Naturally, it is this crowning element which is brought to the highest level of tectonic perfection, evident in the marble revetment and in the cross battened timber rafters which support the roof.

396 Above: open loggia and stone cross
Below: main floor plan
397 Impluvium and sculpture in the center of open loggia

FRANK LLOYD WRIGHT
Falling Water
Bear Run, Pennsylvania, U.S.A.

Initially sketched out in the space of a morning, Falling Water embodied Wright's lifelong ideal of the domestic hearth, firmly rooted in unspoilt nature. As in Wright's design for the Elizabeth Noble apartments of 1929 or, say, his Capital Journal building projected for Salem, Oregon, in 1931, both the structural form and the spatial order of this house depended on the rhetorical use of the reinforced concrete cantilever; a structural device which for Wright was practically synonymous with his idea of organic architecture. This time the structure was cantilevered out to the point of folly, in contrast to the implacable calm of the mushroom structure employed by Wright in his Johnson Wax administration building, under construction at Racine, Wisconsin from 1936. Falling Water projected from the natural rock base into which it was anchored as though it were an effortless floating platform, poised over a small waterfall.

No longer restricted by the extended earth line of his Prairie Style, the terraces of this house appeared as an agglomeration of planes miraculously suspended in space, poised at varying heights above the trees of a densely wooded valley. Tied back into the escarpment like a series of layered concrete trays, Falling Water defies photographic record. Its fusion with the landscape is total, for despite the extensive use of horizontal glazing, painted Cherokee red, nature permeates the structure at every turn. Its interior evokes an atmosphere of a horizontally layered and sparsely furnished grotto rather than a house in the traditional sense. That the rough stone walls and flagged floors intend some primitive homage to the site is borne out by the living-room stairs which, dropping through the floor to the waterfall below, have no function other than to bring man into intimate communion with the surface of the stream. Wright's perennial ambivalence towards technique was never more singularly expressed than in this house, for although concrete had made the design feasible, he still regarded it as an illegitimate material — as a "conglomera" that had little quality in itself. His initial intent had been to cover the concrete of Falling Water in gold leaf, a kitsch gesture from which he was saved by the discretion of his client. He finally settled for finishing its surface in apricot paint!

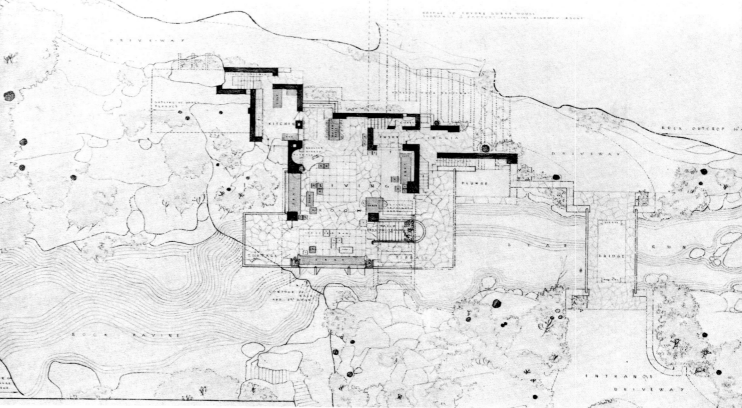

398 Above: exterior view
  Below: ground floor plan
399 Above: living room
  Below: living room, guest house

The S. C. Johnson & Son Administration Building has its origins in the Capital Journal newspaper building projected for Salem, Oregon in 1931, a project in which Wright first hit upon the idea of a "forest" of mushroom columns supporting a single roof covering the main working area. This motif was to be returned to again in the Johnson's Wax Building of 1936. Henry-Russell Hitchcock's appraisal of the evolution and realisation of this work can hardly be equalled: "Preliminary construction . . . began in the early fall of 1936, when the Kaufmann house was nearly finished. But so novel were the hollow tapered piers, reinforced by tissues of expanded metal lath and supporting only their own lily-pad-like tops, that a building permit was not issued until the following spring. Nor was the building finally completed, with furniture and fittings designed by Wright and specially made, until the spring of 1939. . . . It has often been pointed out that the area could easily have been roofed with metal trusses and quite un-broken by piers. Hence the unimaginative — who do not include the general public who have flooded to the building ever since it was finished — have never comprehended the piers. . . . The piers do not support anything. They stand like so many plants, providing the solid part of the roofs with their own extensive circular tops, in a fashion somewhat like Maillart's Swiss type of mushroom columns, but entirely opposed to the post-and-lintel principle of most American concrete construction. Amazingly small at their bases, which rest in nine-inch bronze holders, they do not break up the working space in a functional sense. While in an esthetic sense their lithe repeated shafts, as organic as those of some hollow-stemmed plant, really create the interior space.

For the interior space is here entirely cut off from the outside. The light, coming straight down from the open spaces between the lily-pad pier tops, and entering also in bands below the surrounding balcony and at the top of the wall, is extraordinary even. Perhaps because of its points of origin, perhaps because of the pyrex glass tubes which fill the openings, the light has a very special quality. With the special forms of the piers, there is a certain illusion of sky seen from the bottom of an aquarium."

The hollow pyrex tubes delicately supported by the piers which Wright called *dendri-* *forms,* and the piers themselves whose hollow cores serve as storm water pipes, and whose bases are hinged so as to reduce the bending at the hinge to zero, were to represent the apotheosis of Wright's technical imagination. This was the tectonic embodiement of his mythical new America, seen by him as rising from the ashes of Mumford's paleotechnology and the Depression; this was the destiny of his imagined Usonia — a poetry of miraculous technique arising out of the daring inversion of traditional components. Thus, where one would have expected solidity (the roof) one found light, and where one would have expected light (the walls) one encountered solidity. Of this inversion he was quite aware when he wrote: "Glass tubing laid up like bricks in a wall composes all the lighting surfaces. Light enters the building where the cornice used to be. In the interior the box-like structure vanishes completely. The walls carrying the glass ribbing are of hard red brick and red Kosota sandstone."

The continuous sweeping bands of engineering brick with raked joints, curved corners and inlaid glass tubes, imparted to the structure a streamlined appearance which as Hitchcock was to note, evoked some large scale piece of machinery more successfully than the work of those architects who had long since praised the virtues of machinist architecture.

As with the equally progressive Larkin Building of 1904, the Johnson's Wax Building pioneered a number of unorthodox servicing techniques. Thus its 288 feet by 288 feet by 30-foot-high volume was entirely heated by radiant tubular panels hidden in the ground and mezzanine floors, while its air-conditioning was centralized and fed in and out of the building at the central core, via what Wright was to term "nostrils" in the published plans.

As in the Larkin Building, Wright envisaged the workplace as the place of sacrament and as the only institution capable of reuniting an otherwise uprooted automotive society. To this end he urged his paternalistic clients to provide communal facilities for their employees so that a sense of community could be established in the workplace. This accounts for the 250-seat mezzanine auditorium on the central axis of the main volume which was clearly intended to provide for lectures, film shows, general meetings, etc. This in many respects was the equivalent of the organ installed in the attic floor of the Larkin Building.

In Racine, additional communal facilites

were provided in the form of a squash court fed by a glass tube and metal-framed passerelle running between the penthouse executive offices and the roof of the garage block adjacent to the entry. That Wright was well aware of the historical and environmental context into which this whole utopian complex was inserted, is borne out by the fact that this introspective structure was specifically designed, like the Larkin Building, to stand against the "unimpressive surroundings bounded by three ordinary village streets." It was for Wright a "new social condenser," oriented towards the automotive disurbanized landscape; towards an industrial revolution which as far as Wright was concerned, had already "run away" into the vistas of Usonia.

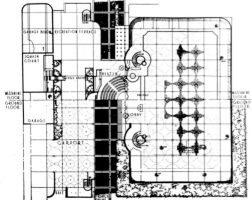

400-1 *Panoramic view*
401 *Lobby*
402 *Above: main office*
    Below: ground floor plan
403 *Reception area of publicity department*

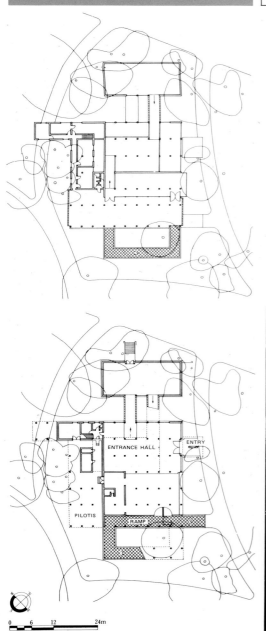

After a five-year apprenticeship with Le Corbusier in the *atelier* at 35 Rue de Sevres, the thirty-six-year-old Sakakura designed this remarkable pavilion for the Paris Exposition Universelle of 1937. Representative, in some sense, of both the cultural policy of the French Popular Front and the modernization of Japan, this building attempted to reconcile traditional Japanese tea-house architecture with both modern technique and progressive western architectural thought. Thus, from a spatial point of view the building is at first glance rather occidental, not to say Corbusian, particularly in terms of its split-levelled and ramped organisation which closely resembles the inner axial structure of Le Corbusier's own Pavillon des Temps Nouveaux built for the same occasion, and even his project for a pavilion in Liege projected in the same year. The system of circulation is induitably a *promenade architecturale* and the rich spatial sequence which follows from the concept may be judged from the fact that the general route comprises a fractured "figure of eight" causing the visitor to traverse a complex sequence of ramps and pass through four different floor levels.

From a technical point of view the building was a *tour de force* in adapting western technique to a reinterpretation of Japanese form; the basic system being a structural steel frame with joisted floors and timber braced walling. This lightweight framework and timber in-fill facilitated both erection and demolition; concrete being reserved

sorely for the point foundations, the ground slabs and the low retaining walls faced in rubble stonework. The external walls where unglazed were finished both inside and out in asbestos cement sheet.

This lightweight system had no doubt been deliberately evolved by Sakakura in order to mediate between occidental and oriental form. While this structure facilitated the simulation of traditional Japanese building methods, the spatial planning sought to evoke the four primary characteristics of tea house architecture; its open plan formation, its constructional clarity, its resonant use of natural materials and its integration of house and garden. Perhaps the most overtly Japanese formal reference was the anti-*torii* or anti-gate over the entrance, which while traditionally profiled, was atypically supported on a single column. This, together with the five bar, horizontal balustrading used throughout, clearly helped to give a decidedly Japanese connotation to the work; a sense which was reinforced by the colour scheme and by the quality of materials employed. Thus a certain oriental feeling was imparted by the dark brown stanchions, the brown linoleum, the ramps painted in Indian red and by the white artificial stone paving in the entrance hall. On the other hand, the colour scheme adopted in the enclosed galleries was Corbusian; pale burnt sienna, cobalt blue, and pale yellowish green. On the northwest wall the letters bearing the inscription *Japon* were of varnished oak and finished with white edges. The most ambiguous detail in the whole pavilion was surely the diagonally laticed timber screens, freely used throughout; a grid which was Japanese in terms of its density and Western in terms of its criss-cross pattern which evoked the tradition of French wall grillwork.

404 Left: ground floor plan (below)
and first floor plan (above)
Right: exterior view toward entry
405 Entrance hall
Photos: Kollar, Paris

Between his own Munkkiniemi house of 1934 and his masterly Villa Mairea of 1939, Aalto produced this pivotal work which combined the modified Neoclassical plan evident in his Viipuri Library of 1935, with an irregular atrium plan-form which now seems to have been derived from the traditional Karelian farm. Premiated in an open competition and designed in collaboration with Aino Aalto, Aarne Ervi, and Viljo Rewell, this pavilion bore as a competition psuedonym the title, *Le bois est en marche* and this phrase served not only to characterize its form, executed almost entirely in timber, but also alluded to the most common material employed in the exhibits. This is the first work by Aalto to employ the "head and tail" theme and as such, it is clearly a fundamental break with the compositional strategy of elision which had been employed in the final version of the Viipuri Library. This configuration is to be employed in a number of subsequent works including the Villa Mairea of 1939 and the Säynnätsalo Town Hall, which came a decade later.

To a greater degree than in his own house or the Villa Mairea, Aalto establishes a tension here between classical and vernacular references and never more so than in the small open-air atrium that punctuates, at midway, the covered *promenade architecturale* meandering from the garden entrance to the windowless, timber-battened, mass of the main building. The surviving photographs suggest that a brilliant condensation of

metaphors was set up in this atrium through the use of regularly spaced vertical poles, which, occupying the full height of the court, were stabilized by a strictly orthogonal wire grid, centering the top of each shaft. Viewed obliquely, these poles evoked once again the irregular spacing of natural forest growth but when approached on axis, this pattern crystallized, so to speak, into the regularity of a hypostyle hall, supporting a ceiling plane whose only perceptual register was the wire grid. This was just as much a Neoclassical allusion as the regularly spaced circular top lights to the main volume — a lighting device which Aalto had already employed in Viipuri.

As far as the vernacular is concerned, this manifested itself most clearly in the irregular exhibition promenade and above all in the various techniques of wooden fabrication and revetment employed, which demonstrated a potential for achieving expressive form in timber construction. And it was just these forms — columns stiffened by inset, radial battens or lashed and braced with bamboo — which tied the whole design back to the Finnish National Romantic movement.

406 Entry to main hall
407 Above left: lashed column detail
    Below left: upper floor plan with exhibition rooms
    Right: open-air atrium
    Photos:
    The Museum of Finnish Architecture, Helsinki

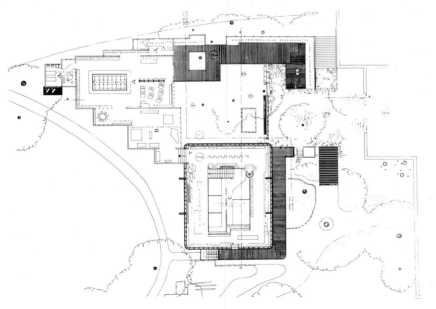

1937

*LE CORBUSIER
& PIERRE JEANNERET
Pavillon des Temps Nouveaux
Paris World Exhibition
Paris, France*

Built for the Paris World Exhibition of 1937, the Pavillon des Temps Nouveaux reflected much of the ethos of the French left-wing coalition of the so-called *Front Populaire* although the specific cultural programme embodied in the exhibit was Syndicalist and Saint Simonian rather than Social Democratic in the accepted sense. It was clear that this small pavilion was conceived as some kind of surrogate church complete with the icons and edicts of a new social order, as represented by the various elements of Le Corbusier's utopian proposals for the Radiant City. Nothing less than an ecclesiastical allusion was intended by the placement of the temporary wooden speaker's platform with its reflective "cloud-like" acoustical shell on which was inscribed the Popular Front slogan, "a new era has begun, an era of solidarity," and the same can be said for the axial placement of the articles of the CIAM, Athens Charter of 1933, setting forth the commandments of a new urbanism.

However, this was by no means the only religious aspect of this temporary building, for the actual structure itself was derived from a reconstruction of the Hebraic temple in the wilderness — a form which Le Corbusier had first advanced as exemplary in the pages of *Vers une Architecture* in 1923. In fact it can be claimed that this pavilion was both a condensation and inversion of the reconstructed nomadic tabernacle, since unlike the Hebraic form, the tented roof is suspended here in a catenary curve rather than a traditional pitch.

This nomadic form facilitated the incorporation of a number of significant metaphors for, on the one hand, as we have seen, the building alludes to a temple, while on the other, the latticework pylons, supporting the catenary, can be seen as refering to airship

construction. In fact in some respects, the Pavillon des Temps Nouveaux is also an *inversion* of the dirigible. Comparable aeronautical metaphors are evident in the aerofoil profile of the centrally pivoted door and in the model of an aircraft (the modern crucifix) situated on the central axis of the volume. One may also note in passing, the National-Socialist symbolism involved in the division of the front panels into blue, white and red (the tricolour) while the main door and the inner back wall were finished in "revolutionary" red. With these complex and contradictory overtones the Pavillon des

Temps Nouveaux, (like Le Corbusier's vaulted weekend house built in Paris two years before) asserted itself as the symbol of a new age which was to be at once both ancient and modern. This conjunction was emphasised by the fact that tented fabric was an ancient technique, whereas steel latticework and suspended cable construction was quintessentially modern. The significance of this mixture resided in the fact that by this date Le Corbusier had lost his faith in the manifest destiny of the machine age and had instead begun to embrace the notion of an intermediate technology; one which would

judiciously combine together, traditional and modern methods.

The Pavillon des Temps Nouveaux returns Le Corbusier to the didactic building type, to the distant annular ring plan of Le Play's Exposition Universelle of 1867, and above all to his own *Musée à Croissance illimitée* which he had first projected for Christian Zervos in 1931. While the logarithmic plan of this project is not present in the Pavillon des Temps Nouveaux, its inner volume was nonetheless structured about the concept of a *promenade architecturale*, which by virtue of a series of interconnected ramps and

elevated platforms, established a didactic itenerary within the luminous volume of the tent. Following a serpentine route, the visitor left the initial CIAM statement on axis to pass through an outer a sequence of rooms dealing with urban history, slum clearance, current urban planning and finally a disquisition on a new type of community center. After further sections treating with CIAM theory the route terminated in various projects dedicated to rural renewal; above all to Le Corbusier's proposals for the "radiant" farm and village.

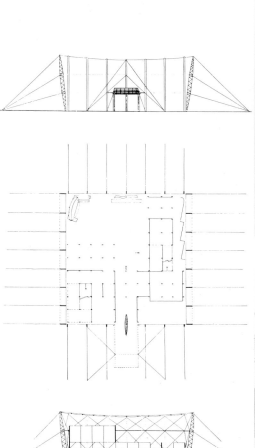

408 *Entry facade*
409 *Left, from top: main elevation, ground floor plan and section*
Right: main hall

Photos reproduced from Le Corbusier & P. Jeanneret 1934-1938, *Verlag für Architektur Artemis*

Aalto's definitive return to the precepts of Finnish National Romanticism came with his own house, designed and erected in Munkkiniemi, Helsinki in 1936. Thus the Villa Mairea designed and realized for Maire Gullichsen, between 1937 and 1939 was basically a further development of a *parti* which had been first tentatively broached by Aalto some four years before. The elaboration of this idea involved a deconstruction and reintegration of typological elements drawn from many different sources. In the first place, the fragmented U-shaped plan clearly derived from the typical Gothic Revival domestic layout which had already enjoyed a certain popularity with the National Romantic movement. On the other hand, as the recently published early projects would indicate, it was also related to the Mediterranean atrium and above all, to the random agrarian aggregations to be found in the traditional Karelian village.

This return to the vernacular is extremely subtle and involves a kind of bricollage in which various heterogenous parts are disjunctively impacted on each other, so that no one simplistic reading may be admitted. Moreover, one may discern an encoded revetment in this building where the material finish employed gives an indication as to the relative status of the respective elements. Thus the more honorific or *public* parts of the dwelling are finished in timber while the less honorific or *private* sectors, that is to say the bedroom and service wing, are of masonry and rendered externally in plaster.

410

This code is maintained even in Mrs. Gullichsen's studio which, set at the head of the plan, is treated like a public room. The reciprocal to this is the sauna attached to the "tail" of the composition; a form which, while of traditional rustic construction, is equally honorific and given its function, equally public. Nevertheless, this grass-roofed primitive hut, rooted in terms of both form and ritual, serves an appropriate foil to the refined syntax of the whole.

All this fails to exhaust the multiple layers of meaning in Aalto's work, for topographic metaphors patently abound in the Villa Mairea where the *porche-cochère* to cite only one instance, apparently refers to the Finnish landscape at two separate levels; first in the organic lakelike outline of its canopy (echoed in the similar profiles adopted for the studio and plunge-pool) and then in the uneven syncopated rhythm of the flanking bamboo screen, the irregular iterations of which surely allude to the random placing of pine trees in the surrounding woods.

Once accepted, the metaphors never cease to recochate — the one upon the other — so that no unequivocal connotation can be finally determined. Thus the curvilinear sculptural moulding of the return to the living room chimney breast remains open to multiple associations. It is at one and the same time not only a reference to the chimney in Gallen-Kallela's studio of 1898, but also an allusion to natural glacial form and finally a harking back to the lost profiles of classical architecture. In a similar way, the black lacquered steel columns to the main living volume, are both an allusion to nature, in their irregular grouping and an evocation of primitive construction, in their being bound together.

410 Overall view
411 Living room

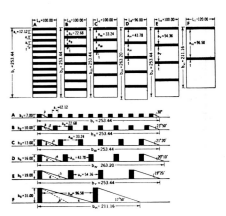

163 Gropius, CIAM Diagram, 1930. Zailenbau *layout showing alternative low-and high-rise settlement patterns.*

1. Socialist Culture and Industrial Norm: The Weimar Republic 1923-31

In the uneasy but fertile interregnum of the twenty-year period between the two world wars, modern architecture played a prominent role in the process of societal modernization. As one would expect, this role was greater where modernization was vigorously pursued by emerging societies rather than in the well established, colonial or industrial powers such as France and England. In the aftermath of the First World War, in Germany, Holland, Czechoslovakia and Sweden, the programme and content of the modern movement was enthusiastically received by the authorities and as such it became a vehicle for furthering the welfare state policies which these countries were variously attempting to advance. Thus in Gustav Stresemann's Weimar Republic — effectively established by the stabilization of the *Rentenmark* in November 1923 — modern architecture was extensively adopted by municipalities, co-operatives and trade unions as a singular sign and hope for the prospects of a new Germany. From Otto Haesler's Italienischer Garten built in Celle, Hannover in 1923 to Ernst May's Bruchfeldstrasse development realized in Frankfurt in 1925, aggregations of flat-roofed, white rendered houses came to be adopted as an appropriate format for the housing of the postwar era. Around the same time the traditional form of the perimeter block gave way to a more normative type of housing, then known as the *zeilenbau* or the row-house system. The row-house *siedlungen* or colonies built in Germany during the Weimar period still withstand scrutiny today as appropriate forms of inner-city development. In fact, Berlin still displays some of the finest suburbs built anywhere in Europe during the inter-war period.

The *zeilenbau* was predicated on an economy of repetition and above all on the provision of optimum sunlight and ventilation to every habitable room. The economy was assured by the orthogonal order of the units themselves, while sun and air were guaranteed by building parallel rows a standard distance apart and orienting them north-south so as to facilitate cross ventilation and the penetration of eastern and western light. Otto Haesler, working in Celle, was to establish the basic pattern of the Weimar Republic's *zeilenbau* system in his Georgsgarten estate of 1924 where the four-storey development comprised three and four bedroom apartments which were stacked in pairs, about access stairs. In general, these blocks were built to new standards of hygiene and convenience, although individual bathrooms were still considered to be more than what the society could afford. Despite this parsimony, radiant central heating, regarded as a minimum standard, was fitted throughout, just as steel casements were used for the fenestration and ergonomically planned kitchens were installed in accordance with the then current concern to Taylorise all forms of production. This applied even to the domain previously reserved for the most traditional rites of domesticity— namely the daily preparation of food. As Barbara Miller-Lane has pointed out in her study of 1968, *Architecture and Politics in Germany 1918-1945*, the labor-saving kitchen had an impact on the behaviour patterns of the ordinary German family, since up to the invention of the minimum kitchen, the living-kitchen (*wohnkuche*) had remained the family forum in the traditional dwelling. It seems fairly clear that the urbanization of the labor force was conceived by the technocratic elite as a normative procedure, as a prerequisite

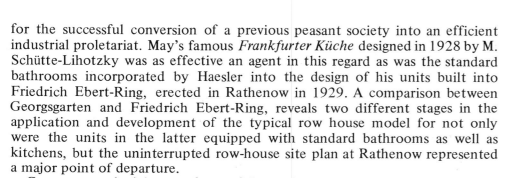

164 Haesler, Georgsgarten, Celle, near Hannover, 1924. Plan of typical 4-bed unit.

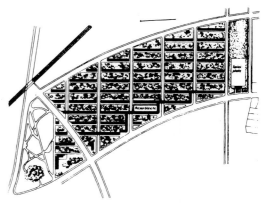

165 Haesler, Friedrich Ebert-Ring, Rathenow, 1928-29. Site plan.

for the successful conversion of a previous peasant society into an efficient industrial proletariat. May's famous *Frankfurter Küche* designed in 1928 by M. Schütte-Lihotzky was as effective an agent in this regard as was the standard bathrooms incorporated by Haesler into the design of his units built into Friedrich Ebert-Ring, erected in Rathenow in 1929. A comparison between Georgsgarten and Friedrich Ebert-Ring, reveals two different stages in the application and development of the typical row house model for not only were the units in the latter equipped with standard bathrooms as well as kitchens, but the uninterrupted row-house site plan at Rathenow represented a major point of departure.

Georgsgarten had been a form of "crisis housing" in the full sense of the term, for over two thirds of the site was devoted to allotments for the direct cultivation of home grown produce in order to supplement the scant food supply available in metropolitan districts in the aftermath of the War. Friedrich Ebert-Ring, on the other hand, displays a different type of anxiety; one which is ultimately concerned with the symbolic representation of the community, for it is clear that Haesler was motivated to reinforce the fragility of a physical composition which consisted of nothing more hierarchic than an endlessly repeated series of parallel, four-storey blocks. Haesler seems to have tried to compensate for this open-endedness by closing the open-ends of the rows with a continuous strip of terrace housing, thereby creating a zig-zag boundary connecting the nursery school and playground to the south with the public park located to the north.

This bounding device was applied on a number of other occasions, by

architects such as Fred Forbat in his Haselhorst development of 1928 or even Hans Scharoun in his plan for Siemensstadt, Berlin of 1929. However, there were those who regarded such last minute manipulations as being incapable of defining the physical identity of the community in a satisfactory way; above all such figures as Bruno Taut and Martin Wagner, who, in their Berlin-Britz development of 1925, were to structure an entire *siedlung* about a central horseshoe-shaped segment of housing, into which was integrated cooperative stores and other social amenities.

With Ernst May's appointment as city architect of Frankfurt in 1925, the building of workers' settlements began on an unprecedented scale. Due to his early training with both Theodor Fischer in Munich and Raymond Unwin in England, May's rationalism was tempered by a feeling for tradition. Where Haesler had created more or less open-ended layouts at Georgsgarten and Rathenow, May, closer to Taut and Wagner, was more concerned with the creation of bounded urban space. Thus May's first work for Frankfurt, his Bruchfeldstrasse development of 1925 (designed with C.H. Rudloff), consisted of a large courtyard, compiled of zig-zag housing enclosing a community center and an elaborate garden. In May's Frankfurt master plan of 1926, this bounded layout was followed by more generalised forms of settlement as in his Römerstadt, Praunheim, Westhausen and Hohenblick settlements built as parts of the Nidda Valley complex between 1926 and 1930. And yet even Römerstadt, despite its use of rationalized building components, maintained the neighbourhood as a clearly bounded domain.

The 15,000 units completed under May's direction account for more than

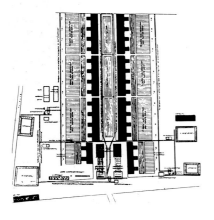

166 Gropius, Törten Housing, Dessau, 1926. Site plan. Spiral layout about the tracks of tower cranes.

90 percent of the housing built in Frankfurt during the Weimar period. This impressive figure could hardly have been achieved without May's insistence on efficiency in terms of both design and construction. Such an objective approach, reinforced by the realities of building costs, led inevitably to the formulation of *Existenzminimum* standards which became the contentious theme of the second CIAM Frankfurt Congress of 1929 (Congrès International d'Architecture Moderne). In contrast to Le Corbusier's idealistic appeal for an 'existence-maximum'. May's minimum standards were dependent on the extensive use of built-in storage, fittings and on the development of the *Frankfurter Küche.* As the world depression began to take hold, escalating costs prompted May to introduce prefabricated concrete construction – the so-called May system which was used after 1927 to construct both Praunheim and Hohenblick. Towards the end of his Frankfurt career May was forced to build to even more restricted standards of construction and space as in his very austere Goldstein Siedlung started in 1928.

Walter Gropius's almost equally reductive Törten housing (1926-28) represents a definitive stage in his own conversion to materialist planning standards, for Törten was determined not only by the standardization of its parts but also by the linear process of its prefabricated assembly; achieved, in this instance, by a travelling tower-crane running down the centre of the scheme. Some time in the second half of the twenties Gropius was to abandon his earlier formal approach to the organization of architectural form, still evident in his Dessau Bauhaus building finished in 1926. During this same period – just prior to his resignation from the Bauhaus in February 1928 – Gropius's views as to the reformation of the legal and social infrastructure of the society moved decidedly to the left of the typical Social Democratic position. This accounts, perhaps, for the radical tone of his essay *Sociological Premises of the Minimal Dwelling* published in 1929, in which he was to advance the radical notion of the *master-household*; a proposition which in its essentials was extremely close to the Russian Soviet concept of the *dom-kommuna.* Gropius elaborated the precepts of the *master-household* in the following terms:

Recognition of the shortcomings of the individual household awakens thoughts about new forms of centralised master households which partially relieve the individual woman of her domestic tasks by means of an improved centralised organisation which is capable of performing them better and more economically than she can perform them herself even when she applies all her efforts. The growing shortage of domestic help further emphasizes such desires. In the hard battle for subsistence faced by the entire family, the woman seeks ways of gaining free time for herself and her children while participating in gainful occupations and liberating herself from dependence upon the man. Thus this process does not seem to be motivated exclusively by the economic plight of urban populations, but it is the manifestation of an internal drive which is connected with the intellectual and economic emancipation of woman to equal partnership with man.... To allow for the increasing development of more pronounced individuality of life within society and the individual's justified demand for occasional withdrawal from his surroundings, it is necessary, moreover, to establish the following ideal minimum requirement: every adult shall have his own room, small though it may be!

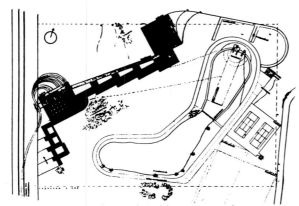

167 Meyer, Federal School of the GGTUF, Bernau, Germany, 1929. Site plan.

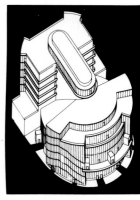

168 Gropius, Total Theatre for Erwin Piscator, 1927.

This essay was patently a response to the general urban chaos then emerging under the aegis of monopoly capitalism. Gropius argued that the government should prepare the ground for the *master-household*, first by preventing the waste of public funds for apartments of excessive size, while facilitating the financing of minimum dwellings, and then by reducing the initial costs of roads and utilities. He went on to insist that building sites should be removed from the hands of speculators and that zoning regulations and building codes should be liberalized.

While Gropius was never to realize a prototypical *masterhold* (the closest he came was the middle-class apartments he projected for the Wannsee in 1931) this document nonetheless demonstrates how close he was at the time to the materialist views held by his successor at the Bauhaus, namely the Swiss architect Hannes Meyer, for if we turn to Meyer's essay *Bauen* (Building) of 1928, we are at once struck by a certain similarity in both the substance and style of the argument:

The new house is a social enterprise. It gets rid of partial unemployment in the building industry during the off-seasons, and it does away with the odium attaching to unemployment relief projects. By putting housework on a rational basis it saves the housewife from slavery in the home, and by putting gardening on a rational basis it saves the householder from the dabbling of the small gardener. It is primarily a social enterprise because, like every DIN (*Deutsches Industrie Normen*) standard, it is the standardized industrial product of a nameless group of inventors.

Meyer was to argue that building was only organization — "social, technical, economic, psychological, organization" — and loseness in attitude was to reflect in the *constructivist* works which both Meyer and Gropius designed during the late twenties; a fact which is evident when one compares, for example, Meyer's school for the General German Trade Unions Federation, built at Bernau, Berlin in 1930 to Gropius's 1927 Total Theatre, projected for Erwin Piscator.

The Total Theatre was Gropius's most unequivocal constructivist work in as much as it was designed to satisfy Vsevolod Meyerhold's concept of the bio-mechanical stage as a theatre of action. The actor-acrobat was the ideal type of this theatre, in which a circuslike gestural performance was invariably presented on an apron stage. Meyerhold's prescriptions for a bio-mechanical production — his October Theatre Manifesto of 1920 — made a certain political content more or less mandatory. To satisfy this agitatory programme Gropius attempted to provide Piscator with an auditorium which could be rapidly transformed into any one of the three traditional forms; the proscenium, the apron and the arena. How this provision was to be made, has been best described in Gropius's own words:

A complete transformation of the building occurs by turning the stage platform and part of the orchestra through 180°. Then the former proscenium stage becomes a central arena entirely surrounded by rows of spectators! This can even be done during the play . . . This attack on the spectator, moving him during the play, and unexpectedly shifting the stage area, alters the existing scale of values, presenting to the spectator a new consciousness of space and making him participate in the action.

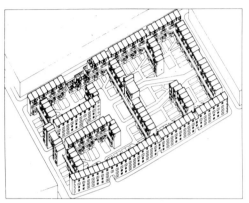

169 Brinkman, Spangen Perimeter Block, Rotterdam, 1920.

170 Oud, Tusschendijken Housing, Rotterdam, 1920-23.
Interior of perimeter block.

2.   From Perimeter Block to Open City: Holland 1915-39

By virtue of its neutrality in the First World War, Holland was able to sustain a continuously progressive housing policy from the passing of the *Woningwet* legislation of 1901, right through to the outbreak of the Second World War. Naturally the greatest impact of this legislation was felt in the two major cities of the country: that is to say in the contributions that numerous architects made to the building out of Hendrik Petrus Berlage's 1915 plan for Amsterdam South and in the various perimeter blocks and garden city developments which Michiel Brinkman and J.J.P. Oud achieved on the outskirts of Rotterdam. From a typological point of view the initial Dutch model for urban housing was the perimeter block which was maintained as a preferred type until the late twenties when Oud, Stam and Van Tijen began to project the Weimar row-house pattern as a new prototypical form.

Apart from Michel de Klerk's highly expressive Eigen Haard development built in Amsterdam in 1917, the most advanced perimeter block of the immediate postwar era was Michiel Brinkman's double-decked, four-storey scheme erected in Spangen, Rotterdam, in 1920. In many ways Spangen has proven to be one of the most remarkable models built in the inter-war period, since while conforming to the street pattern profiles of the surrouding fabric, it also asserted itself as a 'city in miniature'; that is as a microcosm with an internal sequence of garden courts and its own elevated pedestrian street system focused on a central laundry and communal block. This one-off experiment was followed in Rotterdam by a continuous piece of perimeter urbanism; that is by Oud's eight block development known as Tusschendijken,

under construction from 1920 to 1923. Aside from their built-up urban areas, the Dutch also projected denser and more urbane versions of the Anglo-Saxon garden city: most notably in Jan Wils's two-storey Papaverhof estate built at Daal-en-Berg near The Hague in 1920, in Dick Greiner's Betondorp, built between 1922 and 1928 and, last but not least in Oud's Kiefhoek estate in Rotterdam, structured as an urban village and under construction from 1925 to 1929.

The second half of the twenties, however, saw the gradual abandonment of continuous urban fabric in favour of free-standing blocks and slabs. The first theoretical formulation of this open city pattern came with Mart Stam's 1926 proposal for the Rokin district of Amsterdam, where Stam sought to subvert the existing context of the city by introducing a continuous elevated office block into the middle of a traditional thoroughfare. Stam projected this mega-building as being served by a suspended mono-rail; the ground then being given over to display, parking and pedestrian movement. Stam's Rokin project was a constructivist work; that is to say it intended the reduction of built form to the status of being a machine. Apart from this it demonstrated Stam's concept of the 'open city' of which he wrote:

The ever increasing volume of traffic due to the growing economic struggle makes traffic organization the determining factor in architectural town planning. Architectural thinking must break free from aesthetic attitudes left over from earlier generations. The conception of a town as an enclosed space is one of these and must give way to the open town.

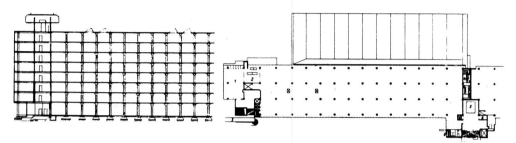

171 *Brinkman & Van der Vlugt (with Stam), Van Nelle Factory, Rotterdam, 1927. Plan and elevation.*

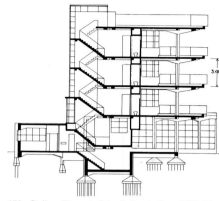

172 *Duiker, Open-air School, Amsterdam, 1928-30. Section.*

Throughout the twenties progressive architects in Holland — figures such as Oud, L.C. van der Vlugt and above all, Stam, pursued a functional form of expression which was patently influenced by the Constructivist movement in Russia. This was never more true than in the case of Stam, who after having had contact in Germany with the Russian avant-garde artist El Lissitzky, returned to Holland in 1925 to serve as job captain on the reinforced concrete, mushroom columned Van Nelle factory, completed in Rotterdam in 1929. The exposed structure and the moving glass conveyors were patently key elements in the Constructivist aesthetic of this tea, tobacco and coffee plant, which is still used in much the same way today as it was fifty years ago.

Despite Stam's evident participation in this design, the role of Van der Vlugt can hardly be discounted since he went on to design functionalist works of comparable objectivity without the aid of Stam; his steel-framed Feyenoord Stadium and his Bergpolder flats both built in Rotterdam in the early thirties. All the same, Stam has to be credited for consolidating this functionalist tendency even if his extremism served to distance him from certain members of the Rotterdam *Opbouw* group — first constituted in 1920 and later to become part of the Dutch wing of CIAM. Some of the *Opbouw* members such as Brinkman and Van der Vlugt and their main client Cees van der Leeuw, sought to transcend functionalism through a concern for universal, not to say mystical values. It is somehow incongruous that all three men were members of the Dutch theosophical society and that Van der Leeuw was to build a functionalist retreat at Ommen for Krishnamurti and his followers.

While distant from theosophy, similar spiritual concerns seem to have been latent in the functionalism of Johannes Duiker and Bernard Bijvoet who departed from their early Wrightian style in an asymmetrical house (influenced by De Klerk) that they built at Aalsmeer, in 1924. This monopitched house, with its exposed cylindrical staircase, initiated the Nieuwe Zakelijkheid period of Duiker's career. This period culminated in two reinforced concrete and glass structures which have a decidedly constructivist character; his Zonnestraal Sanatorium built at Hilversum in 1927 and his Open-air School erected in Amsterdam in 1930. Despite his concern for direct programmatic expression, as in his handling of the asymmetrical gymnasium wing which protrudes from the symmetrical mass of the Amsterdam School, Duiker's idealism found expression in his preference for the butterfly-plan. Only towards the end of his life did he abandon this preferred plan-form in favour of a more empirical approach, evident say, in his Cineac Cinema erected in Amsterdam in 1934.

3. Modernization and Machine Form: Czechoslovakia 1918-35

Created as a result of nearly twenty years of unrelenting political agitation on the part of the Czech nationalists Tomas Masaryk and Edward Benes, the Czechoslovak Republic was patently part of the political restructuring of Eastern Europe, after the end of the First World War. The consolidation and development of an independent Czechoslovakia under Masaryk's timely leadership (president of the country from 1918 to 1935) necessitated a governmental policy of societal modernization which not only provided credit for the further exploitation of Czechoslovakia's industrial wealth, but also

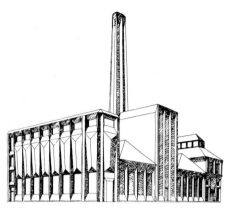

173 *Chochol, study for a factory, 1912.*

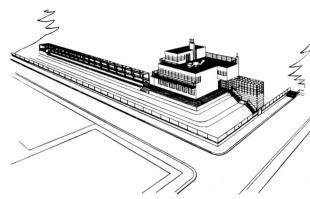

174 *Krejcar, project for Vancura Villa, Zbraslav, 1923.*

maintained a progressive, welfare state approach towards the management of an industrial, multi-racial society.

An independent Czech avant-gardist manner in architecture had already been demonstrated in Prague prior to the 1914-18 war, above all in the separate but related practices of Josef Gočár and Josef Chochol. Gočár's career begins with the Wagnerian Wenke Store built in Jaromer in 1910 and with his strange so-called House of the Black Virgin Mary completed in Prague in 1912. Chochol, on the other hand, tended to be more avant-gardist from the outset above all in his famous Cubistic villas, built in 1913, at the foot of the Vysehrad hill in Prague and bearing a certain resemblance to Raymond Duchamp-Villon's *La Villa Cubiste* exhibited in Paris in 1912. Gočár and Chochol pioneered a post-cubistic syntax which was to be derived in part from Franco-Czech experiments in the field of sculpture and in part from the local Baroque tradition.

Aside from its preferences for prismatic solids, Czech architectural cubism favoured the plastic animation of the surface in terms of faceted planes cast or rendered, in either concrete or plaster. This abstract, nationalistic and yet antirational expression commanded a considerable following including such architects as the prime theorist of the new movement, Pavel Janák and the young Jiri Kroha whose 1921 competition entry for a regional theatre in Olomonc was nationalist in its assembly of grotesque Cubistic form derived from elements in the Czech Gothic and Baroque traditions.

As Dostál, Pechar and Procházka have remarked in their 1980 study, *Modern Architecture in Czechoslovakia*, the conceptual basis of this cubistic expression was basically developed by Janák and Vlastislav Hoffman in the articles which they published between 1911 and 1913 in *Umelecky mesicnik* (Artistic Monthly) which was the joint organ of a group of painters, sculptors and architects known as the Group of Creative Artists, founded in 1911. Janák's formalist views on these appear in his essays, "The Prism and the Pyramid" of 1912 and "The Facade Revival" of 1913, have been recently paraphrased by Ivan Margolius in the following terms:

The Greek, Gothic and Baroque styles used elements based on prism or pyramid forms. The cubist architecture is related to both of them and is based on a positive relationship with mass and a materialistic notion of art. The new trend is concerned above all with form, the material is not considered important; what we see is only the form.

As Margolius explains, the only personality to develop this Cubistic base after the First World War, was Kroha for the sentimental ethos latent in Czech Cubism seemed to degenerate at this point into either the decorative approach of Josip Plecnik's Sacre-Coeur church built at Prague-Vinohardy in 1932 or into that strange style known as Rondo-Cubism, as in Gočár's Legiobank of 1923.

The years 1923 to 1925 are crucial for the evolution of rationalist architecture in Czechoslovakia for 1923 sees the twenty-eight-year-old Jaromir Krejcar's first independent work; his Vancura Villa projected for Zbraslav in 1923. At virtually the same time Kroha starts to design on a technical school which is finally built in Mlada-Boleslav in 1935.

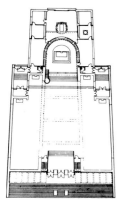

175 Gočár, St. Wenceslas Church, Prague-Vrsovice, 1928. Ground floor plan.

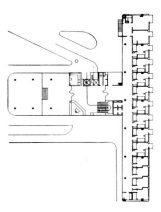

176 Krejcar, Sanatorium Machnac, Trenčiaske Teplice, 1931-32. Ground floor plan.

1924 sees the start of one of the most precocious works of the Czech modern movement, namely the famous Prague Sampler Fair building which was built to the designs of Oldrich Tyl and Josef Fuchs and was to remain under construction until 1928. With its pinwheeling mass, stabilized into a perimeter block and its extensive areas of curtain wall, amply furnished with neon signs, this building appears as a "constructivist" work *avant la lettre*.

In 1927 Gočár was to join the rationalist ranks with his reinforced concrete kindergarten built in that year at Hradec Kralove: — a design which is reminiscent in many respects of the rational classicism of Auguste Perret. In this regard it is interesting to remark on the different forms of rationalism adopted by Gočár and Chochol in their respective works of the late twenties, for where Gočár consolidated his position as a "rational-classicist" above all in his St. Wenceslas Church at Prague-Vrsovice of 1928, Chochol was to embrace the full rhetoric of Constructivism in his project for a Liberated Theatre in Prague of 1927. Last but by no means least among the prewar Czech Cubists who became constructivists in the twenties, recognition has to be made of Pavel Janák who clearly embraced functionalism in his layout of the Na Babe housing estate built in the suburbs of Prague between 1928 and 1932.

The professional high point of the Czech architectural avant-garde came in those nine years between 1928 and 1937 when the continued prosperity of the country, the new political circumstances and the general acceptance of modernization, afforded ample opportunities for architects to build at a generous scale and in this regard Krejcar's practice is exemplary. In 1931 Krejcar received the largest commission of his career, the Machnac spa

building to be erected in Trenciaske Teplice. This 50-room sanatorium, typified Krejcar's constructivist, not to say "biological" approach to planning as did Bohuslav Fuchs's Vesna School built in Brno in the previous year. Both are examples of that pinwheel approach to the organization of complex institutions which Gropius had first demonstrated in his designs for the Dessau Bauhaus.

From the very beginning of his independent professional career, Krejcar was extremely polemical in both a political and cultural sense as we may judge from his editorship of the Marxist Czech Artists Union journal *Zivot* (Life) in 1922, for it was through the pages of *Zivot* that Russian Constructivism and the work of Le Corbusier first came to the notice of Czechoslovakian architects. Krejcar was equalled as a polemicist by the surrealist writer and critic Karel Tiege who first turned to architecture when he assumed the editorship of the magazine *Stavba* (Architecture) in 1923. Four years later he broadened his cultural scope by editing the official organ of the Devenstil Group (International Union of Artists of the Revolutionary Avant Garde) — a journal which was entitled *RED*. Two years later in 1929 he added the editorship of another architectural publication to his multifarious activities, the series known as *MSA* and in 1932 he started to edit the Left Front publication entitled *Za Socialistickon Architektura* (On Socialist Architecture). Of this intense polemical activity Dostál, Pechar and Procházka have written:

At the beginning of the thirties the initiative work of the theorists of functional architecture, headed by Karel Tiege, gave rise to an entirely original and independent theoretical and artistic programme of the Czechoslovak generation between the two wars which sought new stimuli for architecture in its social basis. The architects began to realize the social position and mission of architecture. The Association of Modern Culture (*Devenstil*) which was the principal representative of functionalist ideas in the Czechoslovak culture of the twenties, gave rise to the architectural association of the Left Front, and in 1932, the Congress of Left Architects, prepared by Jan Gillar and Josef Kittrich, saw the foundation of the Association of Socialist Architects . . . A great sense of social values of architecture, linked with the requirements of progressive social changes, was a specific feature of the Czechoslovak architecture of the thirties, the more so as it was suspended in other fields of the European avant-garde, whose unity of ideas was mostly disintegrated. The Bauhaus was closed, the dynamic movement of the Soviet constructivism dissolved, the prominent personalities of functionalism were gradually leaving Europe and emigrating overseas.

The industrialist Tomas Bata represented in his extraordinary career the progressive, yet ambiguous, ethos of the Czechoslovak state throughout the inter-war period. Bata's fortune and his position of industrial and political ascendancy derived directly from the shoe factory that he and his half brother Antonin had founded at Zlín, in Moravia in 1908. Although they were already producing 10,000 pairs of shoes per day and employing a staff of 4,000 workers by the time that the state was founded in 1918, they did not fully engage in the Taylorization of shoe production until 1922 when after an extremely rapid and draconian reorganization, they were down to 1,800 workers and producing 8,000 pairs of shoes per day. And yet this output was nothing compared to the vast expansion they would achieve in the next six

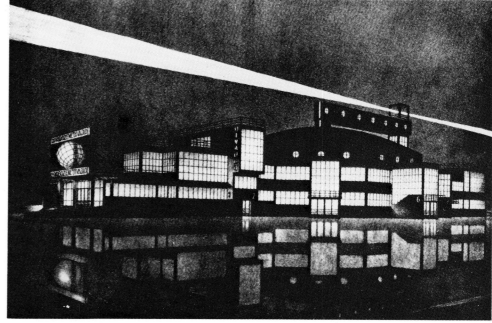

177 Chochol, Liberated Theatre project, Prague, 1927.

178 Gahura, Bata skyscraper project, Brno, 1928.

179 Le Corbusier, Bata Pavilion project, Paris World Exhibition, 1937. Sections with interior murals.

years when Bata expanded his production to become the largest manufacturer of shoes in the world, with some 12,000 employees producing 75,000 pairs of shoes per day. The key to the accelerated growth and success of the company was the so-called Bata System of production in which the labour force was broken down into a series of autonomous ateliers. These ateliers were not only self-disciplining, but their members also participated in a mandatory profit sharing and savings scheme, in which the workers stood to benefit directly on a daily basis, from optimizing the productivity of the firm. This paternalistic and progressive system that Bata liked to describe as "a union between reorganised capital and advanced industrial welfare," seems to have caused him to be progressive in other fields besides industry, and to this end he became a patron of modern architecture beginning as early as 1911 with the hiring of the prime Czech pupil of the Austrian *Wagnerschule*, namely Jan Kotera who was asked to redesign the interior of the Bata family home. While Kotera went on to design a worker's garden city for Bata in 1918, it was not until 1925 that the firm established a full cultural policy with regard to architecture and design, selecting Kotera's pupil Frantishek Gahura as the principal architect to the company. Immediately Gahura began to design and build new reinforced concrete factories at Zlín and in 1926 he turned his hand to the design of a worker's garden city, consisting of 800 dwellings to be built in the village of Tlusta, outside Zlín.

As Bata began to diversify both his ownership and the scope of his production, acquiring farms for leather and food and coal mines for energy and entering into the production of brushes, rubber toys and linoleum, the scope of architectural work increased at such a rate that Gahura was soon joined by the architects Vladimir Karjik and Antonin Vitek. Most of the architectural designs produced in Gahura's office during this period were concerned with maintaining the house style of the Bata shoe stores, which were all modelled on the curtain-walled building which Ludvik Kysela had built for Bata in Wenceslas Square, Prague in 1929. The scope of this Bata distribution system was vast, for by the time of Tomas Bata's death in a plane crash in Zlín in 1935, the firm had 2,000 outlets in Czechoslovakia and 2,000 more in the rest of the world.

This was also the period during which Le Corbusier became involved with the Bata organization, by being commissioned to design a standard system of shops for the future expansion of the Bata market. Perhaps the most remarkable project of this period was his sketch for a publicity pavilion in which he tried to represent every aspect of the Bata enterprise. For reasons which remain obscure, none of this work was every carried out — not even Le Corbusier's designs for a factory and a workers city in France, which was later to become known as Bataville when it was finally built at Hellocourt in France in 1932. In this instance, the architect was again Gahura, who went on to design in 1934, a definitive plan for expansion of Zlín into a regional industrial city, capable of housing some 100,000 people. Here again, Le Corbusier was to add the hopeful post-scriptum in his own plan for the linear development of Zlín, in 1935.

As a consequence of all this, Zlín, while never that sophisticated from a planning point of view, became nonetheless an architectural and social mecca

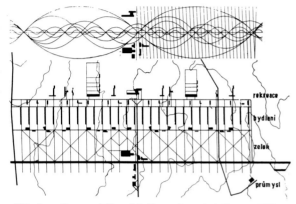

180 Janu, Stursa and Vozenilek, linear city project, Prague, 1932.

for those benighted leftist, modern architects who were either totally constrained in the East due to the stylistic restrictions imposed by the Social Realism of the Soviet Union or alternatively unemployed in the West due to the impact of the economic depression. Like the Van Nelle factory, but on a larger scale, the curtain-walled factories of Zlín — surrounded by modest but well organized worker's settlements and set amid well-groomed lawns and avenues of poplars — became, for sufficient reason, the ideal "green factory" from both an architectural and social point of view. Here May Day was celebrated by the entire plant including the directorate as a kind of social democratic success which despite the paternalism and certain para-military overtones could still be claimed as a triumph of utopian socialism. There was no doubt that Zlín lent conviction to later left wing Czech proposals for new forms of urban expansion which, while based on Soviet pioneering, were at the same time inspired by the reality of Zlín. This is suggested by the urbanistic projects produced by an architectural collaborative known as PAS, (Karel Janu, Jiri Stursa and Jiri Vozenilek) who, in 1932, projected an exceptionally well worked out linear satellite city for the expansion of Prague.

4. Revisionist Modernism and the International Stage:
Paris and New York, 1937 and 1939

In 1932, in the very year that Philip Johnson and Henry-Russell Hitchcock proclaimed the emergence of the International Style, the repercussions of the 1929 Wall Street crash arrived in France, reducing French industrial production to two thirds of its record level three years before. With a mere 300,000 unemployed the social impact in France was at first relatively slight compared to the 6,000,000 who were already out of work in Germany. Nonetheless the crisis was profoundly disturbing for a late nineteenth-century society, which barely fourteen years earlier had emerged from the most violent, divisive and costly war in its history. This is reflected in the fact that after 1932, French governments came and went with alarming rapidity, as one political scandal succeeded another, culminating in the financial and social debacle of the 1933 Stavisky affair which understandably served to feed the flames of French anti-Semitism. By 1934 the rate of exploitation of the workforce had greatly increased with coal miners receiving less than half of what they had earned in 1929 for the same amount of production. The successive political triumphs of Mussolini and Hitler, the first ultimately in 1928 and the second in 1933 had the effect of strengthening the demagogic appeal of the right which in France was represented primarily by Charles Maurras's *L'Action Francaise*. The popular success of the right wing and above all of *Action Francaise* finally compelled the rival left wing factions to organize themselves into a united front, the so-called *Front Populaire* which was created on the 14th of July, 1935, by the formal union of the Socialist, Communist and Radical parties. Enjoying the support of a wide spectrum of the society including the intelligentsia of the international left, Leon Blum went to power as the head of the Popular Front government in June 1936. As France's first socialist prime minister, Blum's authority lasted no more than a year, although he was nonetheless able to introduce important social reforms, including the much disputed 40-hour working week. In March 1936, however,

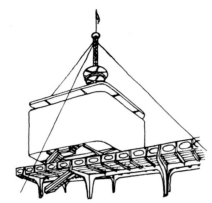

181 Kreskar, Czechoslovak Pavilion, Paris World Exhibition, 1937.

with Hitler's remilitarization of the Rhineland and with the outbreak of the Spanish Civil War in the following July, the stage was set not only for the demise of the Popular Front, but also for the eventual outbreak of the Second World War.

The Exposition Universelle staged in Paris in 1937 reflected the national and international political scene formed by the depression and by the inevitable disruptions of societal modernization. It also revealed the policy of cultural revisionism which was adopted by such a wide spectrum of political constituencies, after the generally progressive and euphoric acceptance of modernism which seems to have been somewhat universal in the previous decade. The 1937 Paris Exhibition encapsulated, in so many ways, the diverse impact that these ideological transformations were to have on the art of architecture. It revealed to a remarkable degree the way in which many countries had either reformed or renounced the early functionalist precepts of modernism.

No building in the 1937 Exposition Universelle was as modern as Krescar's Czechoslovak Pavilion which was erected about an exposed steel frame and clad in a gasketed metal skin. Even by today's sophisticated technical capacity, this structure commands respect for its collage of advanced technological components comprising a riveted cantilevered frame, a suspended deck panelled in glass lenses, delicate neon-lit display panels and a cable bracing system for the support of the central mast and viewing platform. In terms of technical rhetoric this structure was clearly an advance of the avant-garde Constructivist syntax, as this had been formulated by the Vesnin brothers in their Pravda project of 1924.

Nothing could have been further from this constructivist ethos than the 1937 Soviet Pavilion which was an attempt at consolidating the new Social Realist manner. The intent was to make a style which would be readable not only in traditional terms but also in terms of streamlined modern form. Iofan's pavilion came across as a monumental *tour de force*, as a triumphant symbol of the Russian revolution. It was surmounted by the colossal figures of two workers, a man and a woman, bearing a hammer and sickle between them and rushing forward into the ideal socialist future. This crowning symbolic group poised above a "jazz moderne" base, was countermanded both politically and formally by the only other official political pavilion in the exhibition, namely Albert Speer's Neoclassical pylon housing the National Exhibit of the Third Reich. For polemical reasons this structure was sited deliberately opposite the Russian pavilion. In this way the main route of the site, extending from the Eiffel Tower to the Seine, was crossed at midpoint by an axis of symbolic confrontation; an opposition which had its collary in the geopolitics of the time. It is characteristic of the appeasement policies of the thirties that one of the major exhibits in the Third Reich pavilion, namely Speer's project for the Nazi Party rally site – the so-called *Reichsparteitag Gelände*, in Nuremberg – was to be awarded one of the coveted prizes of the exhibition.

The complexity of German architectural culture at this time was also reflected in the German section of the International Pavilion, wherein Mies van der Rohe, on the eve of his migration to the United States, demonstrated

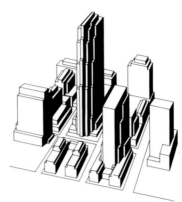

once again his neo-Suprematist taste in a sequence of exhibition stands displaying synthetic plastics, metalurgical goods and scientific equipment. However, Industrial Modernism and State Neoclassicism by no means exhausted the full range of architectural expression institutionalized or condoned under the aegis of the Third Reich. There was also the so-called *Heimatstil* manner which was categorically reserved for worker's housing, that is to say the fake, pitched-roof vernacular in which Speer's own house in Obersalzburg was built in 1937. Even this failed to meet the full range of ideological settings apparently required by the myths of National Socialism. Hence architects were required to simulate mediaeval castles in their designs for the party training headquarters, while Rococo decor was demanded for the recreational facilities of Robert Ley's "strength-through-joy" culture.

It is of import that Speer's Zeppelinfeld stadium in Nuremberg (1938) which was built as part of the Nazi Party rally site, should be conceived as much from the point of view of camera angles as it was in terms of monumental architecture. Zeppelinfeld marks that watershed in twentieth-century culture when the media, that is to say radio and film, took over from architecture as the most effective persuasive instrument of power. At the same time, it is significant that while Mies van der Rohe had become *persona non grata* in the Third Reich as a whole, the functionalist industrial manner that he had helped to evolve could still be employed under the aegis of the National Socialists, since they were realist enough to realize that this was the most economic way to build in the service of industrial production, and that industry hardly needed specific forms of ideological representation.

Although the all pervasive thrust of a totalitarian ideology was absent from the American Art Deco or Jazz Moderne skyscraper culture of the Depression years, it is nonetheless possible to argue that Speer's Zeppelinfeld and Raymond Hood's Rockefeller Center, (the first stage of which was completed in New York in 1930) were to have one thing in common, namely the deference these different architectural expressions were compelled to make to the growing influence of the media. And while Hood may well have been innocent in this regard, the Rockefeller's were not, and it is surely no accident that the principal client in the Rockefeller Center became the Radio Corporation of America or that Roxy's (S.L. Rothafel) conception of the Radio City Music Hall combined, the traditional, representational forms of architecture and theatre with the quintessential media triumph of the film. It was just this apparently popular, not to say populist, need for representation so evidently beyond the capacities of the modern movement, that prompted Sigfried Giedion, Fernand Léger and José Luis Sert to draft in 1943, their *Nine Points on Monumentality*, wherein the first two articles read:

(1) Monuments are human and marks which man have created as symbols for their ideals, for their aims and for their actions. They are intended to outlive the period which originated them, and constitute a heritage for future generations. As such they form a link between the past and the future.
(2) Monuments are the expression of man's highest cultural needs. They have to satisfy the eternal demand of the people for the translation of their collective force into symbols. The most vital monuments are those which express the feeling and thinking of this collective

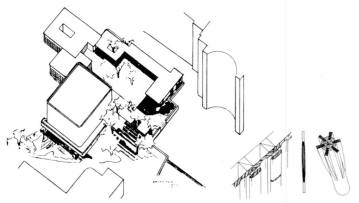

183 Aalto, Finnish Pavilion, Paris World Exhibition, 1937. Axonometric and structural details.

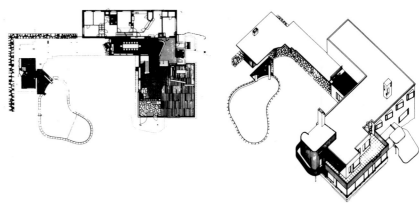

184 Aalto, Villa Mairea, Noormarkku, Finland, 1937-39. Axonometric and living floor plan.

force—the people.

It was out of a similar concern for the ethos of his country, that the Finnish architect Alvar Aalto chose to modify the international modernism which he had largely embraced in his competition entry for the Paimio Sanatorium of 1929, although even in this building there were already inflections which removed it from the main stream of the International Style. Aalto's categoric departure from international functionalism came with two closely related works, his own house and studio completed in the suburb of Munkkiniemi, Helsinki in 1936 and his prize-winning design entitled *Le Bois est en Marche* submitted as a design for the Finnish Pavilion to be built at the Exposition Universelle, Paris of 1937. While both works were a return to the irregular, aggregate plan form of the Arts and Crafts house, Aalto's Pavilion manifested the characteristic head and tail format; the "tail" being a long architectural promenade, while the "head" was a blank, three-storey high, top-lit cubic exhibition building. Aside from this, Aalto's pavilion was a demonstration in modern timber technique, thereby stressing the key resource of Finnish economy, while simultaneously asserting timber fabric as the only material which was capable of expressing Finnish national culture.

Aalto was not only committed to the craft traditions of his country but also to its geological and topographic nature. He was preoccupied with creating a *modern* architecture which would appear as though it had arisen out of the site or had emerged as a slowly assembled and hand-crafted settlement. This led him to reinterpret the precepts of Finnish National

Romanticism and to give particular emphasis to the agrarian building of Eastern Finland. These concerns become increasingly evident in his work over the next decade — that is from the Villa Mairea of 1939 to the Säynätsalo Town Hall of 1949. That the typical Karelian farm suggested to Aalto the possibility of combining in a single work both rustic form and a classic feeling for the grandeur of an archaic site is suggested by his essay *Architecture In Karelia* of 1941:

The first essential feature of interest is Karelian architecture's uniformity. There are few comparable examples in Europe. It is a pure forest-settlement architecture in which wood dominates almost one hundred percent both as material and as jointing method. From the roof, with its massive system of joists, to the movable building parts, wood dominates, in most cases naked, without the dematerializing effect that a layer of paint gives. In addition, wood is often used in as natural proportions as possible, on the scale typical of the material. A dilapidated Karelian village is somehow similar in appearance to a Greek ruin, where, also, the material's uniformity is a dominant feature, though marble replaces wood . . . Another significant special feature is the manner in which the Karelian house has come about, both its historical development and its building methods. Without going into ethnographic details, we can conclude that the inner system of construction results from a methodical accommodation to circumstance. The Karelian house is in a way a building that begins with a single modest cell or with an imperfect embryo building, a shelter for man and animals, and which then figuratively speaking grows year by year. The expanded Karelian house can in a way be compared with a biological cell formation. The possibility of a larger and more complete building is always open.

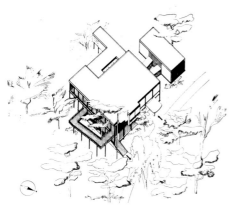

185 *Sakakura, Japanese Pavilion, Paris World Exhibition. 1937.*

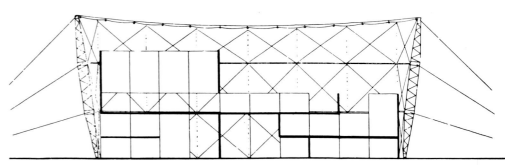

186 *Le Corbusier, Pavillon des Temps Nouveaux, Paris World Exhibition, 1937. Section.*

A nationally indentifiable modern manner was a typical concern of other pavilions built for the 1937 Paris exhibition. It was certainly present in Junzo Sakakura's Japanese Pavilion which was at once both modern and traditional. A traditional reference of Sakakura's which remained at the same time modern was his manner of combining standard steel framing with asbestos cement sheet, as though this lightweight system was the modern equivalent of traditional Japanese construction. Sakakura's pavilion may be thus seen as a technocratic version of the so-called *Sukiya* style, which was later developed by Isoya Yoshida into an exaggerated national manner. The most traditional feature in Sakakura's Paris pavilion was surely the horizontal balustrading to the exposed ramp system which was destined to become a cliche in Japanese modern architecture after the end of the Second World War. A Cubistic licence permitted Sakakura to combine materials and techniques drawn from quite different cultural sources. He would have become familiar with this *collagiste* approach during his apprenticeship with Le Corbusier, lasting from 1931 to 1936. It is significant that Sakakura worked for the progenitor of machinist architecture ("the house is a machine for living in") at a time when Le Corbusier was moving away from doctrinaire Purism towards a subtle combination of traditional and modern architectonic elements, such as we find in the weekend house which he built in the suburbs of Paris in 1935. In this diminutive house, concrete barrel vaults, rubble stone walling, brickwork, plate glass, glass blocks, plywood sheathing and machine-made ceramic tiles were combined into a convincing unity. In a similar vein Sakakura was to apply a form of *adhoc* oriental latticework to the sides of the tea salon which

overlooked the traditional Japanese garden of the pavilion, although this pattern did not apparently derive from traditional Japanese motifs.

In some respects Sakakura's pavilion announced the end of the inter-war Japanese modern movement; a movement which had started with the foundation of the Japanese Secession in 1920, under the leadership of Mamoru Yamada and Sutemi Horiguchi. This development was to reach its height, as a functionalist mode in Tetsuro Yoshida's General Post Office building erected next to Tokyo's central station in 1932; a building which was highly regarded by Bruno Taut when he came to Japan in 1933

With the banking collapse of 1929, the failure of the Japanese silk industry in 1930, and the military right-wing coup d'état of 1932, followed by the invasion of Manchuria — Japanese official cultural policy became unequivocally nationalist. The first architectural manifestation of this swing to the right was Katsushige Takanashi's 1937 design for a memorial pavilion dedicated to the creation of the Japanese Empire. Takanashi's project was designed in the extremely monumental Imperial Crown Style; a style which was also adopted in Hitoshi Watanabe's National Museum completed in Tokyo, in 1937, and in his Dai-ichi Insurance Company building erected in the capital city in the following year. In all these works, the monumentality was in part justified as an effective means of anti-siesmic construction.

It was not that functionalist architecture disappeared from Japan overnight, but rather that, as in the Third Reich, it was kept in the background as a mode of organization and expression which was suitable for utilitarian programmes. The provision of worker's housing in Japan was seen as a corollary

187 Le Corbusier, Maison at Mathes, 1935.

of industrial production and hence as something which could be carried in a functionalist manner.

Built for the same Exposition Universelle of 1937 (but on a separate site) Le Corbusier's Pavillon des Temps Nouveaux embodied much of the ethos of the Front Populaire, although the specific programme of the pavilion's exhibit was Syndicalist and Saint Simonian, rather than Social Democratic in the accepted sense. It is clear that this small pavilion was conceived as a kind of surrogate religious structure in as much as it housed the icons and edicts of a new socio-urban order, as this had already been formulated by Le Corbusier in his Ville Radieuse proposal of 1933. The almost ecclesiastical organization of the tent interior — the entry on axis past the "machinist-cross" of a model aircraft — established certain liturgical connotations. This aura was reinforced by the Athens Charter of 1933 preposterously mounted on axis like an altar-piece. On the left hand side was a rostrum or pulpit, covered by a baldachino, or rather by an acoustical shell on which was inscribed the litany of the faith. This slogan had been borrowed directly from the Front Populaire; it read, "a new era has commenced — an era of solidarity."

This was by no means the only religious aspect of this temporary tentlike building, for the actual structure — the system of suspended canvas and pylons braced by wire cables — was clearly derived from that reconstruction of the Hebrew temple in the wilderness which Le Corbusier had featured in the pages of *Vers une Architecture.* It is now clear that the Pavillon des Temps Nouveaux was the prototypical Corbusian ecclesiastical form which would be reworked in 1950 as the Ronchamp Chapel.

In 1937, however, given the density of the nationalist, political and machinist metaphors, this liturgical reference remained rather obscure. It was literally overlaid by the tricolor subdivision of the front canvas panels of the tent into blue, white and red, and by the left-wing symbol of the red central pivoting door and by the machinist metaphor evident in the aerofoil section adopted for this element. But possibly the most critical aspect of this work (like that of Le Corbusier's weekend house of two years before) was its fabrication out of archaic material and the polemical combination of this material with the modern technique of steel wire suspension. There was in all this, as in Le Corbusier's mono-pitched house built at Mathes in 1935, an indication that progressive development in the future would not reside in the simple-minded optimization of industrial technology, but rather in a judicious combination of modern technique with traditional, not to say primitive methods of construction. By 1937 Le Corbusier was well aware that the future lay not with optimized technology but rather with an intermediate, not to say existential technology, grounded in necessity. A similar level of intermediate technology was evoked by the canvas covered *al fresco* auditorium of José Luis Sert's Spanish pavilion, erected for the same 1937 Exhibition and representing the army of the Spanish Popular Front, then still engaged in the bitter struggle of the Spanish Civil War. This pavilion was focused on Picasso's *Guernica,* which had just then been painted in commemoration of the German terroristic bombing of the Basque town of Guernica, in August 1936.

The picture of the state of international modern architecture on the eve of

188 *Niemeyer, Costa and Wiener, Brazilian Pavilion, New York World's Fair, 1939. Axonometric.*

the World War may perhaps be best completed by the Finnish and Brazilian Pavilions that Alvar Aalto and Oscar Niemeyer contributed to the New York World's Fair of 1939, for both exhibits represented major departures from functionalism. Starting from quite different points of departure, both men were to arrive at very fluid, not to say organic, forms of expression, although the specific tectonic and emotive qualities of these works could hardly have been more different. Where Aalto created a highly sophisticated grotto-like, timber structure in anticipation of the auditorium interiors he would design after the Second World War, Niemeyer articulated the syntax of a modern Baroque manner. This consciously Brazilian style alluded even more directly than Aalto's nationalistic idiom, to the characteristic topography, colouring and climate of Brazil. Niemeyer demonstrated in New York the characteristic syntax of the neo-Corbusian, Brazilian modern movement, which had been underway since Le Corbusier's collaboration with Lucio Costa and Oscar Niemeyer, on the design of the Brazilian Ministry of Education, completed in Rio de Janeiro in 1943. In New York, Niemeyer was to exploit Le Corbusier's concept of the free plan as a framework upon which to suspend a whole gamut of freely distorted neo-Purist elements; undulating walls, irregularly curved access ramps, the characteristic hyperbolic screen announcing the presence of auditoria or the use of circular forms to both accommodate and indicate dance areas. Last but not least, there was the ubiquitous sun-breaker or brise-soleil which animated the surface of the pavilion. This syntax was surrounded by an equally exotic landscape garden, conceived by the painter Roberto Burle-Marx. In 1939 Niemeyer and Burle-Marx

consolidated the essence of a Brazilian modern style but as Niemeyer well knew, a modern national destiny could not be achieved through style alone, but would only arise through a total restructuring of the society. Thus he was to write on the occasion of the publication of his work in 1950:

Architecture must express the spirit of the technical and social forces that are predominant in a given epoch, but when such forces are not balanced, the resulting conflict is prejudicial to the content of the work and to the work as a whole. Only with this in mind may we understand the nature of the plans and drawings which appear in this volume. I should have very much liked to be in a position to present a more realistic achievement; a kind of work which reflects not only refinements and comfort but also a positive collaboration between the architect and the whole society.

5. The Diaspora of the Modern Movement: Russia, Switzerland and England 1930-39

Around 1930, as the political climate in Germany became increasingly reactionary, the architects of the Weimar Republic fled either to the left or right of the world political spectrum depending on their convictions. Naturally enough, those to the left migrated first, that is, those whose political persuasions were communist, for these had to leave as soon as their situation in Germany became untenable. Among those who went to the Soviet Union fairly early was Ernst May who migrated to Russia in 1930 together with a team of German architects and planners, who joined him in order to work on the design of the new industrial city of Magnitogorsk. May's team

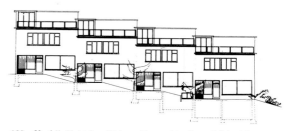

189 *Haefeli, Hubacher, Steiger, Moser, Atraria and Schmidt, Neubühl Siedlung, Zurich, 1930-32. Elevation of row houses.*

included such men as Fred Forbat, Gustav Hassenpflug, Hans Schmidt, Walter Schwagenscheidt and Mart Stam. On his dismissal from the directorship of the Bauhaus in August 1930, Hannes Meyer also migrated to the Soviet Union, initially serving as a teacher at VASI (the Higher Architecture and Building Institute) and later forming the Hannes Meyer Brigade, comprising seven graduates from the Bauhaus. Others such as Bruno Taut and Arthur Korn soon followed suit; Taut went to the Soviet Union in 1932 and Korn migrated to Yugoslavia in 1934.

With the National Socialist rise to power in 1933, the right of center architects also began to leave Germany, above all the architects of the Dessau Bauhaus, such as Walter Gropius who migrated to England in 1934, en route to the United States, where he finally arrived in 1937, to become a chairman of the department of architecture at Harvard. However, one of the most characteristic figures of the German architectural diaspora was Marcel Breuer who while practising out of Berlin from 1928, travelled constantly over the next seven years between Berlin, Budapest, and Zurich. In Switzerland he was to form a liaison with Sigfried Giedion, who in 1931, asked him to design the Wohnbedarf store in Zurich. Wohnbedarf had been founded by Giedion, Werner Moser and Rudolf Graver as an outlet for modern furniture. Like other distinguished designers of the period, including Le Corbusier, Aalto, Bill and Moser, Breuer was to design a number of bent aluminium furniture pieces for Wohnbedarf, including his first attempt at a reclining chair. In 1934, Breuer collaborated with the Swiss architects Alfred and Emil Roth on the design of a series of demonstration apartment buildings for the Zurich suburb

of Doldertal, two of which were finally realized in 1936. For their economy and elegance, these structures (which were sponsored by Giedion) are among the highpoints of Swiss Werkbund architecture between the wars, to be rivalled only by the equally famous Neubühl Siedlung, Zurich of 1932, designed by a group of Swiss architects including Emil Roth, Werner Moser and Hans Schmidt. Breuer, however, remained as nomadic as before, for by the time of the Doldertal commission he was already living in England where he collaborated with F.R.S. Yorke, prior to his definitive migration to the United States in 1937.

Irrespective of whether the German emigres went to Russia first or England, they did not remain in either country for long, moving on to Africa, Japan and Mexico after the Soviet Union; or alternatively, to the United States after a short stay in London. A singular exception to this was Korn, who moved from Yugoslavia to England in 1937, to remain in London on the staff of the Architectural Association School of Architecture for the rest of his career. The true reasons for the relative failure of the Weimar Republic architects in the Soviet Union are many and complex, but among them must be counted the fact that the *zeilenbau* pattern of residential development (as advanced by such figures as May and Stam) was not well received by the advocates of Social Realism, who recognized that such reduced environments were incapable of representing the triumphs of the young Soviet State.

As in the United States, where the International Style was first practiced by Austrian and Swiss emigres, so in England, where its origins lay in the work of outsiders; first in Peter Behrens's house, New Ways, built for the toy

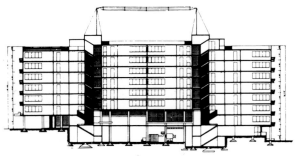

190 *Lubetkin & Tecton, Highpoint 1, Highgate, London, 1934. Cross section.*

manufacturer Bassett-Lowke, at Northampton, in 1926, and then with the New Zealander, Amyas Connell's house High and Over, built for the archaeologist Bernard Ashmole at Amersham, in 1929. Connell was to follow the vaguely Art Deco syntax and the tripartite plan from of High and Over with a work which was altogether more modernist. This was the reinforced concrete house, New Farm, built at Grayswood near Haslemere in 1932; a Cubistic work which displayed all the mandatory features of the time including a glass stair tower, horizontal strip windows and a cantilevered reinforced concrete portico over the entrance. While Connell had obviously read *Vers une Architecture*, which was translated into English by Frederick Etchells in 1927, he seems to have understood little of the Purist principles of composition and it is not until 1933 after the formation of the firm of Connell Ward and Lucas, that his work or rather the work of the firm, begins to move towards more rigorous levels of structural and spatial order. The designing abilities of his compatriot Basil Ward and the Englishman Colin Lucas are decisive in this regard as it is evident from Ward's High and Over estate built at Amersham in 1934 and from Lucas's own house, The Hopfield, built at St. Mary's Platt, Wrotham, Kent, in 1933.

By far the most sophisticated and influential émigré to enter England at this time was the Russian architect, Berthold Lubetkin whose impact on the development of modern architecture in England has never been adequately appreciated. It would be difficult to imagine a more cosmopolitan background than that of Lubetkin. Born in Tiflis in 1901, his studies in the Moscow Vkhutemas and the Petrograd Svomas (1920-22), brought him into contact with such figures as Rodchenko, Tatlin, and Alexander Vesnin. In 1922, he went to Berlin with the Russian art exhibition and remained there for a year to study reinforced concrete construction at the school of building in Charlottenberg. In 1923 he went to Warsaw where he studied formally at the Warsaw Polytechnic. By 1925, however, he moved again, this time to Paris where he was to work for Konstantin Melnikov on the USSR Pavilion for the *Exposition des Arts Décoratifs* of 1925. Lubetkin remained behind after the exhibition to study in the Auguste Perret atelier, of the École des Beaux-Arts. In 1927 he began to practice in Paris with Jean Ginsberg where the immediate result of their collaboration was the small but elegant, eight-storey, in-fill apartment block realized in the Avenue de Versailles, Paris, in 1932. During this period he also worked for the USSR Trade Delegation, for which his most important design was a large demountable timber exhibition pavilion, shifted around to various sites in France between 1926 and 1929, including Paris, Bordeaux, Strasbourg, and Marseilles. After meeting Godfrey Samuel and Margaret Gardener, Lubetkin moved definitevely to England in 1931.

At thirty, Lubetkin was able to bring to Tecton, the firm he founded in London in 1932, an extraordinary wealth of experience in the field of modern architecture and it was this, as well as his specific experience in reinforced concrete construction that gave Tecton a unique edge in the English scene. Aside from this Lubetkin possessed a capacity for logical organization and formal order which was rare in England during the inter-war period. His 1935 block of flats in Highgate, London, known as Highpoint 1, remains a masterpiece and even today it is a model of formal and functional order.

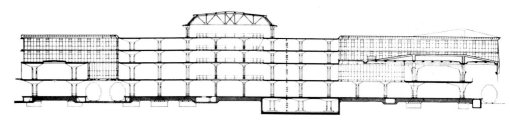

191 *Williams, Boots Factory, Nottingham, 1930-32. Section.*

Despite the facilities and the imaginative settings which they designed for the London and Whipsnade Zoos, Lubetkin and Tecton never attained this level of precision again. Their Highpoint 2 block, built in 1938, already displayed marked mannerist tendencies and one is left to speculate on the extent to which Lubtekin, as an architect of socialist persuasion, had become sensitive to Soviet Social Realism, for certainly his essays on Soviet architecture, written in the mid-1950s, reveal a sympathy in this direction. The shift in expression between Highpoint 1 and Highpoint 2, and the ensuing discussion, set the stage for the ideological struggles that took place in England in the 1950s.

Preoccupied with the need to create a generally accessible modern architecture, Tecton's work after 1938 seems to have been determined by a conscious attempt to assimilate the rhetorical tradition of the Baroque to the rigors of a Cubist syntax. The critical acceptance of Tecton's manneristic neo-Corbusian style, as exemplified by their Finsbury Health Center, London, of 1938, gave Lubetkin influence over the British scene immediately after the war, and the decade following 1945 was effectively dominated by the vocabulary which Tecton had developed. The Royal Festival Hall (1950), to take one of the prominent examples, designed by Leslie Martin, Robert Matthew and Peter Moro, was obviously indebted to Lubetkin, and the connection here is hardly difficult to find since Moro had worked for Tecton during the late thirties and was to continue to do so until the dissolution of the partnership in 1948, when the refusal of the British government to build the Tecton plan for Peterlee New Town, virtually broke Lubetkin's will to continue in practice.

Three other émigrés who were to play salient roles in the evolution of the English Modern Movement were the young Russian Serge Chermayeff who had, in fact, been educated in England, the Australian, Raymond McGrath, and the Canadian, Wells Coates. All three men happened to work together on a set of remarkable studios for the new premises of the British Broadcasting Corporation and thereafter they produced at least one cannonical building apiece: Chermayeff's house at Halland, Sussex completed in 1938, McGrath's semi-circular house built at Chertsey, Surrey, in 1937, and Coates's Lawn Road Flats built in Hampstead, in 1934; this last being destined to become a transient hotel for German emigres who were on their way to the United States. Jack Pritchard, the client of these so-called Isokon flats played an important role in the British movement by founding the furniture firm of Isokon in 1934, for whom Marcel Breuer was to design the Isokon bentwood *chaise longue* in 1935.

The English wing of CIAM, known as MARS (Modern Architectural Research Group) was founded in 1932 on the initiative of Wells Coates who was to represent MARS at the 1933 Athens Congress on board the S.S. Patras in the Aegean. While the MARS group possessed, at least initially, the necessary elan to attract the more avant-garde members of the British profession — including Connell, Ward and Lucas, Lubetkin, E. Maxwell Fry and the critic, P. Morton Shand — its sole achievement aside from its "New Architecture" exhibition staged in the Burlington Galleries in 1938 was its brilliant, if highly utopian, plan for London, drawn up in the early 1940s under the direction of Arthur Korn and the Viennese engineer Felix Samuely. The MARS group naively hoped for a future which, in the words of Coates, "must be planned, rather than a past which must be patched up," and yet, unlike Tecton, it was incapable of formulating a truly progressive methodology for the organization of this future. Lubetkin seems to have been the first to sense this lack of orientation, and he abandoned MARS at the end of 1936 to become affiliated with the left-wing ATO (Architects' and Technicians' Organization), which up to the early 1950s was to concern itself exclusively with the problem of working class housing.

No account of English architecture between the wars can end without mentioning the crucial role played by the engineering profession in the development of the British movement, although here, once again, many of the leading practitioners were of continental origin, among them the Danish engineer Ove Arup and the German trained Samuely; the latter working with Erich Mendelsohn and Serge Chermayeff on the design of the De La Warr Pavilion, built in Bexhill in 1937. In a scene dominated largely by continental engineers, the prime anomaly was the figure of Sir E. Owen Williams whose role has been somewhat difficult to evaluate since he was both an engineer and an architect. However, the fact remains that the scope of English architecture between the wars would have been much reduced had it not been for his remarkable large-scale works and above all for the extraordinary reinforced concrete Boots Pharmaceutical Factory completed to his designs at Beeston, in 1932. Aside from the megastructural scale at which he invariably worked, two unusual features served to give his architecture immediate distinction and enduring authority. The first of these derived from the way in which he developed the programme so as to directly influence the overall *gestalt* of the building; the second turned on the fact that he always employed structurally expressive elements such as counterbalanced cantilevers, mushroom columns, wide-span trusses, elaborately suspended membranes, etc. Williams was to give prominence to structure throughout his major buildings of the thirties from the Empire Pool Wembley of 1934 to the Daily Express Building, Manchester of 1939. In fact he was to continue in this manner until the last major commission of his career, the BOAC large span hanger built at Heathrow, London in 1954.

1937-43
OSCAR NIEMEYER
LUCIO COSTA, ET AL.
in collaboration with Le Corbusier
Ministry of Education
Rio de Janeiro, Brazil

The early career of Oscar Niemeyer is intimately bound up with the extraordinary influence that Le Corbusier exercised on Latin American architecture throughout the second half of the nineteen-thirties. Participating, at his own insistence, as a member of the Brazilian team — which had been commissioned to collaborate with Le Corbusier on a design for the new Ministry of Education — Niemeyer soom emerged as the most fertile mind of the group which included such distinguished figures as Lucio Costa, Alffonso Reidy, Carlos Leão, Jorge Moreira and Hernani Vasconcelos. After three months with Le Corbusier, Niemeyer had not only developed the capacity to initiate Corbusian planning strategies, but had also acquired the ability to reinterpret the Purist syntax in terms of the Brazilian Baroque. As Costa himself, remarked in 1950: "Niemeyer, having assimilated the fundamental principals and planning techniques formulated by Le Corbusier, was able to enrich this acquired experience in a most unforseen way. By giving to basic forms a new and surprising meaning, he created variations and new solutions with local patterns which have a grace and subtlety until then unknown to modern architecture. And all of a sudden, the architects of the entire world found themselves obliged to take notice of the work of this anonymous Brazilian who was able to transform, as with a mere wave of a wand, the most strictly utilitarian program into a plastic expression of the purest refinement."

Niemeyer's sense of elegance was at once evident in the final version of the seventeen-storey Ministry of Education which differed markedly from Le Corbusier's earlier design for the same programme, although the compositional strategies employed by the Brazilian team were virtually identical to those used by their acknowledged master.

With Le Corbusier acting as the catalyst, Costa, Niemeyer, Reidy and Moreira were all involved in the creation of a modern Brazilian style and this much is confirmed by the use they made of Brazilian artists, including the landscape garderner Roberto Burle-Marx, the sculptors Bruno Giorgio and Antonio Celso, and the painter Candido Portinari whose 38-foot-long ceramic tile mural composed of traditional Brazilian *azulejo*, was to enrich the 33-foot-high foyer beneath the *piloti* of the Ministry of Education.

No one, however, could have been more aware than Costa or Niemeyer of the difficulty of creating a truly national style, particularly when the issue as to constitution of the nation and its representative culture was far from being resolved in any profound sense. Could one simply reassert the nation as the culture of the ruling class, or should one attempt to reflect the culture of the people as a whole? This dilemma was touched on by Niemeyer when he wrote in 1950: "I should have very much liked to be in a position to present a more realistic achievement; a kind of work which reflects not only refinements and comfort but also a positive collaboration between the architect and the whole society."

In the same year, Costa summed up the cultural predicament posed by Niemeyer's "new monumentality" in the following terms:

"Since we are dealing with an architectural expression which is still hardly in the process of formation, we should stimulate by our unrestricted support those few architects, very few indeed, who are capable of enriching the current plastic vocabulary. Their work may appear individualistic in the sense that it does not correspond strictly to particular local conditions, or that it does not express faithfully the degree of culture of a given society. This, however, is the kind of individualism that one may term generic and fruitful: it represents a leap forward in time because it is a prophetic revelation of what architecture can mean for the society of the future. Armed with such foresight the artist can contribute much to the cause of the people, to the cause of the culture. For, although at the present moment the interests of the intelligentsia and those of the people do not coincide, the day must come when, because of the widening of the selective process to include the masses, the recuperation of individual values will inevitably occur. We shall then have at last, after a period of an effete twilight, a cultural renaissance unprecedented in the history of civilization."

Apart from its enrichment with art, including a sculpture by Jacques Lipchitz, the Ministry of Education was a strictly rationalist work, its southern sunless facade being faced in a curtain wall of double-hung windows, while its northern face consisted of adjustable horizontal louvers made of asbestos cement and painted blue. The basic organization consisted of a two-storey portico block running southwest-northeast, and a fifteen-storey slab set above and rotated through ninety degrees. The ground floor consisted primarily of a portico, an assembly hall and separate entrances for the minister and the employees. The first floor comprised an exhibition hall and a conference room under the slab, while the second and third floors provided for a number of committee rooms and offices and a general public enquiry area. The roof of the slab itself was given over to a ministerial suite which took the form of a penthouse surrounded by an exotic roof garden designed by Roberto Burle-Marx.

The Ministry of Education in Rio was the first occasion on which Le Corbusier's "Five Points of a New Architecture" were applied at a monumental scale, together with the complementary devices of the *pan verre* and the *brise soleil*. This, together with the small day nursery that Niemeyer built in Gavea, Rio de Janeiro in 1937, was one of the first twentieth-century buildings to be faced with adjustable sun-screens. These works, together with the Brazilian Pavilion for the 1939 New York World's Fair, crystallized the style of the Brazilian modern movement and helped to promote the cause of this Latin "Renaissance" throughout the remainder of the presidency of Vargas.

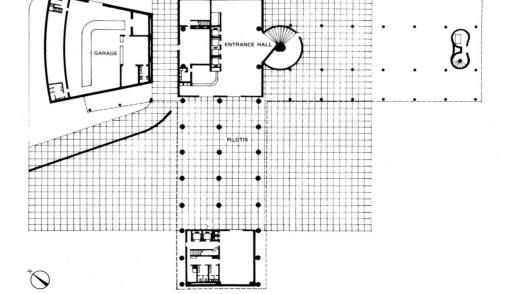

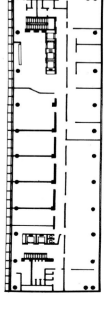

433 *North elevation*
434 *View of north facade*
435 *Above: open ground floor and pilotis*
   Below: ground floor plan and typical floor plan

GARAGE

ENTRANCE HALL

PILOTIS

Wright first confronted his desert destiny in the Ocatillo Camp founded at Salt Range, near Chandler, Arizona in 1927, for the purpose of establishing an atelier close to the site of a desert hotel which Wright never realized the so-called San Marcos-in-the-Desert, which was projected for New Chandler, Arizona in 1927. The first temporary desert settlement vaguely laid out as a protective compound on an octagonal grid, enabled Wright to discover, pragmatically, what was essential to survival in this hostile landscape. To this end he built the Ocatillo Camp as a lightweight canvas and timber, tented structure housing an aggregation of workshops, drafting rooms, garages and living facilities and he was to repeat this strategy a decade later when he organized the podium of Taliesin West about the intersection of an orthogonal and forty-five degree grid.

Taliesin is first approached as an inaccesible mirage lying on the horizon, and one's arrival to the actual point of entry is made deliberately uncertain and circuitous. One finally penetrates the desert compound via a long pergola which brings the visitor to a central terrace and loggia, flanked on one side by a long workroom, and on the other by the master's living quarters. From this central atrium springs a series of low outriding courts and ancilliary buildings; the apprentices' court with its single-storey dormitory and external chess board; the green garden court opening off Wright's sleeping quarters, the sunken desert garden, the pool, the gravel terrace, etc.

The plastic and poetic intention of this complex was to be accounted for in harsh terms by the ninety-year-old Wright, in *An American Architecture*, when he wrote:
"The straight line and flat plane must come here — of all places — but they should become the dotted line, the broad, low, extended plane, textured, because in all this astounding desert there is not one hard undotted line to be seen. The great nature-masonry we see rising from the great floors is ... not architecture at all, but its inspiration. A pattern of what appropriate Arizona architecture might well be, lies here hidden

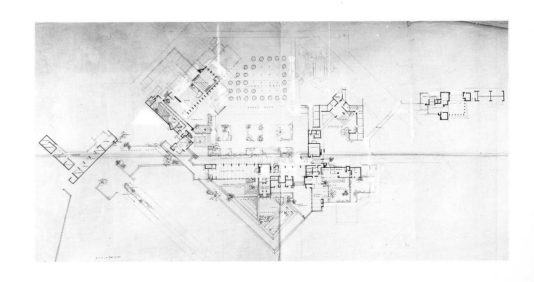

in the sahuaro. The sahuaro, perfect example of reinforced building construction. Its interior vertical rods held it rigidly upright maintaining its great columnar mass for six centuries or more ... Yes, the desert is rockbound earth prostrate to the sun. All life there dies a sun-death. Evidence is everywhere, sometimes ghastly. It is gratifying as we look around us to see how well we fit into this strange, stern, well-armed, creeping cover of abstract land and its peculiar growth, almost as abstract. This inexorable grasp of growing vegetation upon the earth itself is more terrifying to me as a principle at work than what we call death.... There seems to be no mortal escape, especially not in death, from this inexorable — or is it sun principle — of growth: This creative creature of the great sun?"

Taliesin was certainly designed as a desert-sun structure with, on the one hand, its great blocks of purple volcanic stone, laid out in the form of battered walls, canting down into the earth, and on the other its light tented timber roof, equipped with all sorts of ingenious louvers and canvas screens, capable of letting in the air and keeping out the sun.

At Scottsdale in 1938, Wright attempted to create a proto-Indian, mythical American culture, complete with petroglyphs and Navaho rugs, in a jocular, guilt-ridden belief, that "when the Indians come back, 2,000 years from now to claim their land, they will note we had respect for their orientation." Something of the uneasy psychological and physical climate in which this work was brought into being has been testified to by Edgar Tafel when he wrote:

"Mr. Wright soon devised a master plan for the camp, decided on a grammar of building, and was off to a new design concept indigenous to Arizona. Desert stone was placed in forms with a lean mortar mix. Redwood — rough sawn, undried and stained dark brown — was inexpensive and handsome against the white canvas roofs and the sky. Although the redwood had a strong appearance, the climate made it shrink in all directions, it twisted and even exuded nails. Eventually, years later, the wood was replaced with painted steel, in his favorite Indian color: Cherokee Red. ... Mr. Wright actually designed the camp on the site where it was being built. The apprentices were the surveyors laying out the lines for the buildings. Drafting tables were set out in the sun in the blazing light — imagine drafting on white paper in the Arizona sun! ... For sculpture at the terminals of the walls, (he) had us bring down large rocks (decorated with petroglyphs) from the mountainside and set them in a natural-looking orientation."

436 Above: refectories jutting out into the pool
Below: plan
437 Drafting room

It would be hard to imagine a building more characteristic of the so-called International Style, than the Museum of Modern Art, New York, as this was completed to the designs of Philip S. Goodwin and Edward D. Stone in the summer of 1939. The then fashionable, ubiquitous serpentine curve, so ostensibly evocative of liberation, proclaimed itself in the plan profile of the original canopy, extending over the sidewalk and faced in monel metal. This form was sympathetically echoed in the entrance hall, in the sweeping curve of the continuous coat and information counter which forty years ago displayed a much more modest array of catalogues and books. This sole form of plastic relief in what was otherwise a strictly orthogonal building, was also to appear in the bounding plate-glass window wall to the members room on the penthouse level.

The organization of the Museum of Modern Art was originally as follows: The ground level was at first occupied by an entrance foyer, two galleries and a main stair. In a downward direction, this last led to the first and second basement levels which were used to accommodate not only a 470-seat cinema, but also various museum services ranging from receiving and mailing to framing, etc. This same stair led up to the first and second floor galleries, whereupon it terminated, since the third to fifth floors were effectively reserved for curatorial staff and for the membership.

The original site spanned the full block between West 53rd and West 54th streets and from the very beginning the design provided for a sculpture garden. The main body of the museum, however, was structured about a reinforced concrete and steel frame with the 53rd street facade being faced in white marble and a large thermolux curtain wall being adopted for the panelled outer membrane of the second and third floor galleries. Above this level the curatorial offices were faced in horizontal steel glazing, while the penthouse terrace was capped by a cantilevered concrete canopy, pierced by eleven circular holes. The garden court facade which was ostensibly free, was also faced in white marble, its lower face being given a syncopated treatment, comprising alternation between glass lenses and plate glass.

The Museum of Modern Art

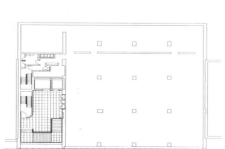

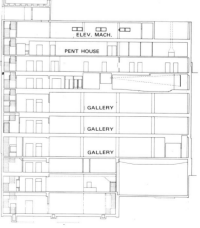

438 *Street facade*
439 *Above: view from garden court*
   Below: third floor plan and longitudinal section

This elementary school for girls opens Villanueva's career as a modernist, although it was by no means his first major work, for it had been preceded by his realized designs for the bullring in Maracay (1931) and the Museo de Los Caobos built in Caracas in 1935. His profoundly French background (his mother was French and he graduated from the École des Beaux-Arts, Paris, in 1938) is all too evident in this building which is clearly heavily indebted to the architecture of Rob Mallet-Stevens (cf. la rue Mallet-Stevens, Paris 1927). There is also a certain affinity with André Lurçat's Karl Marx school, built in the Villejuif, Paris of 1931. As Sibyl Moholy-Nagy has written: "The escuela Gran Colombia in Caracas was the first modern elementary school built in Venezuela. 1939, the year of its construction, marks a time of transition in Villanueva's eclectic rationalism, because it is his first attempt to find a design vocabulary free of historical embellishments. The construction method was again, as in Maracay, concrete frame with brick panels. As late as 1939, reinforced concrete was considered 'experimental' in South America. Contractors did not trust it and insisted on frames of masonry thickness."

In the plan, the school assumes a cranked formation within a rectangular site, with a central cross-axis of classrooms dividing the available area into two unequal courtyards; the larger one being a play court for the older children and the smaller one being devoted to the kindergarten.

The representative elevations of the school open onto the larger entry side of the site and the heavily reinforced frame takes the form of a two-storey arcade running around the playground. The intercolumnation of this facade is still ordered according to traditional classical precepts, with specific axes of symmetry and columns in *in antis* framing entries to specialized teaching units such as the gymansium. Villanueva was to make a liberal use of horizontal cornices and profiles not only as a traditional method for finishing walls and creating accents, but also as a modelling which in places serves to screen the facade from the sun.

Right: view toward entry
Below: plans of first floor and second floor

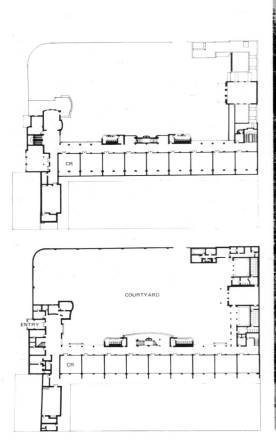

Typical of Neutra's abstract style of the late thirties, this four-storey structure resembles a small apartment building rather than a private residence, with each of the upper floors projecting a terrace eastwards towards the ocean and the Bay Bridge. The house is planned as a set of four self-contained levels with each deck being served by the elevator. The ground floor, cut into the top of Telegraph Hill, serves as a service and work level, while the first floor accommodates everyday living facilities such as the study, the kitchen, the breakfast and dining rooms. Above these two initial levels, the bulk of the sleeping accommodation is contained on the second floor, with the third and final floor given over to formal receptions.

Once again, as in the Lovell Health House, one has the feeling that Neutra was attempting to invent a new residential prototype, with the client's work room on the entry floor, being adjacent to the butler's apartment. Less idiosyncratic perhaps, is the large dining room on the floor above which is designed as a day reception room with tables lowering into position from the ceiling for the purposes of formal dining. The top floor is obviously reserved for a life of ease overlooking the bay, although even here, aside from serving as an observatory, the space was equipped with a retractable cinema screen for the private viewing of films.

Economically constructed about a lightweight steel frame with insulation blockwork, standard horizontal fenestration and a cement rendered finish, this house nonethe-

less displayed the high quality interior finish so typical of Neutra's work at this time. The living areas were equipped with planters wherever possible and most of the casual seating comprised continuous L-shaped corner units with throw cushions. The living areas were generally finished beige, with oyster grey walls, beige curtains and carpeting, reddish brown lacquerwork furniture, white upholstery on the chairs and white plastic table tops. The main access stair was painted reddish brown. The bar on the top floor was finished in light Philippine mahogany, with walls to match and furniture upholstered in green. Typically, Neutra used large sliding plate glass walls at this level in order to separate the salon from the outside terrace.

Formally, the Kahn residence was a neo-Cubist composition of the international period; with the storeys laid up as rectilinear blocks, separated by horizontal bands of steel-framed casements.

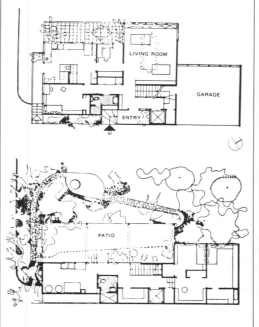

Above: plans of ground floor and first floor
Right: overall view

Niemeyer's Brazilian Pavilion for the 1939 New York World's Fair brought Le Corbusier's concept of the free plan to a new level of fluidity and interpretation. Initially planned around an exotic garden court, laid out to the designs of Roberto Burle-Marx, this pavilion and its tropical garden were partially structured by the Purist concept known a *mariage de contour*, in which organic curves flow uninterruptedly from one form to the next – from the building to the garden and vice versa.

Very much the same spirit informed the Pampulha Casino in which Niemeyer was to reinterpret the Corbusian notion of the *promenade architecturale* in a spatial composition of remarkable balance and vivacity. This was a narrative building in every respect, from the welcoming double-height foyer to the gleaming ramps rising to the gaming floor; from the elliptical corridors leading from the main entry to the restaurant, to the ingenious backstage circulation onto the dance floor. Conceived as a topological labyrinth, the space of the building was structured as an elaborate game; a game as intricate as the habits of the society it was intended to serve. The restaurant with its complex accessways, established not only the routes, but also the class roles of the various protagonists – allocating the available space to clients, entertainers, and serving staff. Strong and hedonistic in its general atmosphere, the building was at times both severe and theatrical; a contrast in mood established in the first place by the propriety of the facade faced in travertine and Juparana stone, and in the second, by the exoticism of an interior lined with pink glass, satin, and brilliantly coloured panels of Portuguese tiles. Closed down as a casino through a state interdiction on gambling, the building now serves as an art museum.

442 *Above: view from main approach*
   Below: floor plan
443 *Above: interior showing chromium-plated finish*
   and mirrors
   Below: entrance hall

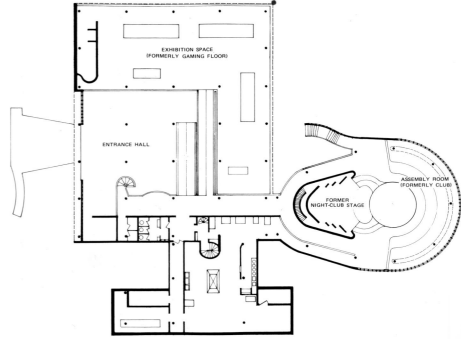

Juscelino Kubitschek first became a patron of modern architecture in 1941 when, as mayor of Belo Horizonte, he sponsored the construction of a new residential neighborhood around the shores of an artificial lake in Pampulha. In order to provide a range of community services for this rapidly expanding suburb, Kubitschek commissioned Niemeyer to design a series of structures around the irregular southern shore of the lake; a casino, a restaurant, a yacht club, and finally this church.

Consisting of a parabolic concrete shell joined to four similar shell vaults which together make the "crossing," this church is a tour de force in reinforced concrete shell construction and is in many respects as much a triumph of engineering as it is a work of architecture, and hence the engineer Joaquim Cardozo must also be given credit for it. Structurally, there is a debt here to the pioneering engineers Freyssinet and Maillart; above all to the latter for his spectacular demonstration of the capacities of concrete shell construction in the Swiss National Exhibition, staged in Zurich in 1937. It would be difficult to find a finer appreciation of Niemeyer's adaptation of this form, than that provided by Stamo Papadaki when he wrote: "The nave is of parabolic design on the plane of the cross section, approaching the form of a half, a frustrum of a cone in the longitudinal section; the space of the altar is prescribed by a smaller parabolic form and the same form is repeated three times on a still smaller scale and is used for the sacristy and the vestry. Light entering the narthex, is modulated by vertical louvers on the front facade.

Beyond, the primary lighting coming from above falls just before the altar, separating it from the worshipers"

One of the most remarkable things about this church is the way in which it was decorated by the Brazilian artist Candido Portinari, who not only covered the external infill of the vaults with a blue ceramic tile — that is, with an *azulejo* mural depicting the life of St. Francis — but he also painted a mural behind the altar, featuring scenes from the life of Christ. In this decidedly Expressionist work, Christ is depicted as the savior from sin and worldly misery. As in all of Niemeyer's works of this period, the artistic ensemble includes yet another exotic garden from the hand of Roberto Burle-Marx.

The concrete canopy supported on tubular steel, the helicoidal stair giving access to the choir balcony and the bell tower with its lattice cross-bracing, are all typical Niemeyer "conceits" of the period and clearly these bestow a somewhat whimsical mood on the entire work. His profound socialist convictions are perhaps reflected in this ironic distance from traditional religious values. It was certainly this that exacerbated local hostility to the work; an aversion which eventually attained such intensity that the building had to be brought under the protection of the National Department of Artistic and Historic Patrimony.

Niemeyer's hedonistic interpretation of the Brazilian Baroque was to reach its apotheois at Pampulha in the deceptively simple "Baile" restaurant of 1942, with its sixty-foot-diameter ballroom-cum-café terrace and its undulating concrete marquee extending out along the serpentine shores of the lake. In general, Pampulha represents a turning point in Niemeyer's career; the critical moment when he finally liberates himself from the stereometric discipline of Le Corbusier and starts to indulge in an organic play of form which is at times lyrical, and at times mannered to the point of being effete.

444 Tiled mural by Portinari on north elevation
445 Left: cutaway drawing of arched structure
Right: mural behind altar depicting St. Francis

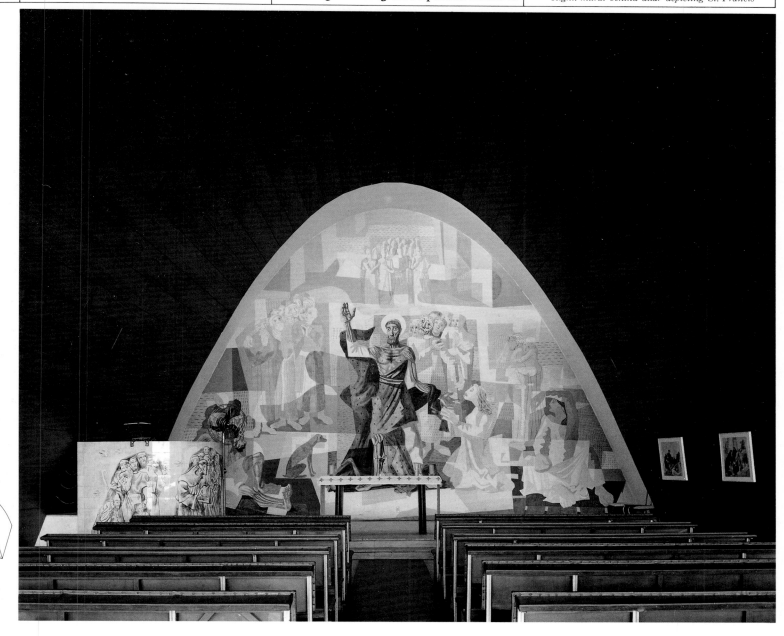

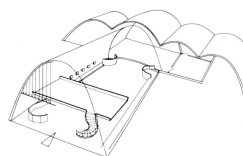

1944-47, 1952-57
CARLOS RAUL VILLANUEVA
Ciudad Universitaria
Caracas, Venezuela

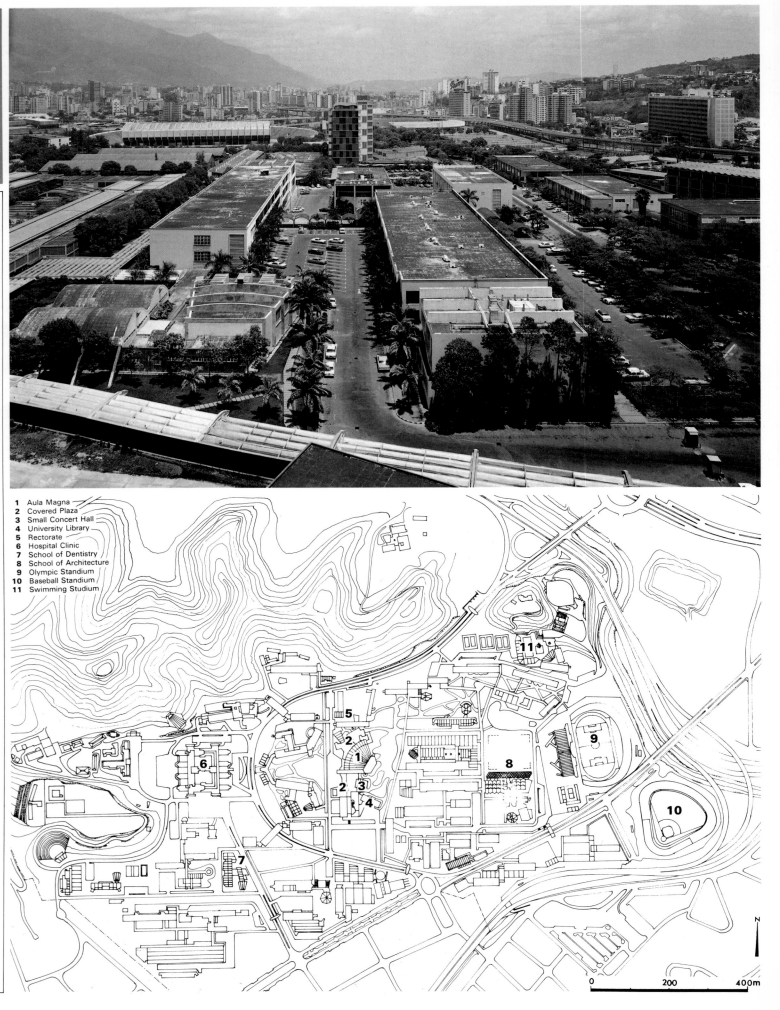

1 Aula Magna
2 Covered Plaza
3 Small Concert Hall
4 University Library
5 Rectorate
6 Hospital Clinic
7 School of Dentistry
8 School of Architecture
9 Olympic Standium
10 Baseball Standium
11 Swimming Studium

This sprawling and perenially unfinished campus by the pioneer Venezuelan modernist, Villanueva, remains, even today, one of the most difficult works to assess, largely because it combines so many different aspects of Villanueva's sensibility. One thing is certain, its most unique feature — namely, the covered cantilevered concrete walkway — is a remarkable "place-making" device, hardly to be found in any other work of the period. This reinterpretation of the traditional Venezuelan colonial section of *corredor y el patio*, extends throughout the campus and reaches its amplified apotheosis in the covered plaza and its adjacent courts, located in front of the Aula Magna. Of this place form Sibyl Moholy-Nagy wrote in 1964: "The covered plaza is the heart of the university body, the central source of energy, giving life to all other members. Here is the Aula Magna, gathering the community at festive occasions that supersede specialization and here is the transition from expedient knowledge to comprehensive wisdom. The student or visitor, approaching from any of three possible directions will be initiated by three patios, cut like light shafts into the concrete roof of the plaza."

Close to the Neo-Baroque sensibility of the Brazilian architect Oscar Niemeyer, the corridor widens and fragments in front of the Aula Magna into a series of irregularly shaped patios, which are both spatially established as well as identified by avant-gardist art works drawn from the mid-twentieth century. In some instances these works are used in combination with each other as in Fernand Léger's mural back drop to Henry Laurens's *Amphion*, or in a comparable way, Mateo Manaure's tiled wall painting which provides a dynamic spatial field for Jean Arp's statue, *Cloud Shepherd*. In both instances the works are constantly transformed by their mutual interaction with each other as induced by the movement of the spectator. These set pierces are also to be read against a deeper ground compounded out of architecture and luxuriant tropical vegetation. That Villanueva enjoyed a unique relationship with the so-called School of Paris in the fifties, is borne out by Léger's letter to him in 1954: "I have left an ajustable space between the elements of the mural, so that you can spread or tighten the composition for the best effect. This is entirely for you to decide, considering light and visual distance.''

What is unique about this large scale attempt to integrate the arts is the aesthetic range employed, running from late Cubist figuration to the Constructivist rigours of Antoine Pevsner or from what is surely Victor Vasarely's finest relief work, to the then current French and South American school of optical art.

Expressive structure was, of course, the primary element in Villanueva's architecture from the concrete ribbed side walls of the Aula Magna to the exposed concrete, ribbed-shell roof of the small concert hall or from the concrete, ribbed-cantilevered shell structures of the various Olympic stadia, to Villanueva's typical trabeated high-rise frame, with its voids variously filled with fenestration, rendered panels and the occasional syncopated pattern of perforated concrete blocks.

Like the American work of Jose Luis Sert, the Ciudad Universitaria, is in many respects a condensation of the late CIAM sensibility, although Villanueva was never a member of CIAM. In 1951, in the eighth CIAM congress held in Hoodesdon, in England, this prewar avant-garde movement was to regroup itself around the forgotten necessity of the monumental urban core — the so-called "heart of the city" which we find reinterpreted here in terms of a continuous arcade culminating in the Aula Magna. This main auditorium of the university (seating 2,600) constitutes a unique attempt at combining art and technique. Alexander Calder's cloud-sculptures suspended from its shell ceiling also double as acoustical distributors while their floating appearance beneath randomly placed spotlights is surely a complex metaphor for cosmic creation.

446 Above: general view of the University
    Below: site plan
447 Above: School of Dentistry, covered plaza
    Below: Aula Magna, corridor
448 Aula Magna, interior

Modern Architects: List of Works 1851-1945

compiled by Anthony Alofsin

Alvar Aalto (1898-1976) Finland/Architect
1921-22	Association of Patriots Building, Seinäjoki.
1922-23	Two-family house, Jyväskylä.
1923-24	Apartment Building, Jyväskylä.
1923-25	Workers' Club, Jyväskylä.
1926-29	Church, Muurame.
1927-28	Farmers' Co-operative Building and Finnish Theater, Turku.
1927-29	*Turun Sanomat* Newspaper Offices, Turku.
1927-35	Municipal library, Viipuri.
1929-33††	Tuberculosis Sanatorium, Paimio.
1930-31	Cellulose Factory, Toppila, Oulu.
1930-33	Villa Tammekan, Tarto, Estonia.
1933	Housing for employees and doctors of Tuberculosis Sanatorium, Paimio.
1934	Stenius Housing Development, Munkkiniemi, Helsinki.
1934-36	Aalto House, Munkkiniemi.
1936	Cellulose Factory, Sunila (first stage of construction).
1937††	Finnish Pavilion, World's Fair, Paris.
1937	Savoy Restaurant, Helsinki.
1937	Nordic United Bank, Karhula.
1937-38	Director's House, Sunila.
1937-38††	Two-story housing, Sunila.
1938	Forestry Pavilion, Agricultural Exhibition, Lapua.
1938	Anjala Paper Factory, Inkeroinen.
1938-39	Three-story housing, Sunila.
1938-39	Finnish Pavilion, World's Fair, New York.
1938-39	Elementary School, Inkeroinen.
1938-39††	Villa Mairea, Noormarkku.
1938-40	Terrace Housing, Kauttua.
1939-45	Ahlström Apartment Buildings, Karhula.
1942-43	Women's Dormitory, Kauttua.
1944	Stromberg Housing Development, Vaasa.
1944-47	Stromberg Meter Factory and Terrace Housing, Vaasa.
1947-48	Baker Dormitory, Massachusetts Institute of Technology, Cambridge, Massachusetts.

Aladar Arkay (1868-1932) Hungary/Architect
1895	Ministry of Defense, Budapest.
1905	Baboesay Villa, Budapest.
1910-13	Villa, Buda Hills, Budapest.
1911-13	Calvinist Church, Budapest.

Arnstein Arneberg (1882-1960) Norway/Architect
1911	Skogsveien, Slemdal, Oslo.
1916	House at Fornebu, Baerum.
1916-24	Telegraph Building, Oslo (with Magnus Poulsson).
1917	Karl Johan St. Building, Oslo (with Magnus Poulsson).
1918-23	Madserud Allé, Oslo.
1918-47†	Town Hall, Oslo (with Magnus Poulsson).

Charles Robert Ashbee (1863-1942) England/Architect
1894-1901	Houses and studios, Cheyne Walk, Chelsea, London.

Erik Gunnar Asplund (1885-1940) Sweden/Architect
1912-18	Karlshamn Secondary School, Karlshamn.
1915-24	Carl Johan Elementary School, Gothenburg.
1917	Workers' Emergency Dwellings, Stockholm.
1917-18	Snellman Villa, Djursholm, near Stockholm.
1917-21	Lister County Court House, Sölvesborg.
1918-20	Woodland Chapel, Stockholm South Cemetery.
1920-28††	Stockholm City Library.
1921	Prince Oscar Bernadotte's Family Vault, Stockholm North Cemetery, Stockholm.
1922-23	Skandia Cinema, Stockholm.
1924-25	Admiral Sten Ankarcrona's Family Vault, Stockholm North Cemetery.
1926-28	Hjalmar Rettig's Family Vault, Stockholm North Cemetery.
1927-35	Stockholm City Library Park.
1928-30	Design of the Stockholm Exhibition.
1933-35	Bredenberg Department Store, Stockholm.
1933-37	The State Laboratory for Biological Research, Stockholm.
1934-37	Gothenburg Law Courts, extension building, Gothenburg.
1935-40††	The Woodland Crematorium, South Cemetery, Stockholm.
1936-40	Kviberg Cemetery Crematorium, Gothenburg.
1937	Asplund Summer Residence (Stennäs House), Sorunca Parish, Stockholm.

Jules Astruc (1862-1935) France/Architect
1899-1901†	Notre-Dame-du-Travail, Paris.

Mackey Hugh Baillie-Scott (1865-1945) England/Architect
1897-98	Village Hall, Onchan, Isle of Man.
1898-99	Blackwell, Bowness, Westmoreland.
1899-1900	The Garth, Cobham, Surrey.
1905	Wertheim Residence (interiors), Berlin.
1906-07	Bill House, Selsey-on-Sea, Sussex.
1908-09	Undershaw, Guildford.
1908-09	Waterloo Court and Multiple Houses, Hampstead Garden Suburb, London.
1909	White Cottage, Biddenham, Kent.
1912	Michaels, Harbledown, Kent.
1912-13	Chludzinski House, Laskowicze, Poland.
1912-13	The Cloisters, Avenue Road, London.
1916-17	White House, Great Chart, Kent.
1919-20	Westhall Hill, Burford, Oxfordshire.
1920-21	Oakhams, Edenbridge, Kent.
1923	The Gatehouse, Limpsfield, Surrey (with A.E. Beresford).
1923	Trunch, Saltwood-in-Hythe, Kent (with A.E. Beresford).
1924	House, Mudeford Green, Hampshire (with A.E. Beresford).
1928-29	Ashwood, Woking, Surrey (with A.E. Beresford).
1931-32	Sandy Holt, Esher, Surrey (with A.E. Beresford).
1931-32	Mena House, Walton-on-Thames, Surrey (with A.E. Beresford).

Victor Baltard (1805-74) France/Architect
1853-86†	Les Halles Centrales, Paris (with F.E. Callet).
1864-65	St. Augustin Church, Paris.

Peter Behrens (1868-1940) Germany/Architect
1900-01†	Behrens House, Matildenhöhe, Darmstadt.
1904-05	Exhibition Pavilion, N.W. German Art Exhibition, Oldenberg.
1905-06	Obernauer House at Sankt Johann, near Saarbrucken.
1906-07	Crematorium, Delstern, near Hagen, Westphalia.
1908-09	Schröder House, Hagen-Eppenhausen, Westphalia.
1909-10†	AEG Turbine Factory, Huttenstrasse, Berlin (with Karl Bernhard).
1909-12	AEG Works, Light Engine Factory, High Tension Factory, Small Motor Factory, Large Machinery Assembly Hall, Humboldthain Complex, Berlin.
1910	Cuno House, Hagen-Eppenhausen, Westphalia.
1911-12	Gasworks, Osthafen, Frankfurt-am-Main.
1911-12	Mannesmann Headquarters, Düsseldorf.
1911-12	German Embassy, St. Petersburg, Russia.
1911-20	Continental Rubber Company, Hanover.
1913	AEG Factory, Riga, Russia.
1914	Festival Hall, Werkbund Exhibition, Cologne.
1917	Werkbund Exhibition, Berne.
1919	Garden Suburb, Neusaberg.
1920	Garden Suburb, Nowawes, Berlin.
1920	Housing Estate, Altona.
1920-24††	Administrative Building, IG Farben AG Dye Works (now Höchst Werke), Frankfurt-am-Main.
1921-25	Hoag Steelworks, Oberhausen.
1924-25	Monastery of St. Peter, Salzburg, Austria.
1925	People's Building, Vienna.
1925	Tomb of Reichspresident Friedrich Ebert, Heidelberg Forest Cemetery.
1926	Fashion House, Frankfurt.
1926	New Ways, Northampton, England.
1926-27	Terrace Housing, Weissenhof Siedlung, Stuttgart.
1929-31	Berokina Building Complex, Alexanderplatz, Berlin.
1931	Clara Ganz Villa, Cronberg, Taunus.
1931-34	New Buildings for the State Tobacco Factory, Linz, Austria (with Alexander Popp).

Max Berg (1870-1947) Germany/Architect
1913†	Jahrhunderthalle, Breslau (now Poland).
1925	Messehof Exhibition Building, entry hall, Breslau (now Poland).
1925	Hydroelectric Station, Norder-Oder and Süder-Oder, Breslau (now Poland).

Hendrick Petrus Berlage (1856-1934) Holland/Architect
1883-84	De Hoop, Restaurant/Hotel, Amsterdam (with T. Sanders).
1892-94	De Algemenne Office Building, Damrak, Amsterdam.
1894-95	De Nederlanden van 1845 Insurance Co., Amsterdam.
1895-96	De Nederlanden van 1845 Insurance Co., Kirkplain, The Hague.
1898	Villa Henny, The Hague.
1898-1900	Diamond Worker Union, Henri-Polaklaan, Amsterdam.
1898-1903†	Stock Exchange (De Beurs), Amsterdam.
1901-09	De Nederlanden van 1845 Insurance Co., Amsterdam.
1913	Simons House, Prinsevinkenpark, The Hague.
1913	Berlage Family House, Violenweg, The Hague.
1914	Meddens and Son, Hofweg, The Hague.
1914	Holland House, Bury Street, London.
1914-20	St. Hubertus, Hunting Lodge, Otterloo.
1925	De Nederlanden van 1845 Insurance Co., Groenhovenstraat-Raamweg, The Hague (with A.D.N. van Gendt and W.N. van Vliet).
1925	Mercatorplein, Amsterdam-West.
1926	First Church of Christ Scientist Building, Zorgvliet, The Hague.
1930	De Nederlanden van 1845 Insurance Co. Building, Utrecht.
1931-35††	Gemeentemuseum (Municipal Museum), The Hague.

Ferdinand Boberg (1860-1946) Sweden/Architect
1890	Fire Station, Gävle.
1892	Electric Works, Stockholm.

Paul Bonatz (1877-1956) Germany/Architect
1909	Henkell Warehouses, Biebricher, Wiesbaden Library, University of Tubingen.
1912	School, Feuerbach, near Stuttgart.
1912	Bonatz House, Stuttgart.
1913	Bridge, near Ulm.
1913-27	Main Railway Station, Stuttgart (with F.E. Scholer).
1914	Hospital, Strasbourg, France (with Karl Bonatz).
1914	Municipal Hall, Corviniusplatz, Hanover.

1916	Assembly Building, Oldenburg.
1916	Zeppelindorf Workers' Housing Development, Friedrichshafen (with F.E. Scholer).
1922	Kriegerfriedhof Monument, Waldfriedhof, Stuttgart.
1924	Scheibler House, Marienburg.
1925	Am Bismarckturm Housing Development, Stuttgart.
1929	Hotel Graf Zeppelin, Station Square, Stuttgart (with F.E. Scholer).
1935	Stumm Company Building, Düsseldorf (with F.E. Scholer).
1936	Locks, bridges, and weirs on the Neckar Canal, Heidelberg, Rockenau, Hirschhorn and Oberesslingen.
1936	Kunstmuseum, Basel, Switzerland (with Rudolf Christ).
1936	Memorial Chapel to the War Dead, Heilbronn.
1941	Bridges for the Autobahn: over the Waschmuhltal near Kaiserslauten; Saale near Lehesten; Donau near Leipheim (Ulm); Elbe near Hohenwarthe (Magdeburg); Elbe near Dessau; Rhine near Frankenthal (Mannheim).
1941	Suspension bridges at Cologne and Hamburg.
1946	Schukru-Saracogu Housing Development, Ankara, Turkey.
1948	State Opera House, Ankara, Turkey.

Marcel Breuer (1902-82) Hungary/Architect

1932	Harnischmacher House I, Wiesbaden.
1935-36††	Doldertal Apartments, Zurich (with Alfred and Emil Roth).
1936	Gane's Stone Exhibition Pavilion, Bristol, England.
1938	Hagerty House, Cohasset, Massachusetts (with Walter Gropius).
1939	Breuer House I, Lincoln, Massachusetts.
1940	Chamberlain Cottage, Wayland, Massachusetts (with Walter Gropius).
1945	Tompkins House, Hewlett Harbor, New York.
1945	Geller House, Lawrence, Long Island, New York.

Johannes Brinkman (1902-49) Holland/Architect
* with L.C. van der Vlugt.

1925-26	Theosophical Union Meeting Hall and Administration Building, Tolstraat, Amsterdam.*
1925-27	Van Nelle Tobacco Company Offices, Aalmarkt, Leiden.*
1926	Theosophical Union Building, Ommen.*
1926	Van Nelle Company Boilerhouse, van Nelleweg 1, Rotterdam.*
1926-27	Public Housing, Mathenesserweg, Rotterdam.*
1926-29††	Van Nelle Tobacco Company Factory, van Nelleweg 1, Rotterdam.*
1928-29	Van der Leeuw Villa, Kralingseplaslaan, Rotterdam.*

1929-31	Grain Silos, Maashaven, Rotterdam.*
1930-31	Mees and Zoonen Bank Building, 's-Gravendijkwal, Rotterdam.*
1930-32	Van Stolk and Zn. Office Building, Abraham van Stolkweg, Rotterdam.*
1932-33	Sonneveld Villa, Jongkindstraat, Rotterdam.*
1933-35	Steel Skyscraper Block, Bergpolder, Rotterdam (with Willem van Tijen).
1935-36	Feijenoord Stadium, Olympiaweg, Rotterdam.
1935-36	Airport Reception Building, Ypenburg.
1938-40	Low-cost Housing, Tarwebuurt, Rotterdam-Sud.
1940-41	Workers' Housing, Rotterdam.
1941-43	Tollens and Company Dye and Lacquer Factory, Overschieseweg, Overschie.
1941-43	Public Housing, Rotterdam-Sud.
1941-45	Gispen N.V. Factory and Office Building extensions, Stationsweg, Culemborg.
1941-48	Strijp I Terrace Housing, Strijp, Eindhoven.
1942-43	Van Nelle Company Warehouse extensions, van Nelleweg, Rotterdam.

Samuel Brown (1776-1852) England/Engineer

1818	Dryburgh Abbey Bridge, Scotland (260 ft), Union Bridge, Norham Ford, Tweed River.
1822	Chair Pier, Brighton.

Isambard Kingdom Brunel (1806-59) England/Engineer

1829-62	Clifton Suspension Bridge, Bristol.
1839-40	Temple Meads Station, Bristol.
1852-54†	Paddington Station, London (with Matthew Digby Wyatt).
1859	Royal Albert Bridge over the Tamar River, Saltash, Cornwall.

Daniel H. Burnham (1846-1912) USA/Architect

Until the untimely death of the talented John W. Root in 1891, all of Burnham's work was carried out with the participation of Root, under the title of Burnham and Root. After 1891 Burnham practised under the title of D.H. Burnham & Co. until his own death in 1912.

1881-82	Montauk Building, Chicago.
1884-90†	Monadnock Building, Chicago.
1885-88	The Rookery, Chicago.
1886-87	Art Institute, Chicago.
1888-90	Rand McNally Building, Chicago.
1890-92	Masonic Temple Building, Chicago.
1890-95†	Reliance Building, Chicago.
1892-93	World's Columbian Exposition, Chicago (Master plan with Frederick Law Olmsted).
1898-1902	Union Station, Pittsburgh.
1902	Marshall Field Department Store, Chicago.
1903	Flat Iron Building, New York.
1903-07	Union Station, Washington, D.C.

1909	Wanamakers Department Store, Philadelphia.
1912	Filene's Department Store, Boston.

William Butterfield (1814-1900) England/Architect

1844-45	Coalpit Heath Vicarage, Gloucestershire and Bristol.
1847-90	Perth Cathedral, Scotland.
1847-78	Adelaide Cathedral, Australia.
1849-59	All Saints, Margaret Street, London.
1850-52	Osnaburgh Street Convent, London.
1850-63	St. Dunstan's Abbey School, Plymouth, Devon.
1851-53	Huddersfield St. John, Yorkshire.
1854-55	Langley Church and School, Kent.
1854-57	Milton Church, Oxfordshire.
1854-57	Balliol College Chapel, Oxford.
1855-63	Wareseley Church, Huntingdonshire.
1856-62	Bamford Church and Parsonage, Derbyshire.
1859-61	Braunstone Cottages, Leicestershire.
1860-86	Rugby School, Warwickshire.
1861-62	Hunstanton Town plan, Norfolk.
1866-75	Keble College, Oxford.
1870-75	St. Mary Brookfield, London.
1877-86	Melbourne Cathedral, Australia.
1885-86	Ascot Priory Chapel, Berkshire.

Jan W.E. Buys (1889-1961) Holland/Architect

1924	Reconstruction and Expansion of the Communal Gymnasium, Haarlem.
1926	Wilhelminahaus, Benoordenhoutseweg, The Hague.
1928††	Die Volharding, Cooperative store, The Hague (with J.B. Lürsen).
1930	De Arbeiderspers, Amsterdam (with J.B. Lürsen).

Pierre Chareau (1883-1950) France/Decorator

1918-19	Dalsace Apartment interiors, rue Saint-Germain, Paris.
1925	Embassy Office interiors, Salon des Arts Décoratifs, Paris.
1927	Golf Club, Beauvallon (with Bernard Bijvoet).
1928	Hotel interiors, Tours.
1928-31††	Dalsace House (Maison de Verre), rue St. Guillaume, Paris (with Bernard Bijvoet and Dalbet).
1931-32	Compagnie du Téléphone offices, Paris.
1937	Djemel Anik Country House, near Paris.
1937	Office interiors, Ministry of Foreign Affairs, Paris.
1937	Union des Artistes Modernes Pavillon, International Exhibition, Paris (with others).
1939	Soldat Colonial Foyer, Grand Palais, Paris.
1940-50	Exhibition Design for the French Cultural Center, New York.
1940-50	Robert Motherwell House, near New York.
1940-50	Chareau House, East Hampton, Long

	Island, New York.

Georges Chedanne (1861-1920) France/Architect

1901-09	French Embassy, Vienna.
1902-03†	Le Parisien, office building, Paris.
1903-04	Hôtel Mercedes, Paris.
1904-06	Galeries La Fayette, Paris.

Charles Robert Cockerell (1788-1863) England/Architect

1837-47	Fitzwilliam Museum, Cambridge (with George Basevi).
1841-55	University Galleries (Ashmolean), Oxford.
1849-55	Bank Chambers, Liverpool.

Victor Contamin (1840-93) France/Engineer

1889†	Machinery Hall, International Exhibition, Paris (with Ferdinand Dutert [1845-1906]).

P.J.H. Cuijpers (1827-1921) Holland/Architect

1885	Rijksmuseum, Amsterdam.
1887	H. Maria-Magdalena Church, Spaarndammerstraat, Amsterdam.
1889	Main Railway Station, Amsterdam.

Raimondo D'Aronco (1857-1923) Italy/Architect

1902†	Pavilions for Turin Exhibition, Turin.
1903	Mosque in Karakeny Square, Galata, Turkey.
1903	Pavilion of Fine Arts, National Exhibition, Udine.
1907	Fountain and Library, Yildiz, Turkey.

Anatole de Baudot (1834-1915) France/Architect

1884-1904†	Saint-Jean-de-Montmartre Church, Paris (with Paul Cottacin).
1905	Saint-Etienne-de-Nevers, Church, Paris.

Michel de Klerk (1884-1923) Holland/Architect

1911-12	Hillehuis Housing Block, Johannes Vermeerplein, Amsterdam.
1913-18†	Eigen Haard Housing (first stage), Spaarndammer District, Amsterdam.
1914	Billeke Country House, Hilversum.
1917-20†	Eigen Haard Housing (second stage), Spaarndammer District, Amsterdam.
1922††	De Degeraad Housing Estate, Takstraat and Henriette Ronnerplein, Amsterdam.
1922	Bloemenlust Flower Market, Oosteinde, Aalsmeer.
1923	Barendsen House, Aalsmeer.
1923	Country House, Wassenaer.
1923	Plan Zuid Housing Estate, Amstellaan, Amsterdam.

Willem Marinus Dudok (1884-1974) Holland/Architect

1916	Secondary School, Leiden.
1917	Leidse Dagblad Offices, Leiden.
1918	Residential development, 1st Municipal Quarter, Hilversum.
1920	Rembrandt School, Hilversum.

1920	Huize Sevensteijn, Zorgvliet Park, The Hague.
1921	Residential development, Naarden.
1921	Municipal Baths, Hilversum.
1921	Dr. H. Babinck School, Hilversum.
1921	Residential development, 4th Municipal Quarter, Hilversum.
1922	Oranje Primary School, 5th Municipal Quarter, Hilversum.
1923	Slaughterhouse, Hilversum.
1925	Jan van der Heyden School, Hilversum.
1925	Minckelers School, Hilversum.
1926	Juliana School, Hilversum.
1926	Fabritius School, Hilversum.
1926	Columbarium, Westerhaven.
1926	Dudok House, Hilversum.
1927	Van Heutsz Monument, Gambir, Indonesia.
1928	Netherlands House, Cité Universitaire, Paris.
1928	Ruysdael School, Hilversum.
1928	Nassau School, Hilversum.
1928-30††	Town Hall, Hilversum.
1928-30	De Bijenkorf Department Store, Rotterdam.
1929	Vondel School, Hilversum.
1929	Noorder Cemetery, Hilversum.
1930	Multatuli School, Hilversum.
1930	Johannes Calvijn School, Hilversum.
1930	Valerius School, Hilversum.
1930	Marnix School, Hilversum.
1931	Snellius School, Hilversum.
1933	Monument on the Zuyderzee Dyke.
1934-35	H.A.V. Bank, Schiedam.
1936	Aquatic Sports Pavilion, Hilversum.
1936	Garden Theater and Lighthouse Cinema, Calcutta, India.
1937	Harbor Master's Office, Hilversum.
1938	De Burgh Garden City, Eindhoven.
1939	Bridge over the River Vecht, near Vreeland.
1939	Erasmushuis Office and Apartment Building, Rotterdam.
1939	De Nederlanden van 1945 Insurance Company Office Building, Arnhem.
1940	Reception and Office Building, Crematorium, Westerveld.
1941	Municipal Theater, Utrecht.
1945	Plan for the reconstruction of The Hague.

Johannes Duiker (1890-1935) Holland/Architect

1917-19	Karenhuizen Old Peoples' Housing, Alkmaar.
1918	Two houses, Eikstraat, The Hague.
1918	Housing and shops, Thomsonplein 10-15, The Hague.
1920	House, Jacob Catslaan 12, The Hague.
1920	Housing Development, Johan van Oldebarneveldlaan and Doornstraat, The Hague.
1920	Housing Block, Doornstraat, The Hague.
1920	Housing Development, Scheveningselaan, Kijkduin, The Hague.

1924	Country House, Stommerkade 64, Aalsmeer.
1924-25	Copper Rods Fund Soap Factory, Diemerbrug.
1925	Chemist's Shop, Haltestraat 8, Zandvoort.
1926-28††	Zonnestraal Sanatorium Complex, Hilversum (with Bernard Bijvoet).
1927-30	Nivana Flats, Benoordenhoutseweg and Willem Witsenplein, The Hague (with Wiebenga).
1929-30††	Open-air public school, Cliostraat, Amsterdam.
1930	Third Technical Training School, Scheveningen.
1930	Basic Housing Units, International New Building Congress, Brussels.
1932	Zonnestraal Servants' Quarters, Hilversum (with Bernard Bijvoet).
1934	Handelsblad-Cineac Cinema, Regulierbreesstraat, Amsterdam.

F.A. Duquesney (1800-49) France/Architect

1847-52	Gare de l'Est, Paris.

James Eads (1820-87) USA/Engineer

1867-74	Great St. Louis Bridge, Mississippi River, St. Louis, Missouri.

Karl Ehn (1884-1957) Austria/Architect

1922	23-24 Balderichgasse, Vienna.
1923	Gemeindesiedlung Hermeswrise, Vienna.
1923	Zentralfriedhof, Vienna.
1924	Lindenhof, Vienna.
1925	Bebelhof, Vienna.
1925	Szidzinahof, Vienna.
1926	Svobodahof, Vienna.
1927††	Karl Marx Hof, Vienna.
1932	Adelheid Popp-Hof, Vienna.
1932	Housing development, 24 Hauslabgasse, Vienna.

Gustave Eiffel (1832-1923) France/Engineer

1866-67	Universal Exhibition, Paris (with J.B. Krantz).
1868-69	Railway Viaducts, Gannat-Commentry Line, Massif Central.
1871-73	Railway Viaducts, built in France and exported to Spain and Portugal, Austria, Rumania, Egypt, Peru, and Bolivia.
1876†	Bon Marché Department Store, Paris (with L.C. Boileau).
1877-78	Maria-Pia Bridge, Porto, Portugal.
1880-84	Garabit Viaduct, Massif Central.
1883	Tardes Viaduct, Massif Central.
1884	Observatory Cupola, Nice.
1885	Statue of Liberty, New York (metal superstructure only, sculptor, Bartholdi).
1887	Panama Canal Works, Panama.
1887-89†	Eiffel Tower, Paris.

John Eisenmann (1851-1924) USA/Engineer

1888-90†	Cleveland Arcade, Cleveland, Ohio (with George H. Smith).

Charles Ellet (1810-62) USA/Engineer

1841-42	Schuykill River Bridge, Philadelphia.
1846-49	Ohio River Bridge, Wheeling, West Virginia.
1847-48	Niagara River Bridge, Niagara Falls, New York.

Harvey Lonsdale Elmes (1814-49) England/Architect

1841-54	St. George's Hall, Liverpool (with C.R. Cockerell).

Eugène Freyssinet (1879-1962) France/Engineer

1914-19	Bridge at Villeneuve-sur-Lot.
1916-24†	Airship Hangars, Orly, near Paris.
1926-29	Plougstel Bridge, Elorn River Estuary, Brittany (partially destroyed 1944; rebuilt).
1932	Tranenberg Bridge, Stockholm.
1937-39	Harbour structures, Brest.
1946-52	Ocean Terminal, Le Havre.

Frank Furness (1839-1912) USA/Architect

1869-71	Rodef Shalom, Synagogue, Philadelphia, Pennsylvania.
1871-76	Pennsylvania Academy of Fine Arts, Philadelphia, Pennsylvania.
1873-76	Guarantee Trust Company, Philadelphia, Pennsylvania.
1875-76	Philadelphia Zoological Gardens, Philadelphia, Pennsylvania.
1876-79	The Provident Life and Trust Company, Philadelphia, Pennsylvania.
1887-91	Library, University of Pennsylvania, Philadelphia, Pennsylvania.

J.-L. Charles Garnier (1825-98) France/Architect

1863-74	L'Opéra, Paris.

Tony Garnier (1869-1948) France/Architect

1904-14†	Cité Industrielle (Project).
1908-24	Slaughterhouse and Stockyard, Lyons (*Abbatoirs de la Mouche*).
1910	Villa Tony Garnier, Lyons.
1911-27	Grange Blanche Hospital, Lyons.
1913-18	Municipal Stadium, Lyons.
1920	Housing Sector, Quartier des Etats-Unis, Lyons.
1924	Monument to the War Dead, Parc de la Tête d'Or, Lyons (with the sculptor Larrive).
1925	Loyons-St. Etienne Pavilion, Expositions des Arts Décoratifs, Paris.
1927	Moncey Central Telephone Exchange, Lyons.
1930-33	Textile School, Croix-Rousse, Lyons.
1931-34	Town Hall, Boulogne-Billancourt, Paris (with Debat-Ponsan).

Antonio Gaudí (1852-1926) Spain (Catalonia)/Architect

1878-82	Mataro Workers Cooperative, Barcelona.
1878-80	Casa Vicens, Barcelona.
1883-85	El Capricho, Comillas.
1890-1930†	La Sagrada Familia, Barcelona.
1855-89	Palau Güell, near Barcelona.
1889-1914	Colonia Güell, near Barcelona.
1889-94	Santa Teresa de Jesus, Barcelona.
1900-10	Bellesguard, Barcelona.
1900-14	Parque Güell, Barcelona.
1905-07†	Casa Batlló, Barcelona (with J.M. Jujol).
1905-10†	Case Milà, Barcelona.
1909†	Parochial School, La Sagrada Familia, Barcelona.

Josef Gočár (1880-1945) Czechoslovakia/Architect

1910	Concrete Stairway, Marienkirche, Hradec-Kralove.
1910-11	Department Store, Jaromer.
1910	Kralovo House, near Brno.
1912	Cerna Matka Bozi, Department Store, Prague.
1912	Health Spa, Bohdanec.

Ilya Golosov (1883-1945) Russia/Architect

1919	Basman Hospital, Moscow.
1926††	Club for Professional Association of all Community Workers, Lesny Street, Moscow.
1926	Telegraph building, Moscow.
1926	Textile building, Moscow.
1934	House of Books, Ogize.
1934	Workers' Housing, Yausky Building, Moscow.
1936-40	Hydro-electric station, Gorky.
1936	Tass Newspaper Building, Moscow.
1939	Kominturn Executive Building, Moscow.
1939	Markomstral Building, Progovsky Street, Moscow.

C. S. Greene (1868-1957) **& H. M. Greene** (1870-1954) USA/Architects

1896-97	Kinney-Kendall Building, Pasadena, California.
1900	John C. Bentz Building, Pasadena, California.
1902	James A. Culberton House, Pasadena, California.
1902-03	Arturo Bandini House, Pasadena, California.
1904	Freeman Ford House, Pasadena, California.
1906	Z.A. Robinson House, Pasadena, California.
1906	Theodore Irwin House, Pasadena, California.
1907	R.R. Blacker House, Pasadena, California.
1908	William R. Thorsen House, Berkeley, California.
1908†	David B. Gamble House, Westmoreland Place, Pasadena, California.

1909	Pratt House, Ojai, California.
1911	Cordelia Culbertson House, Pasadena, California.
1913	Crowe House, Pasadena, California.
1914	D.L. James House, Carmel, California.

Walter Burley Griffin (1876-1937) USA/Architect

1901-02	William H. Emery House, Elmhurst, Illinois.
1908	Orth Houses, Kenilworth, Illinois.
1909	Sloan House, Elmhurst, Illinois.
1909-10	Gunn House, Chicago, Illinois.
1910	Carter House, Evanston, Illinois.
1911	Ricker House, Grinnell, Iowa.
1911	Solid Rock, Kenilworth, Illinois.
1912	Hurt Comstock House, Evanston, Illinois.
1912	Melson House, Mason City, Iowa.
1912	Page House, Mason City, Iowa.
1912-13	Plan for the Capital City of Canberra, Australia.
1913	Stinson Memorial Library, Anna, Illinois.
1913	Blyth House, Mason City, Iowa.
1921	Walter Burley Griffin House (Philiota), Eaglemont, Victoria.
1939	Pioneer Press Building, Lucknow, India.

Walter Gropius (1883-1969) Germany/Architect

1906-09	Workers Houses, Janikow, near Dramburg, Pomerania.
1911†	Fagus-Werk, Alfeld-an-der-Leine (with Adolf Meyer).
1913-14	Rural Houses, von Brockhausen Estate, Pomerania.
1914†	Office Building and Exhibition Hall (Model Industrial structure), Werkbund Exhibition, Cologne (with Adolf Meyer).
1921	Sommerfeld House, Dahlem, Berlin.
1922††	Chicago Tribune Tower, competition project with Adolf Meyer.
1922	War Memorial, Weimar.
1922	Bauhaus Housing, Weimar.
1923	City Theater, Jena (with Adolf Meyer).
1924	Auerbach House, Jena (with Adolf Meyer).
1924	Fröbel Institute, Bad Liebenstein (with Adolf Meyer).
1924	Hanover Paper Mill, Alfeld-an-der-Leine (with Adolf Meyer).
1924	Reis Tomb, Berlin.
1924	Mendel Tomb, Berlin.
1924-25	Fagus Shoe Factory Annex, Alfeld-an-der-Leine (with Adolf Meyer).
1925	Kappe Warehouse, Alfeld-an-der-Leine (with Adolf Meyer).
1925-26††	The Bauhaus, Dessau.
1925	Masters' Houses at the Bauhaus, Dessau.
1925	Gropius residence, Dessau.
1926	Müller Factory, Kirchbraach.
1926	Terrace Houses, groups I and II, Törten, Dessau.
1927	Terrace Housing, group III, Törten, Dessau.
1927-28	Dammerstock Housing, near Karlsruhe.
1927	Zuckerkandd House, Jena.
1927-28	Municipal Employment Office, Dessau.
1928	Lewin House, Zehlendorf, Berlin.
1928	Co-operative Store, Törten, Dessau.
1928	Terrace Houses, group IV, Dessau.
1929-30	Siemensstadt District (Supervising architect with Bartning, Forbat, Häring, Henning, and Scharoun).
1930	Exhibition, German Werkbund, Paris.
1931	Prefabricated Copper Houses, Hirsch Kupfer-und Messingwerke AG, Finow.
1931	Beinert Tomb, Dresden.
1931	Building Exhibition, Berlin.
1933	Bahner House, Berlin.
1933	Maurer House, Dahlem, Berlin.
1935	Apartments, St. Leonard's Hill, Windsor, Berkshire, England (with E. Maxwell Fry).
1936	London Film Productions Film Laboratories, Denham, Buckinghamshire, England (with E. Maxwell Fry).
1936	Levy House, 66 Old Church Street, Chelsea, London (with E. Maxwell Fry).
1936	Donaldson House, Sussex, England (with E. Maxwell Fry).
1936	Impington Village School, Cambridgeshire, England (with E. Maxwell Fry).
1938	Gropius House, Lincoln, Massachusetts (with Marcel Breuer).
1938	Breuer House, Lincoln, Massachusetts (with Marcel Breuer).
1938	Professor J. Ford House, Lincoln, Massachusetts (with Marcel Breuer).
1938	Hagerty House, Cohasset, Massachusetts (with Marcel Breuer).
1939	Chamberlain House, Sudbury, Massachusetts (with Marcel Breuer).
1939	Frank House, Pittsburgh (with Marcel Breuer).
1939	State of Pennsylvania Pavilion, World's Fair, New York (with Marcel Breuer).
1941	Abele House, Framingham, Massachusetts (with Marcel Breuer).
1941-43	Aluminum City, New Kensington, near Pittsburgh (with Marcel Breuer).
1945	Catholic Church, Torreon, Mexico (with J. Gonzales Rejna).
1949	Harvard Graduate Center, Cambridge, Massachusetts.

Hector Guimard (1867-1942) France/Architect

1891	House, 34 rue Boileau, Paris.
1892	Victor Rose Tomb, Batignolles Cemetery, Paris.
1893	House, 63 avenue de Clamart, Issy-les-Molineaux.
1893	Villa, 41 rue Chardon-Lagache, Paris.
1894	Devos-Logie Family Tomb, Gonards Cemetery, Versailles.
1894-98†	Castel Béranger, 14-16 rue La Fontaine, Paris.
1895	École du Sacré-Coeur, 9 avenue de la Frillière, Paris.
1895	House, 1 rue Molitor, Paris.
1895	House, 39 Boulevard Exelmans, Paris.
1896	House, 72 avenue de Montesson, Le Vessinet, Paris.
1897-1901	Humbert de Romans Auditorium, rue Saint-Didier, Paris.
1898-1900	Coilliot House and store, 14 rue de Fleurus, Lille.
1898	House, 9 and 9 bis Hameau-Boileau, Paris.
1899-1905†	Métro station entrances, Paris.
1899-1900	Castel Henriette, Sèvres (ruins).
1899	Villa La Houle, Hermanville, Calvados.
1899	House, 18 rue Alphonse de Neuville, Garches.
1902-03	House, rue de Meulières Chaponval, near Anvers-sur-Oise.
1903-05	Apartment Building (Jassedé Block), 142 avenue de Versailles, Paris.
1904-07	House, 8 Villa de la Réunion, Paris.
1905†	Castel Orgeval, 2 avenue de la Marc Tambour, Villemoisson.
1908	Chalet Blanc, 2 rue du Lycée, Sceaux.
1908	House, 16 rue Jean Doyon, Eaubonne, Paris.
1909-12	Guimard House, 122 avenue Mozart, Paris.
1910-11	Mezzara House, 60-62 rue la Fontaine, Paris.
1910	Apartment building, 11 rue François Millet, Paris.
1911-13	Synagogue, 10 rue Pavée, Paris.
1911	Apartment buildings, 8-10 rue Agar (now 9-11 rue Moderne), Paris.
1911	Apartment buildings, 17, 19, 21 rue la Fontaine, Paris.
1913	House, 3 rue de Crillon, St. Cloud, Paris (altered).
1919	Office building, 10 rue de Bretagne, Paris.
1921	Albert Adès Tomb, Montparnasse Cemetery, Paris.
1922	House, 3 Square Jasmin, Paris.
1925	Town Hall of a French Village, Exposition des Arts Décoratifs, Paris.
1925-26	Apartment building, 18 rue Henri Heine, Paris.
1926	Apartment building, 2 Villa Flore, Paris.
1927-28	Apartment building, 36 rue Greuze, Paris.
1928	Villa Guimard, Vaucresson.
1928-29	Apartment building, 38 rue Greuze, Paris.

Paul Hankar (1859-1901) Belgium/Architect

1893	Hankar House, rue Defacqz, Brussels.
1896	Magasin Claessen, rue de l'Ecuyer, Brussels.
1897†	Ciamberlani House, rue Defacqz, Brussels.
1898	Janssens House, rue Defacqz, Brussels.

Hugo Häring (1882-1958) Germany/Architect

1916-18	Manor House, Gr'Plauen, East Prussia.
1916-19	Hans Romer House, Neu Ulm.
1917	Reimann Shop and Living Quarters, Allenburg, East Germany.
1922	Gaffre Quinle Hospital, Rio de Janeiro.
1923††	Gut Garkau Agricultural Building, near Lübeck.
1924	Auction Rooms, Lübeck.
1925	Tobacco Goods Factory, Neustadt, Holstein.
1926	Terrace Housing, Zehlendorf, Berlin.
1927	Max Voythaler Building, Lankwitz, Berlin.
1928	Art Exhibition Hall, Tattersalle, Berlin.
1928	Adler Weekend House, Wansee Country Club, Berlin.
1928-29	Frenzel House, Elbing, East Prussia.
1930	Behrendt House, Berlin.
1930	Karlshorst Housing Development, Treskowallee, Berlin.
1930	Rodenstrasse Housing Development, Lichtenberg, Berlin.
1930-31	Beck/Segmehl House, Biberach.
1932	Eichkamp Housing Development, Berlin.
1933	Design of Werkbund Siedlung, Stuttgart.
1937-41	Von Prittwitz Building, Tutzing.
1938	Open-air school, Torbole sul Garda, Italy.
1942	Kunst and Werk School, Berlin.

Jacob-Ignace Hittorf (1792-1867) France/Architect

1838-40	Place de la Concorde, Paris.
1839	Cirque de Champs-Elysées, Paris.
1842-43	Rotonde des Panoramas, Paris.
1852	Cirque d'Hiver, Paris.
1861-63	Gare du Nord, Paris.

Josef Hoffmann (1870-1956) Austria/Architect

1899	Villa Moser, Hohen Warte Colony, Vienna.
1903-04	Purkersdorf Sanatorium, near Vienna.
1903-11	La Villa Ast, Vienna.
1905-11†	Palais Stoclet, Brussels, Belgium.
1911	Austrian Pavilion, Rome.
1913	Primavesi House, Winkelsdorf, North Moravia, Czechoslovakia.
1913-14	Austrian Pavilion, Werkbund Exhibition, Cologne, Germany.
1914-15	Villa Skywa, Vienna.
1916-17	Salesroom, Fashion Department, Wiener Werkstätte, Vienna.
1918	Pazzani Palace, Vienna.
1920-22	Berl House, Freudenthal (now Bruntal), Czechoslovakia.
1922-23	Dunckel House, Budapest.
1923	Josef Hoffmann Apartment interiors, Vienna.
1923	Grohmann Company Workers' Housing, Würbenthal (now Vrbno pod Praded), Czechoslovakia.

1925	Austrian Pavilion, Exposition des Arts Décoratifs, Paris.
1928	Altmann and Kuhne Pastry Shop, Vienna.
1928	Pre-fabricated house in steel, Vienna.
1929	Design of the Austrian Werkbund Exhibition, Vienna.
1930	Austrian section, International Exhibition, Stockholm.
1930	Otto Wagner Monument, Vienna.
1932	Four low-cost terraced houses, Werkbund Estate, Vienna.
1934	Austrian Pavilion, Biennale, Venice.
1937	Boudoir for a Great Actress, World's Fair, Paris.
1939-44	German Officer's Club, Vienna.
1950	Public housing, Blechturmgasse, Vienna.
1952	Public housing, Silbergasse, Vienna (with Josef Kalbac).
1954	Public housing, Heiligenstätterstrasse, Vienna (with Josef Kalbac).

Johannes Friedrich (Fritz) Höger (1877-1949) Germany/Architect

1920	Administration Offices, Schleswig-Holsteinischenstrom A.G., Rendsburg.
1921-24††	Chilehaus Shipping Headquarters, Hamburg.
1926	Grosse Bliechen, Broschek & Co. Publishing House, Hamburg.
1926-28	Sprinkenhof, Hamburg (with Hans & Oscar Gerson).
1926-29	Reemtsma Building, Cigarette Factory, Hamburg-Wandsbek.
1927-28	Anzeiger Building, Hanover.
1928	Administration Offices, Bentheimer Railway A.G., Bentheim.
1928	Flughafen Estate, Hamburg-Fuhlsbüttel.
1928-29	Townhall, Wilhelmshaven-Rustringen.
1930-33	Evangelist Church, Hohenzollernplatz, Berlin-Wilmersdorf.
1935-38	Siebetsburg Housing Estate, Wilhelmshaven.

Raymond Hood (1881-1934) USA/Architect

1922-25††	Chicago Tribune Tower (with John Mead Howells).
1924	St. Vincent de Paul Asylum, Tarrytown, New York (with J. André Fouilhoux).
1924	American Radiator Building, New York.
1925	Raymond Hood House, Stamford, Connecticut.
1926	Bethany Union Church, Chicago.
1927	McCormick Mausoleum, Rockford, Illinois.
1927	Morris House, Greenwich, Connecticut.
1927	National Broadcasting Company Studios, New York.
1928	Apartment Building, 3 East 84th Street, New York (with John Mead Howells).

1928	National Radiator Building, London (with S. Gordon Jeeves).
1929	Masonic Temple and Scottish Rite Cathedral, Scranton, Pennsylvania (with Godley, Fouilhoux, and H.V.K. Henderson).
1929	*Daily News* Building, New York City (with John Mead Howells).
1930	DuPont Building additions, Washington, D.C. (with Godley and Fouilhoux).
1930	Patterson House and Garage, Ossining, New York (with John Mead Howells).
1930	McGraw Hill Building, New York (with Fouilhoux).
1930-31	Beaux-Arts Apartments, New York (with Godley and Fouilhoux; plan by the firm of Kenneth Murchison).
1931-34††	Rockefeller Center, New York (Consultant architect; with Fouilhoux; Reinhardt and Hofmeister; and Corbett Harrison and McMurray; died before completion).
1933	Electricity Building, Hall of Social Science and Radiator Pavilion, Century of Progress Exhibition, Chicago.

Victor Horta (1861-1947) Belgium/Architect

1889	Lambeaux Building (Temple of the Human Passions), Parc du Cinguantenaire, Brussels (altered 1905).
1892-93	Tassel House, 6 rue Paul Emile Janson, Brussels.
1895-1900†	Hôtel Solvay, 224 avenue Louise, Brussels.
1896-98†	Maison du Peuple, Place Emile van de Velde, Brussels.
1897-1900	Van Eetvelde House, 4 rue Palmerston, Brussels.
1898	Horta House, 23-25 rue Americaine, Brussels (altered 1911, now Musée Horta).
1901-03†	L'Innovation Department Store, rue Neuve, Brussels (destroyed by fire, 1967).
1902	Belgian Pavilion, Exposition des Arts Décoratifs, Turin, Italy.
1902	Monument to Brahms, Vienna.
1903	Grand Bazaar Department Store, Frankfurt, Germany (with the sculptor, Van der Stappen; destroyed).
1903-05	Waucquez Department Store, 2 rue des Sables, Brussels.
1903	Hallet House, avenue Louise, Brussels.
1903-28	Musée des Beaux-Arts, Tournai, Belgium.
1906	Wolfers Building, 11-13 rue d'Arenberg, Brussels.
1906-26	Brugmann Hospital, Jette, Brussels.
1914-52	Halte Centrale, Main Railway Station, Brussels (construction begun 1924, completed by Brunfaut).
1920-28	Palais des Beaux-Arts, Brussels.
1925	Belgian Pavilion, Exposition des Arts Décoratifs, Paris.

1930	Wolfers Building extensions, 11-13 rue d'Arenberg, Brussels.

Charles-Edouard Jeanneret [Le Corbusier] (1887-1965) Switzerland/Architect

1905	Villa Fallet, La Chaux-de-Fonds.
1908	Villa Stotzer, La Chaux-de-Fonds.
1908	Villa Jacquement, La Chaux-de-Fonds.
1910	Applied Art School Project, La Chaux-de-Fonds.
1912	Villa Jeanneret, La Chaux-de-Fonds.
1912	Villa Favre, le Locle.
1914	Garden City Project, La Chaux-de-Fonds.
1914	Workers' Housing Project, St. Nicholas d'Aliermont.
1916	Cinema La Scala, La Chaux-de-Fonds.
1916†	Villa Schwob, La Chaux-de-Fonds.
1917	Water Tower, Les Landes.
1920	Citrohan House (first project).
1922	Besnos House, La Chataigneraie, Vaucresson, Paris (now altered).
1922	Ozenfant House, 53 Avenue de Reille, Paris (now altered).
1922	Contemporary City for 3 Million People, Salon d'Automne, Paris (exhibition project).
1922	Citrohan House (second project).
1923-25††	Villa La Roche-Jeanneret, 8-10 Square du Docteur Blanche, Paris (now Foundation Le Corbusier).
1923-25	Jeanneret House, 21 Route Lavaux, Corseaux-Vevey, Switzerland.
1924	Lipchitz/Mietschaninoff House, 9 Allée des Pins, Boulogne-sur-Seine, Paris.
1924	Tonkin House, Bordeaux.
1924	10 houses, Lège, near Bordeaux (now altered).
1925††	Pavillon de l'Esprit Nouveau, Exposition des Arts Décoratifs, Paris.
1925-26	Housing Colony, Pessac (now altered).
1925-27	Two Houses, Weissenhof Siedlung, Stuttgart.
1926	Ternisien House, 5 Allée des Pins, Boulogne-sur-Seine, Paris.
1926	Cook House, 6 Rue Denfert-Rocherau, Boulogne-sur-Seine, Paris.
1926	Salvation Army Dormitory (Palais du People), 29 rue des Cordelieres, Paris.
1926	Guiette House, Antwerp.
1927††	Villa Stein or de Monzie (Les Terraces), 17 rue du Professeur Victor Pauchet, Garches (now altered).
1927	Plainex House, 24 bis Boulevard Massena, Paris.
1927	League of Nations Headquarters, Geneva (Competition Project).
1928	Villa Baizau, Carthage, Tunisia.
1929	Salvation Army Floating Dormitory, Pont d'Austerlitz, Paris.
1929-31††	Villa Savoye (Les Heures Clairs), 82 Chemin de Villiers, Poissy.
1929-33	Centrosoyus Building, Kirova, Ulitsa, Moscow (now altered).
1930-31	Charles de Beisteguy Penthouse Apart-

	ment, Paris.
1930-31	Mandrot House, Le Pradet.
1930-32††	Swiss Students' Hostel, Cité Universitaire, Paris (now altered).
1930-32	Clarté, 2 rue Saint-Laurent, Geneva.
1932-33††	Cité de Refuge (Salvation Army), Paris.
1933	Apartment Block, 24 rue Nungesser-et-Coli, Paris.
1935	Weekend House, 85 Boulevard de la Republique, La Celle-Saint-Cloud, Paris.
1937††	Pavillon des Temps Nouveaux, World's Fair, Paris.
1937-43††	Ministry of Education and Health, Rio de Janeiro (with Lúcio Costa, Oscar Niemeyer, Alfonso Eduardo Reidy, and Jorge Machao Moreira), now the Palace of Culture.

Peter Vilhelm Jensen-Klint (1853-1930) Denmark/Architect

1896	Holm Villa, 27 Sofievej, Copenhagen.
1897-98	Rasmussen Gymnastic Institute, 49 Vodrofsvej, Copenhagen.
1905-06	Rødsten Villa, 12 Onsgårdsvej, Copenhagen.
1907	Aagard House, Ryslinge.
1913-40††	Grundtvigs Church and surrounding housing, Copenhagen (completed by his son, Kaare Klint, in 1940).
1921	St. Hans Tveje Church, Odense.
1923	Young Men's Christian Association Building, Odense.

Albert Kahn (1869-1942) USA/Architect

1903	Conservatory and Aquarium, Belle Isle Park, Michigan.
1903	Packard Motor Car Company Plant, East Grant Boulevard, Detroit, Michigan.
1903	Engineering Building, University of Michigan, Ann Arbor, Michigan.
1905	Factory for Burroughs Adding Machine Company, 2nd Avenue, Detroit, Michigan.
1905	Country Club, Grosse Pointe, Detroit, Michigan.
1905	Packard Motor Car Company Building No. 10, Detroit, Michigan.
1906	George N. Pierce Company Automobile Plant, Buffalo, New York.
1907	Grabowsky Power Wagon Company Plant, Detroit, Michigan.
1907	Chalmers Motor Car Company Plant, East Jefferson Avenue, Detroit, Michigan.
1907	Kahn House, Detroit, Michigan.
1907	Trussed Concrete Building, Detroit, Michigan.
1907	Mergenthaler Linotype Company Plant, Brooklyn, New York.
1908	Casino Building, Belle Isle, Michigan.
1909	Ford Motor Company Main Building and Machine Shop, Highland Park, Detroit, Michigan.

1910	Packard Motor Company, Forge Building, Detroit, Michigan.
1910	Hudson Motor Car Company Display Room, Detroit, Michigan.
1910	The National Theater, Detroit, Michigan.
1910	Dodge Brothers Corporation Plant, Hamtramk, Michigan.
1910	Dodge Brothers Corporation Office Building, Hamtramk, Michigan.
1910	Hudson Motor Car Company Plant and Office Building, East Jefferson Avenue, Detroit, Michigan.
1910-11	Hill Auditorium, University of Michigan, Ann Arbor, Michigan.
1912	Continental Motor Company Plant, East Jefferson Avenue, Detroit, Michigan.
1912-19	Burroughs Adding Machine Company Plant Additions, Detroit, Michigan.
1913	Ford Motor Company Plant Expansion, Highland Park, Detroit, Michigan.
1913	Ford Motor Company Service Building, Detroit, Michigan.
1913-15	Detroit Athletic Club, Detroit, Michigan.
1917	Laboratory Building, U.S. Aviation School, Langley Field, Virginia.
1917	Ford Eagle Plant, Ford Rouge River Complex, Detroit, Michigan.
1917-21	The General Motors Building, Detroit, Michigan.
1919	Buick Motor Car Company Plant, Flint, Michigan.
1921	Ford Motor Company Main Power House, Rouge River Complex, Detroit, Michigan.
1921	Fisher Body Company Plant, Cleveland, Ohio.
1922††	Glass Plant, Ford Rouge River Complex, Detroit, Michigan.
1922	Coke Ovens and By-Products Plant, Ford Rouge River Complex, Detroit, Michigan.
1922	Detroit Institute of Arts, Detroit, Michigan.
1922-24	Ford Motor Company Glass Plant, Rouge River Complex, Detroit, Michigan.
1922-25	General Motors Building, Detroit, Michigan.
1923	Cement Plant, Ford Rouge River Complex, Detroit, Michigan.
1923	Job Foundry, Ford Rouge River Complex, Detroit, Michigan.
1924-25	Open Hearth Building, Ford Rouge River Complex, Detroit, Michigan.
1924-25	Motor Assembly Building, Ford Rouge River Complex, Detroit, Michigan.
1925	Ford Motor Company Engineering Laboratory, Dearborn, Michigan.
1925	Pressed Steel Building, Ford Rouge River Complex, Detroit, Michigan.
1927-29	The Fisher Building, Detroit, Michigan.
1928	Chrysler Corporation, Plymouth Plant,

	Detroit, Michigan.
1929-32	Kahn Branch Office, Moscow. Chelyabinsk Tractor Plant, Kuznetsk and Stalingrad (Ford) Assembly Plants, etc., Soviet Union.
1929-39	Glen Martin Plant, Middle River, Maryland.
1931	Hudson Motor Company Office Building, Detroit, Michigan.
1933	Ford Motor Company, Rotunda Building, Dearborn, Michigan.
1935	Chevrolet Motor Division, Commercial Body Plant, Indianapolis.
1936	Chrysler Corporation Press Shop, De Soto Division, Detroit, Michigan.
1936	Ford Motor Company Tire Plant, Rouge Plant, Dearborn, Michigan.
1936	Republic Steel Corporation Hot and Cold Strip Mills, Cleveland, Ohio.
1936-41	De Soto Division Press Shop, Detroit, Michigan.
1937	Chrysler Half-Ton Truck Plant, Detroit, Michigan.
1937	Glen L. Martin Addition to Manufacturing Building, Baltimore, Maryland
1937	General Motors Corporation Manufacturing Plant Diesel Engine Division, Detroit, Michigan.
1938	Curtiss-Wright Corporation Stack Shops and Storage Building, Buffalo, New York.
1938	Chrysler Corporation, Half-Ton Truck Plant Assembly Building, Dodge Division, Warren, Michigan.
1938	Ohio Steel Foundry Company, Roll and Heavy Machine Shed, Lima, Ohio.
1938	Burroughs Adding Machine Company, Office and Factory, Plymouth, Michigan.
1939	Ford Exposition Building, New York World's Fair, New York.
1941	Chrysler Corporation Tank Arsenal, Warren, Michigan.
1941	American Steel Foundries, Cast Armor Plant, East Chicago, Illinois.
1941	Curtiss-Wright Corporation Airport Plant, Buffalo, New York.
1942	Chrysler Tank Arsenal, Warren Township, Michigan.
1942	Amertorp Corporation Torpedo Plant, Chicago, Illinois.
1942	American Locomotive Company Factory, Auburn, New York.
1942	The Amertorp Corporation, Ordnance and Torpedo Plant, Chicago, Illinois.

Jan Kotera (1871-1913) Czech./Architect

1902	The Manes Pavilion, near Kinsky Garden, Prague.
1902-03	Trmal House, Strasnice-Prague.
1905-07	The National House, Prostejov.
1906	Tonder House, St. Gilgen.
1906-13	Municipal Museum, Hradec Kralove.
1908	Chamber of Commerce, Prague.
1908	Kotera Villa, Vino Rrady-Prague.

1908-09	Laichter House, Prague.
1911-13	Urbanek House (Mozarteum), Prague.

Pieter Lodewijk Kramer (1881-1961) Holland/Architect

1919-22††	De Dagaraad Housing, Amsterdam (with Michel de Klerk).
1921-22	Residential Complex, Henriette-Ronnerplein and P. N. Takstraat, Amsterdam (with Michel de Klerk).
1922	Bridge, Keyersgracht, Vizzelstraat, Amsterdam.
1924	Bridge, Amstelkanaal, over the Ansteldijk, Amsterdam.
1924-26	De Bijenkorf (Department Store), Wagenstraat, The Hague.
1925	Residential complex, Hoofdweg and Postjesweg, Amsterdam.

Willem Kromhout (1846-1940) Holland/Architect

1898-1901	American Hotel, Amsterdam.
1917-18	Noorzee Building, Rotterdam.

Henri Labrouste (1801-75) France/Architect

1843-50	Bibliothèque Ste. Geneviève, Paris.
1855	Bibliothèque Impériale, Paris.
1862-69†	Bibliothèque Nationale (Palais Mazarin), Paris.

Jules Lavirotte (1864-1924) France/Architect

1901	229 avenue Rapp, Paris.
1904	Hotel Céramique, avenue Wagram, Paris.

Odon Lechner (1845-1914) Hungary/Architect

1871	Bela Mandel House, Budapest.
1884	City Hall, Szeged.
1884	Pension Fund, Hungarian National Railways, Budapest.
1889	Thonet House, Budapest.
1896	Museum of Applied Arts, Budapest.
1897-99	Geological Institute, Budapest.
1900	Postal Savings Bank, Budapest.
1913	Memorial Church of Arpadhazi St. Elizabeth, Pozsony (Bratislava), Czechoslovakia.

William Lescaze (1896-1969) Switzerland/Architect

1929	Dreyfus Apartment, New York.
1929-30	Howe and Lescaze Office, Philadelphia (with George Howe), Pennsylvania.
1929-30	Porter House, Ojai, California.
1929-32††	Philadelphia Savings Fund Society Office Building, 12th and Market Streets, Philadelphia (with George Howe), Pennsylvania.
1930-32	Headmaster's House (Curry House), Dartington Hall, Totnes, Devon, England.
1930-32	Frederick V. Field House, Hartford, Connecticut (with George Howe).
1931	Trans-Lux Theater, New York.

1933-34	Wilbour Library, Brooklyn Museum, New York.
1934	Lescaze House, 211 East 48th Street, New York.
1936	High School, Ansonia, Connecticut.
1936-38	CBS Radio Building, Hollywood (with E. T. Heitshmid).
1937	Administration Building, Kimble Glass Company, Vineland, New Jersey.
1937-38	Aeronautics Pavilion, World's Fair, New York.
1938-39	Cherry Lawn School, Connecticut.
1939	Swiss Pavilion, World's Fair, New York.
1939-41	Longfellow Building, Washington, D.C.
1941	House, 124 East 70th Street, New York.

William Richard Lethaby (1857-1931) England/Architect

1891	Manners House, Avon Tyrell, Christchurch.
1900	Eagle Insurance Building, Birmingham.
1901-02	All Saints' Church, Brockhampton.

Selim A. Lindquist (1867-1939) Finland/Architect

1906	Villa Johanna, Helsinki.
1908-13	Sulvilahti Power Station, Helsinki.

Adolf Loos (1870-1933) Austria/Architect

1898	Goldman and Salatsch Shop, Vienna.
1899	Café Museum, Vienna.
1904-06	Karma Villa, Montreaux, Switzerland.
1907†	American Bar, Vienna.
1907	Steiner Plume and Feather Shop, Vienna.
1909-13	Knize Store, Graben, Vienna.
1910†	Steiner Villa, Vienna.
1910	Goldman and Salatsch (Loos House), Michaelerplatz, Vienna.
1912	Scheu House, Vienna.
1913	Café Caupa, Vienna.
1913	Northartgasse House, Vienna.
1913	Bellatz Apartment, Vienna.
1913	House, Northartgasse/Sauragasse, Vienna.
1913	Paul Mayer Apartment, Vienna.
1914	Emil Lowenbach Apartment, Vienna.
1915	Gymnasium, Schwartzwald School, Semmering, Vienna.
1918	Director's House, Rohrbach Sugar Refinery, near Brno, Czechoslovakia.
1919	Rohrbach Sugar Refinery Factory, near Brno, Czechoslovakia.
1919	Peter Altenberg Tombstone, Central Cemetery, Vienna.
1922	Steiner House reconstruction, Vienna.
1926-27††	Tristan Tzara House, Paris.
1928	Moller House, Potzleinsdorf, Vienna.
1929	Josef Vogl Apartment, Pilsen, Czechoslovakia.
1929	Hans Brummel Apartment, Pilsen, Czechoslovakia.
1930	Leo Brummel Apartment, Pilsen, Czechoslovakia.
1930	Eisner Apartment, Pilsen, Czecho-

	slovakia.
1930	Müller House, Prague.
1931	Semi-detached House, Werkbund Exhibition, Vienna.
1931	Willy Kraus Apartment, Pilsen, Czechoslovakia.
1931	Small timber house for Mitzi Schnabel, Vienna.
1931	Babi Workers' Estate, near Nachod, Northern Bohemia.

Berthold Lubetkin (1901-   ) Russian/Architect

1927	Apartment Building, 25 Avenue de Versailles, Paris (with Jean Ginsberg).
1932	Gorilla House, London Zoo, Regent's Park.
1933††	Penguin Pool, London Zoo, Regent's Park (Tecton).
1934-35	Giraffe and Elephant Houses, Whipsnade Zoo, Bedfordshire (Tecton).
1934-35††	Highpoint I Apartment Block, Highgate, London (Tecton).
1937-38	Highpoint II Apartment Block, Highgate, London (Tecton).
1938	Finsbury Health Center, London (Tecton).
1942	Lenin Memorial Monument, Holford Square, Holborn, London.

Colin Lucas (1906-   ) England/Architect

1927	Silver Birches, Burghclere, Hampshire.
1930	Noah's House, Bourne End, Buckinghamshire.
1931	Sun House, Ashdown Forest, Sussex.
1933††	The Hopfield, Wrotham, Kent.
1934	Four Houses, High and Over Estate, Amersham, Buckinghamshire (with Basil Ward).
1935	Kent House Flats, Chalk Farm, London (Connell, Ward and Lucas).
1935	Two pairs of semi-detached houses, Parkwood Estate, Ruislip, Middlesex (Connell, Ward and Lucas).
1935	The Firs, Redhill, Surrey (Connell, Ward and Lucas).
1936	Dragons, Woodmancote, Sussex (Connell, Ward and Lucas).
1936	Concrete House (Ronald Gunn House), Westbury-on-Trym, Bristol (Connell, Ward and Lucas).
1937	House, Virginia Water, Surrey (Connell, Ward and Lucas).
1937	Geoffrey Walford House, 66 Frognal Rise, Hampstead, London (Connell, Ward and Lucas).
1937	House, Worcester Park, Surrey (Connell, Ward and Lucas).
1937-38	H. Tarburn House, Moor Park, Hertfordshire (Connell, Ward and Lucas).
1938	Potcraft (Dr. Thomas House), Sutton, Surrey (Connell, Ward and Lucas).
1938-39	Proudman House, Roehampton, London (Connell, Ward and Lucas).

Edwin Landseer Lutyens (1859-1944) England/Architect

1896	Munstead Wood, Godalming, Surrey.
1897-1908	The Pleasaunce (Lord Battersea's House), alterations, Overstrand, Norfolk.
1898	Les Bois des Moutiers (Guillaume Mallet house), Varangeville, France.
1899-1902	Deanery Gardens, Sonning, Berkshire.
1899	Togbourne Court, Witley, Surrey.
1901-04	Marsh Court, Stockbridge, Hampshire.
1901-12	Folly Farm additions, Sulhampstead, Berkshire.
1902	The Hoo (Alexander Wedderburn House), alterations and gardens, Willingdon, Surrey.
1902	Blackburn House, Little Thakeham, Sussex.
1903-04	Papillon Hall, Leicestershire.
1903-07	Lindisfarne Castle, conversion, Holy Island, Northumberland.
1904-07	Heathcote, Ilkley, Yorkshire.
1905-08	Nashdom, Taplow, Buckinghamshire.
1908	Plan for Hampstead Garden Suburb, London (with Raymond Unwin).
1909-11	St. Jude's Church, Hampstead Garden Suburb, London.
1910-30	Castle Drogo, Drewsteignton, Devon.
1911	The Salutation, Sandwich, Kent.
1912-31	Viceroy's House, New Delhi, India.
1924	Marsh Court, great hall addition, Stockbridge, Surrey.
1928	Edward Hudson House cottages, entrance, gate, and bridge, Plumpton Place, Sussex.

Charles Rennie Mackintosh (1868-1928) Scotland/Architect
(Most of Mackintosh's work was achieved while in the employ of Honneyman and Keppie)

1890	Redclyffe, Springburn, Glasgow.
1894-95	Queen Margaret's Medical College, Glasgow.
1895	Martyrs' Public School, Glasgow.
1897-99†	Glasgow School of Art, Glasgow (first stage).
1897-99	Queen's Cross Church of Scotland, Glasgow.
1899-1901	Davidson House, Windyhill, Kilmacolm.
1901	Ingram Street Tea Rooms, Glasgow.
1902-03†	Blackie House, Hill House, Helensburgh.
1903-04	Willow Tea Rooms, Glasgow.
1905	The Dutch Kitchen Tea Rooms, Argyle Street, Glasgow.
1906	Shand House, Auchinibert, Killearn.
1906	Collins House, Mosside, Kilmacolm.
1906	The Oak Room Tea Rooms, Ingram Street, Glasgow.
1907-09†	Glasgow School of Art, Glasgow (second stage).
1911	The Chinese Room Tea Rooms, Ingram Street, Glasgow.
1915-17	Basset-Lowke House (interiors), 78

	Derngate, Northampton, England.
1920	Harold Squire Studio House, Glebe Place, Chelsea, London.

Arthur Heygate Mackmurdo (1851-1942) England/Architect

1873	Halcyon House, Enfield, Middlesex.
1886-87	Brooklyn House, Enfield, Middlesex.
1886	Century Guild Stand, Liverpool International Exhibition, Liverpool.
1889	Savoy Hotel, Thames Embankment, London.
1890	Gymnasium, St. Helens, Lancashire.
1891	House, 12 Hans Road, London.
1899	House, 25 Cadogan Gardens, London.
1900	Cold Storage Warehouse, Charterhouse Street, London.

Robert Maillart (1872-1940) Switzerland/Engineer and Architect

1920	Textile Hall, Sallent, Spain.
1920	Benet Factory, Barcelona.
1920	Arve Bridge, Marignier, France.
1924	Rempen Aqueduct, Schwyz.
1924	Schrahbach Bridge, Innerthal.
1924	Flienglibach Bridge, Innerthal.
1924	Ziggenbach Bridge, Waggital.
1925	Magazzini Generali S. A., Chiasso, Ticino.
1925	Chatelard Aqueduct, Wallis.
1925	Val-Tschiel Bridge, Donath.
1926	Sihl Post Office, Zurich.
1929-30††	Salginatobel Bridge, Schiers.
1930	Landquart Bridge, Klosters.
1931	Spital Bridge, Frutigen-Adelboden, Berne.
1931	Ladholz Bridge, Frutigen, Berne.
1931	Hombach Bridge, Schangau, Berne.
1931	Luterstalden Bridge, Schangau, Berne.
1931	Aqueduct, Gadmen, Berne.
1932	Traubach Bridge, Habkern-Bohl, Berne.
1932	Bohlbach Bridge, Habkern, Berne.
1932	Tessin Bridge, Giubiasco-Sementina, Ticino.
1932	Gorge-du-Trent Bridge, Wallis.
1932	Quai Perdonnet, Vevey.
1933	Screw Factory, Gerlafingen.
1933	Schwandbach Bridge, Berne.
1934	Viaduct, Sarajevo, Yugoslavia.
1935	Rhine Bridge, Schaffhausen.
1936	Quai Turrettini, Geneva.
1937	Gründlischwand Bridge, Berne.
1939	Zementhalle, Swiss Provinces Exhibition, Zurich (with Hans Leuzinger).
1939	Rhone Bridge, Aire-la-Ville-Peney, Geneva.
1940	Simme Bridge, near Laubegg, Berne.
1940	Simme Bridge, Garstatt, Berne.
1940	Footbridge, Lachen, Altendorf.

Giaccomo Matté-Trucco (1869-1934) Italy/Naval Architect

1915-21†	Fiat Automobile Factory, Lingotti, Turin.

Bernard Maybeck (1862-1957) USA/Architect

1896	Mining Building, University of California, Berkeley, California.
1899	Hearst Hall, University of California, Berkeley, California.
1900	Men's Faculty Club, University of California, Berkeley, California.
1902	Wyntoon, Phoebe Apperson Hearst residence, McCloud River, California.
1905	Outdoor and Clubhouse, Mill Valley, California.
1906	Hopps House, Ross Valley, California.
1907	Lawson House, Berkeley, California.
1910†	First Church of Christ Scientist, Church, Berkeley, California.
1910	Randolph School, Berkeley, California.
1913	Chick House, Berkeley, California.
1915	Palace of Fine Arts, Panama Pacific International Exposition, San Francisco, California.
1917	Bingham House, Montecito, California.
1917	Clyde Hotel, Clyde, California.
1919	Forest Hills Association Club Building, 318 Magellan Avenue, San Francisco.
1920	James J. Fagan House, Portola Drive, Woodside, California.
1921	Alpine Glen Springs Resort buildings, El Dorado Country, California.
1923	R. H. Mathewson House, Berkeley, California.
1924	O. K. McMurray House, 2357 Le Conte Avenue, Berkeley, California.
1926	Packard Automobile Showroom, Van Ness Avenue, San Francisco (with Powers and Ahnden).
1927	R. I. Woolsey House, Kensington, Contra Costa County, California.
1928	Earl C. Anthony House, 3435 Waverly Place, Los Angeles.
1933	Wallen W. Maybeck House No. 1, 2751 Buena Vista Way, Berkeley, California.

McKim, Mead and White (1836-1909), (1846-1928), and (1853-1906) USA/Architects

1876-77	Moses Taylor House, Elberon, New Jersey (McKim).
1879-80	Short Hills Casino, Short Hills, New Jersey.
1879-81	Newport Casino, Bellevue Avenue, Newport, Rhode Island (White).
1880-81	Victor Newcomb House, Elberon, New Jersey.
1883-85	Tiffany Residence, New York (White).
1887	William Low House, Bristol, Rhode Island.
1888-98	Boston Public Library, Boston, Massachusetts (McKim).
1890-91	Century Club, New York (McKim & White).
1892-93	Agricultural Building, World's Columbian Exposition, Chicago (McKim).
1893-1913	Columbia University, New York.

1894-1916	Harvard Club, New York.
1895-1904	Rhode Island State Capitol, Providence, Rhode Island (McKim).
1897-1900	The University Club, New York (McKim).
1902-07	Morgan Library, New York (McKim).
1903-06	Tiffany & Co., New York.
1905-11†	Pennsylvania Station, New York (McKim).
1912-14	American Academy, Rome.
1916-19	Racquet and Tennis Club, New York.

Konstantin Melnikov (1890-1974) Russia/ Architect

1917	Facade for main building of AMO (now Likhachev) automobile factory, Moscow.
1917	Three small factory structures, AMO automobile factory, Moscow (with A. F. Loleidt).
1923	Makhorka Pavilion at the first All-Union Agriculture and Cottage Industries Exhibition, Moscow.
1924	Bar administrative building, Sukharevka Market, Moscow.
1924	Sarcophagus for V. I. Lenin, Red Square, Moscow.
1924	Sukharevka Market, Moscow.
1925	Soviet Pavilion, Exposition des Arts Décoratifs, Paris.
1925	Display kiosks, Torgsektor Exhibit, Paris.
1926	Bus garage, Bakmetevskaia, Moscow.
1926	Baldachin for funeral of Leonid Krasnin, Moscow (November).
1927	K.S. Melnikov House, Krivoarbatskii Pereulok, Moscow.
1927††	Rusakov factory, workers' club, Moscow.
1927	Kauchuk factory, workers' club, Moscow.
1927	Frunze factory, workers' club, Moscow.
1927-28	*Pravda* factory, workers' club, Dulevo.
1928	Kauchuk factory cafeteria, Moscow.
1929	Burevestnik factory, workers' club, Moscow.
1929	Parking garage, Novo-Riazanskaia Ulitsa, Moscow.
1929	Gosplan parking garage, Moscow (with V. I. Kurochkin).
1930	Reconstruction of Moscow Chamber Theater.
1949	Interior of central department store, Saratov.

Erich Mendelsohn (1887-1953) Germany/Architect

1911	Chapel, Hebrew Cemetery, Allenstein (now Olsztyn, Poland).
1919-23	Hat Factory, Steinberg, Herman & Co., Luckenwalde.
1919-24††	Einstein Tower, Astro-Physical Institute, Potsdam.
1921-22	*Berliner Tageblatt*, Administration Building addition, Berlin.
1921-22	Semi-detached private residences, Charlottenburg, Berlin.
1921-22	Weichman Silk Store and Offices, Gleiwitz (now Gliwice, Poland).
1923	Sternfeld House, Heerstrasse, Berlin.
1924	Herpich-Furriers' Building, Leipzigerstrasse, Berlin.
1925	Manufacturing Plant for the Leningrad Textile Trust, USSR.
1926-27	Schocken Department Store, Nuremberg.
1926-27	Jewish Cemetery, Koenigsberg.
1926-27	Petersdorff Department Store, Breslau (now Poland).
1926-27	Offices and Showrooms for German Clothing Center, Berlin.
1926-27	Power Station, *Berlin Tageblatt*, Berlin.
1926-27	Shop for C. A. Herpich & Sons, Berlin.
1927-28	Mosse Pavilion, Press Exhibition, Cologne.
1927-28††	Universum Cinema, Kurfuerstendamm, Berlin.
1927-28	Block of Flats, Cicerostrasse, Berlin.
1928-29	Schocken Department Store, Chemnitz (now Karlmarkstadt).
1929-30	Mendelsohn House, Rupenhorn, Berlin.
1929-30	Hebrew Youth Center, Essen.
1929-30	I. G. Farben Administration Building, Berlin.
1931-32	Zinc Factory, Magdeburg.
1931-34	Bachner Department Store, Moravska-Ostrava, Czechoslovakia.
1933-35	De La Warr Pavilion, Bexhill-on-Sea, England (with Serge Chermayeff).
1935-36	Cohen Residence, Old Church Street, Chelsea, London.
1935-36	Professor Weizmann Residence, Rehovot, Palestine (now Israel).
1935-36	Mr. Salman Schocken Residence and Library, Jerusalem.
1937-38	Town Plan, Hebrew University, Mount Scopus, Jerusalem.
1937-38	Hadassah University Medicinal Center, Mount Scopus, Jerusalem.
1937-38	Government Hospital, Haifa, Palestine (now Israel).
1937-38	Anglo-Palestine Bank, Jerusalem.
1937-38	Trade School, Jagur, Palestine (now Israel).
1939	Agricultural Institute, Rehovot, Palestine (now Israel).
1939	Daniel Wolf Research Laboratories, Rehovot, Palestine (now Israel).
1942	Kaplan House renovation, Long Island, New York.
1946-50	Temple and Community Center, Cleveland, Ohio.
1951-53	Atomic Energy Commission Laboratories, Berkeley, California.

Giuseppe Mengoni (1829-77) Italy/Engineer/Architect

1865-67†	Galleria Vittorio Emanuele II, Milan.

Ludwig Mies van der Rohe (1886-1969) Germany/Architect

1907	Riehl House, Neubabelsberg, Berlin.
1914	Mies van der Rohe House, Werder.
1924	Mosler House, Neubabelsberg, Berlin.
1925	Municipal Housing Development, Afrikanischestrasse, Berlin.
1926	Wolf House, Guben.
1927††	Werkbund Exposition, Weissenhof Siedlung, Stuttgart.
1927	Apartment House, Weissenhof Siedlung, Stuttgart.
1927	Silk Exhibit, Exposition de la Mode, Berlin (with Lily Reich).
1928	Addition to Fuchs House (originally Perls House), Zehlendorf, Berlin.
1928	Hermann Lange House, Krefeld.
1928	Esters House, Krefeld.
1929††	German Pavilion, International Exposition, Barcelona (with Lily Reich).
1929	Electricity Pavilion, International Exposition, Barcelona.
1929	Industrial Exhibits, International Exposition, Barcelona.
1930	Apartment interior, New York (for Philip Johnson).
1930††	Tugendhat House, Brno.
1931	House, Berlin Building Exposition, Berlin.
1931	Apartment for a Bachelor, Berlin Building Exposition, Berlin.
1932	Lemcke House, Berlin.
1934	Mining Exhibits, Deutsche Volk, Deutsche Arbeit Exposition, Berlin.
1942-43	Minerals and Research Building, IIT, Chicago, Illinois (with Holabird & Root).
1944	Engineering Research Building, IIT, Chicago, Illinois (with Holabird & Root).
1945	Alumni Memorial Hall, IIT, Chicago, Illinois (with Holabird & Root).

Doménech y. Montaner (1850-1923) Spain (Catalonia)/ Architect

1881-85	Montaner y Simon Offices, Barcelona.
1888	Café Restaurant, Universal Exhibition, Barcelona.
1902-12	Saint Paul Hospital, Barcelona.
1905-08	Palace of Catalan Music, Barcelona.

Karl Moser (1860-1936) Switzerland/Architect

1924-25	Lesesaal Kunsthaus, Zurich.
1925-27††	St. Antonius Church, Basel.

Pier Luigi Nervi (1891-1979) Italy/Engineer

1927	August Cinema, Naples.
1930-32††	Municipal Stadium, Florence.
1936	Aircraft Hangars, for the Italian Air Force, Orvieto.
1942	Underground gasoline storage tanks, Italy.
1945	Ferro-Cemento Warehouse, Rome.

Richard Neutra (1892-1970) Austria/Architect

1927	Jardinette Apartments, Los Angeles.
1927-29††	Lovell Health House, Los Angeles.
1933	Neutra House, Silverlake, Los Angeles (destroyed by fire 1963; rebuilt by Neutra, with his son Dion, 1964).
1935	Beard House, Altadena, California.
1935	Corona Avenue School, Bell, Los Angeles.
1936	Plywood Model House, Los Angeles.
1936	California Military Academy, Los Angeles.
1937	Beckstrand House, Palos Verdes, California.
1938	Strathmore Apartments, Westwood, Los Angeles.
1938	Emerson Junior High School, Westwood, Los Angeles.
1939	National Youth Administration Centers, Sacramento and San Luis Obispo, California.
1939	Amity House, Compton, California.
1940††	Kahn House, Telegraph Hill, San Francisco.
1941	Avion Village, Texas.
1942	Nesbitt House, Brentwood, Los Angeles.
1942	Channel Heights Housing, San Pedro, California.
1942	Kelton Apartments, Westwood, Los Angeles.
1944	Rural School Buildings, Puerto Rico.

Oscar Niemeyer (1907-) Brazil/Architect

1937	Obra do Berco Nursery and Maternity Clinic, Rio de Janeiro.
1937-43††	Ministry of Education and Health, Rio de Janeiro (with Le Corbusier, Lúcio Costa, Jorge Machado Moreira, and Elfonso Eduardo Reidy; now the Palace of Culture).
1938	Oswald de Andrade House, Sao Paulo.
1939	Brazilian Pavilion, World's Fair, New York (with Le Corbusier).
1941	National Stadium, Rio de Janeiro.
1941	Water Tower, Rio de Janeiro.
1942-46††	Pampulha Development, with the Church of St. Francis Assisi, Yacht Club, and Restaurant, Minas Gerais.
1942	Oscar Niemeyer House, Gavea, Rio de Janeiro.
1943	Kubitschek House, Pampulha, Minas Gerais.
1944	Prudente de Morais Neto House, Rio de Janeiro.
1944	Recreation Center, Rodrigos de Freitas, Lagoon, Rio de Janeiro.
1945	Yacht Club, Rio de Janeiro.

Joseph Maria Olbrich (1867-1908) Austria/Architect

1897-98†	Secession Building, Vienna.
1899-1901†	Ernst Ludwig House, Mathildenhöhe, Darmstadt, Germany.
1899	Herman Bahr House, Vienna-Oberst Veit.

1900	Olbrich House, Mathildenhöhe, Darmstadt, Germany.
1900	Christiansen House, Mathildenhöhe, Darmstadt, Germany.
1900	Habich House, Mathildenhöhe, Darmstadt, Germany.
1900	Glueckert House, Mathildenhöhe, Darmstadt, Germany.
1900	Bosselt House, Mathildenhöhe, Darmstadt, Germany.
1900	Keller House, Mathildenhöhe, Darmstadt, Germany.
1900	Deiters House, Mathildenhöhe, Darmstadt, Germany.
1900	Gauss House, Mathildenhöhe, Darmstadt, Germany.
1901	Entrance Portal, Artists' Colony Exhibition, Darmstadt, Germany.
1901	Exhibition Gallery, Artists' Colony Exhibition, Darmstadt, Germany.
1901	Restaurant, Artists' Colony Exhibition, Darmstadt, Germany.
1901	Stade House, Prinz Christians Weg, Darmstadt, Germany.
1902	Kuntze House, Halskestrasse, Berlin-Steglitz.
1905-06†	Wedding Tower (Hochzeitsturm), Mathildenhöhe, Darmstadt, Germany.
1906-08	Tietz Department Store, Düsseldorf, Germany.
1907	Krnska House, Cologne-Lindenthal, Germany.
1908	Feinhals House, Cologne-Marienburg, Germany.
1908	Althoff Store, Gladbeck, Germany.

Ragnar Östberg (1866-1945) Sweden/Architect
1901-03	Ebbagarden, Tureberg.
1904-05	Villa Pauli, Djursholm.
1905	Villa Ekarne, Stockholm.
1906-10	Ostermalms School, Stockholm.
1906	Theatre, Umea.
1906-23†	Stockholm Town Hall, Stockholm.
1907	Villa Larsson, Storangen, Nacka.
1909	Villa Nedre Manilla, Stockholm.
1911-13	Odd Fellows' Building, Stockholm.
1911-21	Patents' Office, Stockholm.
1930	Värmland National House, Uppsala.
1933	Secondary School, Kalmar.
1934	Marine Historical Museum, Stockholm.
1935	Crematorium, Hälsingborg.
1939	Zoorn Museum, Mora.

Jacobus Johannes Pieter Oud (1890-1963) Holland/Architect
1906	Alida Hartog-Oud House, Purmerend.
1907-08	House, Purmerend.
1910-12	Brand House, Beemster.
1911	Vooruit Building, Purmerend.
1912	House, Julianastraat, Purmerend.
1912	Gerrit Oud House, Aalsmeer.
1913	Van Lent House, Heemstede.
1914	Van Bakel House, Heemstede.
1914	Workers' Housing, Leiderdorp (with Dudok).

1915	Van Essen-Uinker House, Blaricum.
1917	Vacation Home, Noordwijkerhout.
1917	Villa Allegonda, Katwijk Aan Zee.
1919	Spangen Estate, Rotterdam.
1920-21	Tusschendijken Estate, Gijsingstraat, Rotterdam.
1922	Out-Mathenesse Estate, Rotterdam.
1924-27††	Hoek of Holland Housing Estate.
1925	Kiefhoek Workers' Village, Rotterdam.
1927	Row Housing, Weissenhof Siedlung, Stuttgart, Germany.
1928	Church, Kiefhoek Workers' Village, Rotterdam.
1938-42	Schell Company Corporate Headquarters, The Hague.
1943	Central Saving Bank, Rotterdam.

Sir Joseph Paxton (1801-65) England/Gardener/Engineer
1836-40	Great Stove, Chatsworth.
1843-77	Birkenhead Park, Liverpool.
1851†	Crystal Palace, Hyde Park, London.
1852-54	Crystal Palace, Sydenham, London (re-erection).

Auguste Perret (1874-1954) France/Architect
1902	Apartments, avenue de Wagram, Paris.
1903-04†	Apartments, 25 bis rue Franklin, Paris.
1905†	Garage, rue Ponthieu, Paris.
1910-13†	Théâtre des Champs-Elysées, Paris.
1919	Esders Factory, avenue Philippe-Auguste, Paris.
1921	Madame Paul Jamot Monument, Montparnasse Cemetery, Paris.
1921	Marinoni Workshops, Wallut Foundry Buildings, and Grange Foundry Buildings, Montataire, Oise.
1921	Rozanes Jewelry Shop, rue de la Paix, Paris.
1921	FER factory, Aulnois.
1922	Société Marseillaise de Crédit Building, 4 rue Auber, Paris.
1922-23††	Notre-Dame du Raincy, le Raincy.
1923	Durand Décors Workshops, rue Olivier-Metra, Paris.
1923	Grand-Quevilly House, near Rouen.
1923	Pont d'Argent, Théâtre des Champs-Elysées, Paris (temporary aluminum structure).
1924	Church Bell Tower, Saint Vaury, Creuse.
1924	Palais de Bois, Porte Maillot, Paris (temporary exhibition building).
1925	Theater and Albert Levy Pavilion, Exposition des Arts Décoratifs, Paris.
1925	Crédit Hôtelier Building, rue de la Ville-l'Évêque, Paris.
1925	Church of St. Thérèse, Montmagny, Seine et Oise.
1925	Observation Tower, Grenoble Exhibition.
1926	Cassandre House, Versailles.
1926	Veret House, Noyon.
1926	Chana Orloff House, rue de la Tombe-Issoire, Paris.

1926	Aghia House, Alexandria, Egypt.
1927	Braque House, rue du Douanier, Paris.
1927	School, Parc Montsouris, Paris.
1928	Bresy House, Villa Said, Algeria.
1928	Chapel, Arceuil, Seine.
1929	Mela Muter House, Villa Seurat, Algeria.
1929	Eiffel Monument, Paris.
1929	Chapel, Chalons.
1929	Hure House, Boulogne-sur-Seine, Paris.
1929	Galerie Katia Granoff extensions, Quai Conti, Paris.
1929	Oblates Convent, Saint Benoit.
1930	Lange House, Avenue Ingrès, Paris.
1931	Nubar Bey House, Garches.
1931	Society of Naval Works and Construc-
1931	Chapel, Vanves.
1932	Apartment Building, 51-55 rue Raynouard, Paris.
1932	Marine National Building, Paris.
1932	Awad Bey House, Cairo.
1933	Aghun House, Alexandria, Egypt.
1934	Paul Lefèvre House, Sceaux.
1934	Mobilier National (National Guard) Building, Paris.
1935	Pont de l'Arc, Paris.
1937	Museum of Public Works, Paris.
1939	Iron and Aluminum Foundry, Issoire.
1939	Clock and Watch Factory, Besançon.
1939	Barbier Hospital, Algiers.
1945	Master plan for the reconstruction of Le Havre.

Hans Poelzig (1869-1948) Germany/Architect
1906	Villa Poelzig, Leerbentel, near Breslau (now Poland).
1908-12	Terraced houses, Breslau (now Poland).
1911-12†	Chemical Factory, Luban, near Posen (Poznan, now Poland).
1911†	Water Tower, Posen (Poznan, now Poland).
1913	Colonnade and Exhibition Building, Breslau (now Poland).
1916	Gasworks, Dresden-Reick.
1919†	Grosses Schauspielhaus, Berlin.
1920	Filmsets for Der Golem.
1924	Meyer Company Administration Building, Vinnhorst, Hanover.
1924	Myer Company Storage Depot, Hanover.
1925	Capitor Cinema Building, with shops, Berlin.
1926	Deli Cinema, Breslau.
1927	Sigmund Goeritz Factory, Chemnitz, (now Karlmarxstadt), East Germany.
1927	Single-family house, Weissenhof Housing Estate, Stuttgart.
1928	Single-family housing, Gafgah District, Zehlendorf, Berlin.
1929	Power Station, Schulau (with Werner Issel).
1929	Babylon Cinema, Berlin.
1929	Cassirer and Company Ltd. Cableworks, Spandau, Berlin.
1929	Community Center, Kammin.

1930	I. G. Farben Administration Building, Frankfurt.
1930	Trade Fair, Berlin (with Martin Wagner).
1930	Broadcasting House, Berlin.
1931	Savings Bank, Wolgast.

Willis Polk (1867-1924) USA/Architect
1889	Presbyterian Church, Liberty, Missouri.
1912	Pacific Union Clubhouse, San Francisco, California.
1918†	Hallidie Building, San Francisco, California.

Antoine Pompe (1873-1980) Belgium/Architect
1910†	Dr. van Neck Clinic, Saint Gilles, Brussels.
1913	Maison Gheude, 174 avenue Molière, Ixelles (with F. Bodson).
1916	House and shop, 33 rue d'Ecosse, Saint Gilles.
1919	Garden City, Batavia, Roulers (with F. Bodson).
1921	Garden City, Hautrage-Nord.
1922	House with garage, 25 avenue J. Sermon, Ganshoren.
1922	House, 15 rue Servais-Kinet, Woluwé-St. Lambert (altered).
1922	Apartment house, 129 rue des Atrébates, Brussels.
1922-26	Kapelleveld Garden City, Woluwé-St. Lambert.
1924	Double Houses, 131-133 rue des Bouleaux, Boitsfort.
1925	Medical Institute Extension, rue Buduognar, Saint-Josse-Ten-Noode.
1926	Villa, avenue de la Sapinière, Uccle.
1928-30	Double Houses, Rhodes St. Genèse.
1928-30	Housing group, avenue de la Forêt de Soignes and avenue du Nouveau Rhode, Rhodes St. Genèse (with Rubbers).
1931	Jewelry shop, place de Meir, Anvers.
1933	Villa, avenue du Sanatorium, Alsemberg.
1934	Country house, avenue Hellevelt, Uccle.
1947	Van Neck House, Ganshoren.
1953	V. Pompe House, Hertogenweg, Wozembeek-Oppem.

Bruce Price (1845-1903) USA/Architect
1866	St. Paul's Evangelical Lutheran Church, Baltimore, Maryland.
1871	R.E. Lee Memorial Church, Lexington, Virginia.
1875	Woodward Monument, Wilkes-Barre, Pennsylvania.
1876	First Methodist Episcopal Sunday School, Wilkes-Barre, Pennsylvania.
1877	Tick's Drug Store, Wilkes-Barre, Pennsylvania.
1879	Union League Club House, New York, New York.
1879	The Craigs, Bar Harbor, Maine.

1880 Cathedral, Demerara, British Guiana.
1882 Neff House, Cincinnati, Ohio.
1883 Seacroft, Seabright, New Jersey.
1884 Seaverge, Seabright, New Jersey.
1884 Casa Far Niente, Bar Harbor, Maine.
1885 First Methodist-Episcopal Church, Wilkes-Barre, Pennsylvania.
1885 Tuxedo Park Village and Gate House, New York.
1885 Barbey House, Tuxedo Park, New York.
1885 Breese House, Tuxedo Park, New York.
1885 Kent House, Tuxedo Park, New York.
1885 Chamber of Commerce, Cincinnati, Ohio.
1885 Parlor car, Boston and Albany R.R.
1886 Windsor Station, Montreal, Canada.
1886 Chandler House, Tuxedo Park, New York.
1886 Van Buren House, Tuxedo Park, New York.
1886 Lorillard House, Tuxedo Park, New York.
1886 Japanese Cottage, Tuxedo Park, New York.
1886 Howard House, San Mateo, California.
1887 Levey House, Elizabeth, New Jersey.
1889 Carisbrooke, Schroon Lake, New York.
1889 Osborn Hall, Yale University, New Haven, Connecticut.
1890 Boulder Point, Tuxedo Park, New York.
1890 Turtle Point, Tuxedo Park, New York.
1890 Rock Ridge, Tuxedo Park, New York.
1892 Jersey Central Railroad Station, Elizabeth, New Jersey.
1893 Chateau Frontenac, Quebec, Canada.
1893 The Turrets, Bar Harbor, Maine.
1897 Georgian Court, Lakewood, New Jersey.
1900 Ross House, Montreal, Canada.

Edward Prior (1852-1932) England/Architect
1883 Red House, Byron Hill, Harrow.
1885 Pier Terrace, West Bay, Bridport.
1895-98 The Barn, Exmouth.
1904-07 St. Andrew, Roker, Near Sunderland.
1911-14 Greystones, Highcliff-on-Sea.

Ernest L. Ransome (1884-1911) USA/Engineer
1903-04 Kelly and Jones Machine Shop, Greensburg, Pennsylvania.
1903-05 United Shoe Machinery Plant, Beverly, Massachusetts (additions 1911).
1904-05 Foster-Armstrong Piano Co. Factory, East Rochester, New York.

Henry Hobson Richardson (1838-86) USA/Architect
1866-69 Church of the Unity, Springfield, Massachusetts.
1867-69 Grace Church, West Medford, Massachusetts.
1869-71 Worcester High School, Worcester, Massachusetts.
1870-72 Brattle Square Church, Boston, Massachusetts.
1871-73 Hampden County Courthouse, Springfield, Massachusetts.
1872-80 State Hospital, Buffalo, New York.
1872 F. W. Andrews House, Newport, Rhode Island.
1872-77 Trinity Church, Boston, Massachusetts.
1873 B. F. Bowles House, Springfield, Massachusetts.
1874-76 William Watts Sherman House, Newport, Rhode Island.
1875-76 Cheney Building, Hartford, Connecticut.
1877-78 Winn Memorial Library, Woburn, Massachusetts.
1877-79 Ames Memorial Library, North Easton, Massachusetts.
1878-80 Sever Hall, Harvard University, Cambridge, Massachusetts.
1878-81 New York State Capitol, Albany, New York.
1879 Ames Monument, Sherman, Wyoming.
1879-81 Ames Memorial Town Hall, North Easton, Massachusetts.
1879-81 Trinity Church Rectory, Boston, Massachusetts.
1880-81 F. L. Ames Gate Lodge, North Easton, Massachusetts.
1880-83 Crane Memorial Library, Quincy, Massachusetts.
1880-82 City Hall, Albany, New York.
1881 Anderson House, Washington, D. C.
1881 Boston and Albany Station, Auburndale, Massachusetts.
1881-82 Old Colony Station, North Easton, Massachusetts.
1881-83 Austin Hall, Harvard University, Cambridge, Massachusetts.
1882-83 Grange Sard, Jr., House, Albany, New York.
1882-83 Ames Wholesale Store, Kingston and Bedford Streets, Boston, Massachusetts.
1883-84 Emmanuel Church, Allegheny City, Pittsburgh, Pennsylvania.
1883-84 Boston and Albany Station, Chestnut Hill, Massachusetts.
1883-88 Billings Memorial Library, University of Vermont, Burlington, Vermont.
1883-85 Converse Memorial Library, Malden, Massachusetts.
1884-86 Allegheny County Buildings, Pittsburgh, Pennsylvania.
1884-86 John Hay House, Washington, D.C.
1885-87 Marshall Field Wholesale Store, Chicago, Illinois.
1885-87† J. J. Glessner House, Chicago, Illinois.
1885-88 Chamber of Commerce, Cincinnati, Ohio.
1886-94 Lululand, Herbert Herkomer House, Bushey, Hertfordshire, England.

Richard Riemerschmid (1868-1957) Germany/Architect
(Compiled by Dr. Winfried Nerdinger, Technische Universität, Munich, Germany, from the catalogue of Riemerschmid's collected works, Prestal Verlag publisher, 1983.)
1898 Richard Riemerschmid House, 11 Lützowstrasse, Munich.
1900-01 (1928-34) Schauspielhaus, 26-28 Maximilianstrasse, Munich.
1901-03 Villa Franz House, 16 Heinrich-Knothestrasse, Oberpöcking.
1902 Fieser House, 33 Bernhardstrasse, Baden-Baden.
1905-06 Adolph Sultan House, Delbrückstrasse, Berlin-Grunewald (destroyed).
1904-05 Admiral Fischl House, 127 Niemannsweg, Kiel.
1905-13 Max R. Wieland House, Herrlingen.
1906-11 Fritz Frank country house 2 Am Johannisberg, Witzenhausen.
1906-07 Dr. Adolf Frank House, 2 Baurat-Gerberstrasse, Göttingen.
1907 Garden City Dresden-Hellerau, with factory of the Vereinigten Werkstätten.
1907 Housing Hagener Textilindustrie Hagen, Westphalia.
1909-13 Max R. Wieland House, 129 Olgastrasse, Ulm.
1910 Dr. Ing. L. Hoffman, 10 Ernestus-Strasse, Halle am der Saale.
1910-14 Dr. Hans Carl House, 35 Höhenbergerstrasse, Feldafing.
1911 Dr. Naumann House, Riesa.
1912-13 Dr. Oskar Blank House, 7 Heilmannstrasse, Munich.
1913-14 Friedhof cemetery.
1923 Max Krause Residence, Mittenwald.
1927 Munich Broadcasting Center "German Hour in Bavaria," 14 Marsstrasse, Munich.
1928-29 Dr. Schaffer House, 4 Peststrasse, Klingenmünster.
1929-31 Wefelscheid House, 45 Vierwindenhöhe, Bendorf am Rhein.
1935 Lieutenant-Colonel Techow residence, 7 Dinarstrasse, Starnberg.

Gerrit Thomas Rietveld (1886-1964) Holland/Architect
1919 Cornelis Begeer Shop, Oudkerkhof, Utrecht.
1920 Dr. Hartog Interior, Maarssen.
1920-22 G. Z. C. Shop. Kalverstraat, Amsterdam.
1923 Exhibition Room, Greater Berlin Art Exhibition, Berlin (with Vilmos Huszar).
1923-24†† Schröder House, Prinz Hendriklaan 50, Utrecht.
1923-24 Wessels Shop, Oudkerkhof, Utrecht.
1926-27 Marie Lommen House, Wassenaar.
1927-28 Garage and chauffeur's living quarters, Utrecht.
1929 Gohsenheimer Shop, Cleef, Germany.
1930-31 Van Urk House, Zwaluwenweg, Blaricum (with Mrs. Schröder).
1930-31 Row Houses, Erasmuslaan 5-11, Utrecht (interior with Mrs. Schröder).
1930-32 Row Houses, Wiener Werkbund Siedlung, Vienna.
1931 Klep Family House, Montenspark 8, Breda.
1932 Row Houses, Robert Schumannstraat, Utrecht.
1932 Music School and House, Henriette van Lyndenlaan 6, Zeist.
1933 Dr. Nuyens House, Montenspark, Breda.
1934 Row Houses, Erasmuslaan and Prinz Hendriklaan, Utrecht (with Mrs. Schröder).
1934 Szekley Family House, Joh. Verhulstweg 70, Santpoort.
1935 Hillebrandt Family House, Van Soutelandelaan 42, The Hague.
1935 Summer House for Mrs. V. Ravesteyn-Hintzen, Breukelerveen.
1936 Cinema, Vreeburg, Uredenburg, Utrecht.
1936 Smedes Family House, Bloemlandschweg 3, Blaricum.
1936 Portable Summer Houses (with Mrs. Schröder).
1936 Mees Family House, Van Ouwenlaan 42, The Hague.
1938 Wijsman Family House, Lieshout.
1939 Wijburg Family House, Van Ouwenlaan 44, The Hague.
1939 Murk Lels Family House, Maarsbergenseweg 3, Doorn.
1939 Brandt-Corstius Family, House, Petten.
1940 Penaat Family House, Tongeren.
1940 Pot Family House, Rijksdijk 22, Krimpen Aan Der Lek.
1941 Nijland Family House, Bilthoven.
1941 Verrijn-Stuart Summer House, Breukelerveen.

John Augustus Roebling (1806-69) USA/Engineer
(Bridges marked with an asterisk were designed and built in collaboration with his son Washington A. Roebling, 1837-1926.)
1844-45 Pennsylvania Canal Aqueduct, Allegheny River, Pennsylvania.
1845-50 Rondout, Neversink, Delaware and Lackawaxen Aqueducts, Pennsylvania.
1846 Smithfield Street Bridge, Monongahela River, Pittsburgh, Pennsylvania.
1851-55 Niagara River Bridge, Niagara Falls, New York.
1857-60 6th Street Bridge, Allegheny River, Pittsburgh, Pennsylvania.*
1856-67 Cincinnati Bridge, Ohio River, Covington, Cincinnati.*
1869-83† Brooklyn Bridge, New York.*

Anton Rosen (1859-1928) Denmark/Architect
1895 Worker's Clubhouse, Silkeborg.
1906-07 Office Building, 34 Vesterbrogade (Savoy).
1907 Office Building, 16 (Frederiksberggade

(Metropol), Copenhagen.
1907-10 Palace Hotel, Copenhagen.
1909 Denmark Exhibition, Århus.
1912 Savoy Hotel, Copenhagen.
1912-17 Gerthas Minde (garden city), Odense.
1914-15 Tuborg Administration Building, Copenhagen.
1915 Denmark House, San Francisco, Calif.

Eliel Saarinen (1873-1950) Finland/Architect
1899-1900 Finnish Pavilion, Paris Exposition 1900.
1902-05 Hvitträsk, near Helsinki.
1902 Suur-Merijoki, near Viborg.
1902 National Museum, Helsinki.
1904 Nordiska Foreningsbanken, Helsinki.
1904 Railway Station, Viborg.
1904-14† Main Railway Terminus, Helsinki.
1905-07 Molchow-Haus, Mark Bradenburg, Germany.
1909-13 Joensuu City Hall.
1910-15 Munksnas-Haga Plan, Helsinki.
1911-12 City Hall, Lahti.
1918 Greater Helsinki Plan, Helsinki.
1922†† Chicago Tribune Tower Competition.
1926-30 Cranbrook School for Boys, Bloomfield Hills, Michigan.
1926-41 Cranbrook Academy of Art, Bloomfield Hills, Michigan.
1928-29 Saarinen House, Bloomfield Hills, Michigan.
1929-30 Kingswood School for Girls, Cranbrook, Bloomfield Hills, Michigan.
1929-30 Hudnut House, New York (with Ely Jacques Kahn).
1931 Stevens Institute of Technology, Hoboken, New Jersey.
1931-33 Institute of Science, Cranbrook, Bloomfield Hills, Michigan.
1937-38 Community House, Fenton, Michigan (with Eero Saarinen).
1938 Berkshire Music Center, Tanglewood, Massachusetts (with Eero Saarinen).
1938-40 Kleinhaus Music Hall, Buffalo, New York (with Eero Saarinen).
1939-40 Crow Island School, Winnetka, Illinois (with Eero Saarinen; Perkins, Wheeler and Will).
1940-42 Tabernacle Church of Christ, Columbus, Indiana (with Eero Saarinen).
1940-43 Museum and Library, Cranbrook Academy of Art, Bloomfield Hills, Michigan.
1941 Houses, School and Community Hall, Center Line, Michigan (with Eero Saarinen and J. Robert Swanson).
1941-42 A. C. Wermuth House, Fort Wayne, Indiana (with Eero Saarinen).
1942 Schools, Willow Run, Michigan (with Eero Saarinen and J. Robert Swanson).
1942 Summer Opera House and Chamber Music Hall, Berkshire Music Center, Tanglewood, Massachusetts (with Eero Saarinen).
1943 Lincoln Heights Housing Area, Washington, D.C. (with Eero Saarinen and J. Robert Swanson).
1944-48 Edmundson Memorial Museum, Des Moines Art Center, Iowa.

Junzo Sakakura (1901-69) Japan/Architect
1937†† Japanese Pavilion, World's Fair, Paris.
1941 Iihashi House, Todoroki, Setagaya-ku, Tokyo.
1941-50 Prefabricated Wooden Houses, Tokyo.
1944 Tatsumura House, Takarazuka, Hyogo Prefecture, Japan.

Antonio Sant'Elia (1886-1916) Italy/Architect
1912 Monza Cemetery (Project).
1912 Milan Station (Project).
1913 Villa Elisi, S. Maurizio, near Como.
1913 Casa di Risparmio, Verona (Project).
1914† Citta Nuova (Project for a Futurist City).

Jules Saulnier (1817-81) France/Architect
1871-72† Chocolate Factory, Noisiel-sur-Marne.

Henri Sauvage (1873-1932) France/Architect
1896 Furniture designs (influenced by Serrurier-Bovy).
1898-1900 Villa Majorelle, 1 rue Louis Majorelle, Nancy.
1900 Théâtre de la Loïe Fuller, Exposition Universelle, Paris.
1902 Villa Oceana, Biarritz.
1903 Apartments, 7 rue Tretaigne, Paris.
1903 Apartments, 111 avenue Victor Hugo, Paris.
1905 Apartments, 10 rue Danville, Paris.
1905 Apartments, 20 rue Severo, Paris.
1907 Apartments, 1 rue de la Chine, Paris.
1907 Villa Leubas, Biarritz.
1908 Villa Majorelle, avenue Thiers, Compiengne.
1912 Apartments, 26 rue Vavin, Paris.
1913 Majorelle Offices/Shops Complex 126 rue de Provence, Paris.
1919 S.E.C.B. Director's House, Mimizan.
1922† Low-cost Housing, 13 rue des Amiraux, Paris (with Charles Sarazin).
1923 Hotel, America House, and other buildings for the 1925 exhibition (project).
1924 Apartment Building, 50 avenue Duquesne, Paris.
1924 Apartment Buildings, 14-16, 19, 137 Boulevard Raspail, Paris.
1925 Apartment Building, 42 rue de la Pompe, Paris.
1925 Apartment Building, 6 rue de Sully Prudhomme, Paris.
1925 Galerie Constantine, Primavera Pavilion, and Electric Transformer Station, Exposition des Arts Décoratifs, Paris (with Zette Sauvage).
1926 Studio Building, 65 rue la Fontaine, Paris.
1926 Sauvage House, Saint-Martin-la-Garenne.
1926 Garage, rue Campagne-Premiere, Paris.
1926 Prefabricated building components, Salon des Appareils Ménagers, Paris, erected at Auteuil.
1927 Varilla House, Orsay, Seine-et-Oise.
1927 Le Sphinx Club, Boulevard Edgar Quinet, Paris.
1928 Apartment Building, 27 rue Legendre, Paris.
1928 Apartment Building, 8 bis Boulevard Maillot, Paris.
1928 Pyramid-shaped Tower, Montparnasse Cemetery, Paris.
1929 Office Building, 10 rue Saint-Marc, Paris.
1929 Hotel, Neuilly, Paris.
1932 Apartment Building, 42 Quai des Orfevres, Paris (now Auberge du Ver-Galant).

Hans Scharoun (1893-1972) Germany/Architect
1913 Kruchen House, Buch, near Berlin (with Paul Kruchen).
1917 Community Hall, Kattenau, East Prussia.
1917-18 Farmhouse, Thierfeld, near Gumbinnen, East Prussia.
1918 Semi-detached houses with stables, near Insterburg, East Prussia.
1920 Two houses, Pregelstrasse, Insterburg, East Prussia.
1920 Kamswyken Housing Devleopment, near Insterburg, East Prussia.
1922 Granary Building, Wertheim, East Prussia.
1922 Gobert House, Sodehnen, East Prussia.
1923-24 Apartment Blocks, Parkring, Insterburg, East Prussia.
1924-25 Public Buildings, Bad Mergentheim Spa, Württemberg.
1927 Transportable Wooden House, German Garden and Industry Exhibition, Liegnitz.
1927 Single-family house, Weissenhof Siedlung, Stuttgart.
1928-29 Apartment Block, Kaiserdamm, Charlottenburg, Berlin.
1929†† Single People's Apartment Block, Werkbund Exhibition, Breslau (now Poland).
1929 Housing, Kaiserstrasse, Bremerhaven.
1929-30 Apartment Block, Hohenzollerndamm 35-36, Wilmersdorf, Berlin.
1930 Housing Development, Siemensstadt, Berlin.
1932 Apartment Block, Hohenzollernring, Spandau, Berlin.
1932 Schuldenfrey House, Garystrasse 26, Dahlem, Berlin.
1932 Wenzeck House, Frohnau, Berlin.
1933 Apartment Block, Zwerbruckerstrasse 38-46, Spandau, Berlin.
1933†† Schminke House, Löbau, Saxony.
1933 Housing Development, Kladow-Hottengrund, Berlin.
1935 Baensch House, Hohenweg 9, Spandau, Berlin.
1937 Housing, Elbestrasse, Bremerhaven.
1937-38 Noack House, Potsdam.
1938 Housing, Blessmannstrasse, Bremerhaven.
1939 Mohrmann House, Falkenstainstrasse 10, Lichtenrade, Berlin.
1940 Housing, Kaiserstrasse 240-254, Bremerhaven.
1940 Endell House, Kleinen Wannsee 30b, Wannsee, Berlin.
1942 Weigand House, Borgsdorf, near Berlin.
1943 Muller-Oerlinghausen House conversion, Kressbroon/Bodensee.

Rudolf Schindler (1887-1953) Austria/Architect
1916 Remodeled house for J. B. Lee, Maywood, Illinois.
1917-18 Buena Shore Club, Chicago, Illinois.
1920 Director's House, Olive Hill, Los Angeles.
1921-22 Schindler/Clyde Chase Double House, Hollywood.
1923 C. P. Lowes House, Eagle Rock, California.
1923 Pueblo Ribera Court, La Jolla, California.
1923 O. S. Floren House, Hollywood.
1924 John C. Packard House, South Pasadena, California.
1924-25†† Dr. Phillip Lovell Beach House, Newport Beach, California.
1925 S. Breacher House, Los Angeles.
1925 J. E. Howe House, Los Angeles.
1928 Braxton Gallery, Hollywood.
1928 Grokowsky House, South Pasadena, California.
1928 C. H. Wolfe Summer House, Avalon, Catalina Island, California.
1930 R. F. Elliot House, Los Angeles.
1931 Hans N. Von Korber House, Hollywood Riviera, Torrance, California.
1932-34 Sardi's Restaurant, Hollywood.
1933 Standard Oil Service Station (prototype).
1934 W. E. Oliver House, Los Angeles.
1934 John J. Buck House, Los Angeles.
1934-35 Elizabeth Van Patten House, Silver Lake, Los Angeles.
1935-36 Ralph C. Walker House, Los Angeles.
1936 C. C. Fitzpatrick House, Los Angeles.
1937 Henwar Rodarkiewicz House, Los Angeles.
1938-41 Apartment Building for A. L. Bubeshko, Los Angeles.
1938 Guy C. Wilson House, Los Angeles.
1939 Apartment house for Mrs. S. T. Falk, Los Angeles.
1940 Alber Van Dekker House, Canoga Park, California.
1941 Hilaire Hiller Studio-house, Hollywood.
1942 Rose L. Harris House, Los Angeles.
1944 Bethlehem Baptist Church, Los Angeles.

1945 F. Presuburger House, Studio City, California.
1946 M. Kallis House, Studio City, California.
1948 R. Lechner House, Studio City, California.
1949 Eileen Janson House, Hollywood.
1949-50 Adolph Tischler House, Bel Air, California.
1950-52 Samuel Skolnik House, Los Angeles.

George Gilbert Scott (1811-78) England/Architect
1865-74 St. Pancras Station, London (shed designed by W. H. Barlow, Engineer).

Richard Norman Shaw (1831-1912) England/Architect
1866-68 Glen Andred, Groombridge, Sussex.
1867-71 All Saints' Church, Bingley, Yorkshire.
1868 English Church, Lyons, France.
1869 Leys Wood, Groombridge, Sussex.
1869-72 Cragside, Rothbury, Northumberland.
1872 Pain's Hill, Oxted, Surrey.
1872 Bingley Church Schools.
1872 Hammerwood, East Grinstead, Sussex.
1872 New Zealand Chambers, Leadenhall Street, London.
1873 Meanwood, Leeds.
1873 Lowther Lodge, Kensington, London.
1875-77 18 Chelsea Embankment, London
1875-77 Swan House, Chelsea, London.
1876 Pierrepont, Farnham, Surrey.
1878 S. Michael's Church, Bedford Park, London.
1878 61 Fitzjohn's Avenue, Hampstead, London.
1879 Albert Hall Mansions, South Kensington, London.
1879 10, 11 Chelsea Embankment, London.
1879 9 Chelsea Embankment, The Clock House, London.
1881 Baring Brothers' Office in Bishopsgate, London.
1881-83 Alliance Assurance Co., Pall Mall, S. W. London.
1882 Frognal Priory, Hampstead, London.
1885 Kate Greenaway House, Frognal, London.
1885 180 Queen's Gate, London.
1888 New Scotland Yard, London.
1888 42 Netherhall Gardens, Hampstead, London.
1890 Bryanston, Dorset.
1893 All Saints' Church, Swanscombe, Kent.
1900 New Scotland Yard (extension), London.
1902 The Gaiety Block, Strand, London.
1905-08 Piccadilly Hotel, London.
1906-23 Regents Street Quadrant, London (after 1912 executed by R. Blomfield).

Guiseppe Sommaruga (1867-1917) Italy/Architect
1901-03 Palazzo Castiglioni, Corso Vanexi, Milan.
1906 Palazzino Salmoiraghi, Milan.

1907 Mausoleo Faccanoni, Sarnico.
1907-12 Villa Romeo, Milan.
1909-12 Grand Hotel Tre Croce, Campo dei Fiori, near Varese.
1915 Villino Poletti, Portineria.

Lars Sonck (1870-1956) Finland/Architect
1895 Saint Michael's Church, Turku.
1895 Villa Sonck, Finström, Ålands.
1902-07 St. Johns Church (Cathedral) Tampere.
1905 Telephone Building, Helsinki.
1905 Eira Hospital, Helsinki.
1908 Mortgage Bank, Helsinki.
1909-12 Kallio Church, Helsinki.
1911 Stock Exchange Building, Helsinki.
1923-35 Warehouses, Jätskaari, Helsinki.
1928 Church, Ålands.
1935 Church of St. Michale Agricola, Eira district, Helsinki.
1939 Town Hall, Mariehamina.
1940 Funeral Chapel, Mariehamina.
1945 Villa Klami, Virolahti.

J . F. Staal (1879-1940) Holland/Architect
1916-18† Park Meerwijk, near Alkmaar. (with Kropholler, Kramer, and others).
1922 Housing Block, Coenenstraat/Barth.
1925 Housing development Jan Evertsenstraat, Amsterdam.
1925 Dutch Pavilion, Exposition des Arts Décoratifs, Paris.
1927 Mennonite Church, Aalsmeer. Holland.
1928 Flower market building, Aalsmeer.
1929 Torrenhaus, and the residential complex, Daniel Willinkplien, Amsterdam.
1930 Building for the newspaper, *De Telegraaf*, Amsterdam (with G.L. Langhout).

Rudolf Steiner (1861-1925) Germany/Philosopher
1908-28† Goetheanum I and ancilliary buildings (with Carl Schmidt-Curtius, Ernst Aisenpries, and others).
1923-28† Goetheanum II.

Edward Durell Stone (1902-78) USA/Architect
1933 Mandel House, Mt. Kisco, New York.
1937 House, 4 Buckingham Street, Cambridge, Massachusetts (with Carl Koch).
1938-39†† Museum of Modern Art, New York (with Philip Goodwin).
1939 Goodyear House, Old Westbury, Long Island, New York.

Louis Sullivan (1856-1924) USA/Architect
(Between 1881 and 1894 Sullivan worked as the partner of Dankmar Adler; thereafter he practiced alone.)
1881 Rothschild Store, Chicago, Illinois.
1884 Ryerson Building, Chicago, Illinois.
1885-86 Adler Residence, Chicago, Illinois.
1886-90 Auditorium Building, Chicago, Illinois.
1888-89 Walker Warehouse, Chicago, Illinois.
1889 Ryerson Tomb, Greenland Cemetery,

Chicago, Illinois.
1890-91 Dooly Block, Salt Lake City, Utah.
1890-91† Wainwright Building, St. Louis, Missouri.
1892 Charnley Residence, Chicago, Illinois (Frank Lloyd Wright assistant).
1892 Wainwright Tomb, Bellefontaine Cemetery, St. Louis, Missouri.
1893-94 Transportation Building, World's Columbian Exposition, Chicago, Illinois.
1894-95† Guaranty Building, Buffalo, New York.
1899-1904† Schlesinger and Mayer Store (now Carson, Pirie, Scott & Co.), Chicago, Illinois.
1907-08† National Farmer's Bank, Owatonna, Minnesota.
1907 Babson Residence, Riverside, Illinois.
1911 St. Paul's Methodist Episcopal Church, Cedar Rapids, Iowa.
1914 Merchant's National Bank, Grinnel, Iowa.
1917-18 People's Savings and Loan Association Bank, Sidney, Ohio
1919 Farmers' and Merchants' Bank, Columbus, Wisconsin.

Vladimir Tatlin (1885-1933) Russia/Artist
1919-20†† Monument to the Third International.
1920 Café Pittoresque, Moscow (with Giorgi Jakulov).
1923 Staging of Elimir Khlebnikov's transational play, *Zangezi*, Petrograd.
1930-31 Letatlin flying machine (model).

Bruno Taut (1880-1938) Germany/Architect
1910 Tragerverkaufkontors Pavilion, Berlin.
1913 Monument of Steel, Steel Industries Pavilion, Building Trade Exhibition, Leipzig.
1914† Glass Pavilion, Werkbund Exhibition, Cologne.
1914-22 Public Assembly Hall, Magdeburg.
1922 Stadt und Land Agricultural Exhibition Hall (now Hermann-Giesler Sports Hall) Wilhelm-Kobelt-Strasse, Magdeburg.
1925 Eichswald Housing Development, stage I and II, Wedding, Berlin.
1927 Hufeisensiedlung Housing Estate, stage I, Britz, Berlin (with Martin Wagner).
1927 Housing Development, Paul-König-Strasse, Hohenschönhausen, Berlin.
1927 Bruno Taut House, Wiesenstrasse, Zossen Dahlewitz.
1927 Three apartment buildings, Neuköln, Berlin.
1927 Terraced houses, Westrasse, Johannisthal, Berlin.
1927 Workers' apartments, Weissenhof Siedlung, Stuttgart.
1928 Housing development, Grellstrasse, Prenzlauerberg, Berlin.
1930 Housing development, Buschallee 21-107, Weissensee, Berlin.

1931 Forest Housing Development, stage I, near Onkel Toms Hütte, Zehlendorf, Berlin (with Hugo Häring and O.R. Salvisberg).
1931 Housing development extension, Parchimer Allee, Britz, Berlin.
1934 Ikoma Mountain Housing Development, near Osaka, Japan (project).
1936 Okura House, Tokyo (now altered).
1936 Hingo House interiors, Atami, Japan.
1938 Bruno Taut House, Ortakoy, Turkey.
1938 Ataturk Lyceum, Ankara, Turkey (with Asim Komurcuoglu).
1938 Language and History Faculty buildings, University of Ankara, Turkey.
1938 Ministry of Culture Exhibition Buildings, International Exposition, Izmir, Turkey.
1938 Kemal Ataturk Catafalque, Ankara, Turkey.

Giuseppe Terragni (1904-42) Italy/Architect
1928 Novocomum Apartment Building, Como.
1930 Vitrum Store, Como.
1930 Strecchini Tomb, Como.
1930 Ladies' hairdressers shop, Como.
1932 Sala del '22, Mostra della Rivoluzione Fascista, Rome.
1932 War Memorial Erba Incino, Italy.
1932 Ortelli Tomb, Cernobbio.
1932 Tailor's shop, Monza.
1932-36†† Casa del Fascio, Como (now the Casa del Popolo).
1933 Ghiringhelli House, Milan (with Pietro Lingeri).
1933 Toninello House, Milan (with Pietro Lingeri).
1933 Artist's Lakeside House, Triennale, Milan (with Gruppo di Como).
1933 Covered Market, Como.
1933 War Memorial, Lake Como (with Enrico Pampolini, from a design by Sant'Elia).
1933 School, Malpensata Quarter, Lecco.
1935 Rustici House, Milan (with Pietro Lingeri).
1935 Lavezzari House, Milan (with Pietro Lingeri).
1935 Post Hotel, Piazza Volta, Como.
1935 Sarfatti Monument, Col d'Echele.
1935 Pedraglio House, Como.
1935-36 Piravano Tomb, Como.
1937 Bianca House, Siveso.
1937 Casa del Floricoltore, Rebbio.
1937 Nuovo Campari Restaurant, Milan (with Pietro Lingeri and Alberto Sartoris).
1937 Asilo Sant'Elia, Kindergarten, Como.
1937 Danteum, Via dell'Impero, Rome (with Pietro Lingeri).
1937 Satellite Quarter, Rebbio (with Alberto Sartoris).
1939 Giuliani-Frigerio House, Como.
1939 Housing Development, Via Anzani,

Como.

Eduardo Torroja y Miret (1899-1961) Spain/Engineer
1925 Tempul Aqueduct, Guadalete River, Jerez de la Frontera.
1926 Sancti-Petri Bridge.
1933 Market Hall, Algeciras (with Manuel Sánchez Arcas).
1933 Aire Aqueduct, University City, Madrid.
1933 Cantarranas Retaining Wall, Madrid.
1934 Operating theater and Sun Balconies, University City Hospital, Madrid.
1935†† Zarzuela Racecourse, Madrid (with Carlos Arniches and Martin Dominguez).
1935 Church, Villaverde.
1939 Brick Water Tower, Zarzuela Racecourse, Madrid.
1939 Alloz Aqueduct, Alloz.
1939 Martin Gill Viaduct, Esla River, near Leon.
1939 Tordera Bridge, near Barcelona.
1939-47 Bridge over the Muga River.
1942-45 Torrejon Aircraft Hangar, Madrid.
1942-45 Aircraft Hangar, Barajas.
1943 Las Corts Football Stadium, Barcelona (with J. M. Sagnier).

Charles Harrison Townsend (1851-1928) England/Architect
1892-94 Bishopsgate Institute, London.
1892-95 St. Martin's Church, Blackheath, near Guilford.
1896-1901 Horniman Museum, London.
1899-1901 Whitechapel Art Gallery, London.

William Van Alen (1882-1954) USA/Architect
1927 Bank of Manhattan Building, 40 Wall Street, New York.
1929†† Chrysler Building, New York.
1936 "House of the Modern Age," exhibition model.

Henry van de Velde (1863-1957) Belgium/Architect
1895-96† Bloemenwerf House, Uccle.
1895 Sèthe House, Uccle.
1900-02† Folkwang Museum, Hagen, Germany (interiors).
1901-03 Leuring House, Scheveningen, Holland.
1902-03 Esche House, Chemnitze (now Karl Marx Stadt), Germany.
1904-06 Arts and Crafts School, Weimar, Germany.
1906 Hohenhof (Karl Osthaus Country House), Hagen, Germany (now the Henry van de Velde Gesellschaft).
1908 Monument, Jena, Germany.
1911 Springmann House, Hagen, Germany.
1911 Frose House, Hannover, Germany.
1912-13 Durckheim House, Weimar, Germany.

1913-14 Henneberg House, Weimar, Germany.
1913 Korner House, Chemnitz, Germany.
1914† Werkbund Theatre, Werkbund Exhibition, Cologne, Germany.
1921 Van de Velde House, Wassenaar, near The Hague.
1925 Fyffes Company Offices, Rotterdam.
1927 La Nouvelle Maison (van de Velde House), Tervueren, Belgium.
1929 Old Peoples' Housing, Hanover, Germany.
1930-54 Kröller-Müller Museum, Otterlo, Netherlands.
1931 Colman/Saverys Duplex House, Zoute, Brussels.
1937 Belgian Pavilion, World's Fair, Paris (with I. Eggeriey).
1939 Belgian Pavilion, World's Fair, New York (with Victor Bourgeois).
1939-40 Library, University of Ghent.

J. M. van der Meij (1878-1949) Holland/Architect
1911-16 Scheepvaarthuis, Amsterdam (with de Klerk and Kramer).
1917 General Plan Tuindorp Nieuwendammerham, Amsterdam Nord.
1917-18 De Lairesse, residential complex for N. V. Bouwmaatschappij, Amsterdam.
1919-20 Plan for Blijdorp, Rotterdam.
1928-30 Residential complex, Hoofddorplein.

Theo van Doesburg (1883-1931) Holland/Artist and Architect
1917 De Vonk holiday residence, Noordwijkerhoùt. Staircase, entry hall, corridors and stained glass (in collaboration with J.J.P. Oud).
1918 Design for a monument, Leeuwarden.
1921 Studies for architectural color application to Terrace Housing and Agricultural School in Drachten.
1923 Project for a University Hall, University of Amsterdam (in collaboration with Cor Van Eesteren).
1923 Project for Studio House and Villa, exhibited at Leonce Rosenberg's Galerie L'Effort Moderne, Paris, 1923 (with Cor Van Eesteren).
1923 Project for Leonce Rosenberg Villa, Paris (with Cor Van Eesteren).
1924 Winkelgalerij Shopping Arcade and Apartments, The Hague (with Cor Van Eesteren).
1924-25 Flower Room for Comte de Noailles' Villa, Hyères, France.
1926-28†† Café L'Aubette, Strasbourg, France (with Jean and Sophie Tauber-Arp).
1927 Project for Twin Houses (Arp and Van Doesburg), Meudon, near Paris.
1929 Traffic-Town, Office Towers.
1929-30 Van Doesburg House, Mendon, Paris.
1930 Barthelome Por, Studio, Paris.

Carlos Raúl Villanueva (1900-75) England (Venezuelan)/Architect

1929-30 Church of San Francisco de Yara, Caracas.
1929-30 Bolivar House restoration, Caracas.
1931 Bullring, Maracay, Venezuela.
1935 Museo de los Caobos, Caracas.
1937 Venezuelan Pavilion, World's Fair, Paris.
1939†† Gran Columbia School, Caracas.
1941 Redevelopment of the El Silencio Quarter, Avenida Bolivar, Caracas.
1943-44 General Rafael Urdaneta Housing Development, Maracaibo, Venezuela.
1943-45 Dos de Diciembre Housing Development, Caracas (with José Manual Mijares, José Hoffman, and Carlos Branco).
1944-47†† Master plan for University City, University of Venezuela, Caracas.
1945 Medical Center, University City, Caracas.

Charles Francis Annesley Voysey (1857-1941) England/Architect
1888-89 The Cottage, Bishop's Intchington, Warwick (addition 1900).
1890 Cazalet Walnut Tree Farm, Castlemorten, Malvern (altered 1894).
1891 W. E. F. Britten Studio, 17 St. Dunstan's Road, West Kensington, London.
1891 J. W. Forster House, Bedford Park, London (wing added 1894).
1891-92 Houses, Hans Road, Kensington, London.
1893 Studio, Aynho Road, Brook Green (destroyed).
1893 J. W. Wilson House, Perrycroft, Colwall, Malvern (additions 1903-04, 1907-08).
1895 Wentworth Arms Inn, Elmesthorpe, Hinckley, Leicestershire.
1895 Annesley Lodge, Platts Lane, Hampstead, London.
1896 Six cottages, Elmesthorpe.
1896 Julian Sturgis House and stables, Hog's Back, near Guildford.
1897 Dixcot, North Drive, Tooting Common (modified).
1897 Norney, Shackleford, Surrey (alterations and additions 1903).
1897 New Place, Haslemere, Surrey (alterations and additions 1899, 1901).
1898† Broadley's Gill Head, near Windermere.
1898 Moor Crag, Gill Head, near Windermere.
1899 H. G. Wells House, Spade House, Sandgate (addition 1903).
1899 Cottage Hospital, Beaworthy, Devon.
1899 Pavilion, Oldbury Park, Birmingham.
1900 Prior's Garth, Puttenham, Surrey.
1899-1900 The Orchard, Chorley Wood, Hertshire (altered 1913).
1902 Wall-paper factory, Chiswick (destroyed).
1902 Vodin, Pyrford Common near Woking.
1902 Interiors and furniture, 37 Bidstone Road, Oxton and 30 Shrewsbury

Road, Birkenhead.
1903 White Cottage, Lyford Road, Wandsworth.
1903 Dr. Fort House, Chorley Wood, Hertshire.
1904 Lady Somerset House, Higham, Woodford, Essex.
1904 Myholme (convalescent home for children), Merry Hill Lane, Bushey (altered 1911).
1904 Housing and Institute, Whitwood Colliery, Normanton, Yorkshire.
1905 White Horse Inn, Stetchworth, near Newmarket.
1905 Dr. Leigh Canney House, Assouan, Egypt.
1905 Holly Mount, Knotty Green, Beaconsfield.
1905 The Homestead, Frinton, Essex.
1906-07 Littleholme, Guildford (gardener's cottage, 1911).
1909 St. Winifred's Quarry, Combe Down, near Bath.
1909 Holiday Cottage, Slindon, Barnham Junction, Sussex.
1911 R. Hetherington House, Malone Road, Belfast, Northern Ireland.
1912 Memorial to the Earl of Lovelace, Ashley Combe, Somerset.
1912 Lady Lovelace House, Lilycombe, Porlock, Somerset.
1919 War Memorial, Malvern Wells.
1920 Memorial to King's Own Yorkshire Light Infantry, York Minster.
1920 War Memorial, Potter's Bar.
1920 Memorial, Manor House, Tonbridge School.

Otto Wagner (1841-1918) Austria/Architect
1871 Synagogue, Budapest.
1886-88 First Villa Wagner, Hutterlbergstrasse, Vienna.
1890 Palais Wagner, Rennweg 3, Vienna.
1894-98 Nussdorf Dam, Danube Works, Vienna.
1894-99 Stadtbahn System, Vienna (Karlsplatz Station with J.M.Olbrich).
1902 Die Zeit, Telegraph Office, Vienna.
1904-12† Imperial and Royal Post Office Savings Bank, Vienna.
1904-08 Kaiserbad Dam, Vienna.
1905-07† Church of St. Leopold, Am Steinhof, Vienna.
1912-13 Second Villa Wagner, Huttelbergstrasse, Vienna.

Warren & Wetmore (1894-1943) & (1866-1941) USA/Architect
1899 New York Yacht Club, New York.
1906 Lexington Avenue Post Office, New York.
1909 Fort Gary Station, Winnipeg, Manitoba, Canada.
1910-13 Grand Central Station, Biltmore Hotel and the New York Central Terminal Yards, New York.

1917   Equitable Trust Building, New York.

Philip Webb (1831-1915) England/Architect
1859†   The Red House, Upton, near Bexley Heath, Kent (with William Morris).
1861   Bentfleet Hall, Cobham, Surrey.
1863   Arisaig, Invernesshire, Scotland.
1868   Howard House, 1 Palace Green Kensington, London.
1873   Joldwynds, Dorking, Surrey.
1879-86   Clouds, East Knoyle, Salisbury, Wiltshire.
1892   Standen, near East Grinstead, Sussex.
1902   Cottages at Kelmscott, Lechlade, Gloucestershire.

Sir E. Owen Williams (1890-1969) England/Architect and Engineer
1912   Shipyard in reinforced concrete, Poole, Dorset (with Reinforced Concrete Engineers).
1912   Gramophone Company factory, Hayes, Middlesex (with Truscon; now the E.M.I. Building).
1913   Prototype airplanes for Wells Aviation Ltd.
1914-18   Concrete ships.
1919   Walls Factory, Acton, London.
1920   Tannery, Runcorn, Cheshire.
1921   Ice-making plant, Hull, Yorkshire.
1923   Palace of Industry, British Empire Exhibition, Wembley, London.
1925   Parc des Attractions, Exposition des Arts Décoratifs, Paris.
1925   River Spey Bridge, Scotland.
1925-30   Wansford Bridge, Huntingdon.
1925-30   Findhorn Bridge, Scotland.
1925-30   Montrose Bridge, Scotland.
1925-30   Lea Valley Viaduct, North Circular Road, London.
1926   Cotton and Crushing Mill, Adana, Turkey.
1930   Cumberland Garage, near Marble Arch, London.
1932†   Boots factory, Beeston, Nottingham.
1932†   *Daily Express* Building, London (Consulting engineer with Ellis and Clarke).
1933   Cement factory, Thurrock, Essex.
1934†   Empire Swimming Pool and Sports Arena, Wembley, London.
1934   Pioneer Health Center, Peckham, London.
1934   Sainsbury's Warehouse, Southwark, London.
1935   Lilley and Skinner Warehouse, Pentonville Road, London.
1936   Housing, Stanmore, Middlesex.
1937   Odhams Printing Works, Watford, Hertfordshire.
1937   Removable restaurant, Wembley Stadium, London.
1937   Synagogue, Dollis Hill, London.
1937   *Daily Express* Building, Glasgow (consulting engineer).
1939   *Daily Express* Building, Manchester

(consulting engineer with Ellis and Clarke).
1939-45   Concrete ships.
1945   Motorway design for the United Kingdom Ministry of Design (consulting engineer).

Frank Lloyd Wright (1867-1959) USA/Architect
1887   Hillside Home School, Spring Green, Wisconsin.
1889-95   Frank Lloyd Wright House and Studio, Oak Park, Illinois.
1891   Charnley House, Astor Street, Chicago, Illinois (with Louis Sullivan).
1892   Twin Houses for Thomas H. Gale, Oak Park, Illinois.
1893   Walter Gale House, Oak Park, Illinois.
1893   Municipal Boathouse, Madison, Wisconsin.
1893†   William Winslow House, River Forest, Illinois.
1895   Chauncey K. Williams House, River Forest, Illinois.
1899   Joseph Husser House, Chicago, Illinois.
1900   Warren Hickox House, Kankakee, Illinois.
1902   Ward W. Willits House, Highland Park, Illinois.
1902   Arthur Heurtley House, Oak Park, Illinois.
1902   Francis W. Little House, Peoria, Illinois.
1903†   Larkin Company Administration Building, Buffalo, New York.
1903   Susan L. Dana House, Springfield, Illinois.
1904   Darwin D. Martin House, Buffalo, New York.
1904-08†   Unity Temple, Oak Park, Illinois.
1906-09†   Frederick C. Robie House, Chicago, Illinois.
1907-09†   Avery Coonley House, Riverside, Illinois.
1908   Isabel Roberts House, River Forest, Illinois.
1909   Mrs. Thomas H. Gale House, Oak Park, Illinois.
1913-14†   Midway Gardens, Chicago, Illinois.
1915   Bach House, Chicago, Illinois.
1916-22†   Imperial Hotel, Tokyo.
1920   Barnsdall Houses A and B, Los Angeles.
1921   Mrs. Thomas Gale Summer Cottages, Whitehall, Michigan.
1921   Jiyu Gakuen School of the Free Spirit, Tokyo.
1922   Lowe House, Eagle Rock, California.
1923††   La Miniatura (Millard House), Pasadena, California.
1923   Little Dipper (Barnsdall Kindergarten), Los Angeles.
1923   Storer House, Los Angeles.
1923   Ennis House, Los Angeles.
1923   Moore House, Oak Park, Illinois (rebuilding).
1924   Freeman House, Los Angeles.

1925   Taliesin III, Spring Green, Wisconsin (living quarters).
1927   Arizona Biltmore Hotel, Phoenix (with Albert McArthur).
1927   Martin House, Derby, New York.
1928   Ocatillo, Chandler, Arizona.
1929   Jones House II, Tulsa, Oklahoma.
1933   Taliesin Fellowship Complex, Spring Green, Wisconsin (addition to Hillside Home School).
1934   Broadacre City model and exhibition plans.
1934   Willey House II, Minneapolis, Minnesota.
1936††   Falling Water (Kaufmann House), Bear Run, Pennsylvania.
1936   Roberts House, Marquette, Michigan.
1936-39††   S.C. Johnson Administration Building, Racine, Wisconsin.
1937   Hanna House, Palo Alto, California.
1937   Jacobs House, Westmoreland, Wisconsin.
1937   Wingspread (Johnson House; The Last Prairie House), Racine, Wisconsin.
1937   Edgar J. Kaufmann, Sr., Offices, Pittsburgh, Pennsylvania.
1938   Midway Farm Buildings, Taliesin, Spring Green, Wisconsin.
1938   Rebhuhn House, Great Neck, Long Island, New York.
1938††   Taliesin West, Scottsdale, Arizona.
1939   Guest House for Falling Water, Bear Run, Pennsylvania.
1939   Armstrong House, near Gary, Indiana.
1939   Goetsch-Winckler House, Okemos, Michigan.
1939   Rosenbaum House, Florence, Alabama.
1939   Schwartz House, Two Rivers, Wisconsin.
1939   Sturges House, Brentwood Heights, California.
1939   Suntop Homes, Ardmore, Pennsylvania.
1940   Baird House, Amherst, Massachusetts.
1940   Bazett House, Hillsborough, California.
1950   Christie House, Bernardsville, New Jersey.
1940   Community Church, Kansas City, Missouri.
1940   Euchtman House, Baltimore, Maryland.
1940   Lewis House, Libertyville, Illinois.
1940   Manson House, Wausau, Wisconsin.
1940   Pauson House, Phoenix, Arizona.
1940   Pew House, Madison, Wisconsin.
1940   Pope House, Falls Church, Virginia.
1940   Sondern House, Kansas City, Missouri.
1940   Auldbrass Plantation, near Yemassee, South Carolina.
1940-59   Florida Southern College, Lakeland.
1941   Affleck House, Bloomfield Hills, Michigan.
1941   Oboler Gatehouse and Retreat, Malibu, California.
1941   Richardson House, Glenridge, New Jersey.

1941   Snowflake (Wall House), Plymouth, Michigan.
1944   Solar Hemicycle (Jacobs House), Middleton, Wisconsin.
1944   S.C. Johnson Research Tower, Racine, Wisconsin.
1945   Friedman Vacation Lodge, Pecos, New Mexico.
1945   Taliesin Dams, Spring Green, Wisconsin.
1946   Grant House, Cedar Rapids, Iowa.
1946   Griggs House, Tacoma, Washington.

George H. Wyman (? – ?) USA/Architect
1889-93†   Bradbury Building, Los Angeles, California.

Architectures marked with † are appear in MODERN ARCHITECTURE 1851-1919, and †† are appear in MODERN ARCHITECTURE 1920-1945.

Acknowledgments

The publisher greatly appreciates the cooperation received from authorities and parties who have charge of any illustrations and photographs used in the issue.

Text illustrations

Architectural Design, London: Figs. 124, 126, 128
Architectural Record, New York: Fig. 162
The Architectural Review, London: Fig. 190
Courtesy of Professor Hans Asplund: Figs. 109, 110
Courtesy of Göteborgs Stadsarkiv: Fig. 114
Courtesy of Guggenheim Museum, New York: Fig. 145
Courtesy of Novosti Press Agency, Publishing House, Moscow: Figs. 120 (axonometric), 121 (axonometric), 127, p. 226
Courtesy of Rockefeller Center: Fig. 182
R. M. Schindler Architecture Collection, University Art Galleries, University of California, Santa Barbara, California. Reproduced by permission: Fig. 151
The Swedish Museum of Architecture, Stockholm: Figs. 111, 112, 113
Courtesy of Professor Bruno Zevi. Reproduced from his book *Poetica dell'architettura neoplastica*, Giulio Einaudi Editore, Torino, 1974: Figs. 105, 137, 138, 139

Illustrations have been reproduced from the following publications by permission.

Alvar Aalto Band 1, edited by Karl Fleig, Verlag für Architektur Artemis, Zürich, 1963: Fig. 184 (plan)
Die Architektur des Expressionismus by Wolfgang Pehnt, Verlag Gerd Hatje, Stuttgart, 1973: Figs. 77, 78, 80, 81, 107
Contemporary Town Planning by Waclaw Ostrowski, IFHP-The Hague and CRU-Paris: Fig. 94
Le Corbusier & P. Jeanneret 1910–29, edited by W. Boesiger & O. Stonorov, Verlag für Architektur Artemis, Zürich, 1964: Figs. 96, 98, 100, 101, 102, 104
Le Corbusier & P. Jeanneret 1934–38, edited by Max Bill, Verlag für Architektur Artemis, Zürich, 1964: Figs. 179, 186, 187
The Mathematics of the Ideal Villa and Other Essays by Colin Rowe, The MIT Press, Cambridge, 1977: Fig. 99
Modern Housing Prototypes by Roger Sherwood, Harvard University Press. © 1978 by the President and Fellows of Harvard College: Figs. 91, 153, 169
Die Neue Architektur 1930–40 by Alfred Roth, Verlag für Architektur Artemis, Zürich, 1975: Figs. 185, 189, 191
Olanda 1870–1940 by M. Casciato, F. Panzini, S. Polano, Gruppo Editoriale Electa, Milano, 1980: Fig. 170
Oppositions 18, Fall, 1979. Reproduced by permission of Stefanos Polyzoides: Fig. 152
Richard Neutra 1923–50: Buildings and Projects, edited by W. Boesiger, Verlag für Architektur Artemis, Zürich, 1964: Figs. 154, 156, 158
Transparenz Le Corbusier Studien I by Rowe,

Slutzky & Hoesli, Birkhäuser Verlag, Basel, 1968: Fig. 97
URSS architettura 1917–1936 by Vittorio De Feo, Editori Riuniti, Roma, 1963: Figs. 115, 116, 120, 121, 125
The Work of Oscar Niemeyer by Stamo Papadaki. © 1950 by Reinhold Publishing Company. Reproduced by permission of Van Nostrand Reinhold: Fig. 188

Illustrations have been reproduced from the following publications.

L'architecture contemporaine en Tchécoslovaquie, Editions Orbis, Prague, 1928: Fig. 178
L'Architecture Vivante, Editions Albert Morancé: Figs. 82, 83, 85, 88, 89, 92, 93, 95, 106, 134, 135, 136, 166, 167
Architettura moderna in Olanda by G. Fanelli, Marchi & Bertolli, Florence, 1968: Fig. 84
Die Baukunst der Neuesten Zeit by G. A. Platz, Propylaen Verlag, 1927: Fig. 79
Encyclopédia de L'Architecture: Constructions Modernes: Tome XI, Editions Albert Morancé, Paris: Fig. 181
Histoire de l'architecture by Auguste Choisy, 1899: Fig. 90
Modern Architecture in Czechoslovakia by Dostál, Pechar, Procházka, Obelisk, Prague, 1970: Figs. 173, 174, 175, 176, 177, 180
Wendingen (Special Issue), Oct. 1930: Fig. 87

Other illustrations

Akademie der Künste Berlin, Sammlung Baukunst, Scharoun-Archiv: pp. 340, 383
The Architectural Review, London: pp. 349, 387
Courtesy of Professor Hans Asplund: p. 396
Bauhaus-Archiv, Berlin: p. 281
Haags Gemeentemuseum, The Hague: p. 237
Courtesy of Hoechst Aktiengesellschaft, Frankfurt am Main: pp. 230, 231
The Museum of Modern Art, New York. Redrawn from the blue prints provided by the Museum: p. 439
Rijksdienst voor de Monumentenzorg, Amsterdam: pp. 222, 227
Studio Nervi, Roma: p. 356
The Swedish Museum of Architecture, Stockholm: p. 233

Illustrations have been reproduced from the following publications by permission.

Alvar Aalto Band 1, edited by Karl Fleig, Verlag für Architektur Artemis, Zürich, 1963: pp. 350, 394, 395, 407
Die Architektur des Expressionismus by Wolfgang Pehnt, Verlag Gerd Hatje, Stuttgart, 1973: pp. 224, 247
Chicago Tribune Tower Competition and Late Entries by Stanley Tigerman, Rizzoli, New York: pp. 238, 239
Designing for Industry: The Architecture of Albert Kahn by Grant Hildebrand, The MIT Press,

Cambridge, Massachusetts, 1974: p. 241
GA 13, A.D.A. EDITA Tokyo. Drawings by Richard Meier: p. 344
Geschichte der modernen Architektur by Jürgen Joedicke, Verlag Gerd Hatje, Stuttgart, 1958: p. 253 (Fig. 86)
Henri Sauvage 1873–1932, Archives d'Achitecture Moderne, Bruxelles: p. 254
I mobili di Gerrit Thomas Rietveld by Daniele Baroni, Gruppo Editoriale Electa, Milano: p. 250
Le Corbusier & P. Jeanneret 1910–29, edited by W. Boesiger & O. Stonorov, Verlag für Architektur Artemis, Zürich, 1964: pp. 248, 258, 294
Le Corbusier & P. Jeanneret 1929–34, edited by W. Boesiger, Verlag für Architektur Artemis, Zürich, 1964: pp. 379, 380, 381
Le Corbusier & P. Jeanneret 1934–38, edited by Max Bill, Verlag für Architektur Artemis, Zürich, 1964: p. 409
Lotus 10, Lotus International, Milano: p. 303
Die Neue Architektur 1930–40 by Alfred Roth, Verlag für Architektur Artemis, Zürich, 1975: pp. 358, 393
Das Neue Schulhaus by Alfred Roth, Verlag für Architektur Artemis, Zürich, 1966: p. 329 (Fig. 172)
Nordische Baukunst by Steen Eiler Rasmussen, Verlag Ernst Wasmuth, 1940: p. 218
Perspecta 12: The Yale Architectural Journal, "Maison de Verre," by Kenneth Frampton, p. 86, ill. 29, New Haven, CT.: p. 333
Richard Neutra 1923–50: Buildings and Projects, edited by W. Boesiger, Verlag für Architektur Artemis, Zürich, 1964: pp. 300, 441
Robert Maillart, Bridges and Constructions by Max Bill, Verlag für Architektur Artemis, Zürich, 1949: p. 342
Rockefeller Center by Carol Herselle Krinsky, Oxford University Press, Inc. Redrawn by Nancy Jane Ruddy: p. 336
Shell Construction by Jürgen Joedicke, Karl Krämer Verlag, Stuttgart, 1963: p. 391 right
Wendingen, vol. 6, no. 8, De Sikkel, Antwerpen, 1924: p. 256
Die Weissenhofsiedlung, Karl Krämer Verlag, Stuttgart, 1968/1977: p. 297

The drawings of Frank Lloyd Wright are Copyright © The Frank Lloyd Wright Foundation:
Fig. 142 (© 1955); Figs. 141, 146, 147, 148, 149, 150 (© 1942, renewed 1970)
pp. 244 left (© 1942, renewed 1970), 244 bottom left (© 1962), 244 bottom right (© 1982), 398 (© 1976), 402 (© 1976), 436 (© 1977)

Photographic Acknowledgments

Akademie der Künste Berlin, Sammlung Baukunst, Scharoun-Archiv: pp. 340, 341, 382, 383
Dienst Verspreide Rijkskollekties, The Hague: p. 328 top & bottom
Albert Kahn Associates: p. 240
Colin Lucas: p. 386
The Museum of Finnish Architecture, Helsinki: pp. 406, 407
Studio Nervi, Roma: p. 357
Verlag für Architektur Artemis, Zürich. Reproduced from *Le Corbusier & P. Jeanneret 1934–38*, edited by Max Bill: pp. 408, 409
Ville de Strasbourg, Conservation des Musées: p. 328 center

Courtesy of The Museum of Modern Art, New York. Collections, Mies van der Rohe Archive, The Museum of Modern Art, N.Y.: pp. 220, 221 (Gift of Ludwig Mies van der Rohe), 331 (below: Gift of Ludwig Mies van der Rohe), 332, 338, 339 (below left: Gift of Ludwig Mies van der Rohe)

Courtesy of Novosti Press Agency (Moscow & Tokyo) for their cooperation in photographing: pp. 282–3, 325–6
Courtesy of Sakakura Associates, Tokyo (Photo: Kollar, Paris): pp. 404–5

The editors have sought as far as possible, the right of reproduction to the illustrations contained in this publication. Since some of the sources could not be traced, the editors would be grateful to receive information from any copyright owner who is not credited herein. Acknowledgment will be gladly made in future editions if appropriate.